To my father . . . I wish you were still around.

Acknowledgements

My thanks above all to Anthony Bowman, who aided and abetted me with this book so comprehensively, as well as providing me with so many friendly faces to call upon in Australia and America. Also to John Blake, Pat Lovell, Cassandra Kirton, Mark Sandelson, Jeanie Bowman, Louise Frogley, Jonathan Margolis, Anthony Clarkson, Joan Wong, Tina Rothwell, Charlie Sungkawess, Som Pol Sungkawess, Alex Johnson, David Johnson, John Bremmer, Peter Nowlan, Graham Fowler, Ed Stinson, Carol Rowell, Ralph McCoach, Kathleen Lyons, Pat Grasso, Don McClennan, Maeva Salmon, Hare Salmon, Coco Dexter, Tevaite Vernette, Maimiti Kinnander, Irene Fuller, George Logue, Noetia Guy, Maco Roometua, Daphne Fuller, Scan Denis, Maurice Lenoir, Andrew Urban, Lisa Offord, Mitch Matthews, Michelle Adamson, Monroe Reimers, Emile Minty, Yvonne Perotette, Jeremy Connolly, Carmel Smith, Eileen Leiden, Tim Burstall, John Dowding, Don Bennetts,

ACKNOWLEDGEMENTS

Scott Murray, Dan McDonnell, Robert Lawrence MC, Peter Wilson, Rhonda Schepisi, Robert Menzies, Mark Griffin, Rea Francis, Hugh Keys-Burn, Mark McGinnity, Judy Holst, Linda Newton, Deborah Foreman, Miranda Brewin, Chris O'Mara, Terri DePaolo, John Philip Law, Phil Avalon, John Bell, Jim Mitteager, Wendy Kane, John McShane, Di Blackwell, Bunty Avieson and every other person who agreed to be interviewed for this book, but requested that I do not reveal their identities. Also Globe Library, Associated Newspapers Library, News International Library and the Motion Picture Library, Los Angeles.

In addition, *Mel Gibson* by Keith McKay (Sidgwick and Jackson 1986), *Mel Gibson* by David Ragan (W.H. Allen 1985), and *Reluctant Star* by James Oram (Fontana 1991), provided some invaluable information re Mel Gibson and I am extremely grateful to them.

And lastly, but by no means least, a special note of thanks to my literary agent, Peter Miller.

"*Stars are essentially worthless – and absolutely essential.*"
Adventures in the Screen Trade by William Goldman.

"*To be or not to be; that is the question; whether 'tis nobler in the mind to suffer the slings and arrows of outrageous fortune or take arms against a sea of troubles, and by opposing end them? . . . For who would bear the whips and scorns of time, the oppressor's wrong, the proud man's contumely, the pangs of despised love, the law's delay, the insolence of office . . .*"
Hamlet by William Shakespeare.

"*Write a book? Ha ha ha! Hell, what would I write about? My life as as movie star? Actors only write books when they run out of money. Anyway, there's enough people writing about me. There is someone doing it even as we speak. Does it get on my nerves? There's a sense of outrage that somebody's wandering about talking to everyone I've ever known.*"
Mel Gibson.

Prologue

Let me upstage a star and beat him to the draw in stating something: you are starting a study which is bound to disturb, distress and infuriate its subject, Mel Columbcille Gerard Gibson.

For the great paradox of one of the screen's best-known men is that hardly anyone knows him. Stonewalling his way through reluctantly-granted interviews or dancing out of range behind smokescreens of ingenuous charm and engagingly mocking flippancy, Mel Gibson is intent on keeping it that way. The up-front guy of the movies is a fiercely private person.

Accordingly, and strangely, Gibson will resent disclosure of a record in which most people would take pride: a child growing up in hard times, under an equally hard paternal regime, with virtually no material advantages, who has triumphed in the most competitive, least forgiving arena on earth – Hollywood.

This book is clear-eyed rather that rosy-tinted, certainly. You must decide whether Gibson emerges as its hero, anti-hero or merely the central character. To him such findings are irrelevant. Refusing to write his own life story, he resents anyone else daring to . . . simply *because it is about him*, and that's enough to rankle with an embattled man who loathes undue scrutiny and is almost superstitiously anxious to keep himself to himself and his family circle.

Mel would be extremely happy if the printing press had not been invented. Partly because he has managed to persuade himself that he's pretty good at just another job, as it might be plumbing or running a supermarket. The customers ought to be content to judge him on whether the taps have been fixed, the produce is fresh – or if they have been taken out of themselves by his latest picture. Leave it at that, huh?

Ain't never going to happen, as the modern American proverb goes. Having elevated the Ordinary Joe to titanic stature, or at least, wide-screen scale, Mel Gibson suffers from the iron law that anyone kindling the imaginations of untold millions is bound to ignite their curiosity as well. What's he *really* like, what makes him tick?

Good questions, especially since he hoards the answers. Depressingly few Great Big Stars are very interesting people. Many bear a drab family resemblance: either their college major was performing arts, leading on to theatre work, or they had high school dreams and broke through via modelling or TV soaps and . . . ho-hum. Mel Gibson, thank God – to whom his extremist, vastly influential father, 'Red' Gibson believes he may have a direct line, by the way – isn't like that.

Yes, he went to drama school, more or less by accident and not particularly willingly, either. That's the only sugges-tion of Hollywood cookie-cutter uniformity. This man is a true original, a one-off on two legs.

Little about the erstwhile Mad Max is stereotyped, predictable. (Even his hell-rising, while its wine, women and song trail was blazed by bygones like Errol Flynn, has unique ingredients of flinty honesty and good old-fashioned Catholic guilt.)

Other mega-stars drive themselves to get bigger, or at worst, cling to their rung on the platinum ladder. Mel Gibson dreams of giving it all up, to farm beef-cattle full time. His peers prattle, between one divorce and the next, of family values and their wonderful wife and kids. The one sure bet about Mel Gibson is that if forced to choose between fame and career or his adored family, he'd be out of there and back home for good, the moment the choice was presented.

Named after a brace of saints, Irish and Italian, Gibson was raised – brainwashed might not be too strong a term, conditioned a fairer one – to fear hellfire and shun sin. Yet heaven-sent talent and good looks have drawn him to Hollywood, where hedonism, self-indulgence, brazen carnality, the whole fleshpots thing, goes with the territory.

Even then, he never went the classic route of a hooker in the limo or a leading lady in her dressing room trailer. Mel's scrapes have an almost comical, essentially working-class ambience. Like the blue-collar Average Guy he yearns to be, Mel Gibson is always terrified that his wife will find out. And he clings to a cop-out that sheepish husbands from Birmingham, England to Birmingham Alabama have deployed for generations – he always tells them he's married and would never leave Mrs Gibson, so that's it.

A potent part of Gibson's appeal is that he is the Ordinary Guy writ large, not to mention high, wide and handsome. And just as 'Real men don't eat quiche', they do go in for blondes. However, it's worth pointing out that his playing around is firmly past-tense, these days.

He'll never be a New Man; nobody would want him to be. But he's doing his level best to be a New Mel . . .

But this is only one facet of a rich, deep and unexpected character. Just as intriguing is that chain of chance, the random connections, placing Mel Gibson on our planet and putting him where he is today. One example: a would-be priest quits the seminary in disgust and joins the army, making it possible – after a gory detour to Japanese-held Guadalcanal during the Pacific battles of World War Two – for him to meet and marry a girl living hundreds of miles from his old home town.

If Pop Hutton hadn't become a GI, Mel Gibson wouldn't exist. Now there is a thought.

And then there's the excruciating irony of a kid forcefed on fanatical, Father-knows-best religion of the kind that some folk label Papism, going into the one trade notorious for rampant egoism, lively libidos and airy disdain towards traditional moral values.

The wonder is not that Mel, a.k.a. Mad Max, has kicked over the traces and flirted with bad craziness, on occasion. The miracle is that give or take his recourse to Alcoholics Anonymous and some worrying lapses in health, he has kept his head together and his heart more or less in the right place.

Movie-making is much like war, which has been said to be ninety per cent boredom while waiting for ten per cent of frenetic activity. Making movies outside a studio, often right off the map, is worse, through offering fewer home comforts. Steam needs letting off, empty evenings must be filled – when it comes to disgraceful behaviour, the main difference between a film team and a rock group, out on the road, is that the band generally sings in key . . .

This has led to a conscience-salving aphorism: 'On

location it doesn't count.' In other words, when cameras stop rolling and the picture is over, so are the affairs.

Given Mel Gibson's tendency to run off the rails, one would expect him to have taken full advantage of being on location. Not so: he seems consciously to distance himself from the actresses and female technicians, many of whom would love to hang his celebrity scalp from their suspender-belts.

The message seems to be that Mel prefers the company of non-industry people, especially on occasions when he has lost self-control and gone over the high side. Intriguingly, he has only ever been tempted when away from film business territory. Apart from a genuine, unpatronising liking for 'real people', Mel still does not really trust Hollywood, or the motives of its denizens when they are eager to be his buddies.

As we shall see, his doubts are well-founded.

Until Christmas of 1990, he fought a losing battle against alcohol – one unfortunate side-effect being a string of brief, generally boozy, encounters with women outside the business.

This Hollywood star made no protestations of love. (Actually Mel on the rampage is very far from a smooth operator, and tight-fisted to boot.)

Astonishingly, none of these women has anything unkind or even reproachful to say about him. He was, they could argue, deceiving nobody – except his wife. It's likely that Mel Gibson subscribes to the philosophy that what a wife doesn't know, can't hurt her. Certainly his strict Catholic upbringing, at Gibson Senior's hands, appears to have given him some highly reactionary views on women.

Modesto, California, in 1990, saw the watershed of his off-the-leash relationships with pretty, dazzled but undemanding girls. For the first time, Mel had been literally caught in the act. Well, captured on film in mildly compromising, candid-camera action.

But as his advisers stress, all that was before Mel gave up drinking. So while it reaped a sensational harvest of embarrassing publicity, worsened by a ham-fisted hush-up operation which didn't help things, Modesto-gate could well have been a farewell performance.

To the sneerers, Mel Gibson – the American who took Hollywood, or perhaps it hi-jacked him, by way of Australia – is a typical Vegemite and Foster's man, an Ocker glorified by an overdose of raw sex appeal. When it suits him, he encourages that misconception.

Even when complimented on his performance in *Hamlet* (lauded by more than one critic, while grudging ones conceded that the Action Man and sex-symbol was a genuine actor) all you got from him was a shrug and a dead-pan refusal to admit that he's smarter and more gifted than the average hunk. 'Good. I've fooled another one.'

In recent years, Mel has grown good at telling journalists everything and nothing. He's a naturally reticent person and that is his means by keeping contractual obligations to promote and publicise his films, while restricting personal data . . . hugging something of himself, to himself.

Anyway, that his game-plan. Somebody called Mel Gibson keeps blowing it out of the water. Efforts to match past-masters of the privacy game, like Sean Connery and a few other wary, laconic veterans, keep failing because he's too genuine for his own good. Honesty keeps letting him down.

Take the notorious Gay Shock-Horror-Disater. When Mel spoke in bluntly homophobic terms about homosexuals, he was simply telling it like it is, in his perception. Somebody asked, so he answered, shooting from the lip. Now those quotes are a media millstone around his neck. Wrenched out of the context of a tour of hs attitudes on countless current topics from politics to the price of eggs, just a handful of unguarded sentences was pounced on and promptly recycled as a major news story, right around the world.

Burned not once but several times, Mel Gibson is a hundred times shy, these days. Many intimates whom I approached for help insisted on checking with him or his family first. They were all strongly discouraged from speaking to me. One relative was even 'instructed' not to loan out some innocuous photographs of the actor as a child. I tried to contact Mel's Hollywood agent, Ed Limato, but never got past his fax machine.

Then one of Mel's oldest friends advised me, 'Drop the project altogether.' Gibson, he warned, would oppose me very vigorously if I tried delving into his background. In Los Angeles, at least half a dozen people who had worked with or for Mel's production company (tellingly named Icon Productions) retreated into total silence. A former employee explained, 'I would be finished in Hollywood if I gave you so much as the time of day'.

Thankfully, I eventually met a number of refreshingly open men and women who were happy to speak their minds and defy Tinseltown rules.

Obviously, many witnesses were mindful of what happened over that recent tabloid exposé of Mel's raffish romp with a trio of nubile women in Modesto. Heavy-hitter lawyers started pursuing them with 'confidentiality contracts' in a bid to seal the girls' mouths. It's likely that Mel's regiment of attorneys will suggest a similar damage control exercise concerning this book, trying to discount, deny and cover up its findings.

But if they do that, they will entirely miss the point of this biography: Mel is no better or worse than the guy next door. Which is exactly what he has maintained from the start, when accused of mega-star glamour. He's a fine, concerned father and loving, good-provider husband who has occasionally erred. In fairness, countless less gifted or famous players have made utter pigs of themselves after hitting the gusher of big bucks and bigger adulation. By contrast, Mel Gibson has hardly dipped a toe in the trough . . . and often scorned temptation.

So why the wall of silence and the lurking lawyers? The answer lies in Mel's upbringing and his priorities. Throughout his career, his family has been the lodestar and life-raft. He'd do virtually anything to protect his wife and children, which accounts for sensitivity over less savoury stories leaking out. No hypocrite, he still feels obliged to come out fighting . . .

If he thought it through, Mel Gibson could raise a far better defence. He's unique or thereabouts. Not for having had a drink problem, nor dabbling with blondes, nor telling what he sees as the truth, and darn Political Correctness – but because he is still in one piece. Still married to the same woman. Still sincerely in love with his wife and adoring his children.

To Mel, unlike the vast majority of his professional peers, they really are all that matters. Few people knowing them doubt that he will remain married to maternal, self-contained Robyn for the rest of his life. She and the children provide a safe haven from the moral and emotional hurricane known as international stardom. Or to change the metaphor, Hollywood has given so many good men a poisoned chalice, but Mel Gibson keeps the antidote at home.

The real reason for this unauthorised biography is that no one had written a comprehensive book about him. Strings of facts, not all accurate, for sure. Fan-magazine-cum-filmography essays, sure. But there's been no attempt to address the paradoxes and strokes of fortune, the interplay genes and environment, the sheer believe-it-or-not quality of an obscure outsider's charge to the top of his profession.

I am an unreconstructed admirer. If for no other reason,

I would have been bound to tell the Mel Gibson story because I feel such empathy with him. It may be imagination, but at moments I have sensed what has been going through his mind.

Let me explain: we are both the same age, both married young and have stayed with the same partner ever since, and both of us have raised a multitude of children, with all that means.

Use 20-20 hindsight and it's easy to say that Mel's time would have come, whether or not he had won the roles of Max Rockatansky or Martin Riggs. He was a virile, macho youngster with that elusive quality of making a audience take notice, just at the time of a great sea-change and renaissance of the arts, especially film-making, in Australia. Of course, as an All-American kid who a few years before seemed rooted in a flyspeck-on-the-map corner of upper New York State, Mel Gibson had no business being in Australia . . . for an overt fatalist insisting that he's never expected much and thus escapes disappointment, he has had an unusual share of luck.

Maybe Mel isn't kidding about indifference to stardom, and his impatience to hand it back and get on with his real life.

Stardom has to be the most over-used and under-defined word in any actor's dictionary. It means everything and nothing. Great acting? Great popularity? Skill and charisma? Sexiness? Is it torment and self-destruction, as with Garland and Clift, or high-profile, excessive consumption, like Burton and Taylor in their lurid heyday? If so, and if craft and art need not be involved, then where do Olivier, Gielgud and Brando fit in?

Thus the crown Mel wears, so carelessly and frequently unwillingly, is invisible and indefinable. the one sure thing about stardom is the *every* actor, whatever they say, dreams of achieving it. Many famous people fear that if that dream is taken away, the initiative goes with it.

Include Mel Gibson out of that. His dream, fully realised, was to have a good wife and lots of children, and look after them. The guy has no *right* to have got where he is!

And as you will have gathered by now, he is not the easiest subject to analyse. None of that glib, manufactured charm of most Men-About-the-Movies. He's been described as shy but his taciturnity owes less to diffidence than a constant campaign to hide his reel feelings. No matter, the challenge has made the quest all the more satisfying. I have followed in his footsteps, often literally, around the globe, and thanks to a fact or anedote here, an insight and a revelation there, rather like a photograph building to definition in a tank of developing fluid, a portrait began to emerge.

It's not the publicity-pack image, airbrushed, cunningly lit, essentially two-dimensional. Here is a surprising picture, downright startling by contrast with the face on the posters.

Mel denies strangers clues to the guilt, unease and even anger fuelled by his rigidly Catholic unbringing under a father who, even to this day, rarely praises his son. There are manifest tensions and contradictions in a boy squeezed into that rigid mould, springing up into a man making money in telephone-numbers profusion for what some
people refuse to regard as work – and in the notoriously profligate, near-pagan, Celluloid Circus, to boot.

No wonder that his gorge rose on being hailed as owning 'The most kissable lips', or that he was so appalled and scornful when an American magazine poll pronounced him the Sexist Man Alive.

His fans expect Mel to be himself, and the knack of fooling them into accepting that what they see is what they get, is a key to his primacy. Except that there is a heck of a lot more to Gibson than that; on the record he talks of getting through life by faking it, freewheeling. But preparing for *Hamlet*, the longest and most taxing single role in the Shakespeare canon, he read every text, tome and manual he could lay hands on.

Mel the scholar-thinker-thespian, then. Until the marathon was over, and deadpan-impish, he claimed that Marty 'Trust Me' Riggs of *Lethal Weapon* was a far harder character to sell. See what I mean? Even his facets have facets and, personality-wise, he's a moving target.

Sexist Man or no, those who have been around at the time report that he can just be there, glancing ever so casually at a female – regardless of age, race or status – and those magnificent, trapped-sky, opalescent orbs reduce them to a dreamlike state.

Mel has been called handsome, but he's better than that. He is actually attractive, which is more accessible and less threatening. Significantly, female fans love him and far from resenting and scoffing at him for it, their men like, admire and wish they were Mel. That is the rarest of cross-overs, a wild talent that cannot be learned, bought or simulated . . .

For all his striving to be a worthy Hamlet, Mel Gibson does not have to persuade you that he is anybody else but Mel. The screen likes actors but it adores stars.

The snag is that stars are deceptive, unknowable. Simplest proof of that – Mad Max and madder Marty Riggs are extroverts, and then some. Mel Gibson, though he puts on a show, is much more of an introvert.

Yet there is a bond. And as this book will demonstrate, the one common factor between Max, Marty and Mel is intriguing, engaging, and uncommonly worth attention . . . all three are magnificent mavericks!

If you have no great expectations, you're not going to be disappointed.

She had the audience in the palm of her hand.

They demanded encore after encore. The Sydney Town Hall was packed to capacity for the farewell concert of famed contralto Eva Mylott. If there are such things as show business genes then it must have been Eva who passed them on to her grandson Mel Gibson.

In February, 1902 Eva, then 27, was giving her last performance before setting off for Europe, a land of hope and opportunity which – naturally – she intended to take by storm. Australia had been good to her and her family ever since Eva's father Patrick Mylott escaped the Great Potato Famine and British repression in Ireland to head Down Under. Eva became renowned as a free spirit in a land where society was a bastion of male domination. She wanted the sort of artistic freedom and licence that everyone had told her existed in Europe. It was a huge risk for a single woman. It was typical of Eva Mylott.

Her career in Australia had been nurtured by the legendary Dame Nellie Melba, acclaimed around the world as one of the greatest operatic sopranos of all time. Melba took the talented Eva under her wing and became her confidante and mentor. She also incurred the wrath of Eva's father, who fled the horrors of life in Ireland, only to find his beloved daughter headed back for that same corner of the world.

But Eva had a reckless streak within her. She spent her lifetime balancing precariously along a thin line between taking outrageous risks and enjoying life to the full. It is something Mel Gibson can definitely relate to.

Eva spent a total of five years in Europe. The black clouds of World War One were not yet on the horizon and the emphasis was on living well and playing hard. She fell in and out of love as regularly as her emotions decreed. The artistic opportunities of cities like Paris, Rome and Madrid made them even more seductive places to Eva. She had so much to learn.

But there was an even bigger, more exciting land of opportunity beckoning from across the Atlantic and she grew ever more inquisitive about America. There was growing interest in opera in the United States and travellers spoke of vast concert halls and enthusiastic crowds desperate to welcome entertainers.

When another love affair crumbled, Eva found the appeal of America too hard to resist. It was a perfect time, once again, to start afresh.

Most immigrants toiled hundreds of miles by foot just to reach the European ports where cramped ships packed them on board like sardines for the difficult voyage across the Atlantic. Eva travelled in much more style. As the hard-pressed found themselves sleeping often on open decks in chafing, saltwater-damp blankets, Eva slept peacefully in her cabin and dreamt of how she was about to take the new land of opportunity by storm.

In the summer of 1907 she entered Upper New York Bay, sailed past the Statue of Liberty and stood on the upper deck for the final three-quarters of a mile towards Ellis Island. Eva's eyes were dazzled as she stared out at her new home and unknown future.

But this was a time when tens of thousands of immigrants were pouring into the United States every week. To immigration officers, Eva was just another potential problem. Inspectors boarded to survey the latest delivery from crowded Europe and insisted that she travel on a barge to Ellis Island like everyone else. All those who have walked down the gang-plank and up the quay to the New World can recall the noise of the ground-floor baggage room. Above the smell of the masses there was the welcome aroma of thick soups, stews and freshly-baked bread. Medical examinations took place in the Great Hall upstairs.

Eva had to wait her turn on one of the endless wooden benches, just another supplicant. Then she was asked thirty questions in two minutes of machine-gun dialogue from a grim-faced immigration officer. "What is your name?" "Where were you born?" He looked confused when Eva said Australia. Many Americans did not even know where Australia was – and she had just arrived from Europe after all! The questions continued. "Are you an anarchist?" "Do you have a criminal record?" "Do you have any skills?"

Eva Mylott was outraged. She considered herself a skilled and talented singer. But that did not cut much ice with her interrogator. By the time Eva officially stepped on to American soil, she was starting to wonder if she had made a dreadful mistake. But with typical steely deter-mination she held her head high and got on with a new life in a new land.

Within months, Eva was winning rave notices for her performances at concerts in Chicago, Boston, Philadelphia and Montreal. She was rapidly gaining a reputation as a superb contralto. Back in Australia, Dame Nellie Melba was proud of her success. She pored over every word of each letter Eva sent her. Her prodigy had well and truly made it.

Life in America could not have been kinder to Eva. She swept audiences up with her magnetism.

"She had a way of handling crowds. They adored her," explained old Gibson family friend Ed Stinson.

Eva also had those incredible blue eyes that movie audiences across the globe have found so irresistible in her grandson. Child behavioural experts have long been convinced that personality patterns frequently skip a generation. In other words, you are more likely to resemble your grandparents than your own mother and father. Eva Mylott was a warm, attractive, hypnotic personality, scornful of risks, and capable of grabbing attention in a crowded room. Little wonder that Mel Gibson found his calling in Hollywood's movie industry.

But in 1914, Eva – who was then nearly 40 and still unmarried – met millionaire businessman John Hutton Gibson after a sellout concert in Chicago. Gibson, a shy, reserved, handsome man was, perhaps not surprisingly, bowled over by the beautiful, exotic Eva. She in turn felt attracted to him because he was the exact opposite of the flighty, flirty men whom she usually encountered during life on the road. Too many love affairs had crumbled after Eva fell for predatory fellows interested only in a brief liaison with a spirited opera star.

In Gibson she found a man who truly cared for her – and as partner in a successful Chicago metal foundry, he could provide her with the security she desperately craved. It was a last chance for Eva. She had lived life in the fast lane but now it was dawning on her that she had so little to show for it. No husband. No children.

Marriage to Gibson brought her more happiness than a thousand encores. She helped raise money to send medical supplies to Australian hospitals during World War One, spurred on by her family links Down Under. The couple moved to the tranquillity of Montclair in New York State where, at the age of 43, Eva's dream came true in 1918 when she gave birth to Hutton Peter Gibson, father of Mel.

Typically, Eva defied doctors in the first place by getting pregnant at an age when many women are about to become grandmothers. But she angered medics even further by trying for more children after the birth of Hutton. Fifteen months later, just weeks after giving birth to another son, Alexander Mylott, serious post-natal complications set in.

Eva knew she was dying. And according to family lore, she grasped her heartbroken husband's hand as he sat by her hospital bedside and told him: "It is God's will. We have two wonderful boys. The Gibson name will carry on."

A month after giving birth to Alexander, she died. Gibson was understandably distraught at the funeral service in Chicago held a few days later. He felt betrayed to have found love late in life, only to have it snatched away so cruelly. In a pledge of loyalty that would become characteristic of his son and grandson, he swore that he would never marry again. No one could replace Eva in his affections and the very suggestion of another woman entering his life brought an indignant response. Widower Gibson turned to the Roman Catholic Church for his solace and strove to ensure that his two sons did likewise.

Hutton and his baby brother were, as is often the case, different as chalk and cheese. For the first few years after their mother's death they led a wealthy if not exactly inspiring existence in the Gibson mansion. Papa brought in an elderly, stern housekeeper to keep the boys in check until they were old enough to attend parochial school in Rockford, Illinois. Most of their early upbringing was centred around the doctrines of the Catholic Church.

Gibson senior worked long hard hours at the metal foundry. The Great Depression was on the horizon and he was fighting a losing battle to prevent the business from sliding into bankruptcy. He would arrive home exhausted after yet another stressful day. The boys were desperate for contact. More often than not, he would bury himself in a religious manual and order the housekeeper to get them to bed.

Hutton Gibson was barely into his early teens when the Depression hit the family very badly. Gibson senior's income halved; eventually he lost his stake in the metal foundry and suffered poor health for the remainder of his life. The Gibsons were no longer the richest kids on the block and a paper round became an important source of income for young Hutton. He rose at four every morning to complete not one, but two rounds in a desperate effort to augment the family income. His doggedness has become a hallmark of his clan.

In the evenings, Hutton Gibson accepted the lack of attention from his father and threw himself into Catholicism, often reading avidly until the early hours. His deep commitment to the faith was growing by the day. Like many before and since, he used his unswerving beliefs to feed eternal optimism that everything would once again be fine in the world. He studied devotedly, and years later, still insisted: "The greatest benefit anyone can have is to be a Catholic. You have the lifelong satisfaction of being right."

Such blinkered dedication, easily mistaken for smug self-confidence, caused many to remember Hutton as "distant" or "uncommunicative". Indeed he prides himself on an unswerving view of the world in blacks and whites.

"There's right . . . and wrong," he declares, "and that's ALL there is!"

Back in the Depression-ridden early Thirties, Hutton and kid brother Alex were forced into the Civil Conservation Corps, set up to train young people for non-existent jobs. More than half a million unemployed youngsters were in CCC camps at the time, making the places hotbeds of insecurity, cynicism and potential rebellion.

Hutton got back to his sombre family home each night, increasingly disillusioned by this futility. His spare time dominated by religious exploration, he sensed that his vocation waited elsewhere – the Church.

Chicago's Society of the Divine Word was a dour, imposing place, but as combined college and recruit-barracks for the priesthood, seminaries are supposed to be that way and Hutton was undaunted. He thrived in an ascetic, intellectually demanding regime. Catholicism was his calling, his new home. He had no qualms about the vow of celibacy: temptations tripping most hot-blooded kids were mere hurdles to be vaulted, for Hutton.

His initial year went well enough. An ideal seminarian at first, Hutton welcomed the discipline, structure, and above all, the company of like-minded men on the same road. At home, there had been tension and friction with his sprightlier young brother, and the implicit gloom generated by his father's declining health and spirits. At last he had a clearly defined goal and means of reaching it.

But as the would-be priest adjusted to seminary restrictions and routine, his questioning began. It wasn't a matter of the yoke of self-denial starting to chafe. Quite the reverse: young Hutton's distaste was for the Roman Catholic Church's belated, very mild and minor attempts to move with the times. His attitude did not go down well. Many priests at the seminary were in favour of reform and he was regarded as something of a pest. *Callow* reactionaries can be the most tiresome . . .

More than twenty years later, Hutton's unbending religious creed captured headlines, but then, it simply convinced the softly-spoken yet stubborn American that the priesthood was not for him. Freed from celibacy, he might better serve Christ by fathering children who would be trained in the good old, true old faith. Just after the outbreak of World War Two, Hutton abandoned the seminary.

Weeks later, his father died and Hutton became doubly orphaned, parents and vocation lost. Whether it was patriotism or panic at being rootless and aimless, young Hutton opted for another all-male, highly structured society – he joined the army. Enlisting in the infantry may have been the most illuminating and shocking move of his life. It wasn't the grisly, hand-to-hand conflict in the Pacific that shook Hutton Gibson, but fellow GIs' total disdain for God.

"There are no atheists in foxholes," was a wartime saying; but such was not soldier Hutton's experience. As he saw it, he was surrounded by blasphemers, unbelievers, modern pagans. They might die at any moment, unshriven, *and so many of them didn't care*. The teachings of Our Lord did not extend to the killing fields and that baffled and disturbed him, far more than the very likely prospect of dying in tropical mud.

It was a crucial insight, not only for the World War Two warrior, but one of his sons, whose birth lay years ahead. Because Hutton – Second Lieutenant Gibson by then, a combat veteran – made up his mind that *his* children would never abuse God in the cause and course of war. When Hutton Gibson reaches a decision, it's set in concrete: long afterwards, he took his vast family halfway around the world, a modern Moses leading his tribe in flight from Pentagon Pharaohs, sooner than allow his boys to be conscripted.

(Here's another paradox: Mel Gibson landed up in Australia, the right place at the right time, because his father detested soldiering, on moral grounds. Yet his most successful son's career owes much to playing exactly the profane, violent type of characters whom, long ago Second Lieutenant Hutton Gibson deplored. Go figure it.)

Leaving that lone crusader, Mel's father, in the Pacific for the moment, we must switch to the maternal branch of the family tree. Cue for more conflict.

In Ireland, towards the turn of the century, the Reilly family was experiencing – in their and Mel's perception, you understand – the horrors of British rule. The notorious Black and Tans were an army of ex-servicemen sent over from the mainland to "teach the Irish a lesson". In Republican demonology, "the ***** Tans" are arch-fiends. Beyond doubt, many of the Auxiliaries were out of control on occasions, behaving in such a brutal and heartless fashion that the locals held them in complete contempt as well as healthy fear. Not only IRA propagandists believe that the Black and Tans were a significant element of a wind that, as in the Bible, is being reaped as the whirlwind on the streets and in Bandit Country fields of Northern Ireland and the border, to this day.

Long-time family friend Ed Stinson says that the behaviour of the British towards the family of Mel's mother Anne (and especially her own mother) remains unforgotten to this day.

"There was and still is great resentment towards the English. The Black and Tans came to Ireland when Mel's grandmother lived there. They were nothing more than thugs and they attacked many women over there. Mel's mother in particular hated the English. Anne told me that women in her family were raped by the Black and Tans; those stories have been handed down over the years."

Stories of female members of the Reilly family being

raped and brutalised by the Black and Tans are still spoken of in hushed tones in the Gibson household. Rumours abound that Mel's own grandmother suffered at their hands. Certainly Mel and the rest of the Gibson clan share a distrust of the British as a result of whatever incident did actually occur.

And Mel himself has talked in interviews about his feelings towards the British for the way they handled America and then Australia.

"Both countries started for the same reason. They were places where Mother England put her cast-offs, her undesirables – a lot of Irish and English criminals. Then you guys [the Americans] got strong enough to sort of say to the British: 'Get lost, we don't want you around here any more. You got rid of us; we're doing something good here; leave us alone.' But the Australians never did that."

To this day, the Gibson household believes that the modern Irish struggle is a problem created by the British.

Mel's mother's family, the Reillys, settled in the Bushwick section of Brooklyn, New York. This predominantly Irish and German community had sprouted up during the preceding twenty years and the Reilly home on Granite Street was right in the centre of it all. Ironically, Anne Patricia Reilly actually ended up being born in the home country after her mother returned to Ireland to visit her own mother, who had refused to move to the new world despite the horrors inflicted on her by the dreaded Black and Tans. Paid just 10/- (50p) a day, the Tans (named after their mix of army and police uniforms) were first sent to Ireland in March, 1920.

Anne's grandmother was a widow suffering from regular bouts of ill health and living in the picturesque country area of Marley, in County Longford. But the pregnant mother's visit to Ireland coincided with some of the worst outbreaks of civil unrest and she witnessed the full, horrifying impact of the Black and Tans. In the middle of all this violence, Anne was born.

Eventually, they arrived back safely in New York. Mel's mother attended a parochial school in the parish of Our Lady of Lourdes and then went on to graduate from Bushwick High, a state school. Anne showed a particular talent for drawing and she was greatly interested in photography. Later, she even attended art school in Manhattan.

Anne was a homely sort of girl, enjoying a fine relationship with her parents. And like any good Catholic girl, she continued living at home after getting a job at a photographic firm near Penn Station, on Seventh Avenue. Anne relished family life and happily obeyed the rigid rules of a traditional Catholic household. That was something which definitely made her a good catch for the deeply religious Hutton Gibson when they eventually met and fell in love.

At that time, Anne's elder sister Kathleen married a young man who worked for the New York transit company as a motorman on trolley cars. One of his best friends was fellow worker Harold Cardello, who came from the Flatbush area of Brooklyn. When Cardello enlisted in the infantry he was sent to Fort Benning, Georgia, where he became acquainted with Hutton Gibson, a fellow GI.

"At first, I might say, he did not seem a very lovable person, not until you got to know him," says Mel's aunt Kathleen.

"I didn't think too much of him and seeing he seemed likely to marry my sister, there was some defensive mechanism early in the piece. He seemed strong and single-minded."

But then Hutton was in his early twenties, with no parents and a wild kid brother who had taken off to do his own thing years earlier. He was unsure how to handle friendships, let alone actual relationships.

Earnest, worthy Hutton started being called "Red" by his newly-adopted family. It was a name that was to stick for the rest of his life. But, at Gibson's insistence, only his family could call him that. To the rest of the world he was "Hutt".

"Red is the only name I've ever called him by because 'Hutton' seemed kind of far out to me. Anyway, Red just fell into the family. With that red hair, he looked mickey, Irish mickey, like we did," recalls Aunt Kathleen.

"Red was very pleasant and very well educated, more so than we were. He wasn't outgoing, but kind of shy and distant. He made people feel uncomfortable at first. Once you got to know him he was a real warm person though."

Aunt Kathleen could just as easily be describing Mel Gibson. It is a common bond between father and son. They hold their distance until they are absolutely certain.

However, Kathleen went on to reveal: "We all got on together and very soon loved each other. Then Anna, who came to visit us often, met Red through us."

Hutton Gibson hardly swept Anne Reilly off her feet. He quietly got to know her. Family members say that he wanted to make sure she shared his religious beliefs before they even so much as held hands.

"It was a very, very austere affair, to say the least. Because Red was a very religious person – cool but at the same time affectionate. And Anna was a very plain, very soft, very nice girl – a good conversationalist and talented – but she didn't have all the knowledge that Red had."

A few months later, Hutton was sent to officer cadet school, in the Signal Corps at nearby Fort Monmouth, New Jersey. It was the perfect transfer for the young soldier. His affection for Anne was slowly but surely growing and he was able to travel to Kathleen's home every weekend.

"It didn't take us long to grab her and say: 'Don't let this guy get away'," admits Kathleen.

But it wasn't just Hutton's interest in his sweetheart that incited his regular visits. He adored playing with Kathleen's children. "He loved our kids and our kids loved him," she explained years later.

Almost inevitably, Hutton – whose own mother had been too old to have more than just two children – had already decided that he wanted a huge family. In some ways it might recompense him for missing out on all the fun of being part of a big family when he was a child. He went out of his way to play with Kathleen's children to make up for what he had forfeited. Interestingly, Mel Gibson appears to have been equally adept at handling his relatives' children, even when still in his teens.

"Mel loved children even when he was still at drama school. He was always talking about his nieces and nephews. He was the sort of uncle who would take them all to the park," said one of Mel's former girlfriends from student days.

Back in those far-off days during World War Two, Hutton soon received his second lieutenant's bars. And earned them all over again, in the thick of the action in the Pacific. Many months of gruelling combat action followed. Hutton's ever-present belief in God, and his Catholic education, he said later, helped him survive the horrors of war. But he could not come to terms with the atheism of many of his fellow soldiers.

"Hutt had a lot of problems with the way the army was run. He did not approve of the morals. He did not care for it," says Ed Stinson now.

It was during the war that Hutton Gibson made his first visit to Australia. He and brother Alexander had hoped to visit their mother's birthplace but they were both recalled to active service before they had a chance to organise the trip.

Hutton made a pledge, there and then, to return one day. The vow altered many lives.

Towards the end of the war, Gibson was wounded in the battle of Guadalcanal and sent home. Anne Reilly was there to greet him when he set foot on American soil. Hutton did not hesitate in asking her to marry him that very day but he made her make one solemn promise.

"Hutt told Anne she had to read up on all the Catholic writings on birth control and the marriage vows before they could wed," explained Ed Stinson.

Once again the Hutton Gibson black-or-white philosophy on life was uncompromising. Not to mention the fact that he made it clear he would only marry a virgin – an attitude he appears to have passed down to many of his children, including Mel.

The happy couple were married in a simple ceremony at the church of Our Lady of Good Counsel in Brooklyn, on the morning of May 1, 1944.

"We're going to have ten children," announced Hutton with a mischievous smile to the assembled guests. Just like every word he ever speaks, Hutton meant it . . .

And even Aunt Kathleen was impressed.

"As we got to know him there was this wonderful warmth and he truly loved Anne."

And Anne was equally determined to have lots of children in a marriage that would last until death did them part. More than forty years later she argued:

"Look at Cary Grant. He had five wives and died with only one child. That's a completely unproductive life as far as I'm concerned."

A few weeks before his wedding, Hutton had taken a job on the New York Central Railroad. Strange career choice for a well-educated man from a fine middle-class background, but the wages were better-than-average and that would give Hutton the freedom to start the family he longed to raise.

"Starting that family meant more to Hutton than anything else and I never once heard him complain about his lot in life," said one close family friend.

The newly-weds set up home in a large sunny apartment near 212th Street, Manhattan. It was a fine, safe area and Hutton felt that for the first time in his life, things were going his way. Both he and Anne were thrilled when their first child, Patricia, was born on April Fool's Day in 1945. Anne was just 24 years old when that baby was born – almost twenty years younger than Hutton's tragic mother had been when she gave birth to him. He was determined that he and Anne would live to enjoy the growing up of all the children they were planning to have. So far, everything had gone precisely to plan.

More babies followed with the sort of regularity that alarmed friends and colleagues but delighted Anne and Hutton. There was Sheila, then Mary, Kevin and Maura Louise.

Wisely, Hutton decided the city was no place to bring up an ever-growing family and they moved thirty miles north of the city to Croton-on-Hudson. It was a quiet, friendly little community and Hutton managed to transfer to working on the freight trains travelling to and from the huge Croton-Harmon railroad yard. With the arrival of baby number four, Kevin, Hutton's family outgrew their small, one-storey home so they headed for the peaceful hamlet of Verplanck nearby.

Verplanck's Point, to give its full name, is one of several historic villages on the eastern bank of the Hudson River, settled by the Dutch in the late seventeenth century. Nestled on the banks of this vast river, with the shadow of Dunderberg Mountain and its cliff-edge roads to the north and other mountains to the south, it is hard to imagine that the sprawling metropolis of New York lies just forty miles to the south.

This now predominantly Irish/Italian town looks across the river to Tomkins Cove and Stony Point. It is girdled by thick forest and during winter, snow-clad roads and lush pastures have definite picture-postcard appeal. Winter in these parts is by far the longest season and the Gibsons spent many months huddled in front of their one and only fireplace while the dozen or so streets in Verplanck remained deserted for much of the day and night.

Home was a modest shingled one-storey house on Seventh Street. The property was right next to the entrance to the Sun Oil Company depot, which meant a steady procession of heavy tanker trucks thundered past the Gibson front door, by day and night.

Some evenings Hutton would sing with the St Patrick's church choir and as one parishioner recalls: "You could always hear Hutt above everybody else. He had a fine voice." Hutton was also an active member of the church group that put on minstrels and other musical entertainments.

Hutton Gibson continued working for the railroad but as his family grew his income covered less and less.

"He was far too bright a guy to be working in such a menial job but he just didn't have the opportunity or time to branch out and try something more testing," explained one old family friend.

Hutton's outgoings were rapidly overtaking his salary. Yet it would take a tragedy long after the birth of five more children finally to help him realise his true potential . . .

I don't go in for personal heroes but I do have one – my old man. My admiration for him cannot be measured.

A son to Mr and Mrs Hutton Gibson, of Verplanck, at the Peekskill Hospital, 4.45 p.m. January 3.

It was a simple announcement, typical of Hutton. No fuss. Plain and to the point. The year was 1956 and the births column of the *Peekskill Evening Star* (cost 5 cents) the following day contained only one other announcement. The paper's front page revealed vital up-to-the-minute news such as the fractured wrist suffered by 9-year-old Diane Wyatt and the ten stitches required by 10-year-old Anne Mason after she put her arm through a window.

At the bottom of the page a three-column story informed readers that President Eisenhower planned to present his much-discussed farm plan to Congress. And inside the paper, columnist George E. Sokolsky fulminated over the evils of Pandit Nehru and his alleged involvement with the Communist Party. But it was some of the advertisements in the paper that day which say it all about life in upstate New York in the mid-Fifties: A sale at Windsor's department store in South Street, Peekskill, proudly offering men's suits for $15. Around the corner at Peekskill Ford Motors Inc., you could pick up a brand-new Tudor Mainline Six, "a 6-passenger car with the lean low-to-the-ground look of Thunderbird styling" for just $1,775.

Not that Hutton Gibson could afford a new model. He whisked Anne and latest arrival Mel away from hospital in the family's scruffy blue station wagon just a day after the birth.

"They never had good cars and often whatever one they did have would be broken down and they'd all have to walk," recalled family friend Ed Stinson.

And as the family grew, it became more and more taxing to fit mother, father and the children all in the car at the same time.

Then there was Hutton Gibson's professed distrust of the medical profession. Mainly fuelled by the high cost of medicine in the United States, it was also influenced by a natural suspicion about non-Catholic doctors and a reluctance to part with any of his hard-earned cash.

The end result of this was that Hutton shovelled vitamin pills into his children at an astonishing daily rate. He also tried to grow organic vegetables. He firmly believed that by keeping his children fit he could avoid doctors completely.

"In all the years I knew them I never saw a doctor at the house. That is pretty amazing when you raise that number of kids," Ed Stinson points out.

This obsession with vitamin pills is yet another habit that Hutton passed down to Mel, who swallows at least thirty different brands each day. He even made a commercial for American television recently, for free, to tell viewers that vitamins are healthy. The public service announcement was for the Supernutrition Life Extension Foundation, who are fighting the US Food and Drug Administration's attempt to make certain vitamin dosages available by prescription only.

And today, Mel and his family regularly tuck into porridge made from fresh oats bought by Hutton at the feed store near their Australian farm.

In January, 1956, Mel was baptised at St Patrick's in Verplanck by Rev. Monsignor Daniel Doughtery. He was christened Mel Columbcille Gerard Gibson.

Columbcille is the name of the rural diocese in Ireland where Mel's mother was born. Columba of Iona – sometimes called Columbcille – is one of the best-loved Irish saints, a descendant of Niall, the first high king of Ireland. It is pronounced "Colum-kill". Gerard is for Saint Gerard, an Italian saint of the eighteenth century, the patron saint of expectant mothers, to whom Anne Gibson prayed each time she was expecting another child.

And it wasn't long before her constant prayers were answered. She provided Mel with four younger brothers and sisters: twins Danny and Chris, Donal and Ann. The house in Verplanck was becoming a bit of a tight squeeze to say the least, so Hutton – already working sixteen-hour shifts on the railroad – set about extending the property, single-handedly. It was mid-July and seemingly the correct time to be ripping the roof off to enlarge the attic. The only problem was that the Gibson clan had no place else to stay, so they slept under the stars – literally.

Then Hutton Gibson went off to work in New York City one evening, leaving Anne and the ten children roofless in Verplanck. Good friend and neighbour Ed Stinson takes up the story.

"Early one morning a huge clap of thunder woke me up. It began raining buckets and I knew the kids were there alone with their mother. I jumped in my car and got down to the house as fast as I could. The house was flooding and all the kids – big and little – were running around with pots trying to catch the water, but they were fighting a losing battle.

"I pulled them all out and took them to my office nearby and got some tarpaulins to put over what was left. But there was a lot of damage."

Now some wives might have been really annoyed by their husbands leaving them in the lurch like that – but not Anne Gibson. She had, according to Ed Stinson, an inborn gift for "riding the tide". He says: "Anne went along with practically everything Hutt said. It takes a good woman to go through something like that and come up laughing, but Anne did. We always laugh about that experience."

Ed says they even laughed about it when Anne and Hutton and some of the children paid a nostalgic trip to Verplanck after moving to Australia. In 1979, Mel's mother went to the house on Seventh Street for one last look. It was an emotional tour of her old home.

Current owner Ralph McCoach recalled: "She walked around the various rooms and stopped as if she were listening out for those children's voices. It was obviously very moving for her."

Most of the eight rooms in the single-storey property are still as they were when the Gibsons lived in Verplanck, but it is hard to imagine how ten noisy, energetic children fitted into such a modest place.

Predictably, the stresses and strains of living a hand-to-mouth existence with ten children did abrade and shorten Hutton Gibson's temper at times. Thirty years ago, child abuse was a term restricted to battering and sexual molestation. The rule of the stick was common in most households and there was certainly nothing illegal (or even immoral) about inflicting corporal punishment on a child who misbehaved. These days, it sometimes seems as if shouting at your child in the street can spark a child abuse charge.

Ed Stinson testifies: "Hutt was very, very strict with his family. He had them toeing the mark the whole time. He was a stern person. When he had to do his duty, he was right there as far as discipline was concerned. But they still adored him. Believe me, he was not bashful at dusting them off. He let them know every now and again if they were being bad. Hutt believed in the power of the hand. If the children did not behave they got hit. But he also believed he was doing it for the good of the family."

More than twenty years later, Mel admitted that he was a chip off the old block, saying that sometimes he smacks his own children to make them behave. This was yet another example of the influence that his father has had on him.

Life in Verplanck sounds very insular by today's standards. Hutton the old-time religionist naturally banned all television in the house and comics were hidden under mattresses like contraband for fear that father Gibson might find them and let fly with his explosive temper.

The children were brought up on a staple diet of reading the classics. Cursing was strictly forbidden and punishable with a right-hander. Smoking and drinking were (and still are) considered two of the deadliest sins. Human nature has ensured that nearly all the Gibson offspring – including Mel – have enjoyed their fair share of booze and cigarettes over the years.

"I never saw Hutt have a drink, ever. Even at Christmas there was no alcohol in the house," says Ed Stinson.

In fact, the most popular beverage in the Gibson household was tea.

But despite the iron hand of Hutton Gibson, the family was basically happy and above all, highly self-contained.

"I think the kids all knew their limits as they grew up. They never tested Hutt except on the odd occasion," recalls Ed Stinson.

Older sister Sheila had a rebellious streak and ran away from home after a furious argument with her father – only to return, tail firmly between her legs, just a few hours later. Like all the other children, she had been brought up to believe in the family as the number-one priority. They protected and loved one another and were not that eager to make friends outside the home.

"Sheila was the only one of the children who got the bright red hair of the father and she was the only hothead in the bunch. After she gave him that hard time he made sure she didn't forget it!

"But they all had each other. They used to make their own enjoyment. The children worshipped their father and mother. There was no question that they were the two most important people in their lives," adds Ed Stinson fondly.

By all accounts, the children excelled at amusing themselves. There were few toys in the Gibson household. Hutton laid the law down partly because he could not afford to buy many possessions but also because he distrusted the outside, materialistic world and all its "evil" influences.

But there was a downside to his overbearing personality. While Christmas sounded a solemn affair, birthdays seem to have been positively depressing occasions.

"They got a cake and that was it," says Ed Stinson. "Virtually no presents. That was Hutton's way."

There was another underlying motive for this apparent obsession with not enjoying oneself. Hutton was a *very* tight-fisted fellow. He was seriously stretched financially to the extent that the children sometimes did not get birthday presents.

A few years ago Hutton, mellowed with age and free of the cashflow problems associated with bringing up such a large family, made a candid confession that he is so mean he "can squeeze an American dime until the Indian on one side ends up riding the buffalo on the other side".

Back in Verplanck, the Gibsons' social life was bounded by church, school and family. Occasionally they would visit relatives in Brooklyn. Movies were a very rare occurrence. Hutton Gibson's strict regime meant that films were out of bounds for the most part.

Sometimes, if the kids were well behaved and did their homework, they were allowed to go round to a school pal's home to watch "The Mickey Mouse Club" on television. But that tended to be a treat given on the most part after Hutton had set off for a night shift on the railroad. He would most certainly not have approved of such hedonistic behaviour from his offspring.

It was around this time that an extraordinary incident occurred, involving Hutton and his only brother Alexander. It provides a vivid insight into the lengths to which Papa Gibson would go in order to make those near him submit to his religious convictions.

Alexander had fallen in love with a beautiful Asian girl and decided to visit his sole close relative to present the woman he intended to marry. Hutton was naturally keen to see his younger brother, even though they had not been close for many years; Alexander had settled in California, on the other side of the United States.

The reunion between the brothers followed an awkward scenario, as unofficial family historian Ed Stinson explained. "Hutt was so strict that he would not let his brother and his fiancée stay at the house. They could come and have meals but nothing else."

Hutton's belief in the strong moral values of no sex outside marriage were preached by him to his children constantly, and no one – not even his brother – was going to be allowed to break those rules.

Tragically, Alexander died not long after marrying his fiancée and, according to Ed Stinson, Hutton could not afford to attend the funeral of his only near relative.

Vacations just did not exist in the Gibson household: too many kids and not enough money. However the surrounding countryside in Upstate New York was the backdrop and arena for many juvenile adventures – swimming in the river, sledging on nearby hillsides, skating and ice hockey on the lake, walks through the forest.

And despite their lack of spare cash, Anne Gibson managed to keep herself and her family well fed – in fact by today's standards some of the children would undoubtedly be classified as overweight. But then Mom liked eating as well as cooking.

"Anne was not what you would call thin," explained Ed Stinson. "She took up two seats whenever the family went out in their automobile."

Even Mel at the age of five was hardly wasting away. His chunky physique more than made up for his lack of inches. And it wasn't until his early twenties and fame had struck that he managed to lose weight – which he proudly tells friends he has never regained since.

"We always had enough to eat. My mother would stuff us full of Irish soda bread flan with raisins, or stews, pies and hotpots," said Mel many years later.

One friend, Carol Rowell, vividly recalled how surprised she was by the vast amount of food consumed by the Gibson clan when she went to their house. "I had graduated with Mel's sister Sheila and we went back to their house. Well, within minutes of arriving, the mom brought out this huge pan of pork chops," she explained.

Needless to say, each of the chops was grabbed instantly by the assembled children, who devoured every morsel within minutes. As is often the case in large families, it was the girls who seemed to put on the most weight. Patricia, Sheila and Anne's weight fluctuated wildly throughout their childhood.

Others I spoke to in Verplanck remembered how immaculately dressed the Gibson children always were – although they wore each other's hand-me-down clothes. "Anne could make a small amount of money go a long, long way," said one former neighbour.

Margaret Smith Saladino was Mel's first babysitter when she was a 16-year-old schoolgirl in Verplanck. She remembers the family vividly.

"It was not long after Mel was born but he was always giggling and smiling even then. My mom was great friends with the Gibsons. They were always pitching in like big families do and my younger sister Eileen was close friends with Patricia."

To most of the residents of Verplanck, the Gibsons are unforgettable for two notable reasons: the unusual size of the family and their overt religious beliefs.

"They were a very strong family unit. I think their religious faith kept them very close," Margaret believes.

Her sister Eileen, Patricia's special friend, has even fonder memories of Mel.

"Mel was always my favourite. I don't know why. Probably because of his personality. He was kind of a happy-go-lucky kid. All smiles. The kind of kid you enjoy having around. He may have been kind of a little devil, but he was the sort who could get away with it because he was so cute."

More than thirty years later, Mel proudly labelled himself someone who "could get away with it" during the making of a documentary about *Lethal Weapon III*, one of his most successful movies. Whether he was referring to life in general or certain aspects of his character he alone knows.

But there seems little doubt that Mel's mischievous ways were signalling something special, even in Verplanck.

"He was like a comedian, always doing different kinds of comic things, making fun of this or that. Mel was very smart, sharp as a tack . . . and he was a little devil," says Aunt Kathleen.

Mel loved to act the clown, even when aged just 5. He adored entertaining anyone who happened to be around, with fake falls from scooters and bikes and by walking into doors and walls. He was a disciple of his favourites, the Three Stooges, without knowing about them.

Sometimes, his brothers and sisters would try and emulate his pratfalls.

"But they were never as good as Mel," chuckles Ed Stinson. "If he made you smile, or laugh, he was happy. There was never any malice in Mel's heart and I don't think there ever will be."

Years later Mel confirmed: "Of course I enjoy entertaining people. I have been doing that since I was little. You know how little kids do it. They love the attention – especially if they come from a big family. I used to get a kick out of affecting people, no matter what sort of effect. That is what drives you on."

Many members of the Gibson clan look on their eleven years in Verplanck as the happiest times of their lives. But for Hutton Gibson that timespan represented an intensely hard period of work on the railroad during which he strove to keep the family unit afloat, financially.

Colleagues on the railroad remember him as an ambitious man who sometimes lacked a sense of humour, especially when it came to listening to dirty jokes. But Hutton Gibson had other priorities. He had to get himself promoted in order to earn more money – it was as simple as that. He had no intention of living on the breadline for the whole of his life. Several times he received minor promotions while working on the New York Central line. Finally, he became a freight conductor.

His work routine involved boarding an engine at the Croton-Harmon yard, then with his small crew he would continue down the winding tracks alongside the Hudson River to the sleepy town of Tarrytown, just a few miles south of Verplanck. There they would switch freight cars all night into and out of the massive General Motors yard. It was tough, gruelling work. But Hutton never complained. He had a master plan extending well beyond the railroad.

Gradually, increased earnings enabled him to build up a modest nest-egg. He had always dreamed of owning a house in the middle of the real countryside way north of Verplanck. Hutton wanted his children to have the freedom to roam the fields at will and he wanted a spread of his own land to farm.

In the spring of 1961, Hutton announced to his family and friends that he had found the perfect property among the white wooden houses and picket fences of Mount Vision, a community of just a few thousand nestled in the high country between mountains and lakes, almost two hundred miles north of New York. So the family set off in their newly-purchased bone-shaker of a Volkswagen van for a better life . . .

The farmhouse itself was a picturesque two-storey double-fronted property with more rooms and space than any of the Gibson children had imagined living in. Ten acres of wilderness backed on to the main building. The site looked down on to the village of Laurens, three miles across a small valley, and the little-used Highway 205. The hamlet was exactly halfway between the bustling towns of Oneonta and Cooperstown, in a stretch of unspoilt landscape. To Hutton Gibson this was paradise. The sort of place he had been looking for to fulfil his dreams since those distant days when he promised himself he would some day have a huge, happy family.

Hutton's scheme was to continue working on the railroad while setting up the farm in such a way that he would eventually be able to quit his day job and run his own business. It was a pipe dream inspired by an abiding determination to give his children a good, wholesome life. But the practicalities of farming the land were not as easy as they must have appeared.

"I told him I thought it was a very big undertaking and that financially it was not the most rewarding life," explained Ed Stinson. "But they thought they could be self-supporting and make a go of it. Most of all they believed it was the ideal place to raise a family."

One of the first problems encountered by the Gibsons was the sheer solitude of life in Mount Vision. Hutton would take off at dawn most Mondays in the Volkswagen van for work on the railroad and more often than not end up sleeping-over weekdays at his sister-in-law's in New York City, only returning late Friday to his family.

With Anne unable to drive, this left her and the children completely stranded. Even Anne's easy-going nature found it hard to accept that this was, as Hutton claimed, a better life. Just a visit to the village store was a major operation and with all those mouths to feed three times a day, she spent much of her time on the winding road down to Mount Vision.

Luckily a steady stream of visiting relatives and friends broke the monotony, but other children were struck by the lack of activities at the rambling house. There were no horses to ride, no motorbikes to explore the hilly trails. Some of the Gibson clan did not even own bicycles.

But Mel and his five older brothers and sisters did manage to take younger visitors over to some of the swimming holes in nearby Ostego Creek and in those days youngsters could safely thumb a ride into the village to buy sticks of penny candy.

The back yard was soon filled with home-grown vegetables, but Anne never had enough left over to store in the barn. The children tended to gobble them up the moment they were ripe for the picking.

All the children were made to share the chores around the farm. Mel tried hard to avoid cleaning out the cattle pens and often found himself being dragged into the barn by his older and wiser – bigger, anyway – siblings.

The only aspect of life that seriously bothered Hutton Gibson was the lack of a good Catholic school in the vicinity. He had carefully weighed up the pros and cons of life in Mount Vision before buying the farmhouse and decided that he could afford to risk the children at the local public school just so long as they absorbed his special religious teachings at home.

The kids – although none of them would admit it to his face – were no doubt delighted to get a reprieve from a Catholic education. Typically of a large family, they settled into the Laurens School with ease. Hutton Gibson had a family of achievers to be proud of; Mel's sister Patricia soon became the school's assistant librarian as well as appearing in both the junior and senior plays and choruses, the colour guard, the Spanish Club and the girls' volleyball team. She was a highly popular student with this glowing tribute written beneath her graduation photograph in the 1962 edition of the school yearbook: "Lovely voice . . . brothers and sisters galore . . . sugar and spice and everything nice."

Mel was happy as a sandboy when he joined sisters Sheila, Mary B, Maura and brother Kevin on the school bus to Laurens each morning.

Mrs Evelyn Koelliker was Mel's first-grade teacher

followed by Mrs Katherine Sapatek in the second and Mrs Zelma Ainslie (now Shapely) in the third.

"He was a very bright youngster. Actually all the children were," said Mrs Shapely.

Sports teacher Pat Grasso is the only teacher still working at the school who encountered Mel. Every day he held a forty-minute group games session when all the youngsters played kickball, relay races and catching. His memories of the little boy are dim, but Hutton Gibson made a lasting impression on him.

"His father was most concerned about some of the teaching in the school. He seemed to expect there to be more religious instruction. Frankly, he could be quite a pain," recalled Grasso.

Hutton Gibson made it his business to see that his children were receiving a "decent, moral education". He had already promised himself that at the first sign of a breakdown in his children's upbringing he would pull them out of school and teach them at home if necessary. It was by no means the only time that Hutton Gibson stepped between his children and their teachers.

On Sunday, October 7, 1962, just a few weeks after entering his new school, Mel received his first Holy Communion at the small Holy Cross Catholic Church, in the nearby community of Morris. Hutton had fastidiously assessed all the Catholic churches in the area before finding one that lived up to his high standards. He was obsessed with making sure they did not encroach on any of the High Mass observations and ritual to which he strictly adhered.

But there were other more pressing problems in their rural paradise, like the freezing-over of their only supply of drinking water, from the mountains behind the farmhouse, and the persistent problems of rearing cattle in an environment predominantly used for dairy farming. The children got plenty of exercise rounding up the animals which were forever escaping from their pens. Then there were the brief summers that barely allowed the family to work the land before the snow returned, reigning from October to May.

However, the biggest problem encountered by the Gibsons was caused by Hutton's bedrock belief in the doctrines of the Catholic Church. During his search and seek mission to locate the finest Catholic church, he became painfully aware that Upstate New York was overwhelmingly Republican and Protestant. The political part he could easily live with; his own beliefs appear to border on extreme conservatism. But the virulent dislike of the Catholic Church was deeply offensive and very disturbing to Hutton. He had earlier ignored it when overhearing a "friendly" neighbour in the local store refer to the "Catholic invasion". But clear evidence of religious discrimination was everywhere he looked.

The assassination of John Kennedy on November 22, 1963, shocked the world. Yet in the communities around Mount Vision some Protestants were actually celebrating the death of a Catholic President. Hutton's disillusionment with the United States was gradually building. When, in 1964, the Warren Commission report concluded that Lee Harvey Oswald had acted alone in killing the President, Hutton was not the only American citizen who began to question the direction his country was taking.

He read with disdain in August that year how Lyndon Johnson had decided to escalate the war in Vietnam after North Vietnamese torpedo boats allegedly attacked the US destroyers *Maddox* and *Turner Joy*. For all Hutton's conservative beliefs he could not condone war. He had seen the horrors of battle at first hand.

Further, all the Gibsons' close family and friends knew

that the family's dream life on the farm was not going according to plan.

"They'd gone to a place where you really couldn't do much. It was very, very hard, with Red working on the railroad down here [in New York City] and Anna and the children being alone during the week up there," explained Aunt Kathleen.

Old friend Ed Stinson summed it up when he said: "It just did not turn out the way they had planned. The logistics of the situation were proving too much to handle."

At 12.30 on the morning of December 11, 1964, Hutton Gibson was going about his work as usual aboard engine No. 8595 as it waited in the Croton-on-Hudson railroad yard. Another arduous week was coming to an end and he was looking forward to heading home to Mount Vision for a welcome sojourn with the family. He did not see the pool of oil on the engine floor until it was too late. He slipped and fell heavily on to the railroad roadbed and lay there unable to move. Spasms of agonising pain were stabbing through his back.

Fellow workers rushed to help him to his feet, but he could not move. Eventually paramedics arrived and took him to a nearby hospital for overnight observation. There were genuine fears that he might have broken his back in the fall. Hutton Gibson's long ordeal had only just begun.

It wasn't until just before dawn the following day that Anne Gibson got a phone call from a railroad colleague of Hutton's. The news wasn't good at all.

A myelogram – an X-ray procedure in which the outline of the spinal cord and the space surrounding it can be seen – revealed that Hutton had sustained various spinal injuries, including herniated lumbar discs. A series of painful operations followed. A laminectomy was performed to help ease the injury to the spinal cord. This involved an agonising procedure during which the spinal canal is opened by the removal of the posterior wall. Hutton also had to endure spinal fusion of one of his discs. Not to mention the whiplash injury of the cervical spine which resulted in arthritis and degenerative changes.

Much more anguish was to follow. For more than three years the New York Central Railroad refused to admit responsibility for the accident and fought Hutton's claims for reparation.

Throughout these difficult times, papa Gibson did not once lose faith in God. If anything he increased his involvement in the church while accepting that he had to sell the Mount Vision farmhouse and rent a cheaper place nearer the city. Evidently difficult times were ahead, but neither Anne nor the children were heartbroken by the move. They were armoured in Hutton's belief that fate had dealt a cruel blow but that everything would be for the best in the end.

They found a huge, ramshackle house across the river from Verplanck in Salisbury Mills, at a peppercorn rent. It was in an appalling state but its lakeside site made up for that in many ways. The children spent untold hours swimming in the lake, and their landlords, the Seamans, let them take boats out on it for fishing. The lake froze in winter and child skaters congregated from a five-mile radius. Hutton Gibson might have lost his job but still he gave his brood a lifestyle fit to make many a wealthier youngster envious. Most importantly, they were still one happy family.

Rugged, hilly Salisbury Mills lies between two hulking mountain ranges and local weather had a nasty habit of scourging the area with violent, tree-shredding thunderstorms. But climatic tantrums were the least of the Gibsons' concerns. Somehow they had to exist on little or no income.

"They were practically starving. Whatever we could do, we did, but we could do very little," explained Aunt

Kathleen. Ed Stinson affirms, "They were almost destitute during that time in Salisbury Mills."

Not only Hutton's spine was seriously injured. So was his pride and self-image as a hard worker capable of any hardship or sacrifice in the campaign to provide for his family. Now he was disabled, possibly permanently, and unable to function as breadwinner and staunch guardian.

Mel's two elder sisters, having finished high school, found jobs to help the family survive. One became a library assistant and the other worked in a newspaper office at nearby Newburgh. Anne longed to venture out and get a job, but caring for ten children was a full-time occupation. In any case, Hutton would never dream of allowing his wife to work. The other youngsters – including Mel – attended school in Washingtonville, where Hutton again managed to find a Catholic church called St Mary's that conformed to his high standards. There, on May 22, 1965, Mel was confirmed.

Witnessing the service were Mel's older sister Patricia and brother Kevin. They had just announced to a delighted mother and father that they were entering strict religious orders. Kevin was to go to a seminary near Newburgh and Patricia to become a novice at a convent near Albany. Already the teachings of papa Hutton had obviously had a profound effect on two of his children.

Typically, Hutton did not sit around doing nothing with his time. He began reading more and more. He took an avid interest in the changing world and he most certainly did not like what he was seeing.

Tie-dyed T-shirts, sandals, beads and bell-bottom jeans were on the horizon. Acid rockers like Grace Slick, Janis Joplin and Jimi Hendrix were hogging the headlines. They seemed to represent everything that was wrong with America, in Hutton's eyes.

Meanwhile, with his wife and children's encouragement,

he sent off a letter to "Jeopardy", the high-stakes quiz show in New York City. The whole family had never forgotten how, some years earlier, Hutton had won a few hundred dollars on another local quiz programme.

A few weeks later, Hutton swept the board on "Jeopardy", answering a barrage of questions thrown at him by host Art Fleming, and walked off with winnings of several thousand dollars. The family had by this time got one tiny black-and-white TV set, which they crowded around and cheered each time their father came on the small screen. At the "Jeopardy" championship run-off some time later, Hutton went all the way and won $21,000. It could not have come at a better time for the Gibsons as they were on the verge of being evicted from their home for non-payment of the minimal rent.

But Hutton was a realistic type of fellow. Despite his family's joy, he knew he could not feed and clothe them for ever on quiz show winnings – and he was well aware that his battle with the railroad would end with a settlement or the sack (most likely both). So, shortly after marching victoriously off the set of "Jeopardy", he visited the New York Rehabilitation Center, in Newburgh, to be assessed for a new career. The results of an IQ test were astounding. He was pronounced a genius and encouraged to enrol in the then-new and arcane field of computer programming.

Computer school on Fourteenth Street in Manhattan was a breath of fresh air for Hutton. He had begun a new career in his mid-forties and with it came a new lease of life. But there was still one cloud looming – the court case about the accident.

After three years and two months of struggling to support his family, the case of *Hutton P. Gibson versus The New York Central* finally came to trial at the Westchester County Court House, in White Plains. Presiding was Judge

John J. Dillon and representing Hutton was Anthony Ferraro, of the law firm Ferraro, Lombardi and Decaro. Hutton's Catholic tastes even stretched as far as his choice of lawyer!

Figures approaching $2 million were mentioned initially, as Ferraro revealed there had been a recent flare-up of his client's injuries. But when the trial ended after seven days, on Valentine's Day, 1968, the jury awarded Hutton $145,000. Even after paying a big chunk for attorney's fees, there was enough for them to settle their debts and make the biggest decision of their life – to emigrate to Australia.

Hutton as usual had thought long and hard to himself about this move to his mother's homeland. But it wasn't just family ties that were luring him away from the United States; the Vietnam War was being fought out in horrifying conditions and Hutton's experiences in the last war had left him with a lasting obsession – to avoid sending his own children off to die in battle.

Years later, Mel – who has played more than his share of war heroes in his time – was candid in revealing the motivation behind his father's decision.

"My older brother was about to get drafted and my father didn't want to send his sons out to get jungle rot and worse. He didn't want to have to send us off one by one to get chopped up."

Intriguingly, Patricia and Kevin immediately withdrew from their religious orders and insisted on travelling with the rest of the clan to Australia. Not even their vocations could snap the extraordinary bond uniting the Gibsons.

For Hutton, there were contributory factors in quitting the United States. One can't help seeing grimly upright Hutton Gibson as a stranger in a strange land – where he had been born. He'd have made a splendid Pilgrim Father but in the sleek, complacent, Fifties era of Eisenhower he cut a vaguely eccentric figure and during the Sixties his ethical rigidity made him nigh-bizarre. By 1968, with Bobby Kennedy and Martin Luther King gunned down, the permissive society putting its pedal to the metal and Mick Jagger singing the praises of fightin' in the street, Hutton Gibson mourned for vanished values, moral aspirations, and was convinced that his homeland was bound for ruin and perdition.

But he knew of a country where, it was said, folk still upheld the values he deemed essential. Like an Old Testament patriarch he would lead his flock to the Promised Land, otherwise known as Australia . . .

The family's final Stateside day was, by all accounts, a solemn occasion. Gibson relatives and friends gathered for a picnic lunch at Aunt Kathleen's house outside New York. This was no vacation, but emigration and a parting of unknown duration, which accounted for the low-key partying. Hutton, Anne and their brood were in great shape, however; wherever they wandered, they were secure in each other.

Instead of flying direct to Australia, Hutton organised stop-overs turning the life-changing journey into a virtual world tour. He was frugal but never cheap, so this was a startling but not uncharacteristic move. Severing his roots and taking ten children across the globe did not daunt him in the slightest. They were Good People, after all, so what could go wrong?

Whenever they used to have raffles at home, I was the guy who won the turtle. And when my parents took us to Ireland for a family vacation, walking down the streets of Bray, I used to find pound notes and stuff. I was always finding money.

3

In her capacity as mother, Anne Gibson had always been of warm heart and easygoing disposition, but amid the customary chaos at Rome's busy Leonardo da Vinci Airport, she was close to panic stations.

The root of her problem lay in a phenomenon that now, more than twenty years later, would probably be headlined in a newspaper as leaving a child "Home Alone". The child in question was Mel Gibson. All twelve in the family were about to board a plane for Australia, the final destination of their world tour and the place they intended to settle in – when it became clear that 12-year-old Mel was not among them.

Anne had only established the awful truth after doing her customary counting in of all ten children as they queued up at the Quantas check-in desk.

"I counted one . . . two . . . three . . . and there were only nine," explained Anne later.

Fortunately, the Gibsons had showed up hours early for their departure – over-punctuality is a habit that most large families get used to. The simple logistics of getting everyone packed and into a convoy of three tiny Fiat taxis was testing to say the least. But now one of them was missing and that unheard-of word "panic" was setting in.

Then Hutton stepped in and calmly organised search parties into two groups. They spread out and began shouting Mel's name above the noise of Roman neuroses as thousands of Italians (all of them running late, naturally) rushed towards the departure lounge. After five minutes of frantic yelling and searching, the two parties regrouped and retraced their footsteps to the spot whence Mel had disappeared. Even Hutton – usually very calm – began to wonder if this wasn't some message from God warning them off their intended new life Down Under.

"The restroom. The restroom. That's where I last saw him," volunteered one of Mel's brothers.

When they found the mischievous schoolboy he just smiled up at his father and shrugged his shoulders.

"I knew you'd find me so I stayed put."

Even the friendly airline clerk looked shocked as she flicked through the tickets presented at the check-in gate by Hutton Gibson that sunny day in late October, 1968.

"Ten children? Mama mia!"

Papa Gibson beamed. He had grown increasingly proud of his clan during their three-month world trip on the way to Australia. Their first port of call after leaving New York on (aptly) American Independence Day, July 4, had been Ireland.

Where else? For this trip was as much a pilgrimage to Catholicism as it was an adventure-trek to far-off places. In Ireland and Scotland, the Gibsons visited the birthplaces of both Anne and Hutton's relatives. They were understandably proud of their Gaelic heritage and they wanted the children to understand precisely where they came from.

The family spent a few days in England, but it was not the highlight of their world tour. Anne Gibson felt uncomfortable among a nation whose citizens had broken down front doors in her home village of Marley, County Longford, more than forty years earlier.

All the Gibsons agreed that the highlight of the trip was the visit to the Vatican, world capital of the Roman Catholic Church. To Hutton and Anne this was the ultimate pilgrimage. They and the children spent many days praying and attending daily masses. To the older Gibson children like Patricia, then 23, Sheila, 21, Mary, 20, Kevin, 18 and Maura, 14, Rome was a real eye-opener. Cheeky Italian waiters would constantly be trying to chat up the girls and Kevin had never seen such beautiful women in his life.

Stuck in the middle were Mel and the twins Donal and Christopher. The terrible threesome played countless pranks on their brothers and sisters, but they must have wished they had been just a few years older, really to appreciate the sights and sounds of a city that never sleeps.

"MEET THE GIBSONS – 12 OF THEM" was the headline accompanying a king-size photo of Hutton and his clan in the *Melbourne Herald* on November 4, 1968. The family had been talked into posing for an airport press photographer who could see that their pilgrimage across the globe was worthy of a piece in the local newspaper.

"So you think YOU have trouble keeping your children within spanking distance", read the article.

It went on the describe Hutton as an *"American computer programmer"* and quoted him as saying:

"I thought Australia offered pretty good opportunities for me and my children."

Meanwhile Anne Gibson was slightly more frank about the logistics of travelling so far with so many children:

"It's a once in a lifetime thing – thank goodness. It was a little trying and hard to keep things organised. But we made it."

The article rounded off by saying that Anne was really looking forward to one thing.

"I'm dying to get back in a kitchen."

The most intriguing aspect of the photograph that accompanied the article is that the only member of the family dressed in a brightly-coloured jacket is young clown Mel. Little did the journalist know that he had just photographed a child destined to become one of the most famous men in the world.

After visiting all of Australia's main cities, Hutton decided that Sydney was the best place to set up home. This thriving metropolis still retains the atmosphere of a seaside resort, with its hundreds of miles of clean sandy beaches north and south of the city.

The Gibson fell in love with Sydney's beautiful harbour, complete with spotless hydrofoils and regular commuter ferries chugging across the calm waters of the bay. They were mesmerised by the beautiful tropical plants and red-tiled roofs of the rows of Victorian terraced houses often overshadowed by brilliantly coloured purplish-blue jacaranda trees.

It all seemed a million miles away from those long cold winters in Upstate New York. Here, the climate was warm for most of the year and gardens often housed parakeets and other exotic birds.

Hutton swiftly found a property in the Mount Kuring-gai area just north of the city and set about finding schools for his younger children. For Mel Gibson, one of the most miserable periods in his life was about to begin.

As an American in Australia, he was something of an

oddity and he hated the fact that many people could not understand a word he said. But worse than that, his father had found a good old-fashioned Catholic boys' school – run more along the lines of a prisoner of war camp than an educational establishment.

St Leo's College was located in the quiet, leafy suburb of Wahronga and run by a group of Catholic priests known as the Christian Brothers. Outside the school gates were pleasant detached homes occupied by bankers, doctors and lawyers. But inside St Leo's a spirit-crushing regime ruled and Mel, used to the more gentle school system in Upstate New York, was having a very rough time.

To start with, he felt a complete idiot dressed up in the school uniform of straw boater and blazer with grey flannel trousers. St Leo's prided itself on being run on the same lines as the British public – fee-paying – school system.

Then there was the constant teasing by the other boys, anxious to voice their superiority to the "Yank". Within days Mel was getting into regular scraps with his classmates, leading to horrendous beatings from teachers that have emotionally scarred him to this day.

"I got picked on because of my accent. I hated that school," said Mel many years later, but still with a trace of bitterness.

As with many unhappy children, Mel soon shed his shyness and became a trouble-maker in the eyes of his teachers – all of whom were allowed to use the strap on students whenever necessary.

Classmate Mark McGinnity says that Mel was so unhappy at St Leo's that he would deliberately seek to antagonise the teachers. Three boys including himself and Mel even devised a bizarre competition to see who could get the most strappings in one day from a maths teacher who bore the brunt of much of Mel's outrageous behaviour.

"Mel won easily. He annoyed this teacher so much by copying his mannerisms and mimicking his voice that he ended up being strapped twenty-seven times. Mel was crazy."

McGinnity – now himself a teacher in Sydney – claims that Mel was "not very bright". He explained: "Mel was a loner who made his own trouble most of the time. He did not hang around with groups or gangs of kids."

Even in sports, Mel struggled to get to grips with such strange activities as rugby and cricket.

"He didn't know anything about them. He seemed bewildered and in the end he just played a bit of basketball," added McGinnity.

And Mel later confessed:

"I used to think that all those kids had something I didn't, that they had an identity. I carried that with me through and beyond school. I was always considered a bad influence. But I wasn't. It was just an unfortunate manner I had."

Another loner and trouble-maker at St Leo's was Jeremy Connolly. He also shared an Irish heritage and striking, dark good looks. The two boys became firm friends and remained so until very recently.

Jeremy – the more outgoing of the two – openly voiced his hatred of the Christian Brothers who ran the school, and even today casts aspersions on the abilities of many of his teachers.

"They were a joke and so was that place," says Jeremy.

And Mel later admitted to a friend, Deborah Foreman, that he was very deeply affected by his experiences at St Leo's.

"Mel said the priests were very mean. He thought they were wrong in their teachings and he said they were very brutal and the teachers were not properly trained," recalled Deborah.

Mark McGinnity explained why many of the teachers who were allowed to use the strap on boys were not even properly qualified.

"There was a teacher shortage at the time and some of them came from backgrounds that had nothing to do with teaching."

Jeremy Connolly describes the teachers at St Leo's at the time as "a disgrace".

Rumours of furtive "incidents" between certain teachers and pupils were whispered around the school (it has to be stated immediately that St Leo's links with the Christian Brothers were broken some years ago and it is now a standard – and respected – private school for boys and girls). "Such incidents" would help to explain Mel's attitude towards homosexuals, later in life.

The actor himself only once gave a clue as to his true feelings towards those unChristian "punishers" when he said:

"Some of them were regular sons of bitches."

There seems little doubt that St Leo's – along with just about every similar type of one-sex school – had its fair share of homosexual experimentation between boys. But whether Mel's later homophobia had anything to do with such incidents, is unclear.

Classmate Mark McGinnity conceded that many of the less pleasant teachers "moved on when problems were spotted".

Aged just 13, Mel's misery at school soon manifested itself when he took up smoking and drinking beer; during one memorable week, Mel was caught smoking in the school toilets every single day and duly strapped on the bottom on each occasion. Mel even started to think seriously about becoming a priest and entering a seminary. Anything had to be better than the hell he was suffering at St Leo's.

But throughout all this pain and anguish, Mel still

managed to come out smiling. He showed grim determination not to be beaten by the system. And through all the beatings and teasing, Mel continued his pranks. They were a release from all the inner tension of life at St Leo's.

"I used to spend my time trying to get one over on the teachers, pulling pranks. I would walk along normally one moment, the next falling down pretending I was dead," he says now.

Sometimes Mel would pretend he'd lost an arm, walking around the school all day with it tucked up the back of his school blazer. Other days he would adopt a Scottish accent and talk loudly all day. Years later, he admitted: "I wasn't bright at school but I'm no fool – I just didn't like it."

And neither did Hutton Gibson. His dislike of St Leo's had nothing to do with his son's unhappiness. Papa Gibson was most concerned by the fact that the Christian Brothers were not a particularly vigorous religious order. The priests who ran the school may have sanctioned the use of non-stop corporal punishment, but they did fail to make the boys attend mass every day and that bothered Hutton Gibson immensely.

"He came to the school one day in a real mood. He was most unhappy about the way his son was being taught religion," explained Eileen Leiden, St Leo's school secretary at the time.

And Mark McGinnity recalled: "His father dragged him out of the system – that was how strongly he felt."

Hutton Gibson had taken the law into his own hands. That black-or-white philosophy he has preached throughout his life was being put into operation yet again. But then Mel was hardly complaining about his father's intervention. He was delighted to be getting away from the straw boaters, strappings and creepy teachers of St Leo's.

And once Hutton resolved that Mel would be better off

at the local state school and being taught religion at home, the teenager reckoned that perhaps Australia wasn't such a bad place after all. At the Asquith High School, Mel encountered the same sort of Yank taunts, but this time he decided to retort with his fists and it soon gained him wary respect.

"He threw a few real punches and scruffed a few of the boys who had given him a verbal bashing. We had to pull him into line several times a week," says Ken Coleby, a senior prefect at Asquith during Mel's early days there.

"Mel had a controllable energy, was stocky and not easily intimidated. A couple of meeker teachers were horrified and thought Mel was too outrageous for his boots."

And the star himself has agreed: "I was considered a bit of a larrikin, and a bad influence."

Mel was soon performing his stunts. This time the model for his pratfalls was the late, great Peter Sellers.

"He could move very quickly towards a door and seemingly collide with it with a head-splitting sound, a crunch, and fall prostrate to the floor or ground," says Ken Coleby. "He was as good as Peter Sellers. Incredibly co-ordinated."

Another, slightly more disturbing habit was Mel's very convincing impersonation of a head-butt. It all enhanced his reputation as "a bit of a devil".

But there were no overtly or offensively effeminate teachers at Asquith. It was every boy for himself and Mel soon adapted his accent to Australian, buckled down to work (sort of) and immediately began to find life much easier.

At Asquith he even acquired a prophetic nickname – "Mad Mel", after an American disc jockey on Sydney radio, who for reasons known only to himself and the station management always appeared with a hood over his head.

But Ken Coleby says that Mel "showed he could mix it with the best and his schoolwork improved too. I guess he was a rebel in most ways but also did his work at the desk."

At home in Mount Kuring-gai, Hutton Gibson – now working full-time in his new career as a computer programmer – was getting increasingly frustrated by the direction in which his beloved Catholic Church was heading.

Visitors to the house could not help but notice the multitude of religious artefacts spread throughout the living room. Statues of Jesus, the Virgin Mary and Child took pride of place. Hutton could sound more like a priestly Father than the father of ten. Anne, meanwhile, was getting broody again. Intensely maternal, she was now too old to have children, and thirty years of meal-making and nappy-changing were about to become history. The kids were either grown up or away at school each day. And she had no career to revive.

Her sadness and sense of imminent loss may have been sharpened by Hutton's renaissance. Fully recovered from his catastrophic accident, he was making a living in a good job and even managed to get on to some Australian TV quiz shows.

His wife realised that only one thing would make her happy again – another child. Anne had made a secret vow to St Gerard, motherhood's patron saint, that if they arrived safely in Australia, she would adopt an infant. Duly, little more than a year after settling in Sydney, nine-month-old Andrew became the eleventh junior member of the Gibson household; Anne was fulfilled once more.

Recalls one of Mel's friends, "He told me his mother simply could not understand how people could *not* love children. They meant so much to her."

Anne became wrapped up with the new arrival, and Hutton Gibson found an equally absorbing, fulfilling pursuit: he went to war against the Holy See. As a diehard Roman Catholic traditionalist, he detonated fiery debate among

Australia's Catholic clergy.

During the late 1960s, Hutton was shocked by the introduction and spread of the so-called "new order" mass. Implacably opposed to compromise, fudging (and, perhaps, progress in most forms), he was certain that the new style of service was "neo-Protestant" and of dubious validity. Whatever the rights of the matter, beyond doubt Hutton Gibson the spoilt priest is what Robert Louis Stevenson dubbed "a bonny fighter". He began writing campaigning, temperature-raising letters to fellow traditionalists throughout the world, and considered heading an Australian branch of "old-school" Catholicism.

He was driven by a burning conviction that the mass should always be in Latin, not the vernacular, as was then becoming more and more the case. Hutton was further outraged – people sharing his outlook spoke in all sincerity of feeling disinherited, betrayed – by changes in the service, introduced in a bid to make it more accessible and the Catholic Church more attractive and, a Sixties buzz-word if ever there was one, *relevant*.

Within two years of arriving in Australia, Hutton was secretary of the Latin Mass Society, which fiercely challenged the right of Pope Paul VI to amend a rite approved originally by a sixteenth-century Council of Trent "in perpetuity".

Hutton's growing involvement with the society disturbed some of his friends, especially when they learnt of the group's theories about a Communist-Masonic-Zionist conspiracy behind this controversial change in Vatican policy.

"I remember going to mass one day and Hutt refused to go with me and tried to persuade me not to go. He implored me," recalled Ed Stinson, of one occasion in the early 1970s when Hutton visited his old friend back in Verplanck.

But perhaps more disturbing is the fact that Hutton expected all his children to support his views. Mel, even in his middle teens, seemed to be completely spellbound by his father's ideals. Even today, he does nothing to distance himself from what his father has been fighting for.

"Mel is highly respectful of his parents. He really looks up to his father. He felt that Hutton was a very godly father and he respects that deeply. Really, he has modelled himself on his father. Mel can even recite prayers in Latin like his father. He was always saying how wonderful his dad was and how he was taking on the Catholic Church and would challenge people," recalled one of Mel's former girlfriends.

In her essays *Ego and the Mechanisms of Defence*, in particular the chapter "Identification with the Aggressor", Anna Freud writes of children who are afraid of one or both of their parents and cope with their fear by impersonating them. As a small child, Mel had tried to defuse his awe of his father by mimicking paternal mannerisms. And as he grew older his love for rigid, undemonstrative Hutton Gibson drove him to take on his father's attitudes as well. Hutton has taught Mel his standards in life. Hutton had disciplined him and soon it would become Mel's turn to pass those lessons on to his own children.

Hutton's opinions on Communists and Zionists are extreme. They include an open reference to the then Pope's "Jewish connections" – based solely on the fact that he was occasionally photographed wearing the ephod, symbol of Jewish high priesthood. Often Mel's father would refer his children to these pictures of the Pope as positive evidence that the Pontiff was in league with the "dangerous" Jews.

Twenty years later, Mel is himself working with many Jewish people, as they tend to hold a large number of the top producing and creative posts in Hollywood. He has openly – if cryptically – supported his father's controversial views on the Catholic Church, telling one interviewer: "In a nutshell, you take an orange which has pips and flesh and peel and all this kind of stuff. You buy this orange from a fruiterer, and you say this is a true fruiterer because this is a true orange. And you go back to the same guy a year later and somehow he has managed miraculously to give you an orange that looks the same, smells the same. But when you open up the skin you find there are only half as many segments. Then you feel you've been ripped off and the whole thing is false. And if the whole thing is false, the practice of perpetrating the fact that you are what you say you are when you're actually not, is a lie. And a grand lie."

On another occasion, he spoke in more near-riddles when he said about the changes in liturgy: "People started leaving the Church when things changed. See what I mean about shifting foundations?"

Back in Australia, an outraged Hutton had already begun to boycott his local parish church in Asquith in protest against the changes. He especially objected to the way the tabernacle was removed from the altar and placed in a side chapel. He caused a further stir by refusing to allow his youngest daughter Ann to be confirmed by a visiting bishop. Hutton complained bitterly that the new-style service contained "Arianist heresy".

"Hutton was especially obsessed with the Jewish race. He seemed to think there was a Zionist conspiracy to take over the Catholic Church," one friend discloses.

Hutton began seizing on Papal pronouncements, the way committed collectors lay hold of postage stamps. His living room became crowded by icons, candlesticks and sundry religious objects "rescued" from Sydney churches whose progressive priests had discarded them. "Red" Gibson and fellow traditionalists feared that progress was eroding the very structure of their Church – an opinion they have never abandoned.

His most extreme, dramatic action was launched in 1975

when, at the head of a thousand-strong group, Hutton broke away from the main Catholic body to celebrate their cherished "outlawed" mass in secret locations around the city. These included papa Gibson's living room. He gave his children specially recorded tapes as foundation for their religious observances. Thus they could be taught the essentials of Catholicism without crossing the threshold of any recognised church.

"We feel," an indignant Hutton lectured his local newspaper, "like hunted Christians in the catacombs – merely because we want to celebrate the Latin rite which the Church has used since time immemorial."

Within months he added "author" to he accomplishments. Though the book Hutton wrote was not designed for best-sellerdom. *Paul's Legacy: Catholicism?* is a long rant about his traditionalist movement. In a single sentence Hutton crystallises his stance towards life in general: "How do you know you're right when so many in authority disagree with you?" By implication, if you are Hutton Gibson, supremely confident in the justice of your cause, then faith is impervious to disagreement . . .

Later he stressed the point, in the defiant statement: "I like bigots. I know where they stand!"

It was a cast of mind, undoubtedly, either instilled in, picked up or inherited by his offspring, especially Mel.

Throughout the theological jousting, with its faint overtone of a Resistance movement, Anne and the rest of the family gave the patriarch their full support. In turn he expected them to read every word of the regular newsletters he was composing for his splinter group, the Australian Alliance for Catholic Tradition, which he formed after being axed as secretary of the Latin Mass Society.

Ed Stinson received one from Hutton dated December 1990. Titled "Our Greatest Crime is Silence", it is headlined:

"The War is *NOW*!" and has Hutton's name and address printed on the cover. Inside he talks in conspiratorial terms about Spaniards and Catholics who were secret Jews and claims that Jews have infiltrated almost every religion in the world. He claims that Jews have tried to destroy the Catholic Church.

"And this is the doctrine that Hutton taught to his children. It would be perfectly accurate to say that Hutton has painted the Jewish faith in a poor light to them," said one Australian friend.

"To plant those sort of prejudices in the minds of your children seems to be a very dangerous practice indeed."

But Hutton Gibson no doubt sees it in a completely different light. It's that old black-or-white philosophy locking into place again.

"The greatest benefit anyone can have is to be a Catholic. You have a lifelong satisfaction at being right. But we can't go to mass, there are no sacraments and I feel cheated," said Hutton later.

Intriguingly, Mel was at the time already becoming a two-levels personality, even admitting once that he had "this maniac inside, a sort of Jekyll and Hyde thing".

At home, he adored and worshipped the ground that his parents walked on and knelt in prayer at least three times a day with the rest of his family. He knew the Bible backwards and he passionately backed his father's obsessive beliefs about the Catholic Church.

But away from the house, he had become a regular 14-year-old tearaway – smoking, drinking and beginning to think about women, of whom there was no shortage in Sydney. However, Mel's shyness, which he disguised by being aggressive at school, came back to haunt him whenever he was in the presence of females other than his mother and sisters.

He also kept up his friendship with Jeremy Connolly, who was still struggling to survive the terrors of the St Leo's POW camp. Both youths were painfully timid in many ways and would haunt snooker halls and milk bars in the Bondi Beach area, a haven for teenagers from all over Sydney.

Jeremy – taller and the more macho-looking of the two – would buy the beers in local pubs, then sneak outside with a pint mug for his pal. The two would then watch a procession of bikini-clad blondes strolling by seductively from the beach.

The norm in those days (as it still is today on Bondi) was to surf your way into a girl's arms. Unfortunately, Hollywood hero Mel was not a great surfer. Instead, the short and stocky teenager became more and more dependent on booze to fuel his social courage.

It wasn't until a few months after his fifteenth birthday, in the early part of 1971, that Mel actually plucked up the nerve to date a girl he met while out drinking with his pals.

"Wanna come to the flicks?" Mel mumbled the words as quickly as possible in the hope the girl in question would say yes immediately and then he could get back to his beer. The next day, shaking like a leaf, he just managed a lingering French kiss in the back row of his local cinema. Although, typically of Mel, he tried to play down the adolescent rite of passage, years later.

"It was not that exciting. I wondered what all the fuss was about. I was a really shy lad. It was hard asking girls out."

In fact, Mel decided after that first date that it was much easier just to stick to hanging out with a group of mates all the time. That way he could avoid having to make conversation with girls on their own. It was the part he found hardest. A constant flow of wisecracks was not enough to keep a teenage girl content. She wanted warm, romantic conversation – something that Mel did not know anything about. Or want to know, one gathers.

"I was never a womaniser. I didn't have the right chat. I'd go all tongue-tied or say something embarrassing if a girl came near me," says Mel now.

But he certainly left a trail of broken hearts behind him.

Back home as a reserved, still highly religious teenager, Mel faced a grilling from Hutton about what career he would like to take up after school. Mel's initial thoughts of joining the priesthood had disappeared along with his taste for lemonade. Journalism had a vague appeal but Mel did not feel particularly keen on exposing other people's lives – something to which he would fall victim, down the road.

Sitting in the living room with Mel and his father was older sister Sheila. Mel had always been her favourite and she was especially concerned about his future, even though she had by now married an Australian and had her own young family to worry about. She decided there and then that she would influence Mel's career decision, and filled in an application form for him, including his photo and $5 admission fee, then sent it off to Sydney's most prestigious school of dramatic art.

She had witnessed enough of her kid brother's pranks over the years to be convinced that he could one day make a wonderful actor. (Sheila also knew that if she even bothered to mention it to Mel he would never get around to filling out an application form.)

The Australian film industry was in the process of rising from the grave of obscurity where it had been for more than fifty years. Mel was about to ride to fame on the crest of its exuberant revival.

You have to learn to play the game – not because you want to play the game, but because you want to know how to beat it.

Mel was a tad irritated when he got a letter from the National Institute of Dramatic Art, Sydney, telling him that if he cared to go along for an audition he would be considered for a three-year acting course. After all, his sister Sheila had not even bothered to tell him she was sending off an application and acting was something he had never even considered as a career.

But a gruelling three-month stint in an orange juice bottling factory on the outskirts of Sydney convinced him that he had to do something worthwhile, more interesting, so he wandered along to NIDA for the audition. With his shoulder-length hair, and beard, Mel looked more like a juvenile hippy than a would-be matinee idol. Appearances meant little to him in those days. His attitude towards life was relaxed to the extreme. He had been protected by a strong-willed father, a warm and loving mother and five bossy older brothers and sisters, every inch of the way. As a result, you could say that Mel lacked cold ambition. He knew that if all else failed he had his family to fall back on.

Ironically, it was this laid-back attitude that probably helped him get a place at NIDA more easily than most of his peers. For many students this was make-or-break time during which their life's ambition to be a thespian would be realised. Many had pushy parents pressurising them to succeed no matter what. Others took their chosen career so seriously that they spent every waking hour reading plays and books and rehearsing for whatever class they had the next day.

Meanwhile there was Mel. Shy, vulnerable but completely unconcerned about whether he made it or not. That helped him immensely with the audition.

"They made us do all these silly things – improvise, sing, dance. I know I was terrible, but it seemed good then. I guess they saw something raw in me.

"I didn't really give a hoot. I thought 'what's the rush?' you know. Over the years I'd got so good at pretending, convincing people I'd done my homework, that I already knew how to act," he said years later and with wry, trademark modesty.

One friend from NIDA days remembers it slightly differently: "While all the rest of us were taking it deadly seriously, Mel would stroll casually around college as if he did not have a care in the world."

Another peer from NIDA, Monroe Reimers, described Mel as "pretty gawky" throughout the first year at acting academy.

But it was attractive 18-year-old student Linda Newton who probably gained the best insight into then 19-year-old Mel. Every day she shared a ride in her father's car or a train journey to and from NIDA with Mel.

"We both lived in the upper north shore area so it was

natural to share a ride," says Linda, now a successful actress in an Australian sitcom called "My Two Wives".

But life at NIDA was anything but glamorous. The college consisted of a handful of prefabricated huts wedged between two University of New South Wales buildings on High Street, in the Sydney district of Kensington.

"They were more like accommodation cottages," explained Linda. "It was freezing in the winter and boiling in the summer."

Cockroaches and rats shared many classes with Mel and his fellow NIDA students. "And when it rained, water poured through the leaking roof in our classroom," said Linda Newton.

Mel was having real problems settling in. His tutors criticised him for being "too cerebral", for not "externalising" and "keeping too much inside".

Now he admits it did not all come as naturally to him as it did to many of his fellow students.

"I found it difficult to break through the barriers and not feel ridiculous and uncomfortable."

And it took that first year before Mel, as he now says: "started to like or enjoy acting. Enjoy it. Finally NIDA was like another little world that I could get lost in."

During that period most of the students in Mel's class brought in lunches packed by their mothers. On a grant of less than $50 a month, no one could afford to drink in the local pubs at lunchtime.

One of Mel's fellow students was a thin, pale, very nervy 20-year-old. Judy Davies has gone on to receive many acting awards as well as Oscar nominations for films such as *My Brilliant Career* and *A Passage to India*, proving to be the second most famous acting talent to come out of Australia.

Back in those days, Judy was best known because her lunches usually consisted of liquorice sticks and green apples.

"But Mel would eat anything," explained Linda Newton. "He was short, stocky and very good-natured."

However he was already using formidable natural acting abilities to hide his true feelings – he was miserable as hell working alongside all these very serious students. He felt inferior and, worst of all, he had so little money he could not even afford to go to the pub each evening and drown his sorrows.

"I didn't really like it to begin with. But I found it was something I couldn't let go of," admitted Mel just after leaving NIDA.

The truth was that he had no idea why he was there in the first place. When one NIDA teacher went around the entire class asking each student why they wanted to be an actor, Mel stumbled over his reply because he did not know the answer.

To some of his fellow students this complete lack of ambition was very frustrating, even annoying.

Among that section is Monroe Reimers, who still cannot help talking about Mel in faintly sarcastic terms.

According to Linda Newton, Mel kept pulling regular practical jokes as a way of disguising his true feelings about NIDA. That light-hearted attitude did not always meet with the approval of his teachers or students. They saw him as someone who did not take his calling as an actor seriously and some even wondered what on earth he was doing at NIDA, anyway. And he continued hiding his face under a mass of hair.

Today, NIDA officials like director John Clark tactfully insist that "one of the big advantages of going to a theatre school is that you have the opportunity to make all the mistakes in the world, make a fool of yourself, be your silliest, behave well or badly . . ."

But there is no doubt that many at NIDA looked down their noses at Mel. "He definitely wasn't one of us and he knew it," says another erstwhile classmate.

Well aware of these feelings towards him, Mel became

increasingly nervous. He managed to spill an entire drink over drama tutor Richard Wherrett, who took them all out for a get-to-know-you drink before Mel starred opposite Judy Davies in a NIDA production of *Romeo and Juliet*.

"I was saturated and he was mortified," recalled Wherrett, who insists he knew that Mel "was a star in the making" from the moment he cast him as Romeo all those years ago.

As the hours in those scruffy pre-fab sheds accumulated, there developed an experimental element in some of the exercises carried out by the students at NIDA. Both Linda and Mel – by now good friends but "definitely nothing more" – found themselves frowned upon when it came to taking part in one particular class.

She explained: "We had to pretend to be members of different Aboriginal tribes and walk about pretending to make things out of nothing. It was supposed to be creative, good for our imagination. But it was ridiculous."

Mel would regularly collapse in fits of giggles after such exercises and then he and Linda would have a laugh about them on the way home that evening. Hardly the sort of behaviour one would expect from a budding thespian.

And, as Linda revealed, with the end of the first year rapidly approaching there were serious doubts about who would actually be invited back to continue the course.

"We all knew they would probably keep Judy Davies and two others but it was becoming clear that no one else was definitely going to be asked back."

Mel, Linda and the others were all pulled into NIDA administrator Elizabeth Butcher's office and asked if they really wanted to be actors. Miraculously both of them just slipped through the net and were offered places the following term.

"About half the students were not asked back. Well, Mel was not on the throw-away list, but I'm pretty sure he was on the 'grey list' of those who were on a kind of probation for about the first six months of the second year," says Linda now.

"I certainly wouldn't have picked Mel as one of the most talented in the class. He looked more like a surfie. Judy Davies, on the other hand, was always focused and determined – it was obvious she was destined for stardom."

During the summer holidays, Mel plucked up the courage to announce to his closely-knit family that he was planning to cut the umbilical cord and find a place to live. During those first few uncomfortable months at NIDA he had rekindled the friendship with his old pal from difficult days at St Leo's – Jeremy Connolly.

Jeremy also toyed with the idea of being an actor, but as he recalled recently, "It wasn't really for me." Jeremy told Mel that his father owned an empty apartment in the King's Cross area of Sydney – a cosmopolitan district not dissimilar from New York's Greenwich Village. It sounded like the ideal place for him and Mel to live.

It was a big move for Mel. His mother and father had always prided themselves on keeping the family together and Hutton Gibson was particularly concerned that his son might let his Catholicism lapse under the influence of new-found, free-thinking actor friends.

Then there were all those other "evil" areas like drink, smoking and girls. By all accounts Mel was managing to dabble in all three of these sins but he naturally did not want to confess this to his father.

And his incredible effect on women was about to cause him no end of grief – for the first but certainly not the last time in his life. A pretty young blonde in the year below him at NIDA just would not take no for an answer from Mel.

"She was completely obsessed with him. She was just one of those impressionable type of girls," recalled Linda Newton.

Why he rejected the girl is unclear but according to fellow

students, the two had a brief fling and she took things rather more seriously than Mel – something that was to happen on a number of occasions yet to come.

"This girl would follow him everywhere," explained Linda Newton.

Somehow the damsel in question got hold of a copy of the front door key to Mel and Jeremy's apartment in King's Cross. "And every time Mel got home at night she would be waiting there in bed for him," added Linda.

Mel confessed to one friend at the time that he was completely panicked by the situation.

"Instead of sitting down with the girl and trying to work things out, he just ignored her. He just didn't know how to handle it."

For the following few weeks, the girl continued shadowing Mel's every move. But, says Linda Newton, he claimed he had absolutely no idea why the girl was so besotted with him.

"He was not comfortable being chased by women. I think it must have had something to do with his background, and that situation with the woman letting herself into his flat was a very extreme example."

None of Mel's classmates seems to know if Mel actually slept with the girl. But they all recalled how he openly joked about the situation. Once again he was hiding his true feelings behind a mask of good humour. It was already becoming a reflex action.

Eventually, Mel and Jeremy found that life in King's Cross was less than restful. The long-running saga of the female stalker and the wilder aspects of living in such a crowded, colourful (and squalid, in patches) city area spurred them to move to the beach.

Mel asked his NIDA friends Monroe Reimers and Steve Bisley (who later starred with Mel in his first two films) if they wanted to share a flat with him and Jeremy. They jumped at the chance. From being the loner during his early schooldays, Mel now found it much easier to handle life if he blended with a group of friends.

The quartet soon found a rundown four-bedroomed house in Henderson Street, just a stone's throw from Bondi Beach. Mel was about to embark on a period that he suspects to have been one of the happiest of his life.

Steve Bisley – who became a close friend – recalled the first day they all went to see the house.

"It was due to be pulled down and looked like it. But the rent was cheap and we were really poor – so poor that we used to have credit running at the pizza place down the road."

One night Mel and Steve even staged a mock fight at the Astra pub in Bondi by falling over tables and chairs and then crashing down the stairs into the street. It was a typical bit of Mel Gibson tomfoolery carried out because he had had a few beers and "felt a bit bored".

Bisley went on: "This huge crowd gathered around and about three other fights started. We stopped ours and hot-footed it out of there just as the police paddy-wagon arrived."

Linda Newton says the four Bondi flatmates "were like a little gang of guys. They certainly had a good time and Mel was going out with lots of girls."

Mel and his new pal Bisley became renowned keep-fit fanatics at NIDA despite Mel's later claims that he never went to a gym to keep in shape.

NIDA administrator Elizabeth Butcher recalled: "I can tell you that Mel was very hard-working. He and Steve Bisley would come in at eight every morning and work out in the gym so they'd be warmed up to start class at nine."

For the first time, Mel encountered drugs in large quantities. The beachside community of Bondi was and still is a haven for young people doing everything from smoking pot to shooting heroin. In the mid-1970s the drug culture was at its peak. A trip to nearby taverns like their favourite Limerick Castle, at weekends, would invariably involve being offered speed, cocaine or grass, and many of Mel's friends at the time were heavily involved.

When the four friends decided to hold a party at the flat in Bondi, there naturally had to be a supply of drugs on offer.

"We did drink and smoked cannabis at those parties and there were flagons of red and white wine and beers. It was right in the middle of the drug culture," explained Linda Newton during an interview in April, 1993.

"People would sit around drinking and smoking and getting bad hangovers the next day. There would be smooching on the dance floor."

One of those girls who was smooching, and taking heavier drugs than cannabis at one of Mel's parties in Bondi, was a young brunette actress called Debbie Foreman. Stoned on amphetamines, she watched as the handsome host went outside to deal with police sent by angry neighbours fed up with the noise blasting out across the street. Mel never noticed Debbie on that occasion. Less than a year later their paths crossed in a much more dramatic fashion and almost cost her her life.

In those days, Mel and his friends favoured groups like Queen, led by the flamboyant Freddie Mercury, and as the parties went on into the early hours, the lights would be dimmed.

"I was always tripping over people getting up to naughty things," added Linda. "You had to feel your way around in case you bumped into something embarrassing."

Another friend who attended the parties at the flat in Bondi said:

"They were really wild. There were lots of girls around and we all had a go with one or two of them. After all, AIDS did not even exist in those days. We were just out to have fun. As far as drugs are concerned we tried just about everything. It was just the accepted thing to do in those days."

And one ex-girlfriend remembers: "Mel seemed to drink a lot even then and there was always dope at the parties they held."

Flatmate Monroe Reimers's edged verdict is: "Mel was a fun guy."

Best friend Jeremy Connolly is understandably still fiercely protective towards Mel. "As far as any less than savoury incidents are concerned there is no way in the world I would divulge anything. Everyone has their wilder sides and there is no way I could talk about that side of Mel."

Jeremy – now a taxi driver in Sydney – claims he could make "a lot of fucking money" out of revealing some of the wilder secrets of Mel's young life. But he still holds the star in great regard, despite a major run-in with him and wife Robyn a couple of years ago, according to Monroe Reimers.

"Mel got Jeremy to look after his farm when he had to rush out to Hollywood and offered him the measly sum of $5 an hour to look after it while he was away. Jeremy went over there and stayed on his own and rang up all his friends because he was lonely. But when Mel and Robyn got back, she left a message on Jeremy's answering machine threatening to sue him over a $25 parking fine he incurred; and a $400 phone bill."

Monroe Reimers is still bitter about the incident.

"They were just awful. I could not fathom out why they behaved like that. I look at all the hype about Mel and think, fuck, he is not like that."

Jeremy refuses to get drawn into discussing the incident but Monroe Reimers believes it is an incisive example of how much Mel has changed in recent years – and also of the total control Robyn exerts over all domestic matters. Jeremy has not spoken to Mel directly since, although he is still in touch with his brother, Donal Gibson.

Back in Bondi nearly twenty years ago and barely surviving on a peppercorn grant, Mel and his flatmates devised a special way of eating out for nothing. They would all crowd around one of the hamburger stalls littered throughout the Bondi Beach area, order their food and then run off without paying. None of them saw it as dishonesty in the normally accepted sense. Mel rationalised that it was "all a matter of survival".

But one thing Jeremy Connolly happily admits to was that the communal flat was "a fucking mess". There was no phone and they only got a fridge by stealing one from a low-budget film Mel and Steve Bisley appeared in at the end of their course at NIDA. As the only non-drama student in the apartment, Jeremy sometimes felt a little left out, but Mel always went to great lengths to involve him in everything they did outside of NIDA.

The bond of loyalty between Mel and Jeremy was immensely strong and especially illustrated by Jeremy's reluctance to speak about his great friend. "Quite frankly, I have to be careful. It is difficult to talk about Mel. I just don't think I can talk about the things that really happened."

Back at Bondi, the four friends had a rundown Australian Holden station wagon between them.

"It was a very old car and Steve and I used to repair it for Mel to drive," recalled Monroe Reimers, now a scriptwriter living in Sydney.

"Mel was the worst driver in the world and I don't think he has improved much."

Interestingly, Mel was not in the least bit ashamed of his parents. Most people around his age would go out of their way to avoid introducing their family to their friends. But Mel did the opposite. He still worshipped the ground his father walked on. He seemed positively proud of his folks and often took his friends home to sample one of Anne's delicious pies. But the day he allowed Monroe Reimers – a plain-speaking character by anyone's standards – to get into a "heavy" discussion with Hutton Gibson seems to have scarred the ex-NIDA student's opinions of Mel.

"His father is a complete bastard. I just happened to mention something about abortion and the father blew up and threw me out of the house. He branded me a heathen and Mel sided totally with his father – I was banned. You cannot disagree with Mel's father. He just goes on about how fantastic God is all the time."

Under ten years later, one of Mel's closest friends was warned that, "Mel did not like people disagreeing with him." It is clear that he reflects more than just his father's fanatically religious beliefs. They are very similar to each other.

One of Mel's other classmates was Robert Menzies, grandson of former Australian premier Robert Menzies. According to one NIDA pupil, Mel felt completely inferior to the blue-blooded member of the Australian aristocracy.

But Menzies himself prefers to say now:

"I wouldn't want to do a lot of the stuff that he does and I'm sure he feels the same way about a lot of the work I do. I'm certainly not jealous of Mel. No way!"

Mel's biggest struggle at the time was a financial one. Friends remember him as being constantly broke and he seems to have borrowed relatively small amounts of cash from a number of them and sometimes "forgotten" to pay them back. The four flatmates were supposed to share all household bills but there were frequent occasions when Mel just did not have the money.

Recalled ex-classmate Peter Kingston: "Mel was a nice bloke but always broke! He seemed to have a lot of trouble keeping afloat when it came to money."

And Monroe Reimers maintains that Mel – now estimated to be worth at least $50 million – had a car crash but managed to get out of paying for the damage to the other person's car.

"It was Mel's fault but he couldn't afford to pay for the damage, so he went to the guy and said he would give him $2 a week – and pay the rest when he was rich and famous. I don't know what happened with that . . ."

But what most of his NIDA friends conveniently forget is that the traditional source of subsistence – one's own family – did not exist for Mel as his father had so many other children to support; and he was self-confessedly stingy, even when he had the money to spare.

Overall, the four flatmates got on fairly well despite the odd row about whose turn it was to clear up "the tip", as they all called the house.

At NIDA, Mel was starting to be the most talked-about student at school.

"You could never give him a small part, because he'd take over the play," recalled Keith Bain, Mel's movement coach at NIDA.

"He was once given a very small role as a very dumb soldier. When I look back on that production, it is Mel's performance that I remember more than any others."

Mel's first encounter with open homosexuality occurred towards the end of his three-year stay at NIDA. It was hardly surprising that a fairly large quota of both staff and students were gay and even as far back as the mid-1970s, Sydney was fast gaining for itself the reputation of a liberal sort of place where homosexuals could openly live and work, especially in the showbusiness milieu.

One drama teacher deliberately put Mel in the centre of every scene in an end-of-term play because he was so besotted by the young student's good looks.

"I think this man fell in love with Mel," says Linda Newton, who is sure that Mel often had no idea of the sexual impact he had on both men and women.

"Mel just did not realise it a lot of the time but he definitely had this effect on people."

Incidentally, Linda insists that Mel never had that "effect" on her, although she did concede: "I occasionally thought why not? I mean he is a gorgeous-looking man but when you know someone as a friend you do look at them differently."

When rumours started flying around NIDA that Mel had a male admirer, he was the last one to find out and, says Linda Newton, he did not appreciate it. "Mel was not very good at dealing with that kind of stuff."

Linda also remembers going out with Mel and a group of NIDA pals to a notorious gay nightclub called Patches in Oxford Street, in the centre of Sydney. For probably one of the few times in his life, Mel definitely did not want to be in a nightclub. Instead of relaxing with his friends, he tensed up and became very anxious that "something awful" might happen to him. Linda Newton again: "Mel would not let go of my hand. He just hung on to me. He did not want to be in that nightclub."

Mel clung to Linda for dear life in the hope that none of the men throwing admiring glances his way would try to follow through with actual approaches.

"He was not comfortable to be amongst gay people."

For once, Mel's famous ability to laugh his way out of a sticky situation completely failed him.

According to Linda Newton he was "terrified" and even refused to go to the lavatory all that night because "he was convinced he would be raped on sight".

Linda Newton remembers another occasion when Mel found himself the highly embarrassed object of a famous gay singer's desires when he was appearing in a theatre in South Australia.

She explained: "Mel did not cope very well at all. He used to make jokes about it, but he did not like it."

This particular singing star – who was touring Australia from his native Europe at the time – spotted the young actor when he attended the play that Mel was appearing in. That very same evening the overweight recording artist made his first move – by turning up at the stage door in a Rolls-Royce with a bottle of champagne to "entice" the attractive thespian into his arms.

Linda went on: "He tried to offer Mel a ride home."

But the actor rejected the singer's attempts at seduction by completely ignoring him and looking the other way before heading at high speed down the street in the opposite direction from the waiting limousine.

According to Linda Newton, the pop star returned on at least three evenings to try and persuade Mel to change his mind. By the fourth night, Mel was completely panicked by the attentions of his famous admirer and, according to Linda, got very "pissed off".

"He did not like men or women chasing him. I think that is probably why he wanted to share a house with so many people – then girls like that earlier one in King's Cross could not throw themselves at him so easily."

In 1991, Mel provoked accusations of homophobia when he told an interviewer with a Spanish newspaper that during his time at NIDA, he assumed that many people would think he was gay because of his chosen career as an actor.

"But I did it. I became an actor despite that. With this look who's going to think I am gay? It would be hard to take me for someone like that.

"Do I look like a homosexual? Do I talk like them? Do I move like them?" he was reported as saying.

Not surprisingly, Hollywood's powerful gay rights groups were incensed by Mel's remarks – and many of those voicing their disapproval of the actor's apparent homophobia were the very studio employees, technicians and actors with whom Mel comes into contact all the time.

Back at NIDA, Mel's acting abilities were being noticed by more and more people. To some fellow students, Mel had transformed into an ambitious, ingenious player, while others say he had a natural talent that just took time to emerge from within his shy persona.

"In the third year he underwent a change . . . a kind of crazy ambition came over him. He began to play on his image as the leading man – he was always groomed at NIDA for that and it changed him. A part of his personality came out that was quite ambitious and ruthless," says Monroe Reimers with a hint of sourness.

But fellow student Peter Kingston says the opposite.

"He was a very unpretentious guy; unaware of his own talents and charisma. Over the three years, he just kept on blooming and showing new dimensions of himself. He didn't seem to be overly ambitious. I just remember a really unassuming bloke, a pretty ordinary kind of bloke really, who just happened to be really talented."

But all Mel's fellow students and staff at NIDA agree that it was not until he finally agreed to shave off his beard and cut his hair for a role in a 1940s period play, that his now famous matinee idol powers were unveiled.

"We were all shocked because suddenly we all saw this wonderful face. It was as if Mel had evolved before our very eyes," says Peter Kingston. "Until then he had a mane of hair down to his shoulders and looked like a lion."

And Linda Newton concurs: "Once he cut off that long hair and beard I looked at him in a different light."

As if in response, Mel began to excel, although he still plays down his stardom at NIDA by claiming that his favourite classes at the school were . . . fencing.

"I loved plotting out the duels – figuring out the dirtiest, most violent ways of stabbing people."

Linda Newton and Mel remained good friends throughout their three-year stint and often shared their problems with each other.

"He had a girlfriend and I had a boyfriend and we used to talk about how they found it hard to understand the demands of NIDA," recalled Linda.

By all accounts Mel's sweetheart, a girl called Julie from a good middle-class home near him in Bondi, was having real problems coming to terms with his career as an actor – and her parents certainly did not approve of their daughter going out with someone in such an insecure profession.

"Once you go through drama school and do all these strange things it becomes very hard for anyone who is not a part of it. It takes up so much of your time," explained Linda.

For some months, Mel desperately held on to his relationship with Julie and she in turn became increasingly anxious to marry the 20-year-old would-be actor. The situation provoked some intense discussions between Mel and Linda.

"Julie wanted to marry Mel and my boyfriend wanted to marry me and if we had not gone to NIDA then we might well have. But we were completely immersed in drama school and neither of our partners could come to terms with that."

Mel's romance with Julie eventually came to an end, but not until after at least half a dozen on-off off-on interludes between the couple.

As one friend argues: "Mel had a real soft spot for Julie but he was also very ambitious and he knew that marriage at that time would more or less destroy his career."

Eventually Julie went off and married a plumber, with her parents' wholehearted approval. Meanwhile Mel got back to the task in question – building his career. He went out on dates with a number of actresses like Zoe Bertrum and Deborah Lawrence, now a star of the television soap "Home and Away". But actresses did not really click with Mel. The last thing he wanted from a relationship was intense discussions of the stage. His own wisecracking approach was intended to lighten proceedings and many serious-minded young actresses did not find that attitude to their liking.

Mel now looks back on his NIDA grounding with great fondness, and has always been most generous about how much be owes staff and students for his success. In 1991, he even donated the proceeds from the gala openings of *Hamlet* in Sydney, Brisbane and Melbourne (plus, apparently, a percentage of the box-office takings) to help set up a scholarship for actors at NIDA. He was persuaded, after genuine reluctance, to let it be named after him. But Mel's main intention was to encourage more raw talent to take the plunge and go to drama school in just the same way he did.

The worst thing that can happen is you can screw up. I've done that before and it's not too damning. I've done some real stinkers. Luckily most were early on.

By November 1976, Mel had become much more settled at NIDA. His earlier doubts about a career as an actor had completely disappeared and he was fast gaining a reputation as a real talent.

"His confidence was growing by the day. He was really beginning to believe in himself," one classmate recalled.

This new-found confidence was partly due to the fact that Mel had spent the previous year living out of the shadow of his revered father, Hutton. While there is absolutely no doubt that Mel worships his father, papa Gibson expected those living under his roof to adhere to his strict code of ethics. Life at that house on Bondi Beach was gloriously laid-back in comparison. Mel had started learning to fend for himself. How to cope with life away from the protection of his family. Although he still regularly popped back to the Gibson household for a plateful of his mother's finest home-made meat pie.

Flatmate Steve Bisley became an especially close friend during this period. The two young thespians literally ate, breathed and talked acting. They encouraged each other to push performances to the limit – and they both knew how to sink a few pints of beer.

Mel's oldest pal Jeremy Connolly stepped back slightly at this stage and let Mel and his acting friends do their thing. As the only non-thespian in the house, there were times when he felt the odd man out.

Mel was looking forward to the following summer when they would all be leaving NIDA. The real world beckoned, and he was somehow convinced that he would have no problems surviving in such a precarious profession.

"I told Mel it was going to be tough being an actor but he reckoned it would be easy and that he'd fall on his feet," recalled friend Deborah Foreman.

Then in the middle of November, as if to prove Mel's optimism absolutely justified, Australian producer Phil Avalon contacted him and Steve at NIDA and asked if they would be interested in appearing in a little beach movie he was planning. Mel's ability just to happen to be in the right place at the right time was surfacing.

Steve and Mel were delighted. The fact that the movie in question, *Summer City*, was being made for a minuscule budget of less than $100,000 and producer/actor/ screenwriter Avalon intended to offer them the union minimum of $400 (which Mel later claimed he never even received) did not deter them in the slightest. Here they were, still students, yet about to star in a movie.

Neither boy noticed glaring holes in the script or wondered how on earth a film could be produced on such a small budget. They were swept along by the glamour associated with any movie project, however cut-price. Mel learned a lot of lessons during the making of *Summer City*;

many helped turn him into a shrewd, adept Hollywood player. He has also been highly critical of the project, in hindsight.

"It was an abomination, a cheap, nasty flick that was cranked out in three weeks on a tiny budget. My character was a 19-year-old surfer who simply surfed and acted dumb, which was all I could possibly handle at that time. The movie actually got a release, but, fortunately, only in Australia," Mel snapped at one interviewer who dared ask about his debut movie.

Summer City really isn't that bad considering the shoestring budget and its shoot-from-the-hip style. And producer/actor/screenwriter Phil Avalon is still hurt about Mel's attempts to disown the picture, and his taunt that he never got paid for the film.

"This story keeps being run by Mel but it is not true. I personally sent him the cheque and it was definitely cashed. I think it's just become a bit of a publicity stunt to keep claiming he wasn't paid for his first film role," recalled Avalon.

"Of course now he is regarded as something like Jesus Christ within the movie industry it must be very hard for him to remember that time. I look back fondly on those days and I'm really disappointed to hear that some people don't."

Avalon says he even wrote Mel a letter to try and end malicious gossip. "It's more of a mate's note and said the no-pay story was old hat. I don't think it has been mentioned since."

Mel's true motives in denouncing *Summer City* will be investigated further into this chapter, but first let's look at the background to the film that launched Mel Gibson on to an unsuspecting public.

Mel only got the part of a surfer called "Scollop" after Phil Avalon failed to recruit another actor, Nick Papadopoulous. "Unfortunately Nick was going through some personal problems so I asked one of the actors already cast, John Jarratt, if he knew an actor who could take Nick's place and he suggested I look at Mel. He had shoulder-length hair at the time and seemed very timid and introvert but I thought he could be good."

But *Summer City* was, as Avalon points out, really Steve Bisley's film. "Boo", the character that Bisley played, was "an outrageous, self-opinionated mongrel and he enjoyed the part and played it brilliantly".

Avalon is less laudatory about Mel, and revealed that he had to use a stand-in surfer for some scenes because Mel was so bad "on the boards".

Says Avalon: "The couple of times we sent him out to ride a surfboard were a laugh. Mel is not a surfer though when the film went into release everyone thought he was a top surfer. Ross Bailey actually did the surfing for him in the film."

Just as at NIDA, Mel's image was transformed by a good short back and sides, deemed essential by Avalon because *Summer City* was set in the 1960s.

"The transformation was phenomenal. He really suits short hair. He is really handsome and I know a couple of the girls on the film were very keen on him," recalled Avalon.

Mel's first-ever appearance on screen is fascinating in that he is recognisable from the moment he steps in front of the camera – despite having his hair dyed a dreadful blond and looking at least twenty pounds heavier than he does these days. In that initial scene, he used the same swagger that he has deployed to such great effect in recent years and which tells an audience instantly who they are watching.

Years later, a Hollywood executive stated that the difference between Mel and several other young actors pushing for stardom was like comparing a still photograph with film. Even in those novice days during the making of *Summer City*, he was having the desired effect . . .

However the young actor's first words on screen were less than memorable: "I thought we were going bowling tonight," he says, interrupting the Steve Bisley character in the middle of a passionate necking session with a girlfriend in the front of his car.

Considering Mel's attitude towards homosexuality it does seem rather ironic that Mel's very first screen kiss was with a man – Steve Bisley! It occurs about one-third of the way through *Summer City* and for some reason has never been stressed in subsequent publicity surrounding the film and Mel's part in it.

"It does seem hilarious that macho Mel, the guy all the girls love and adore, only got to kiss a *man* in his first movie," comments one Hollywood producer.

The joke is obviously not appreciated by Mel, who has never been asked to kiss a man since. Nor has he ever mentioned this scene in the seventeen years since *Summer City* was made. It has to be said that the scene involves Mel kissing co-star Bisley firmly on the lips as a "gesture of friendship and nothing more", insists Phil Avalon.

"Neither cared about kissing each other. It was just done in jest. It was a bonding thing. They were close friends on and off the screen," he added.

Two other incidents involved mooning, on and off screen. And no one who worked on *Summer City* can recall Mel objecting to either.

First there was an on-screen moon – a popular pastime in those days, that involved baring one's backside – in which Mel and Steve did the dirty deed for a very brief scene. It takes place in a small town called Swanson and can easily be missed if you happen to blink at the wrong moment.

Its only real significance in Mel's career is that for the

following couple of years he consistently refused to go naked in movies and even claimed it was something he would never consider. He first went bare for *Gallipoli* and subsequently appeared unclothed in virtually all his following films – which Hollywood producers now reckon adds at least $20 million at the box office. (Wistfully lusting housewives are said to shout "Turn around! Turn around!" every time Mel's bare bottom appears on screen.)

The off-screen mooning episode was more disturbing altogether and nearly ended violently, as Phil Avalon disclosed.

"We were staying in an RSL Hall in Catherine Hill Bay about sixty miles north of Sydney at the time but we had all been forced to vacate the hall for one day to make way for a wedding reception. Cast and crew had gone to the pub," he began.

In the tavern, the Catherine Hill Bay Hotel, Mel and Steve Bisley decided to get smashed and proceeded to down beers at an alarming rate before struggling across the road to see if the wedding reception was over, so they could bed down for the night in the sleeping bags they had been using all week. It has to be noted here that Catherine Hill Bay is a rough, tough mining town with 1930s-built "gun-barrel houses" and a reputation for being a classic piece of what Australians call "God's country".

When the two drunken pals found the wedding reception was still raging, it seems they took umbrage and, inspired by that scene they had just shot for *Summer City*, dropped their pants in front of a group of giggly girls standing at the entrance to the hall. Then they disappeared in the direction of the pub across the street. Within minutes a lynch mob gathered around Phil Avalon, who was huddled terrified in his car.

They began pounding on the car bonnet and roof, smashing fists up against the windows.

"Dirty bastards," hollered one man.

"Flashers. Bloody flashers," yelled another.

"I thought I was going to be in serious trouble. I even got my .22 rifle from the back of the car because there were so many people surrounding me," recalled Phil Avalon.

"They were out for blood. They had gone from a happy, celebrating group to one that seemed hell-bent on revenge. But I didn't even know what they wanted revenge for. All I knew was they wanted to bash my head in. I played it cool because I had to find out what was happening."

After a few minutes of terror, Avalon managed to persuade the mob to let him go and retrieve his two stars from the pub, where Mel and Bisley sheepishly admitted what they had done.

"My problem was that I was laughing so much I had difficulty finding the right words to apologise. I mean, it was funny. But not to the family folk at the wedding. We got back in the hall the next morning more by luck and guile than approval."

Other mishaps occurred. Avalon and his crew were trying to film a tricky chase scene when a mob of Hell's Angels started dogging their every move before trying to run Steve Bisley, Mel and the rest off the road. In the confusion and panic, the unit camera car hit a telegraph pole, seriously injuring the cameraman, who was rushed to hospital.

The entire shoot – which lasted on and off for more than a month – was a highly informal affair. Actors and technicians mucked in together, loading and unloading camera equipment at each location, and catering consisted of ham rolls bought from the nearest bakery by Phil Avalon – if he had enough spare cash on him.

"I handed out the odd $30 here and there but everyone just chipped in."

Mel and Steve regularly "borrowed" petrol for the huge

black Chevrolet Biscayne, another "star" of the movie, by siphoning it out of parked cars near locations where they happened to be filming.

And at the end, Mel and Steve Bisley were so annoyed about Avalon's cut-price operation that they stole a pinball machine used in the movie.

Avalon complains: "I had to go over to their flat and get it back. They had sawn the legs off. It took me a month of phone calls to get them to let me have it back. The people I'd hired it from were getting very heavy with me about it."

But despite Mel's reluctance even to acknowledge the existence of *Summer City* it undoubtedly taught him a great deal about movie-making. Towards the end of the shoot, he began studying the rushes closely, sometimes wincing and agonising as he saw his image flicker across the screen.

"Hell, is that me?" he would mutter. "Ooh, the eyes are wandering . . . aah, I'm nodding too much . . . I didn't know you would be that close."

One of the leading ladies in *Summer City* was Australian actress Abigail. She recalled being particularly struck by Mel – the person rather than the screen idol.

"He was quiet, even shy, but he wasn't shallow or transparent. Underneath was something brewing. You could see the makings of an actor."

The final weeks of the shoot were completed in very trying circumstances, with Avalon virtually broke and unable to advance even a few dollars for expenses. "I had to borrow from friends, anywhere I could. I'd go out and buy a lot of mince meat, chop some onions and carrots into it, cook it myself, and that was lunch."

A few years later, Mel reflected on his role in *Summer City* by saying: "It was a case of wondering day and night if you ate, slept, got paid or what. There was this madness as we went from day to day, a kind of excitement."

There was another, far more significant reason why Mel has tried to bury the memories of *Summer City* for ever.

"One of the actresses was very keen on Mel. She has married now but she was carrying a torch for Mel and it all ended in a very unfortunate incident. But they were very young at the time," says Phil Avalon.

The actress's name was Deborah Foreman and for almost twenty years she has kept silent about her relationship with Mel Gibson. Now, for the first time, she has revealed the full story of their romance – and how it almost led to her death.

Now happily married and the proud mother of two, Deborah – an attractive 36-year-old brunette – lives in a modest beachside house twenty miles north of Sydney. Her account of her relationship with Mel provides the first-ever glimpse of Mel the lover, the romeo.

He married in his early twenties and no girlfriend has ever come forward before, to talk about her romance with Mel. At times during this interview, Deborah was close to tears; she still holds the movie star in very high regard.

"We were just a bunch of kids having a good time, I guess. Mel had a crush on me and I had a big crush on him. We went out together for about two months. I was crazy in love with him. He was great. We had such fun times together. He was so warm, shy and vulnerable. A very decent chap. A funny, loving character. I really enjoyed that feeling of having someone fall madly in love with me. He was completely different from anyone else. I have never met anyone like that, apart from my husband."

According to Deborah, when she met Mel he was still "very keen" on Julie, that previous girlfriend who eventually walked out on him to marry a plumber.

"He was still a bit in love with Julie at the time I met him. A lot of people on *Summer City* were matchmaking us. They wanted him to get his mind off Julie."

Interestingly, Mel – the man so adored by millions of women throughout the world – certainly was not a born romantic.

Deborah explained: "He never once got me any flowers. He was just not that type and he never even opened doors for me either. Basically he did not like taking girls on dates. You just tended to hang around with him and his mates. There were no candlelit dinners. He is a very Australian man."

But, perhaps even more surprisingly, Deborah says she paid for his rounds of drinks in the pub – not to mention having to chauffeur Mel around town.

"I used to have to buy all his drinks because he had no money. I even drove him around in Steve Bisley's car a lot of the time. Mel was more like a romance you would have when you are about 15.

"We went to pubs, played pool across the road from where we were staying during some of the filming of *Summer City*. Mel had this habit of telling long-winded stories that hit you like a shaggy dog story at the end."

Years later, even Mel admitted what a lousy escort he made.

"I'm not that romantic. I'm not very demonstrative. I don't go around buying flowers or throwing my coat in the mud. I'm just there."

And that's not all. The actor once dubbed the world's sexiest man had some fairly unpleasant table manners – which still let him down occasionally.

At one Sydney press conference to promote a movie in which he starred, assembled members of the media looked on in disbelief, as Mel shoved croissants into his mouth, greedily licked his fingers and then held a ten-inch cigar in his fist, proceeding to puff thick fumes over his audience.

Ironically, Deborah Foreman played the romantic interest in *Summer City* and that meant acting in some very awkward underwater sex scenes with Mel's best pal Steve Bisley, as the other young actor looked on.

According to Deborah, Bisley also "had a crush on me" and tried to persuade her to go out on a date with him after she broke up with Mel some months later.

Both Mel and Deborah were aged 20 when shooting the movie and started their relationship just days after beginning work on *Summer City*.

"Steve and Mel were like a couple of stand-up comics. They were very funny together. I felt like an outsider with them sometimes. Mel was always impersonating people – hiding behind a mask. Sometimes he would play this uncle character and that floored all of us."

About two weeks into the filming, Mel and Deborah took off with Steve Bisley, John Jarratt, another actor and a technician for a week-long holiday in a caravan further north along the coast. They weren't playing truant – Avalon was away too, raising more cash to continue the movie.

She says they stayed together in an annex to the caravan. Sharing a bed with Deborah did not stop young Mel holding forth on morality and marriage . . . By the most forgiving yardsticks it was a dire display of double standards: the stud lecturing his highly-strung mistress on why a girl like her was beyond the pale, when he came to seek a wife.

As the twig is bent so grows the tree, and all that. Mel was no wimp but he could be warm, compassionate, understanding, giving, especially around kids. Yet the same person was crassly insensitive – as good as telling Deborah he was there for the companionship and the sex, forget anything deeper. One need not be fanciful to discern Hutton Gibson's uncompromising script being spoken by his raffish son.

Lord knows what it cost Deborah to replay dialogue evidently branded into her memory. "Mel had very definite ideas about what women should be and how they should behave. He was very old-fashioned and said that women should be virgins. They should be 'nice', he said things like that.

"He had quite a conscience about morals, immorality. It was to do with the way he had been raised. He tried to cover up when he did sleep with someone. He wanted to stay very clean. I think he belonged to my parents' generation. He was more like my dad was. He got around a bit but . . ." her tone is bittersweet, ". . . he wanted to marry a virgin."

And Mel made no secret that he intended to have a large family. "He always said he would marry and have lots of children. He definitely believed in that sort of thing."

Given his upbringing, cynics could snigger that Mel Gibson had no choice in the matter of hordes of offspring. In a controversial interview with the Spanish magazine El Pais, Mel affirmed his detestation of abortion – a stand he had hinted at during his relationship with Deborah.

"God is the only one who knows how many children we should have," he declared, "and we should be ready to accept them."

Talking of double standards, not to mention hypocrisy, about midway through their relationship, Deborah stayed the night with Mel and his parents at their religion-permeated home.

He hadn't taken her there in the courtship ritual of "Meet my folks," of course. The senior Gibsons took pity on her when chauffeuse Deborah drove him there one night.

As she explains, "It was so late they asked me if I wanted to stay the night. The house was built of double brick and had a very long table in the kitchen. It was like a rabbit warren of beds and rooms. But his parents weren't very interested in me because I was an actress. I remember Mel's mom had an incredibly strong American accent."

There is absolutely no suggestion that Deborah slept

with Mel at the family home. It is just surprising that she was even offered a bed for the night.

On at least three other occasions, Deborah says she went to the home Mel shared with his pals in Bondi. But they could only snatch brief kisses and cuddles, more often than not, because Bisley, Monroe Reimers and Jeremy Connolly were always around.

"The flat was very sparse. Nobody ever cleared out of there when we arrived. I would have liked a few more private moments with Mel."

But she says that during one evening out together, Mel told her: "I am really starting to fall for you in a big way."

Deborah recalled that his enthusiasm worried her.

"I was afraid I wouldn't like him any more if he got too close. I was really enjoying feeling in love with him but . . ."

Deborah also revealed that Mel suffered from extreme mood swings.

"He could have very solemn moods and be very miserable, then he would be up again. I remember discussing the fact of there being no middle ground with him. He said he was on an even keel but the truth was that one moment he was funny, the next he was quiet and introvert."

But the one thing Mel and Deborah still share is their opinion of the shoestring project that threw them together.

"I thought *Summer City* was pretty dumb. It was a bad film and there wasn't much good acting in it either. Mel looked pretty silly in it and so did I."

Yet she says that during the film everyone heaped false praise on each other. "In a situation like that you just praise each other. Everybody was brilliant. This was going to be the movie to end all movies. But the truth is that *Summer City* was embarrassing for me to make. It was a crummy film but I had a lot of fun."

Deborah says, needlessly, that her relationship with Mel had its ups and downs.

One particular incident is still painful for her to talk about . . . Deborah will only say, "There was one thing he did to me I would rather not mention. He was pretty mean to me. It was something which a well-brought-up person would not do."

Deborah insists that Mel will know exactly what she is referring to and she would rather keep it between themselves. Tantalisingly, she insists it was the reason they broke up.

"I dropped him because of what he did. It was obvious that he still loved Julie. He hurt my feelings very deeply. I was messed up for a long time afterwards."

Around then, Mel told his good pal Jeremy Connolly about "problems" with Deborah Foreman.

A close friend of both lovers sees it this way: "Deborah Foreman certainly was mad keen on Mel. We were all well aware of it. I think he was very relieved to have finished with her."

That emotional anguish, hinted at by Deborah, led on to a most disturbing incident, shortly after the young lovers parted. Deborah says that for two weeks after their break-up she "went through a pretty painful time. I hardly ate. I drank a lot and took drugs."

Then she bumped into Mel at a party at a friend's house. She was with a friend and he was with a girl.

"I was still very miffed at him. I was drunk and I was stoned and I had dropped a few pills. I was out of my mind. I got really mad at him and then I threw a glass of wine all over him and kicked him. This other girl took me aside and told me that what I had done was atrocious."

Throughout all this, according to Deborah, Mel remained passive, visibly stunned by her onslaught. She went outside, into the garden, and burst into tears. *Then she took a decision she has regretted ever since.*

"I was so out of it on drink and drugs, I slashed one of my wrists. I had considered suicide several times before and struggled with depression. Now I have a scar on my wrists I never want my kids to ever see."

Deborah says that bumping into Mel at that party "was the trigger for what happened. It wasn't so much him. In fact it was more me than him. Now I wish I hadn't done what I did. It was very embarrassing."

In an extraordinary scene, Mel – who had been told what had happened, by the other girl – rushed into the garden and tried to restrain Deborah as her wrist bled. But instead of hugging the man she loved, Deborah started punching him.

"I fought him off. Blood was spouting slowly from my wrist. There was nothing he could do to stop it."

Deborah says Mel was shocked and upset by what had happened and then became especially hurt when she brushed off his efforts to help.

"He was very concerned. I feel such hurt inside my heart about what happened. I was an idiot. I had cut myself extremely deeply but the blood wasn't gushing out. I looked down and thought: 'I don't think God wants me to die yet.'"

Moments later, Deborah was driven to a nearby hospital by a girlfriend, where she underwent microsurgery. She spoke to him just once again, many months later, seeking advice about whether to take a part in a play.

"I got through to him at his parents' house. He was very nice to me considering what had happened and he told me I was a natural actor and should do very well."

Besides seeing him across a crowded cinema during a glitzy Sydney film premiere some years later, Deborah confirms that she has never seen or heard from Mel since their affair.

But she says that her relationship with the world's so-called sexiest man did help her in many ways.

"What happened with Mel did bring things to a head with me. I changed after that."

The nearest Deborah gets to her lost love now is when she finds his photograph in a magazine or newspaper.

"I don't look at him and say if only we had made it."

Then she completely contradicted herself by admitting: "I feel like screaming every time I see his photo. He was very warm."

Deborah's career crumbled after *Summer City*. She never fully recovered from the emotional turmoil caused by her relationship with Mel. But, as is disclosed later in this book, she was only the first of two beautiful actresses who "retired" from movie-making after appearing with him.

Summer City eventually opened in Sydney in December 1977 and was billed as: "The one you have been waiting for! Funnier than *American Graffiti*. Heavier than *Easy Rider*."

It did reasonable business, mainly through being one of the first movies of its genre to come out of Australia. Years later it gained a cult following on video and made a small profit for then 28-year-old producer Avalon, who went on to make more than half a dozen Aussie movies, including *The Sher Mountain Mystery Killings*, starring former world heavyweight boxing contender Joe Bugner, plus *Fatal Bond* with Linda Blair and Donal Gibson, Mel's younger brother.

The most comprehensive review of *Summer City* was written by Stephen Marston in the prestigious Australian magazine *Cinema Papers*:

"*Summer City* is reminiscent of the American 'B' features of the early 1960s in which spoilt young Californians crashed their hot rods, punched each other up, and spent wild weekends which ended in tragedy and moral re-assessment.

"It is a low-budget Australian road film, billed as a 'one-way trip back into the 60s'. But its theme of four young guys heading up the coast for a good-time weekend is still very much a reality in modern Australia. It is, therefore, an ideal subject for social and cultural comment, not to mention exploitation as film entertainment.

"The plot is simple: Robbie (Phil Avalon) and Scollop (Mel Gibson) are blond, blue-eyed, happy-go-lucky surfers, while Boo (Steve Bisley) is an aggressive ocker in constant conflict with Sandy (John Jarratt), a rather proper university graduate. They drive off in Robbie's long, black Chevrolet to a small coastal town where they front up the local surf club stomp. Boo seduces the landlord's virgin daughter, Caroline (Debbie Foreman); Robbie and Scollop go surfing. They get drink, argue amongst themselves and crash the Chevy. They spend the night in the bush and an argument flares between Sandy and Boo. The next morning, with the landlord on Boo's trail, the 'fun' weekend climaxes in a fatal shoot-out.

"What holds the film together is its action-packed plot, the story and characters being portrayed with great energy. Unfortunately, however, the film is directed in a scrappy, disjointed fashion and the camera bumps in and out of the action in a style better suited to gritty documentary or home movie.

"Most of the dialogue is spoken off camera, or viewed from a distance. A particularly frustrating example is when Caroline, desperately searching for Boo, appeals to Sandy for help, but he can only offer text-book morals. A potentially moving scene, it is thwarted by being viewed in a series of long shots amid windswept sand dunes. When the camera does move more closely, the actors seem hampered by the simple-minded script, and their lines rush out quickly to make way for the action.

"None of the performances are weak, they are just rarely

given a chance to be strong. We are only allowed a very limited understanding of Boo and Sandy; just Abigail (as a downtrodden pub wife) *and Mel Gibson (Scollop) emerge as real people.* [My italics.]

"It would have been better if the characters of the four guys were established at the beginning, instead of murky montage of old Bandstand clips which only emphasised the lack of period setting throughout the rest of the film.

"Overall, the treatment of this slice of typically Aussie life is crude, frantic, jumpy and full of missed opportunities. The surf club dance sequence, for instance, is beautifully mounted but lacks any direction – or even good stomping music.

"There are, however, moments of clarity: the sequence in which Boo seduces Caroline in a water tank and her return home are very sensitively photographed and acted. It is one of the few passages with descriptive flow and continuity.

"The film does rattle along very energetically and, at least, it is never slow, boring or pretentious – it can't afford to be. It was produced on a budget of about $200,000 of private money (this figure is heavily disputed), shot on 16mm and blown up (quite successfully) to 35mm.

"Financial and production problems notwithstanding, it is a pity that all the energy apparent in *Summer City* could not have been applied more carefully to the script, production values and direction."

Mel and his good friend Steve Bisley returned, battle-scarred, to the realities of NIDA and their final year of drama school. Both felt disillusioned by the kick and scramble side of film-making, as they considered it left them little time to fine-tune their performances.

But Mel – whose name was now being mentioned throughout the Australian showbusiness community – was soon approached by Sydney agents Faith Martin and Bill

Shannahan. They suspected he had what it took, and they managed to elicit offers of work while he was still at NIDA. On paper, some of these openings looked promising. He happily accepted a two-week stint on the infamous Australian soap opera "The Sullivans", reckoning that a mainstream television project had to be more professional than a low-budget surf movie.

Mel lived to regret making his hasty decision to take the job, rather than toil away at college. Eventually he rued it, as a bigger mistake than *Summer City*.

"It was a shocking experience – terrible scripts, no rehearsals, just knock it over in a day. I did two weeks' work and I was on screen every night for three weeks. I played a naval officer – I inspected navels."

Yet again, Mel felt cheated out of his rights as an actor by not being given sufficient rehearsal time before working under directors who rarely did more than three takes on any set-up. But he was absorbing all these experiences, to throw back at directors and producers when he had gained some power.

As he cruised through those last months at NIDA, he decided that his career needed a return to the theatre. He had jumped at two very poor film and television roles and it just did not make sense to him to continue along that path. In any case, his experiences at NIDA made him hunger for the stage.

A job touring with the South Australian Theatre Company seemed a golden opportunity to get back to what he liked doing best. Mel was soon getting rave reviews for his performance in Beckett's *Waiting for Godot*, which inspired his great friend, actor Sam Neill's shrewd comment: "Mel Gibson is a character actor trapped inside a leading man's body."

In Adelaide, Mel went flat-hunting – and met the girl

who would become his wife. Robyn Moore was one of the people sharing an apartment he was interested in.

For the first few months they did little but exchange the odd casual glance.

NIDA classmate Tony Prehn – who appeared with Mel in *Waiting for Godot* – remembers: "She was a dental nurse and he met her when he was looking for a room to rent."

One of Robyn's classmates at the Woodlands Church of England Grammar School in Adelaide explained that the neatly-presented brunette was "so quiet she was more like a dormouse. She was very skinny and very shy, but she excelled in sports like hockey and softball."

More than ten years later, Mel himself recounted that first meeting with Robyn.

"I woke up one morning and went into the kitchen and there she was making breakfast. She was my new flatmate. We shared the rent on the house. It wasn't a huge romance straight away. We became great friends first and used to do things like go shopping together."

One of Mel's NIDA classmates said that at first Robyn did not consider Mel as anything more than a good friend, "because she had heard stories about what actors are like".

The friend went on: "Robyn came from a quiet, secure background and she wanted to give any suggestion of a real romance with Mel some very careful consideration before she took the plunge."

There was a practical reason why the two did not "connect" instantly. Robyn already had a boyfriend and he was much larger than Mel!

The actor jokingly dismisses this with, "I sort of waited until he fell by the wayside."

While Mel and Robyn played a waiting game, agents Shannahan and Martin were busy spreading the word about their exciting new discovery.

This time, when Mel heard that doctor-turned-director George Miller wanted to discuss the possibility of his playing the lead role in the good doctor's low-budget, futuristic action movie he was much more cautious . . .

People who achieve minor success when they're so young should have a training school to go to. Someone ought to teach you how to handle it.

In September 1977, just before graduating from NIDA, Mel went to Sydney casting agent Mitch Matthews's office to try out for a role in a movie called *Mad Max*. Mitch – a well-liked and respected figure in the Australian film industry – had been given Mel's name by Betty Williams, a voice teacher at NIDA.

"I had asked Betty if she knew any spunky young guys to put in the movie. She immediately suggested Mel Gibson and a few other raw youngsters," recalled Mitch recently.

Those "youngsters" included Mel's classmate Steve Bisley (his *Summer City* co-star) and shy, sensitive NIDA student Judy Davies, who went on to gain an international reputation, specialising in the opposite sort of movies.

The legend of the casting session at Mitch Matthews's tiny studio in North Sydney has been repeated many times and spawned headlines like "Mel's Punch-Up". Or articles that begin, "A wild punch-up in the pub put Mel Gibson on the road to stardom!". But as with all good yarns ("Never let the facts spoil a good story"), truth has been lost in the wind.

Mel claimed in many a subsequent interview that when he went along to that fateful gathering he "looked a mess" after being "really worked over" by three men at a party.

"I ended up with masses of cuts, broken bones, black eyes and a flattened nose. The casting director took one look at my mug. Then she nodded and muttered, 'Yeah-yeah, you look fine.' I did that and ended up playing the lead in the first *Mad Max* movie."

That casting director was Mitch Matthews and she insists that Mel's claims are "absolute, total nonsense".

Speaking at the same little studio where she tested Mel all those years earlier, Mitch ushers dull old reality in with: "There is no way Mel was in a fight. I have seen these stories and I know they are not true."

What's more, Mitch's daughter Celia – who has worked with her mother for almost twenty years – was also present when Mel showed up. She said: "He never came in here with all those fight injuries. It had absolutely nothing to do with why he was cast. He certainly did not have a black eye when we tested him."

Even *Mad Max* co-creator and director Dr George Miller has never referred to this so-called fight, in numerous accounts of how he came to cast Mel in the movie that did more than any other project to make him into a star.

Neither Mitch nor Celia was the least surprised by the fight fable. It is common practice in the movie business to spin legends out of nothing. Their only reason for pointing out the true situation is that Mel did not need a gimmick to help him get the part of Max. Mitch says he got it the moment he went before her video camera for the test.

"I got the shivers up and down my spine when I saw Mel

through the eyepiece. He was just magic. He had great depth and sensitivity."

Steve Bisley – who had "stolen" *Summer City* the previous year – was this time chosen to play a secondary role to his old friend and flatmate. But Judy Davies was deemed to be "too strong" by Mitch Matthews for the role she tried out for, and was rejected.

But there was one big problem about casting Mel as Max – his tutors would not let him leave drama school until he had graduated in October. So the movie's eccentric director, Dr George Miller, held back production until Mel got on a plane for Melbourne, the same day he left NIDA. An official, trained actor at last.

A few hours later Mel was knocking at the front door of a tatty Victorian house in the Melbourne suburbs. A man who looked as if he had just walked out of a hospital casualty ward answered.

"Ah sorry," said the 21-year-old Mel, thinking he had arrived at the wrong address. "I'm looking for George Miller's place, the film people . . ."

The hospital patient looked amused.

"This is the right place. Come on in."

"I'm Mel."

Extending a bandaged hand and grimacing as Mel shook it, the "patient" explained that he was Grant Page, stunt co-ordinator for *Mad Max*.

Mel must have tasted a cocktail of inquisitiveness and caution. He had already experienced the trial-and-error school of film-making on *Summer City*. This operation had that familiar low-budget feel to it, but then Mel met Dr George Miller and realised that this could well turn into something much bigger and more exciting than a hundred movies like *Summer City*.

The Melbourne home housed all the cast and many crew

for the film. It was a definite improvement on the wooden floors of that hall Mel had slept on during the making of *Summer City*, but it was pretty basic all the same. Each room slept six or seven people on a variety of "beds" made out of such things as camp stretchers, beanbags and even mattresses.

And as Mel soon discovered, while everyone else was out filming during the day, the band of real Hell's Angel-types hired to play the Toe Cutters, marauding bikers in *Mad Max*, used the house to sleep and "hang out" in. One of their more bizarre habits was scrawling messages on ceilings to give actors something to think about before dropping off to sleep.

Friendly little notes began appearing on the ceiling like: "Actors are mincemeat – you die today!" and then there was "Watch the toads today – we're out there, you mother-fuckers" and "Care for a lift to eternity, boys and girls?"

Vince Hill, who played the fatalistic Night Rider in the movie, muses: "It was comforting bedtime reading. Basically, the bikies gave tremendous input to the picture. They were the real stuff, even if they were crazy signwriters."

Art director John Dowding says the bike gang was "playing the Method" to its extreme.

Mad Max was set in a distant future in an urban society suffering from terminal decay. Inner-city highways became white-line nightmares where nomad bikers and young cops in souped-up pursuit vehicles had created an arena for a weird apocalyptic death game.

"They say we haven't got any heroes any more. Well, damn them. You and me, Max, we're gonna give 'em back their heroes," says the police chief character in the movie.

The basic premise behind *Mad Max* was, director George Miller admits, to create a futuristic western. The film used the same type of plot and characters.

Miller saw it as a way to counter some of the gloomy portraits of life Down Under, given world-wide critical acclaim during the preceding five years, but which had limited appeal. He could see that they had little chance in the lucrative international marketplace.

Filmgoers were already tiring of artistically valid yet downbeat fare, and Miller knew that what audiences really wanted was escapism.

He was the man to provide it. "It is a western in new clothes. Each country has its own frame of reference. In Japan they liken it to Samurai pictures. In Scandinavia they say it is a Viking picture. All are basically westerns," explained Miller.

John Dowding – who still lives in Melbourne – was just one of 60 per cent of the crew and cast who had never worked on a feature film before. Afterwards, Miller said that all the enthusiasm of this raw talent helped make *Mad Max* a box office megahit, taking more than $100 million worldwide. It also made the actual shooting of the movie a nightmare to organise.

John Dowding – virtually the same age as Gibson – hasn't forgotten the day he was introduced to the young Mel.

"He was beautifully unself-conscious. George had earlier pulled out a photograph of Mel and said, 'This is the man we are going to use.' He described him as pretty, feisty and a good actor. On set, Mel did not make much noise. He would just sit quietly between set-ups."

Miller and his producer Byron Kennedy (who later died tragically at the age of 33 in a helicopter crash) had lovingly developed the *Mad Max* script (with journalist James McCausland) for at least three years before getting the project off the ground. Miller, a doctor who graduated from the University of New South Wales Medical School, worked dauntingly long hours in a hospital casualty ward to raise initial funds for the film. His medical skill had to be shown frequently as stuntmen and cast members were injured . . .

After years of struggle, Kennedy and Miller managed to

raise $250,000 to make the film. It was a minuscule budget for an action film involving virtually non-stop stunts. But the moment Mel met Kennedy and Miller he was infected by their enormous enthusiasm. He even – prime concession from an actor – ignored the fact there were only fourteen lines of dialogue for the main character.

The two young film-makers recognised that in *Mad Max* they had an opportunity to make a movie that could set new standards in Australian film production. Up until then, Aussie movies tended to be homespun family dramas with little scope (or money for that matter) for outrageous stunts. That sort of action genre was left to Hollywood. Kennedy and Miller were about to change all that.

They had agreed before casting the movie that they would use unknown actors so that the characters would be 100 per cent convincing. First choice to play Max was Irish-born actor James Healy, then living in Melbourne. The young actor was desperate for any acting job, as he was "resting" between work by hauling carcases at a local abattoir. But after reading the script, Healy declined the lead role – Max had such meagre, terse dialogue.

Miller tried desperately to convince Healy but he would not budge. In later years, he turned up in Hollywood to star as Joan Collins's manipulative lover Sean Rowan in "Dynasty" and then as a scheming romeo in America's daytime soap, "Santa Barbara". In 1993, Healy was arrested by Los Angeles police after allegedly shooting a relative – quite a Max-like development.

And then Mel turned up to see Mitch Matthews for that infamous casting session . . .

George Miller says, "I still remember the moment I saw the TV monitor with Mel reading this monologue. Suddenly I thought, God, there was something special there. I replayed the screen test and the feeling was still there. I forgot I was a director trying to cast his first movie. I sat and watched and got transported by the moment."

In fact the only comparatively well-known actor in the film was Australian Roger Ward. But Miller made him shave his head for an unrecognisable appearance.

"I was unimpressed by the rather small, spindly youngster who would play Max. But the kid spoke with authority and didn't seem intimidated or frightened to work out various methods and interpretations of certain scenes," Ward concedes.

Before shooting commenced, Miller and Kennedy hosted a get-to-know-you party at the house in Melbourne. John Dowding said it was a raucous event – Mel stood out because he was in a corner looking terrified.

"There was a bit of sex, drugs and rock 'n' roll, and a lot of tequila slammers, but Mel seemed very shy. He gave the impression he was very nervous. I remember shaking his hand at the beginning but he was so shy and retiring."

So, as the rest of the cast and crew "bonded", Mel sloped off to bed early to prepare for his role. Typical of Mel; he was quite capable of being a real party animal some days – more like the local librarian on others.

According to Dowding, the *Mad Max* shoot, mainly at a desolate area just outside Melbourne, was a "very rock 'n' roll" scene. The location consisted of flat plains, an expanse of Australian desert as far as Perth to the west, and an abandoned industrial park with just a handful of horses grazing; little else. To the east a vast range of mountains marked a snaking coastline.

Everyone put in gruelling eighteen-hour days and, as often on film shoots, drugs were available to those wanting to buy.

There is no suggestion that Mel took any illegal substances but by all accounts many of the cast and crew took amphetamines and cocaine, if only to keep going during those long hours.

"The whole film was achieved on the smell of an oily rag and generated by a lot of mind-altering substances, spur-of-the-moment decisions," is Dowding's theory.

"We were like a guerrilla unit. There were some appalling days and a lot of close shaves with the stunts. We were all naive and some stupid risks were taken."

During one action-packed sequence the bike gang, the Toe Cutters, were supposed to spill over the side of a bridge. When it came to shoot the scene, bikes went out of control and ended up bouncing off the rails of the bridge.

"Luckily no-one was hurt," said Dowding. "We all had a sense it would be something special. There had never been a film made like it before."

Mad Max has often been described as a futuristic *Wild Bunch* and some of Mel's closest colleagues believe that the success of the whole series fuelled his obsession with making a western even though they were considered by Hollywood to be passé.

Filming had a chaotic start. Mel and Steve Bisley nearly got themselves arrested as they drove to the *Mad Max* location in the souped-up Interceptor car, specially adapted for the movie. The two actors – kitted out in their black leather uniforms complete with fake guns – were stopped by a curious policeman in a Melbourne street.

"They almost freaked out when they saw the guns," said Mel. The actors avoided instant arrest by showing the officer official documents proving that they had permission to film.

But worse disasters were on the way; four days after the start of shooting, leading lady Rosie Bailey was involved in a head-on car crash, broke her leg and had to be replaced by Australian soap star Joanna Samuel.

George Miller admits that despite its incredible success,

that first *Mad Max* was "a terrible, bitter experience and a nightmare to shoot".

He added that he "finished it feeling the movie had licked me. It was like walking a big dog. You know, you want it to go one way and it wants to go another."

Where it wanted to go was the top. *Mad Max* proved an instant box office hit. Most critics were full of praise for it, particularly the stunt work, all the more creditable because of the tiny budget.

But within Australia there was an element of snobbery about the subject matter. Some of the industry's self-appointed elder statesmen felt that Miller and Kennedy had sacrificed artistic integrity to make an unashamed smash it and grab 'em film.

The chairman of the Australian Film Commission, Phillip Adams, assailed *Mad Max* for having "the moral uplift of *Mein Kampf*" and suggested that it could foster violence. Adams later described Australia's other huge international movie hit *Crocodile Dundee* as "listless" and star Paul Hogan's performance as "lacklustre", so his judgement calls are not exactly impressive.

Mel's aunt, Kathleen Lyons, described *Mad Max* perfectly when she said: "All that noise and car wrecks and people getting murdered. I thought Mel was terrific but the movie was something I just didn't expect. Even with all that dirt, blood and make-up and the passing of the years, it was little Mel up there, the kid who always wanted to play games and have fun. Now he was being paid to do it and everything was like a dream. I had to sit in my seat at the cinema for several minutes before staggering to my feet and going outside."

The critics came up with some fascinating takes on descriptions of the film. Andrew Sarris in *The Village Voice* wrote: "*Mad Max* is an Australian futuristic roadrunner movie so unremittingly violent and kinetic that it makes *The Warriors* look like *Mary Poppins*."

Mel later admitted sneaking into a cinema in Sydney to finally see the film for himself – and getting quite a shock. Firstly he found the theatre full of the very type of bikers portrayed in *Mad Max*. Life, rather worryingly, imitating art? Then he noticed that the movie had a very real effect on the crowd.

"I must admit I didn't like what it seemed to do to them. A lot of them seemed to take it a little too seriously. But I suppose they'll always be those sort of people. I'm just glad a couple of the bikers didn't bother to look at who was sitting next to them."

He also insisted that he "cringed" whenever he saw himself on the big screen.

Miller and Kennedy were infuriated when *Mad Max* was released in the US with Mel's voice re-dubbed because the movie's American distributors claimed that American audiences would not understand the Aussie dialogue. Not surprisingly the film bombed in the US but its world-wide success forced Hollywood to sit up and take notice of star and creators.

And John Dowding – who helped design many of the bizarre futuristic vehicles used in the movie – said: "*Mad Max* represents the Australian film industry's renaissance. It was a captivating piece of writing. It was quite brilliant."

Mel himself varies enormously when asked his feelings about the original *Mad Max*. But his usual verdict is that it was "probably the classiest B-grade trash ever made". Then he often backtracks a bit by adding: "It's actually a fairly good film in a trashy, badly scarred kind of way. It's a cartoon. You have to remember that."

The movie won six Australian Film Institute awards, including the jury prize and best actor for Mel. It also received top honours at Avoriaz, in France, where the world's most prestigious fantasy and science fiction film festival is held each year.

In Sydney, *Mad Max*'s extraordinary success was having a knock-on effect on Mel Gibson's career.

Agents Faith Martin and Bill Shannahan were swamped with inquiries about his availability.

Numerous offers of work came in from home and abroad, and renowned Hollywood agent Ed Limato was pressing Mel to appoint him as his Los Angeles agent.

Mel admitted wonderingly that fate played a vital role in his progress.

"It's all been accidental. There wasn't any plan. It wasn't a considered move until well after I was into it. Fate has a funny way of tipping you into things."

Three years later, Mel was persuaded to put his Max leathers back on and reprise his most successful role thus far.

He had been in a number of much gentler movies meantime but none of them had the same box office clout. With a budget of $4 million and an allegedly less violent script by George Miller and his writing partners Terry Hayes and Brian Hannant, Mel accepted a surprisingly modest fee of $100,000 for *The Road Warrior (Mad Max II)* and didn't object when he discovered even fewer lines of dialogue than the first time around.

Taking up where *Mad Max* left off, the movie opens with a much more battered-looking Max complete with leg brace, at the wheel of his V-8 Interceptor in an eerie, ravaged landscape, travelling at hurricane speed on a long, lonely road towards an ominous horizon.

Miller gave Max a dog, and heroic child, and transformed the gang members into homosexuals, much to Mel's amusement. The result is ninety-four minutes of non-stop action backed by superb Dolby sound effects as Max becomes the reluctant champion of a band of idealistic but bewildered survivors. It climaxes when they find themselves defending their makeshift oil refinery from the marauding gay bikers and their cronies. After fleeing the compound, Max leads them to survival in a remarkable chase sequence.

Mel was once again surprised by the terror instilled in many people watching Max in action again.

"I thought it was funny. It was a comedy almost. A very black comedy. Even the violence in it wasn't that brutal sort of violence. It was just thrill, thrill, thrill."

This time, he uttered one of his classic "Mel-isms": "I regard *Mad Max* as a *Star Wars* in the gutter."

But Mel was still full of praise for George Miller.

"He is a true film-maker, with a completely unique way of going about it, of using film and its techniques to tell a story. It takes somebody pretty talented to actually get that simplicity on film."

Yet he freely confessed that his role of the Road Warrior did not stretch his own talents. He believed so much in George Miller's creation, that any attempt really to *act* the role would have been detrimental to the film. That, claimed Mel, was why he played it with virtually no emotional internalisation.

"If I had tried to do anything more then it would have gone against everything in the film. It would have gone against the style, the classic guy who is a stranger. He operates coldly because that's the only way to survive. It's down to basics. Eating dog food. Running for his life. You just live, you know. He doesn't even sneer. He's beyond that."

Mel insisted that the role had "to be sort of remote, and detached, almost not human" and at the same time manage to reveal something of Max's inner self. He had to strive to "make people think: 'Oh, the poor guy'."

To many of Mel's closest friends and associates those

words come uncomfortably close to one side of his real-life character.

The Road Warrior was shot at Broken Hill, an isolated mining town 800 miles west of Sydney in an even rougher and more desolate area than the first movie. More than 120 crew, forty actors, a hundred extras, nine extremely over-worked stunt men and a full medical team invaded the little town. Then there was a fleet of more than eighty vehicles, including some that were rigged with steel plates to make them look like tanks and battering rams, a gyrocopter (to be flown by actor Bruce Spense as the wacko Gyro Captain) and one camera helicopter.

Producer Kennedy, only 31 at the time but considered a giant of the Australian film industry, explained that at times *Road Warrior* was a logistical nightmare.

"Co-ordinating all the elements in the film was pretty daunting. But the results were worth it. We did things we'd never done before."

More than half of the vehicles used on *The Road Warrior* were written off while filming outrageous driving stunts and it wasn't that unexpected when five people had to be hospitalised following horrendous crashes near the end of filming.

Mel watched in horror when Gary Norris, a 21-year-old stunt man, careened a motorbike into the side of a stationary dune buggy, hitting it at over 60 m.p.h. According to the stunt co-ordinator, Norris was supposed to throw himself forward off the bike, creating the illusion that the impact had "fired" him into mid-air. But as the rest of the cast and crew watched, an explosive charge detonated prematurely, creating a mini-dust storm – then Norris hit the vehicle-escaping with a broken leg.

One of Mel's co-stars was eight-year-old Emil Minty, who played the Feral Kid. Although only just out of his teens himself, Mel befriended Emil, showing that special Gibson charm when it came to handling children.

Minty recalls that Mel taught him how "to throw a boomerang and head-butt people without hurting them" – something that Mel had used to great effect during his own boyhood at St Leo's College.

Minty also remembered how Mel took him out to see *Mad Max I* at a drive-in cinema with wife Robyn and his three children born by then, who were staying with the star on location.

"My mum made me promise I wouldn't actually watch it but Mel did not seem too worried about allowing his own children to see it," says Minty, who still lives in Sydney (Mel disputes this version and insists that *Mad Max II* is the only one of those movies that he had allowed his kids to see).

On another occasion, young Emil enjoyed a barbecue thrown by Mel and Robyn at a house they rented in the Broken Hill area.

"Mel was very easy-going. He was very helpful to me and gave me advice all the time and was really charming."

The Road Warrior broke all Australian box office records in its first five days of screening, grossing A\$802,000 in just fifty-eight cinemas. In Britain it was much the same story. And at the US box office it took a healthy \$24 million and eventually outstripped *Mad Max*'s international revenue of \$100 million. Critic Megan Morris enthused: "There isn't really much to say about *Mad Max II*, except that it is one of the best action spectacles ever filmed."

But other film critics acclaimed little eight-year-old Emil Minty's performance.

Fran Hernon, in the *Sydney Sun*, wrote: "Mel Gibson walks away with the throbbing hearts, Emil Minty walks away with the acting honours and a cattledog walks away with the picture."

But despite being allegedly overshadowed by his young friend, the movie established Mel as a potential Hollywood star.

What set it apart from many other similar action movies was that women were dragging husbands and boyfriends to see it, rather than the other way around. A US fan club was set up around this time and one member proudly announced she had been to see *The Road Warrior* 123 times.

Released on video, *The Road Warrior* sold more than 50,000 cassette units, making it eligible for platinum certification. It also became a firm favourite at Saturday-night late shows in cinemas across the States, running for years.

One critic claimed that females flocked to see Mel "because they love to see him dressed in his Max uniform of black leather".

And fashion expert Frances Roche reported that "refined ladies now dress like thugs with metal studs" because of *Mad Max*.

But all this female adoration did have its drawbacks, as Mel discovered when he attended a premiere of *Mad Max II* in Perth, Western Australia. As he walked through the crowds outside the Paris Theatre 500 screaming ecstatic women pounced on their idol. Completely trapped, Mel looked daunted and tried to find a route through the lusting females. Then he realised that the only way to calm the crowd was to start signing autographs. Our Hero called this incident "one of the most frightening experiences of my life. I found myself horribly trapped. I was petrified. I thought I was going to be ripped to pieces."

Publicist Inge Salisbury agrees: "We thought fifty or so would turn up but the place was inundated. Mel was a bit scared but no one hurt him. They didn't want to. They just wanted to touch him. Some even kissed him." We should all have such troubles . . .

After scrawling at least 400 signatures, Mel managed to persuade the women to release him. Inge Salisbury records: "He was shaking after it was all over."

Mad Max mania was not restricted to Australia, America and Europe. In Japan, Mel was known as the "samurai on wheels" and obliged to do a whistle-stop promotional tour of the land of the Rising Sun. During ten exhausting days he gave interviews to thirteen newspapers, two movie magazines, four weekly papers, five monthlies, seven television and nine radio programmes. The Japanese even compared him to Steve McQueen and Paul Newman.

Yoshio Sakai, editor of Japan's *Cinema Magazine*, attributed the film's success to the fact that "it was able to attract the interest of people who don't normally go to the cinema. In Japan, the main movie fans are young women and children. But *Mad Max* was successful in getting young men into the theatre with its vast and rather violent car scenes."

At a press conference in Tokyo attended by seventy Japanese journalists, Mel endured what he hates most. Answering banal questions like: "Have you been to Japan before?" and fending off leather-clad models offering round-the-clock bouquets of flowers. He looked in a complete daze for much of the trip.

Later, the immense success of the *Mad Max* movies prompted one famous Japanese beer manufacturer to use Mel's image to spearhead an advertising campaign, "because we want to promote a hard image", said a spokesman for the Asahi Brewery.

Gibson filmed a series of commercials for the brewery for a fee of $1.34 million. The project's producer was amazed at how co-operative and accommodating Mel was about the product. "He would drink seven or eight cans of beer in a row and never complain. Even when we offered to fill the cans with tea or another substitute, he refused." But then a million-and-more dollars gives "small beer" a different dimension.

During a twenty-four-hour flying visit to Melbourne, promoting *Mad Max II*, Mel confided to journalist Kim Trengrove that he "expected to be washed up in a year".

This was a remarkable confession from a young actor on the crest of a wave at the time. But Mel was feeling gutted by the non-stop publicity work on *Mad Max II*, he was hating every minute of it, and like any freelance worker, he feared that the work might dry up at any moment.

"It's good to be in demand now but the offers could stop tomorrow. There are high times and there are low times – you have to take insurance out on yourself."

Mel even told the prestigious *Cinema Papers* magazine that "acting is really prostitution, isn't it? Certainly you think of it that way."

There is no getting away from the fact that the suit of fame did not fit Mel comfortably. While other Hollywood stars relished hype-driven attention, Mel, the one who "fell into" stardom, wished it would all just blow away.

In the same interview with *Cinema Papers* he was asked how he would manage to stay realistic amid success. His reply matched Mr Average against the challenge.

"It depends on your upbringing and whether you hang on to what you were taught. It is good to have little reminders along the way – things that put you back in touch with what you have learnt. There is nothing like a good stretch of not working to do that to you, or somebody whom you know very well being brutally truthful in their criticisms."

That "somebody" was Robyn and Mel's parents and brothers and sisters. Unlike traditional Hollywood players, he still remained close to his family and relied on their truthful opinions. His main priority was to keep both feet firmly on the ground.

After the release of *The Road Warrior*, George Miller announced that Max was dead and buried for ever; there would be no more sequels. Mel approved – he was "not particularly keen on the idea".

But few in Tinseltown believed either of them and in June 1983, Miller and his producer Byron Kennedy caused no ripple of surprise when *Variety* announced that Max was on the road again.

The budget this time would be $8 million – double the cost of the second Max and twenty times the budget of the first. In key with that, Mel's new Hollywood agent Ed Limato held out for $1 million for his client. Miller and Kennedy felt it was money well spent; when they agreed to Mel's fee, he became the first Australian-based star to receive a million dollars for a picture.

This time around, Miller brought in stage director George Ogilvie, who had worked in the theatre with Mel, to take charge of the acting, while he concentrated on the stunts that had to surpass the last Max movie. Miller kept details of the plot top-secret and would only disclose: "When we came up with the story it was something festering deep down in our dreams and unconsciousness." Miller insisted he was making a third movie because Max had "become a personal obsession".

But tragedy struck *Mad Max III* (later changed to *Mad Max – Beyond Thunderdome*) just one month after that initial announcement. Byron Kennedy died when his helicopter crashed into Lake Burragorang, south of Sydney.

Mel was deeply depressed by the news and, at one stage, he and George Miller considered whether *Mad Max – Beyond Thunderdome* should even go ahead. They decided that Kennedy would have definitely wanted them to carry on, so the project continued.

In September 1983, Mel announced the inauguration of

with a can of beer – was once again putting his foot in it, helped by a *People* magazine reporter sent to do a piece from the set of *Beyond Thunderdome*.

"I don't even want to be making this film. Don't print that," rasped the allegedly sneering, surly Mel. Naturally, the reporter printed every spit, comma and euphemistic asterisk . . .

But it was his comments about that recurring, haunting theme of fame and how to handle it that conveyed his true feelings at the time.

"It's all happening too fast. I've got to put some brakes on or I'll smack into something. It's hard to keep your head above water when the floodtide of Hollywood hype hits. My brain keeps me sane and my wife and family, who have no illusions about me."

In a classic "Mel-ism" he described being a star as "having your pants down around the ankles and your hands tied around your back so it's a good opportunity for some parasite to come up and throw darts in your chest".

A verbal Impressionist painter, unless he's a Surrealist, Gibson has a wild way with words.

The "parasites" were already gathering for a piece of Mel . . .

Mad Max – Beyond Thunderdome got good reviews on its release in July, 1985. The *New York Times* said Mel has "that stately world-weariness that makes him irresistible". While the *New York Post* suggested: "In the end the crazy images and unthinkable brutality creates and communicates a unique crude poetry that is both primitive and beautiful. Acting is the last thing on anybody's mind, but Mel Gibson gets through it without smiling and Tina Turner, as the barbaric queen of Bartertown, is Grace Jones with soul food."

Even the normally staid *Los Angeles Times* critic Michael Wilmington saluted the movie as "outrageously entertaining . . . It's a hideous world, but it has a hideous energy. It pulses with furious life. Survivors battle tooth and claw in an arena where little of value or beauty is left."

Wilmington even went on to compare director George Miller with John Ford, Howard Hawks and Akira Kurosawa.

Mel read the reviews with bemusement. He had tried to break away from the *Mad Max* mould by starring in numerous other, completely different types of movies. But the character of Max remained the one his adoring public liked best.

Wanting to experience all types of roles, he was starting to learn that he could use his stardom to find new projects that might really test him. The hazard was that many of those scripts did not contain the right ingredients for his fans.

On the set of *Beyond Thunderdome*, some of the stunt men and crew who had become friendly with Mel during the previous two *Mad Max* films voiced very real concerns that the star had changed.

Sydney-based stunt man Frank Lennon (who died in 1989 after falling just ten feet from a balcony) said that Mel was haunted by the box office failure of other, arguably better films.

"He wouldn't accept the basic logic we offered that no one wanted to see the damn things. Word of mouth killed the three of those flicks, not his performance," Lennon said.

"Mel would counter, 'Look at the budgets, man, the leading ladies, the directors . . . class, man, class . . . *River* was a top story. It deserved better . . . *Mrs Soffel*, well, maybe they don't like the main characters getting shot up at the end . . . Diane Keaton was great 'wasn't she?'"

Scott Murray, of *Cinema Papers*, put it all into perspective when he said: "Mel came through during the best period in Australian film history. It was a lucky period for a lot of people. There were no other handsome male movie stars and he filled the void so well. He was also lucky to work with George Miller, the best director in Australia."

In January, 1987, Mel turned down an extraordinary $22 million offer to play Max, one more time. Having already filmed the first in the *Lethal Weapon* series Mel knew that it was best if Max remained dead and buried. Although he did not disclose it at the time, his desperate search for a potential series of movies had ended with *Weapon*.

One of his associates states flatly, "No amount of money will lure him back to play Mad Max again."

In analysing the extraordinary success of the *Mad Max* films, it is especially significant that they appeared when the Australian film industry was in the midst of a boom, and Australians were beginning to believe in their own, home-grown talents. Yet, until *Max*, they tended to churn out nostalgic accounts of the past rather than tackle livelier issues. The *Max* movies did not take safe, soft options. Boldly they confronted the public with a hero who would be equally at home in Dodge City or ancient Rome. The films were brave, innovative and accomplished, with an energy unique at the time.

Long afterwards, George Miller told the *Los Angeles Times* that Mel was and still is the only Australian-based actor capable of making it really big in Hollywood.

"I would have been surprised if you'd told me that any Australian actor would become a mainstream star, but, having said that I'm not surprised it is Mel. Mel is a greater actor than we've seen on the screen."

I don't go for that Freud stuff. It's a load of crap.

But roaring after the *Road Warrior* and his sequels, we've got ahead of the story. Time to get back on chronological track . . .

When filming on *Mad Max I* came to an exhausting end, Mel took off for Adelaide to join the State Theatre Company of South Australia for a stint on the stage where he genuinely believed he belonged. He still considered himself to be learning his craft and paying his dues, as he later put it, "doing Greek tragedy and Shakespeare, and carrying spears and saying, 'I take my leave, my liege'".

He appeared in a number of mainly secondary roles in such plays as *Oedipus Rex*, *Henry IV*, *The Les Darcy Show* and *Cedona*. But almost a thousand miles away in Sydney, his hard-working agents Faith Martin and Bill Shannahan were discovering that Mel's performance in the still unreleased *Mad Max* had created quite a stir. George Miller was raving about the young actor, to anyone who would listen, including one of Australia's best-known film industry figures, Michael Pate.

Pate returned to his homeland after finding fame and fortune in Hollywood as an actor who appeared in more than thirty movies and something like 300 television shows between 1950 and the late 1960s. He had played everything from Chief Sitting Bull to Flavius in *Julius Caesar*, not to mention writing a book on acting and giving drama lectures at colleges. Since returning to Australia, Pate had become a highly respected producer and director.

On hearing about Mel, Pate immediately contacted Faith Martin and Bill Shannahan to ask if the young actor would be interested in the title role of a film he was slated to direct, titled *Tim*. Based on a novel by Colleen McCullough, writer of *The Thorn Birds*, it was a sensitive story of a sweetly innocent, mentally retarded young handyman who became the object of desire of a spinster old enough to be his mother. The agents immediately sent Pate the video of a screen test Mel had made. Hooked the moment he saw it, he booked the next flight to Adelaide and met young Mel. Despite having earmarked his own son Christopher for the role.

Pate remembers his first meeting with then 22-year-old Mel as notably unimpressive.

"I found him ingenuous, naive, charming in a sort of primitive way and I was beginning to think I had really been too optimistic. I had seen him in *Summer City* without realising it at the time. He had his hair dyed."

The veteran movie-maker was studying the scruffy young man in faded Levi's and a jean jacket, tumbling over his coffee, and chain smoking, and wondering if he had been expecting too much.

"Then I had the idea that perhaps this kind of 'face-to-face', casual as I was keeping it, might be too much for him."

So Pate suggested they go to a hotel run by some friends in North Adelaide. Mel insisted he drive.

"You should have seen the inside of that car! It really looked as if he was living in it – which he well could have been."

Even Mel has cheerfully confessed over the years: "I am a bit of a slob. I live in my own squalor. Dirty socks. Pants hanging off the lightbulb."

Pate learned that after a few drinks Mel relaxed more and started to chat away merrily, "generally being the sweet, open boy he was then".

That was enough for Pate. He resolved there and then to take a chance on Mel. It turned out to be an interesting experience for all involved. It was also the first time Mel had been properly directed for a movie role.

Australia's *Cinema Papers* magazine can precis the storyline of *Tim*:

"Mary Horton (Piper Laurie) is an attractive woman in her mid-40s, unmarried, and at ease with her career and her comfortable if undemanding home life. She meets Tim (Mel Gibson) when, as a building labourer working next door, he is asked to hose dust from her garden. Tim is a fine-looking young man, handsome and strongly built. He is 25 years old and good at his work. He is also mentally retarded, a condition that might have been remedied if his parents, Ron and Em Melville (Alwyn Kurts, Pat Evison) were educated and had the money to know how best to help. Instead, they and his sister, Dawnie (Deborah Kennedy) have given him love and understanding; in return Tim loves them and moves through life with a child's gentleness and content.

"Because her usual gardener has injured his back, Mary arranges for Tim to garden for her regularly. Gradually, a friendship develops. On Tim's part it is all admiration for someone who treats him naturally and kindly. For Mary, it is at first an interest in helping him to read, to paint, and to understand a little more of things he never had the chance to learn.

"When Dawnie marries the wealthy Mick Harrington (David Foster), Tim is heartbroken. Mary tries to explain marriage, and Tim asks her to promise never to marry and go away. When his mother has a heart attack and dies, Tim is lost and bewildered. He had never understood death until Mary explained it to her. Ron, without Em and Dawnie, is lonely, and Mary offers friendship. Tim is jealous, though he doesn't understand why.

"Mary sees a television programme in which John Martinson (Michael Caulfield), an expert in the care of mildly retarded children, discusses what can be done to help these youngsters learn. She visits Martinson to ask for guidance with Tim. Without Mary realising it, Tim is also helping her, teaching her, by example, to enjoy simple pleasures, bringing warmth into her life. Mary's employer, Tom Ainsley (Peter Gwynne), warns her that she is becoming emotionally involved. But it is Martinson who tells her: 'Marry him . . . you love him . . . you need each other.' For Mary, the decision seems at first a problem. But most problems can be solved. Mary and Tim, together, work out their solution."

The script was essentially a two-hander for Tim and Mary – which presented some testing scenes for writers, directors and actors. Like all simple movie stories it had to be very real and identifiable to work.

Up-front as ever, Mel told Pate, during the first few days of filming, that he had "never been directed" before. That all be could remember about *Mad Max* – true or false – was being told to stand here, look there, walk here.

"He really had very little film technique in those early days on *Tim*. But he absorbed direction like a great big sponge; he learned very quickly and, I considered, very well. After all, the cast around him were all very experienced and competent film and TV performers," recalled Pate.

Among those performers was twice-Oscar-nominated actress Piper Laurie, playing the older woman who seduces Tim. She and Mel hit it off from the moment they met.

"It's incredible when you realise it was only Mel's second feature film. It's not an easy role, yet he brings a warmth and presence you expect only from an actor who has been around for a long time," says Laurie now.

(Note the reference to his "second film". Already Mel was avoiding any mention of *Summer City*. Studio publicity hand-outs fail to mention his real debut movie.)

Laurie considered, after the film had been completed, that "Mel was fun to work with. When I went back home afterwards I told everyone about this wonderful young actor in Australia."

Shooting of *Tim* was carried out mainly around the picturesque peninsula area, about forty miles north of Sydney. Mel – used to the kick-and-scramble school of movie making – nonplussed the production co-ordinator when he announced the day before filming started that he would be staying at various addresses around the area. It was a situation that every line producer dreads: nightmare scenarios of him not showing up on the set were rushing through the executives' minds.

Initially, Mel suggested he would travel back to his parents' home in Mount Kuring-gai each night, and get up at dawn to make the 7.30 a.m. call-time. But then came his alternative plan – which threw the whole production into chaos.

Production manager Betty Barnard takes up the story.

"We were about to start the shoot and there was this awful problem of getting Mel to the location, after he decided to stay with friends. Either there was something of the nomad in his blood or he had friends everywhere, because we'd get a series of telephone numbers to follow his wanderings."

Even Mel apologised obliquely, after the film had wrapped: "I guess I've been a bit nomadic these past months. But I always come home, don't I, Mum?"

Anne Gibson was sitting just by him when that particular interview concluded. She nodded her head in bewilderment. She was just relieved that her beloved son still wanted to pop home now and again to sample delicious home cooking.

Back on the set of *Tim*, Mel's lack of a home base did nothing to stop it being by far his most enjoyable movie-making experience, until then.

He praised Michael Pate as "an actor's actor and an actor's director. He really knows what it is all about and what to ask for at exactly the right time. Even Piper commented on this. She said it was something that eluded many directors."

And after making two films where money was so tight that most scenes were shot in minimal time, Mel found himself admired for his extraordinary ability to get it right on the first take.

"One-take Mel, we called him," said Betty Barnard. "It was marvellous to see a new face with loads of talent to match."

But what the production team did not realise was that Mel was angry with himself every time he got it right so quickly – because he wanted to develop the character of Tim and try different approaches to each scene. But once Pate and his crew had a good take in the can they simply moved on to the next set-up.

Those two previous films had made Mel, in his

own eyes, much too sloppy. He wanted to slow down. He believed that the key to success in his acting was to do every scene to perfection, but until he actually managed to land a role in a big-budget feature film that opportunity always eluded him.

Michael Pate was blissfully unaware of Mel's inner reservations, doubts. He saw the modest budget of $400,000 as perfectly sufficient to make a film everyone would be proud of. During production he passed on his opinions to anyone who would listen.

"*Tim* will be a beautiful picture. It will look like we spent four or five million dollars."

Pate courted an entry in Pseuds' Corner when he told one interviewer: "Mel was so open and vulnerable and receptive and intrigued and inquisitive of [sic] what he might truly have been thinking at times. And I'm sure there were times when he might have asked himself what in the hell he really was supposed to be doing. But bringing all of his instinctive gifts into play, he came up with a performance of innocence and worth unmatched in the annals of Australian film-making.

"Whatever Mel has done since, and what he will do in the future, cannot quite compare with the giant step forward he took – in many ways on his own, with some assistance, guidance, counselling, and inspiration, I hope, from me – in his performance as Tim."

In fairness to euphoric director Pate, author Colleen McCullough – one of Australia's most celebrated writers – was also full of praise for Mel, whom she saw as the perfect Tim.

"He was absolutely right for the part. Michael Pate is a shrewd judge of talent. *Tim* worked wonderfully and I must admit that Mel Gibson was one of the prime reasons."

Mel himself tried very hard to mould the character of

Tim into something that he thought would appeal to everyone. He made a special point of observing the behaviour of one of his young nephews and made low-key visits to mental institutions to help him understand the role more clearly. He refuses to share the impression left on him by those visits, but they seemed to bring out yet another side of his character.

Those close to him say that he became a more sensitive person during the filming of *Tim*. Many believe that having to play someone retarded made Mel examine his own role in life. He explained during filming:

"I'd read the book and knew how I was going to attack it. It had to be pretty low-key. You can't have a spastic-looking guy. It was more like childlike innocence and obedience.

"It wasn't so much playing someone retarded but rather stressing the innocent aspect of it – as if he were someone normal who has a link missing somewhere. I couldn't play him drooling. It would have been a turn-off."

And, as an afterthought, he added a small clue to his self-image at the time: "It wasn't all that difficult – I'm quite simple myself really."

The truth was that despite the happy atmosphere and Michael Pate's gushing enthusiasm, *Tim* was a fairly amateurish-looking movie that did reasonable business in Australia but totally failed at the all-important US box office. As is sometimes the case in inferior productions, Mel's performance in *Tim* seems all the more impressive because the movie is mediocre.

"It's difficult not to shine when you are in a film like *Tim*," warned one film critic. But the *New York Post*, perceiving Mel's performance as "a thing of beauty, in its subtle shading of an adult with a very young mind", sounded as if their review had been written by Michael Pate himself.

Mel has been relatively noncommittal about *Tim*, in recent years, although it did him more good than harm and earned him an Australian Film Institute best actor award in 1979. It was a remarkable achievement for someone who had made only three films.

Making *Tim* also thrust Mel much more into the public eye. (*Mad Max* had not yet been released in cinemas and there was little hint of the incredible success that film would attain.) On the set of *Tim*, Mel was expected to do his bit in publicising the film.

One particular interview on a radio station is note-worthy, for it ignited his abiding contempt for the press.

"There were some questions that I simply couldn't answer, so I was just sitting there open-mouthed and the interviewer was getting really snotty."

The flare-up that followed received saturation coverage in the Sydney papers and Mel was described as a "typically dreary and inarticulate Australian actor". He was hurt and disillusioned by the reaction. He believed he was simply being honest; that questions as banal as: "How does it feel to be Australia's next Jack Thompson?" did not merit response.

Respected columnist Mike Gibson in the *Sydney Morning Herald* also laid into the hapless actor.

After encountering Mel, he wrote: "Gibson's pants were held up by a pair of faded firemen's braces. Given a script to read, Mel Gibson may be a young man with something to offer, but I'm afraid I haven't the slightest idea what he is all about."

The *Mad Max* furore was deceptive, too – it led people to believe that Mel was as sullen as the character he played in those movies. Liz Porter, writing in Australia's *Cleo* magazine in December 1979, was one of the few writers even to vaguely appreciate what makes Mel tick.

"For Mel Gibson to be identified with the role of strong,

silent Max would be particularly unjust. Mel is anything but sullen . . . or silent. He's a natural clown and an hilarious comic. Not a show-off; clowning just appears to be part of his nature, which makes him a most delightful and entertaining victim for an interviewer," she stated in an article aptly headlined "Mad About Mel".

"Mel doesn't have a great capacity for glib formula answers. One of his most attractive qualities is his total lack of affectation. He's not at all interested in impressing people. If an interviewer expects him to make pronouncements on things such as the Australian film industry and he feels he doesn't have the answer, he just says no. Which might not endear him to people who want an answer, any answer at all costs. However, ask him to talk about other things besides being a sex-symbol and Mel is far from inarticulate and anything but dreary."

During the same interview, an uncharacteristically relaxed Mel unbent sufficiently to give Liz Porter a sample of his girning (face distortion) techniques and pretended to be shot in the crowded King's Cross, Sydney, coffee bar where they met.

The interview with Liz Porter is of special significance because Mel so rarely lets his guard down in front of journalists. Just as well, since on the few occasions he has done so, there have been chaotic results – as we shall see later in his career.

Mel returned to his NIDA lead role in *Romeo and Juliet* at Sydney's Nimrod Theatre around the time that *Mad Max* was finally premiered in January of 1979. With crowds of moviegoers flocking to see him ripping people's arms out of their sockets, and shooting villains galore, it did not go unnoticed that the talented young star was playing exactly the opposite role on the stage.

As Mel put it in deadpan humorous style: "Romeo is a

young guy who is just dying to be loved . . . in fact he does die for it."

Then, waxing a touch more serious about the Bard, Mel continued: "I love the words and the scope of Shakespeare. His words are full of possibilities for interpretation, for nuances in delivery."

Mel's love for live theatre and Shakespeare has endured through his career, of course.

His co-star in *Romeo and Juliet* was Angela Punch McGregor – a well-known Australian stage and television actress. She was stunned when young women in the audience started throwing bouquets at the stage. At first she assumed they were for her; then it dawned on her that the avid stares of lusting young ladies were locked on her young co-star.

Strangely, *Romeo and Juliet* turned into a cursed production. A number of near-disasters resulted in virtually the entire cast and crew being injured. Mel played Romeo first with a dislocated thumb, injured during a swordfight, and then a leg so seriously damaged he could not put any weight on it.

Mel managed to hide his pain on stage by using control of the body – even though he had not shone in his dance training course at NIDA. Mel was (and still is) a reluctant dancer. The only occasions when he has been known to dance have been during alleged dalliances with pretty blondes in nightclubs.

In that era, shy dental nurse Robyn Moore was not engaged to Mel Gibson, far less wed to him. Yet while staying behind the scenes, she was a major if gentle influence. Robyn had crossed an important personal threshold, made an implicit statement, by following him out to Sydney just before shooting started on *Tim*.

But only to personal friends did Mel so much as mention his Robyn. It was as if he was treating her as somebody too special for small-talk with people who didn't matter. Not for nothing has he called her, "my Rock of Gibraltar, only more beautiful".

He picked, in psychological terms, a highly significant and positive symbol. Surely Robyn Moore represented sanity and reality to somebody fighting for recognition in an environment where those qualities are rare as endangered species.

Mel, however, as we are beginning to witness, can be all things to all men – and even more, if only in their fantasies, to all women. His cards stay close to his chest.

So while the likelihood is that he envisaged Robyn as The Girl, journalists still noted him turning up for interviews with pretty actresses and gorgeous models in tow. To gullible onlookers Our Hero was playing the field . . .

Girls for show, and a girl to go home to, after respectful wooing and wedding pomp and ceremony? Perhaps.

The previous year he'd treated poor Deborah Foreman to a smugly brutal declaration of intent about partnering her for as long as it lasted, but marrying a virgin. And now it seemed that Robyn was saving herself for Mel.

For the moment, though, many of his circle were unaware of such undercurrents. Mel Gibson was a hot young actor, and HYAs aren't notorious for settling down with a walk-the-line Little Woman.

A brace of strong stage performances followed *Romeo and Juliet*. Mel appeared in *No Names, No Pack Drill*, playing Rebel, a US Marine who shuns the Halls of Montezuma to go AWOL in Sydney in 1942 and have an affair with an Australian nightclub singer. Then came Samuel Beckett's gnomic masterpiece, *Waiting for Godot* (con trick or classic view of the Human Condition? You decide.)

Rave reviews rewarded Mel's portrayal of Estragon Gogo, lost soul and probably the most famous waiter never to see the inside of a restaurant. Yes, it has been a long and winding – and surprisingly cultured – road to reach Martin Riggs, the living Lethal Weapon.

Mel gave a characteristically straightforward appraisal of his performance. "Now that was something. Strange casting, do you think? I thought so too. I'm sixty years too young for that role. But we used that. It was a very stylised production. We were clowns more than bums. That part required probably the most physical strength I ever had to produce for a role.

"We did vaudeville and we did things that seemed to defy physics and gravity. I had to make myself short without appearing to be stooping or something. Plus stand on tiptoe on one leg with my other stretched out at a forty-five-degree angle for like minutes on end. It was discipline. It was fantastic.

"I lost about ten pounds every night. From sweat. By the end of the show we'd look shithouse. We'd go out there with sort of tramp make-up on – sort of white but with five o'clock shadows – and we'd end up being just mud. Everything running down our faces."

What Mel did not tell the world was that during his stint on *Waiting for Godot* he developed alarming breathing problems, made worse by his thirty-to-forty-cigarettes-a-day habit. Fellow actors recall him having five-minute-long coughing fits backstage which left him gasping, eyes streaming.

He found himself literally struggling to breathe on stage one night. Lying down supposedly asleep while his co-star Geoffrey Rush as Vladimir was in the middle of a long soliloquy, Mel lay there for minutes in absolute agony, praying that he could resist the oncoming coughing fit. Every now and then his body would twitch as he went rigid to try and avoid the inevitable. Gradually tears of pain started rolling down his cheeks but he did not flinch and managed to survive without any embarrassing moments.

Years later as his smoking habit worsened he must have wondered if it would have been better if his coughing fit had occurred that night, then it might have made him stop immediately. As it was, he used the dreaded weed more and more, finding it impossible even to rehearse his lines without a cigarette between his lips. Significantly, he still *never* smoked in Hutton Gibson's household.

Mel would orate about his passion for the theatre with the same level of energy that he put into his performances each evening. He adored the atmosphere, the crowd and the no-safety-net nature of it. He maintains that if he could have supported a family purely on his theatrical earnings he would have been the happiest guy on the street.

But the Australian film industry was re-emerging from decades of inactivity at that time and Hollywood became aware that interesting talent could be found Down Under. Admittedly, some not so desirable film projects managed to thumb a ride on the back of the good name of the rapidly expanding Australian film industry. One such movie was *Attack Force Z*, and it would plunge Mel Gibson into an artistic abyss and, to his mind, put his career into a steep decline.

When Mel and co-stars John Philip Law, who had made a name for himself in *Barbarella*, the New Zealand-born Sam Neill (later to star in films like *The Hunt for Red October*) and two talented Aussies, Chris Hayward and John Waters, signed up for *Attack Force Z* they had no idea of the problems they would encounter or the sexual adventures ahead.

The story sounded, and read initially, like a good old-fashioned World War Two adventure: a bunch of undercover Aussie soldiers, led by a Dutch commando, land on a Japanese-held island in the Pacific and aided by loyal Chinese, bring back a defecting Japanese scientist.

Mel did not hesitate to sign up for the movie when he met highly regarded Australian director Philip Noyce, who had won international acclaim for his newsreel nostalgia drama *Newsfront*. Noyce's own father had been a member of the real-life squad of commandos upon which the story was based, so Mel felt he had a superb grasp of the subject.

The other "bonus" was that *Attack Force Z* was going to be filmed entirely in exotic locations in Taiwan, partly because it looked right but also because it was a cheap place to hire labour and the film was being partly backed by an Asian company, the Central Motion Pictures Corporation of Taiwan. The project's other partner was the successful Australian company John McCallum Productions, makers of the "Skippy" television series.

But even before filming began, director Noyce clashed with producer Lee Robinson, over changes he had made in the script. It was that old familiar story of an artist (the director) being forced to compromise the quality of a movie, thanks to a producer trying to make sure it did not go over budget. The day before shooting was scheduled to commence, Noyce – who went on to direct *Patriot Games*, *Dead Calm* (with Sam Neill) and *Conundrum* with Sally Field – departed. His replacement was Tim Burstall, an experienced Melbourne-based director with some highly praised Aussie films such as *Alvin Purple* and *The Last of the Knucklemen* to his credit. Unfortunately Mel and the other actors, excluding American star John Philip Law, feared that this change in commander would be a complete disaster.

Law was deemed the star because of his work on a string of Hollywood films. He also happened to be a box office attraction in Asia.

Tim Burstall had never spoken about working with Mel on *Attack Force Z*, but in a series of talks he revealed the full story of what really happened during that six-week shoot in Taiwan.

"It was a crazy situation. Chaos. I certainly did not get what I wanted. The film suffered from so many problems."

Within hours of arriving at their base in the capital city of T'aipei, Burstall was facing a deputation of actors led by Mel and Sam Neill, who made it perfectly clear that if they could wriggle out of their contracts they would desert the film immediately.

"I took them aside and said: 'You make me ashamed to be an Australian. What the *fuck* are you doing?' It was the most disgusting example of Aussie unionism. I was pretty angry. I felt like taking them outside and kicking their fucking heads in. I wanted to shame them into doing something."

That night Sam Neill visited Burstall in his hotel and told the director that he had talked to Mel and "we have no choice but to work together".

The director is painfully candid. "The person least happy was Mel. He disgusted me the most. He placed me in a continually difficult position," Burstall accused.

He even suggested that Mel distrusted him partly because of the rivalry that exists between Aussies from Sydney versus those from Melbourne. The truth was far more complex; Mel felt he had yet again been betrayed by the broken promises of cheapskate film producers. Here he was on his fourth movie, with second billing to a major star like Law – yet the problems haunting *Summer City* and *Mad Max* and to a lesser extent *Tim* had returned.

Producer Lee Robinson insists that Mel just did not appreciate the complex nature of any co-production.

"He knew there would be teething problems. But he had this idea the film should be made a certain way. Well, the conditions dictated we should make it another way. And we did. I have no quarrel with Mel's energy and views, but as he was still learning his craft, he should have listened just a little bit more."

But an even bigger chip on the shoulder than artistic integrity was involved – money. Handsome John Philip Law, whose good looks and Hollywood status had helped in part to get the film financed, was being paid $50,000 for his work while Mel and Sam Neill were on exactly $1,000 per gruelling six-day week.

"It wasn't just their roles they were angry about. It was more to do with money," Tim Burstall confirms.

Soon the Aussie actors, not least Mel, were sending up Law behind his back and calling him names that were far from complimentary. The filming of *Attack Force Z* was turning into a real-life battlefield of bitterness.

Law – who today, ironically, lives only a few miles from Mel Gibson's home in Malibu – also broke a long silence to talk about the film. He accepts that, "The movie was blown apart by Philip Noyce's departure. It was a terrible situation for the actors. They felt double-crossed by the producers."

But Law sided entirely with new director Burstall because he knew they had to get the film shot – although he claims that he was constantly "fighting for things on behalf of everybody".

He adds: "We did have our ups and downs and I did get angry over the falling out with the producer earlier."

Mel and the other Aussies were further needled by the fact that Law was staying in a grand hotel overlooking their smaller accommodation in T'aipei, and he was supplied with a car and driver kept at his disposal throughout the shoot. The rest of the actors were given rides in a scruffy old van to and from the location. And told to fend for themselves the rest of the time in this teeming city made up of vast skyscrapers surrounded by shanty towns, with a million bicycles on the streets at any one time.

"They did not fraternise with Law. They were very covert about it. They talked amongst themselves about what they thought of him. They had a contemptuous nickname for him," recalled Tim Burstall.

The Chinese co-stars, including veteran local actor Koo-Chuan-Hsiung (known to everyone as "Mr Koo"), and technicians made up at least 50 per cent of the entire contingent and a number of them seemed to spend much of their time taking rake-offs and demanding bribes to continue working efficiently. The scenario rapidly degenerated into "them and us" nastiness, not helped by the fact that there was an obvious language problem.

In later years, Mel laughed off his experiences in Taiwan, claiming that his skill at miming springs from trying to communicate with the Chinese on the set. "Up there in Taiwan we were all good mimers. As we didn't speak the same language, we used signal language. In the end, we found there wasn't any barrier in communicating."

The truth was that barriers were being set up daily as problem after problem plagued the production of *Attack Force Z*.

Tim Burstall sets the scene: "Mr Koo was the Marlon Brando of the region and he was also a very powerful figure in the city of Kaohsiung. He had a group of henchmen with him the whole time and was always late, and that caused added resentment."

In addition to all this, Burstall was rewriting the script as they went along – a disastrous method when you are shooting to a tight schedule.

Then there was the cinematography of local cameraman Lin Hung-Chung. It could be best described as "choppy" but the biggest omission was that those famous azure blue eyes of Mel's were never even passingly exploited.

Tim Burstall believes that Mel "had some personal

troubles at the time" and cites one flare-up with the young actor that shows just how on edge he was feeling. Those problems at home were rumoured to be something to do with his girlfriend at the time, presumably wife-to-be Robyn Moore.

"There was a fight sequence and I remember explaining something to Mel and halfway through he just threw his gun down and said: 'You're fucking taking away my responsibilities as a hero.' He had failed to grasp the whole point of the fight sequence. He did not realise I was trying to help him. Mel just would not accept what I was saying."

Intriguingly, Burstall says that Mel had trouble acting out the emotional scenes in the film.

"I was unhappy with his approach when he had to show emotion. These were moments that required his internalisation. He just did not give it enough."

Attack Force Z also marked the first time that Mel had cause to regret his lack of height: co-star John Philip Law towered over him at six foot five. In publicity handouts, Mel is said to be somewhere between five foot nine and five foot ten. But, like one of his biggest movie heroes Gary Cooper, Mel is actually often much shorter than many actors around him. Law thinks he is about five foot six, but it would probably be more realistic to estimate his height at around five foot eight. During shooting of *Attack Force Z* they devised all sorts of tricks to make him appear to be a similar height to Law (who, incidentally, believes that he has lost countless jobs because he always towers over "tall" stars. Christopher "Dracula"' Lee makes the same complaint.)

"I am very used to doing that equaliser thing but I was very taken aback by his size," Law says. "I had to regularly kneel down and have him alongside me, standing. That way we could do things together. Often he would stand and I'd duck around the set. There was a lot of effort made to make him look the same height. It was perfectly understandable. A lot of actors are sensitive about it."

Law went on: "I did all my close-ups with my legs spread apart so both our heads could be in the camera frame."

And during filming of *The Year of Living Dangerously* with six-foot-one-inch Sigourney Weaver looming over him, Mel's shoes were secretly given a built-up instep so that he would look taller.

Halfway through the troublesome and unhappy *Attack Force Z* shoot, Chinese star Mr Koo took it upon himself to improve communications by inviting Mel, Law, Burstall, Sam Neill and another Aussie actor on a getaway weekend to Kaohsiung, Taiwan's second biggest city, where Mr Koo was an uncrowned king. The five men gladly accepted Mr Koo's offer, especially when he insisted on paying for the entire trip.

It has never before been disclosed that on the first evening of that trip, Mr Koo actually took the *Attack Force Z* party to a brothel. He believed that by indulging his round-eye colleagues sexually, it might help them all to "bond" better. Tim Burstall takes up the story:

"Koo called it a restaurant but it was basically a brothel, serving Japanese food. It turned out to be an absolute feast. A new girl would come round every second course. All they had on were little towels around their necks and they would pull a chair up and sit next to us. Mr Koo would then say something like 'Touch them, Mr Tim.' We were made to feel like royalty.

"Koo wanted to make us all get along better. He was forcing drinks down us and all these women were made available. This was hospitality Chinese-style. The tradition in China is to fix up Westerners with women and then find out exactly what they like."

John Philip Law has an even more vivid recollection of the Night of the Brothel.

"At first we all sat there shitfaced and didn't know how to act. We were so worried about offending anyone. We had a hell of a time. It was such a bizarre evening. Mr Koo just wanted to do his thing for us, and this was it, boy!"

At first, disclosed Law, none of the party realised where Mr Koo had taken them. Initially they settled down in a huge room with a big round table and waited to be served.

"We were totally unaware of what was to come. I remember there was a bed in the corner with a lamp. It became a topic of conversation between us."

As the night wore on, a girl walked into the room.

"She sat on one of the guys' laps and then the parade started. Koo paid for everything. He was the host and would have resented us offering to pay. Koo would orchestrate a little and say: 'Which one do you like?' and 'Take your pick'. It was like a sample situation. He said have as many as you want. It says a lot about the film that this was the most memorable thing about it."

Law, remarkably, argues "there was nothing sordid" about what happened in that bordello.

"It was an ice-breaker. When in Rome do as the Romans do. There is not the stigma attached to their occupation as there is in other countries. If a girl is from a poor family and she is a knock-out then she can better herself. It was just doing a service. It was very refreshing to see it. It was very amusing. It is hard to be judgemental about situations like that."

Two years later, Mel slammed *Attack Force Z* in a bad-tempered outburst, saying he only played the role "for the money".

"It was just a vulgar attempt at a war-action movie with Aussie WASPs [White Anglo-Saxon Protestants] shooting Chinese dressed up in Japanese uniforms. I don't like to talk about or even remember that film. You do that kind of film because you are starving to death," he recalled.

Attack Force Z was never released in American cinemas and ended up being shown on US cable television, but many believe that Mel's criticisms of the movie are based as much on his real-life experiences during the shoot as they are on the quality of the end-product.

One review in *Variety* concluded that it was "a good example of a well-paced, finely-acted war film, not much short of super . . . ahead of many more-vaunted Aussie productions". The same reviewer heaped praise on much-maligned director Burstall, writing that "he got to grips with essentials of structure and plotting, and developed the characters firmly and economically".

Scott Murray, of *Cinema Papers*, concedes: "It's not as bad as it's made out. It is an okay picture of its kind."

The *Attack Force Z* shoot ended around January, 1980. Tim Burstall was pleasantly surprised when embittered Mel turned up one evening in the cramped editing room in King's Cross, Sydney, where Burstall was trying to knit together the film, some months afterwards.

"We had a drink and he told me he was getting married. He was rather sheepish about it and most of his friends thought it was Disastersville – that the girl was trying to get him and he was just a poor demented Catholic kid."

One of Mel's best friends at the time said there was talk of Robyn being pregnant; it might explain the eventual birth of their eldest child Hannah later that same year.

To most people these days, marrying after conception of a child is hardly a shocking situation. But for Mel it would present a few problems at home – where Hutton Gibson was still passionately fighting the Roman Catholic hierarchy. Now his own flesh and blood was about to undergo a shotgun wedding to a Church of England girl.

I get my ears boxed if I'm not home by midnight. Marriage is hard work.

Mel could not wait to get back to the sanity of Sydney after madness and mayhem in Taiwan. In many ways his lengthy stay in that tiny country had taught him more lessons about life than he cared to admit. He'd escaped from those unhappy work conditions in bottle after bottle of the local beer, and there was that weekend in Kaohsiung with Mr Koo. Mel felt overwhelmed with guilt, the sort you can only really suffer if you have been brought up a strict Catholic.

People who encountered Mel in the early months of 1980 report that he was subdued, more moody. The cocky self-confidence that had seemed so much a part of his character was replaced by something quieter, more thoughtful. But then 1980 threatened to be among the most significant years in his life.

Firstly there was Robyn. She was content to remain firmly in the background, but Mel's experiences in Asia made him realise how much he needed her calming influence. Back in Sydney, Mel was suffering from that classic actor's problem – lack of work. His $6,000 fee for *Attack Force Z* was disappearing fast and he was finding himself more and more reliant on Robyn's hard-earned wage as a nurse. She in turn was more than happy to go out and earn the money while Mel waited for a good, quality job to come up. His experiences in Taiwan had taught him never to accept acting work simply for the money; there had to be some quality to the projects.

He was better off starving than damaging his career.

And to her immense credit, Robyn, still no more than his girlfriend at the start of 1980, was prepared to support Mel all the way. He was amazed by her generosity and deeply touched by her loyalty. Mel also loved the fact that after three years of talking, eating and breathing acting with friends like Steve Bisley and Monroe Reimers as well as a procession of acting girlfriends, here was someone who neither knew nor cared much about the art of being dramatic. In fact, Robyn could not have been less similar to some of the actresses Mel had encountered during his late teens and early twenties.

It also says much about his interest in her that he waited at least a year while Robyn went through that other relationship with a boyfriend before the two even began to consider actually dating.

As the boredom of being unemployed set in, Mel grew even surer that Robyn Denise Moore was just the sort of girl his father Hutton had always advised him to look out for. The little matter of her being brought up in the Church of England was the only minor obstacle. Marriage was being talked about between Mel and Robyn when he bumped into *Attack Force Z* director Tim Burstall in April, during the middle of one of his "lean spells" of unemployment.

There was gossip among his closest friends and stage acquaintances the Robyn was pregnant and a wedding was imminent. Mel for his part volunteered little. After all, he had spent many years preaching the importance of marrying a virgin, even to girlfriends like Deborah Foreman. And his opinions on abortion were absolutely crystal-clear, as he stated very bluntly in an interview with *Cosmopolitan* less than three years later.

"Abortion? It's inhuman because it destroys life. Who presumes to know where life starts? I'll tell you one thing – the foetus grows, its heart beats. It's like when you strike a match . . . is there a flame, or do we just imagine it?" Asked if he would ever force a woman to have an abortion he replied: "Well, I wouldn't get one!"

The irony of the situation was that no one apart from Mel and his family was that bothered about the fact that Robyn was pregnant. The most important thing was that he truly loved Robyn and wanted to spend the rest of his life with her – and there was absolutely no doubting that. Mel found her to be a rare, stable, down-to-earth person, and his is a business where personal relationships crumble with alarming regularity.

When Mel got a call from agent Bill Shannahan to say that an offer of a meaty role in a new Australian television series called "Punishment" was on the cards, he decided that pregnancy or no pregnancy, he should marry Robyn as soon as possible.

The wedding on June 7, 1980, was a restrained affair and no one present has ever provided an account of what actually happened. All that is known is that it took place in a church in the community of Forestville, New South Wales, and the priest who officiated was the Reverend Clement Gailey. Most families would have proudly announced such a wedding in the local press and Mel, by then the veteran of three films, might well have attracted the attention of the media. It was even claimed by one newspaper that the marriage was carried out in such secrecy because Mel did not want to ruin his image as a sex-symbol. The truth seems more likely to be that religious differences, and the possibility of a baby being on the way, made for a hastily-arranged ceremony.

Anyway, whatever the circumstances, Mel felt hugely relieved to be married, though he and his bride were still relatively young at 24. He had been brought up to believe in the sanctity of marriage and he genuinely believed that having a partner like Robyn would stabilise his life. Above all, they truly loved each other.

His mother Anne recalled how Mel broached the subject of marriage in a very round-about way with his parents, shortly before the wedding.

"He was talking about marriage and families in a general way and asked us for advice. Hutton, who's always been Mel's hero, said he should never marry a dumb woman, and pick someone who can be your friend for life. I added the reasoning of a mum, telling Mel he should always be kind to his wife."

In fairness to religious fanatic Hutton, he does not seem to have been as upset by the circumstances surrounding the marriage as some of Mel's friends expected. Both parents had warmly emphasised to their son that true love and happiness in a marriage had little to do with religion, and more with respect and friendship.

Mel and Robyn spent their honeymoon at a friend's beach house up the coast from Sydney. For the first time since leaving home in his second year at NIDA, Mel felt that he was getting his life under control once more. He was more settled and hoped that his acting career would start moving in the right direction.

Unfortunately that direction did not lead to the Channel Ten prison drama "Punishment". Mel regretted accepting the role of an inmate of fictitious Longridge Prison the moment he walked on to the set at the East Sydney Technical College. He had accepted the part after a long stint of unemployment but his heart wasn't in it. The relentless six-day-week shooting schedule evoked the worst aspects of his experiences on "The Sullivans" a few years previously. Television's churn-it-out philosophy was not something that Mel could warm to, let alone welcome.

And then he decided to turn up late on the one day all the Sydney newspapers had been invited to be on the wintry set. Journalists gleefully reported the anger of harassed director Leon Thau following the young actor's non-appearance . . .

"Does anybody know where the hell Gibson is?" shouted Thau furiously.

Mel's co-star Mike Preston looked slightly contemptuously at the director and replied: "No idea mate, he could be anywhere from an aboriginal encampment in Alice Springs to Hollywood. He's that sort of bloke."

Preston knew whereof he spake – he had appeared with Mel in *Mad Max* only eighteen months earlier.

Two hours later, to a round of applause from the crew, Mel finally showed up with a week's stubble, a grubby pair of jeans, a leather jacket and riding a motorbike.

"It looked like *Mad Max* all over again," chortled journalist Andrew Saw.

Director Thau was close to boiling point by this stage, only holding his temper because of the assembled members of the press.

"That has to be shaved off," he said, pointing to the Gibson chin. Mel emerged from make-up ten minutes later, grinning in the direction of the press and ignoring his esteemed director.

No more TV, Mel promised himself, no more television ever again.

Despite these occasional setbacks, agents Bill Shannahan and Faith Martin knew that Mel was a hot property. *Mad Max* might have bombed in the United States, but throughout the rest of the world it was a huge commercial success and Shannahan was particularly adept at exploiting the explosion of interest in his young client. The agent became a showbusiness father figure to Mel as he nurtured and humoured him. Shannahan was not a stock type, get-rich-quick agent. He was a patient, caring man with Mel's best interests at heart. Mel in turn greatly respected the opinion of Shannahan. So both men were delighted when director Peter Weir made an approach to cast Mel in one of the lead roles in his movie *Gallipoli*.

Weir – who had made such a reputation with the wonderfully haunting *Picnic at Hanging Rock* – spent four years honing and moulding the perfect script in conjunction with Australian writer David Williamson. Then he had carted the project around from company to company in a desperate effort to get it financed at a level that would enable him to film a true, authentic version of one of the most tragic events in Australian history.

The battle of Gallipoli began on April 25, 1915, a military disaster that cost the lives of 33,000 Allied soldiers, including 8,587 Australians. The tragedy came about after the generals and politicians running the war decided Turkey should be invaded because of that country's support for the Germans. The force selected included men of the Australian and New Zealand Army Corps (ANZAC), who had been training in Egypt, as well as British, French and Indian troops.

Blamed for the carnage-ridden fiasco was Winston S. Churchill, described by Australian writer Murray Sale as "a hare-brained amateur strategist who had dreamed up the whole disastrous operation".

Out of this tragedy grew a legend so powerful that all

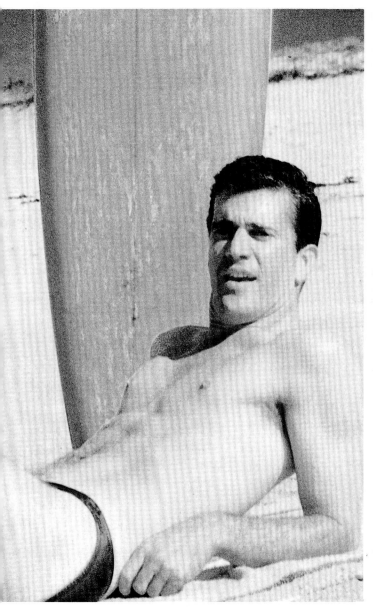

Mel, aged 20, during the making of *Summer City*.

Top: Mel (top row, middle), aged 13 at St. Leo's College, where he suffered a miserable year.

Below left: Mel aged 14.

Below right: St. Leo's today.

Melbourne Herald article after Mel and his family arrived in Australia from America.

Top left: Mel's father, Hutton, and mother, Anne.

Top right: Mel's oldest sister, Patricia.

Top middle left: Mel's granny, Eva Mylott.

Middle right: Mel's first home in Verplank, upstate New York.

Middle left: Mel's brother Kevin.

Bottom left: Mel at his parents' home.

Below right: The farm in Mount Vision, upstate New York, which almost sent his father, Hutton, into bankruptcy.

Mel, aged 21, during the making of *Tim*.

Top: Recent poster for Mel's first film.

Below: Deborah Foreman (right), on the set of *Summer City*, just weeks before attempting suicide after falling in love with Mel.

Deborah Foreman today – almost 20 years after her tragic love affair with Mel.

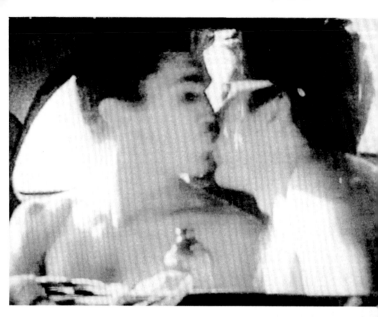

Top: Mel's first screen kiss with fellow actor Steve Bisley on *Summer City*.

Below: Mel in a scene from *Summer City* with Steve Bisley (right).

Top: Mel in *Summer City*.

Below left: Mel enjoys a drink during *Summer City*.

Below right: Mel on the set of *Punishment*, a TV series he did not enjoy working on.

Top: Mel with co-star and brothel owner, Mr. Koo, on location during filming of *Attack Force Z*.

Below: Mel with *Attack Force Z* co-star, John Philip Law, who accompanied him on a sexy adventure in Taiwan.

Mel with *Gallipoli* co-star, Mark Lee, whom Mel helped nurse through the jitters.

Tevaite Vernette, Mel's beautiful *Bounty* co-star, who quit acting after developing a crush on him during the making of the film in Tahit

Mel during one of his many passionate scenes with Tevaite in
Bounty.

Bare-chested Mel in Tahiti during the making of *Bounty*.

Mel, Robyn and Hannah in a rare off camera moment during the making of *Bounty*.

Top: Mel with *Bounty* co-star Anthony Hopkins, whose teetotal ways bored Mel.

Below left: Maimiti Kinnander, one of the topless dancers in *Bounty* who met Mel.

Below right: The disco in Moorea, Tahiti, where Mel was punched by an angry local.

Australians were taught about Gallipoli at school and April 25 was celebrated annually as the day Australia became a true nation. Director Peter Weir wanted to bring all the horror, futility and madness of Gallipoli to the screen through the eyes of two young Australian soldiers who set out to war thinking of it as an adventure only to discover a nightmare.

Weir and Williamson's script floated around Sydney for years until theatrical entrepreneur and record producer Robert Stigwood showed it to his new business partner Rupert Murdoch, the most famous Australian publisher in the world. Stigwood – master of groups like the Bee Gees and backer of *Saturday Night Fever* – and Murdoch were an unlikely partnership but their R and R Films claimed to be committed to backing Australian movies to the tune of $50 million.

Murdoch – owner of the very same tabloid newspapers that would come to stalk and pillory Mel in later years – had another, very deep-set interest in *Gallipoli*, beyond being a patriotic Australian. His own father, the great Australian journalist Keith Murdoch, had covered the battle, landed with the ANZAC troops in Turkey and sent back dispatches that helped expose the tragedy caused by those inept generals and Winston Churchill.

Murdoch – who later went on to purchase 20th Century-Fox – and Stigwood were so taken by the *Gallipoli* script that they immediately contacted Peter Weir and struck a deal. Stigwood told the rather overawed director: "This is the film we want to make."

Weir then made his approach to Mel, who was instantly captivated by the subject matter, especially since it put the British in a poor light – he had never forgotten horror stories of what the notorious Black and Tans did to his relatives in Ireland. Winston Churchill had been behind that as well, he understood. Mel was particularly moved by one scene in the film when the Aussies are ordered by their British superiors to advance into battle, bayonets drawn but rifles unloaded, in spite of the Turks having dug in. Mel saw it as a typical example of the stupidity and cowardice of the British.

The director had always wanted Mel for the key part of Frank. And Mel saw *Gallipoli* as an opportunity to play a role with real depth and compassion – something that had so far eluded him as a film performer.

"I had seen Weir's films and was impressed because they were so full. Peter works on a higher level than I've come across before," he explained shortly after taking the role.

Mel also saw in Frank, whom he was playing, someone he could truly relate to.

"Frank is a strange bag of tricks. More complicated than the average young man at that time. He's funny, but also sneaky. He's the kind of person who would pick up on a phrase or expression to make other people laugh – something smart, off the cuff."

Mel described his approach to such a character as "child-like". He went on: "When things get too complicated you lose a certain truth – which is why you have to fight against becoming hardened, jaded; to retain a sense of wonder."

Mel's words had a certain ring about them. He was really talking about himself rather than a character.

But Mel did make one stipulation to director Weir before agreeing to the $35,000 fee being offered for *Gallipoli*. He steadfastly refused to do any explicit sex scenes although he did bare his torso for a nude bathing sequence.

In an interview with respected movie journalist Dan Yakir, he completely contradicted himself by saying: "I wouldn't take off my clothes" and then went on to insist the bathing scene "was innocent". In later years all sorts of incentives would be dangled in front of him to "persuade" him to go naked.

But to Yakir he provided a unique insight into, perhaps, his true feelings about sex when he said: "I might do a love scene, but nothing too explicit – no close-ups or noises, because it would be an obstacle in my way. It would kill something I want to preserve. I don't want to give too much to the viewers – mystery is important, because the moment they think they know you too well . . ."

On signing up for *Gallipoli*, Mel plunged into weeks of research, reading books by historian C.E.W. Bean, diaries and letters written by soldiers and tracking down and chatting to old soldiers. Mel knew he had to gain a sense of history about Gallipoli, otherwise he could not truly honour the emotions felt by all Australians about this national disaster.

Mel developed a deep respect for the spirit of the soldiers who so bravely marched into action. His character, Frank, knew nothing about the outside world until he got on that battlefield. Mel saw Frank as a knight in shining armour fighting a battle in which men's lives were sacrificed as if they were nothing more than pieces of meat.

The part of the other soldier, Archie, was to be played by blond, blue-eyed Mark Lee. His character – although working-class like Frank – believed all that propaganda about the rightness of fighting the Germans and their allies. Mark had never before acted in a feature film and admitted that he was "terrified" at the prospect.

For the first few weeks of filming he found it virtually impossible to relax, on or off the set, and even out-puffed Mel in the chain smoking department. Lee – a softly-spoken, all-Australian-looking character – never really got out from under Mel's shadow in *Gallipoli* although the other man tried hard to make their relationship work.

Lee sounded completely in awe of his co-star when he said: "Mel has it – he is wonderful in *Mad Max*; he adds a human dimension to a comic strip character."

In Hollywood, stars often go out of their way to overshadow newcomers. But Mel – as the veteran of the pair – did not play his relationship that way at all. He recognised that it was completely in his interests to elicit a good performance from Lee, and so did Peter Weir.

The director at one stage slapped and shook Lee to snap him out of his fear-riddled paralysis.

"Then he would make me laugh by making faces at me and taking his shirt off. He took me by surprise and kept the energy going," said Lee.

"I was going about it all wrong. I would smoke a dozen cigarettes between takes and shake as though I had a fever. I was lost."

Gradually Lee gained sufficient confidence at least to make the relationship between the two characters believable. Mel took pains to win the younger actor's friendship. They grew to like each other and the most moving scenes were shot after they had "connected".

When Weir described Mel's character Frank as "a professional athlete on a yellow brick road to his fate" he could just as easily have been talking about the star himself. And the director seemed to sum up Mel perfectly when he added: "His unpredictable quality, his sense of mystery and exuberance added to the part. He is never quite what he appears." Just so . . .

Weir was so taken by Mel that on the very evening he was signed up to play the part of Frank, Gibson was dragged over to writer David Williamson's house to inject some of Mel's real character into the final draft of the screenplay.

But Mel's meticulous research into the ANZACs plus his athletic training with Olympic coach Jack Giddy was nothing compared to real-life hardships experienced by both actors and crew while making *Gallipoli*. It sometimes seemed as if

Weir was deliberately putting his stars through the mill to make sure they felt the full horrors of war every time they stepped before the cameras.

The first location was near the outback settlement of Beltana in the lower Flinders Ranges in South Australia. Temperatures were consistently above the 100-degree mark and regular dust storms added to everyone's anguish. There were no hotels for hundreds of miles and home for a few weeks was a shearing shed with the occasional sand-gritted meal supplied from the bed of a pick-up truck. Mel started making films under the impression it was a glamorous business, but here he was on his fourth movie and so far he had only stayed in a hotel during the making of *Attack Force Z* – and that had been a dump.

In Beltana, the crew were relegated to a nearby woolshed, although there was serious debate over which building was more smelly. However, all complaints soon subsided when the *Gallipoli* cast and crew got to their next location – an ancient dry salt plain on the edge of the desert, Lake Torrens. This time it was bitterly cold and infested with poisonous funnel web spiders capable of killing a human.

"They're the most vicious spiders in the world," Mel expounded with relish. "If they bite you, you're a goner. Deadliest things around – big, black, hairy and very aggressive." Luckily no one got bitten.

Next stop was Port Lincoln, a quiet fishing town on the South Australian coast. There the fateful ANZAC cove at Gallipoli was painstakingly reconstructed by the production design team – and the cast and crew found pubs complete with cold beer and welcoming locals.

"We embraced the town – and they embraced us," said actor Bill Hunter, who won the Australian Film Institute's award for best supporting actor in his *Gallipoli* performance.

But filming in Port Lincoln was no easier; everyone worked horrendous long hours, dusk to dawn, complete with high temperatures, constant swarms of flies and yet more sandstorms.

However, none of all this seemed to bother Mel in the slightest. He felt as if he truly belonged in *Gallipoli*. When he wasn't needed in front of the cameras he would help prop men load and unload equipment. He enjoyed being one of the boys and the crew warmed to him as "being one of us". But Mel kept one thing very much to himself – Robyn's pregnancy. As the weeks on *Gallipoli* passed, Mel began hoping and praying that filming would end on schedule so that he could get back to Adelaide, where Robyn had gone to be with her family before the birth of their first child.

Sometimes he would climb to the top of the steep cliff overlooking that lovingly re-created beach landing scene and sit there for hours just looking out across the sand towards the ocean. He sensed from the onset that *Gallipoli* was different from those previous films. There was much to ponder. He found himself daydreaming about Robyn and all the children they wanted. He also wondered how he would cope with fast-approaching stardom. Agent Bill Shannahan had briefed him many times on keeping his feet on the ground, but would it all be that simple?

"I would sit up there often by myself and look down on it. I'd think how fantastic the set designer and his team were. It was a work of art. I had huge goose pimples the day they did the master shot of the landing, those little boats going ashore, the ANZACs in the water scrambling . . . I had this feeling about what it would be like to have been there . . . scary, futile . . . but it was to be, I suppose, like the Alamo in America."

"Scary" and "futile" were two labels he gave to

Hollywood, eventually. *Gallipoli* provided memories and images that Mel has frequently said will stay with him for the rest of his life.

But the last two weeks of filming were a race against time for the producers, rapidly running out of funds, and for Mel, who was running out of days before Robyn had that baby. Unfortunately, as Mel later joked, the movie's location scouts had decided that the final place for filming would be Egypt, which took him well beyond reach of Robyn if that baby appeared.

Weir wanted to show scenes of soldiers Frank and Archie enjoying the sights and sounds of Cairo souks and then marvelling at the Pyramids, before leaving for Gallipoli.

Mel joked with producer Pat Lovell that he would walk off the set if Robyn's baby turned up early. But, as with many of Mel's wisecracks, there was a serious undertone.

At the end of November, Mel put one of his daily calls in to Robyn at her family's home in Adelaide. The baby was already on the way and Robyn's sister suggested Mel call back later.

"No way," came the father-to-be's reply. He was seething because he could not be there. Now at least he had a chance to hear the birth, if nothing else. The phone was rested on a bedside table and he sat down on his hotel bed and listened.

So, with an Egyptian hotel telephone operator regularly interrupting to ask if the actor had finished his long-distance call, Mel monitored as a midwife, doctor and close family gathered in that tiny bedroom in Adelaide and Robyn gave birth to a healthy little girl called Hannah.

Mel exulted: "I got through just as the baby's head was appearing. I could hear every sigh and cry. I heard everything and I mean everything – not just somebody telling me."

But the line kept cutting out and the anxious expectant father admitted later it was "touch and go".

Once the baby was born, Mel heard the midwife and Robyn's sister saying, "Oh it's beautiful. Oh-oh. Hell, it's a girl."

"It was a wonderful experience," exclaimed Mel.

Ironically, Mel and Robyn had planned the birth as an all-in-the-family event because, like his father Hutton before him, Mel had a healthy dislike of hospitals and the medical profession and believed his baby should be born at home.

Mel was undoubtedly disappointed he could not be there and he pledged that he would never leave Robyn to have a baby without him, ever again. But it did happen nearly ten years later and caused a huge rift on the set of a $30 million movie.

Robyn meanwhile was gracious as ever. She knew how much Mel wanted to be there and explained afterwards: "I wanted it to be a wonderful experience. And it still was. I enjoyed it immensely."

A few weeks later, Mel told one writer that he was hoping that Hannah would be the first of many children. The couple had already decided not to use any form of contraception, in keeping with Mel's religious beliefs, and he was fully intent on emulating his own parents by having "at least ten children".

Predictably, the reviews of *Gallipoli* were superb, except in Britain where *The Sunday Times* described it as "a curious piece of work . . . by turn sanguine and tragic, schoolboyish and disillusioned, artless and arty". While the normally stuffier *Sunday Telegraph* admitted: "to a large extent it succeeded", and described the final shot of the movie as an "image of considerable poetic resonance".

In Australia, the highly-regarded *Australian Film Review* magazine acclaimed *Gallipoli* as "a symbolic focus for the industry's aspirations – a key event in Australia's history, rich with accumulated mythical force, brought to the screen in irreducibly Australian language by leading talents backed up with enough money to give them range and flexibility".

In the United States, critics described Mel as "excellent" and *Newsweek* called his role "most enjoyable".

Surprisingly, the film was labelled "predictably anti-British" by film-maker and movie writer Scott Murray, editor of Australia's prestigious *Cinema Papers* magazine.

"It was definitely let down by the pommy bashing and it is like a celebration of failure and I felt there was no spark between Mel and Mark Lee."

But Richard Wherrett, who directed Mel in *Romeo and Juliet* in his second year at NIDA, has no doubt that his performance in *Gallipoli* was a turning-point for the young actor.

"It is his physical participation, a sensuality that marks his acting. He is mettlesome, unflappable without being complacent, enormously demanding of his fellow actors and the director. Then there are those intelligent sensitive eyes. It's simple really – he has a head, a body and a heart."

Unlike the disastrous camerawork in *Attack Force Z*, director of photography Russell Boyd managed to light Mel's azure blue eyes to perfection and it was in *Gallipoli* more than any of his earlier efforts that they became his trademark.

Mel himself put the film in his own perspective when he said: "I'm pretty sure it will succeed. It's a very complete movie and while it doesn't have a happy ending, it's emotionally satisfying."

Three months before its release, Robert Stigwood pronounced himself so pleased with the just-edited version of *Gallipoli* that he was signing Mel to an exclusive three-picture deal.

A story in the Sydney *Sun-Herald* announced an "unprecedented deal" with Stigwood and Murdoch. Even fatherly agent Bill Shannahan shared the optimism, saying: "It's a very good deal."

It was reported that Mel and Bill had been flown specially to New York by Stigwood to sign on the dotted line for one Aussie project and two films to be made in the US Within a short time, the deal faded into oblivion. But it did Mel some good, sparking strong interest from Hollywood.

Three months later, in Australia, the *Gallipoli* premiere in Sydney was the biggest event in the country's cinematic history.

"OVATION FOR GALLIPOLI" read a headline in the *Sydney Daily Telegraph* on August 8, 1981. Underneath it was a photo of Mel, Robyn and co-star Mark Lee, still looking painfully uncomfortable, just as he had through much of the shooting of the movie.

The *Telegraph* recorded:

"The world premiere of *Gallipoli*, Australia's most expensive movie, finished to tumultuous applause at the Village Cinema Centre in Sydney last night.

"The audience included the film's stars and producers as well as show-biz personalities and politicians.

"A cavalcade of limousines brought the leading actors to the cinema. Stars Mel Gibson and Mark Lee were applauded as they left the theatre after the screening.

"A pipe band welcomed guests to a supper dance hosted by the movie's backers, entrepreneur Mr Robert Stigwood and Mr Rupert Murdoch, at the Lower Town Hall.

"The hall was decorated as a replica of a Cairo ballroom set used in the movie.

"Chamber musicians played while guests mingled under a Red Cross banner that welcomed 'Australian and New Zealand Corps to the Nile Hotel'.

"Waiters wearing Egyptian-style headgear served champagne as the guests arrived."

Mel and Robyn seemed bewildered by all the attention, and in the photo, he is clutching a glass of beer rather than anything sparkling. He did not particularly like big crowds – a few pints of ale in a rundown bar with his friends was more his scene. At the premiere he told one writer that he thought all the attention "was a complete joke".

Movie specialist Don Bennetts recalled: "Mel was giggling away the whole time. He thought it was so funny that he had even made it. Unlike many stars, he displayed the ability to separate himself from everything."

Rhonda Schepisi – whose husband at that time, Fred Schepisi, was one of the first of many Aussie directors to win acceptance in Hollywood – got the same impression, on meeting Mel at *Gallipoli*'s premiere in Los Angeles.

"He was so shy and quiet. He seemed out of his depth."

Gallipoli picked up many awards, including nine from the Australian Film Institute. Mel won yet another best actor award. The film also did well at the box office considering its $2 million budget, very modest for the epic nature of the movie. In London, it even beat opposition from the latest James Bond movie, while in the US it grossed $4 million, at that time the best figure for any Australian film.

Yet for some reason, soon after the movie's release, the two Rs – Robert Stigwood and Rupert Murdoch – abandoned their well-publicised plans to inject tens of millions of dollars into the Australian film industry. There was talk of inferior projects being offered to the two tycoons, though there is absolutely no doubt they were delighted with *Gallipoli*. Many inside the Australian film industry believe that if Murdoch and Stigwood's plans had gone ahead then Mel might well have resisted the temptation to go to Hollywood.

Meanwhile, after *Gallipoli*, Mel was facing a resurgence of interest from the press. Headlines like "Rebel" and

"Temperamental" were being used, projecting Mel as Australia's answer to James Dean.

"A lot of people think I am a rebel. I get a lot of beat-up articles written about me. It's probably because I don't follow any code, any behavioural pattern. I freak people a bit because they don't know what to think about me but there's nothing I can do about that," he told one interviewer, with brazen unconcern.

Mel was really much more intent on mapping out his career. He told his Sydney agent, Bill Shannahan, that he desperately needed a comic role to play. Shannahan – a wily old hand – agreed with his star that it would be great, but he knew that Mel could fade into oblivion if he stretched himself too far too soon. Instead, he went through the motions as Mel told anyone who would listen:

"I can't seem to get away from playing policemen or soldiers. I'm getting really used to having a crew cut and wearing uniforms and leathers."

Shanahan, in his fatherly way, was more interested in making sure that Mel got his act together now that he had a family to look after. He was worried over Mel's complete inability to turn up on time for appointments – even missing vital casting sessions because he had not noted their time and place. There were also the literally hundreds of tickets that he incurred by dumping his jalopy in restricted parking areas. Shanahan gave his client a diary and told him not to lose it, otherwise his career would be over before it had begun. Bill had seen too many promising careers go down the pan and he truly believed that in Mel, he had found someone very special indeed.

With his fee from *Gallipoli* still partly intact, Mel bought a family home in the pleasant Sydney beach resort of Coogee and tried to get away from the spotlight. Get used to being a father.

He turned down an offer to play a drug addict in *Monkey Grip*, produced by Pat Lovell, whom he had met during the making of *Gallipoli*. Mel insisted he could not play someone whose life revolved around something as immoral as drugs. An interesting decision – because eight years later he agreed to play a similar role for a multi-million-dollar fee.

When I was a little kid, my old man taught me the Ten Commandments. Then he said: "Now I'm going to tell you the eleventh." I said what was that? "Thou shalt not kid thyself, that's all." I knew what he meant. He lives by it.

"Are you feeling brave?"

"What do you want to know that for?"

"Get out or we will kill you!"

Mel slammed the phone down in his Manila hotel suite, wondering if his decision to accept his biggest-ever fee of $150,000 for the lead role in his friend Peter Weir's new film was really worth it. For the first time in his career he was staying in civilised accommodation, only to face death threats from Muslim fanatics determined to disrupt a movie titled, aptly, *The Year of Living Dangerously*.

He and the rest of the cast and crew had been assigned bodyguards on arrival in Manila – a safety precaution following the previous year's death threats to foreign celebrities attending the Manila Film Festival.

Mel found himself shadowed by a huge six feet five Filipino minder carrying a .38 in a holster under his shirt. But no one had anticipated that the film unit would be threatened by a group of Muslims who presumed that *The Year of Living Dangerously* would be insulting to Allah. Protesters started haunting the set. When that failed to persuade the producers to pack up and go home, fanatics began threatening death to the director and stars of this $6 million movie, based on a novel by C. J. Koch.

"The phone would ring and this bloke speaking broken English would ask: 'How brave are you Mr Gibson?' I'd say 'What do you want to know that for?' Then would come the threats – always something to do with bombs and death. The threats were real. They'd come in like clockwork and the phone would be snatched off me by the bodyguard, who would start jabbering down the line in Tagalog, the native tongue. Then he would slam the phone down and tell me not to worry," recalled Mel later.

But director Peter Weir – reunited with Mel after the success of *Gallipoli* – could not just pack up and relocate. He had spent months scouting the area for perfect locations; no amount of threats were going to stampede him.

The movie's Hollywood backers, MGM, were so concerned they contacted the CIA, the Philippines Intelligence Agency, the police and the army in an effort to find out who was making the threats.

Mel for his part tried to remain calm amid all the tension. He mused over having accepted the role of an ambitious journalist because it was a challenging part that would help him get away from the stereotyped tough guy image of *Mad Max*, just enjoying its second dose of international success thanks to *The Road Warrior*. He had also been gratified by Weir's offer of a percentage in the film – something which actors at early stages in their careers are usually not offered. It was only half a per cent but it made Mel feel as if he had broken through. (Unfortunately, the movie never made enough money to pay Mel as much as one dollar in royalties.)

He'd read the script of *Living Dangerously* a few months earlier, between rehearsals of the most controversial project he had ever undertaken – a two-handed play called *Porn No Rape Trigger*. Mel and co-star Sandy Gore played a couple falling out of love and resorting to sexual games and fantasies in an effort to revive passion. It was a brave choice by Mel; against the odds, he was never taken to task about it.

He believed the play – written by Australian David Knight – was artistically valid, worthwhile and well crafted. Theatre critics agreed.

Just a few days after impressing audiences in that play, Mel made his first public appearance at a political rally. Although not eligible to vote in Australia, he had strong views on the Fraser government's decision to slash arts subsidies.

Floats, giant puppets, impromptu bands and 3,000 weirdly-dressed thespians lined the streets of Sydney on Thursday, November 19, 1981, to protest at the cuts. They had real fears that the Australian theatre might die if the grants did not continue.

And Mel, banner in hand, was in no mood for compromise.

"The Fraser government must be forced to accept that the theatre is the very lifeblood of Australia's cultural health," he asserted. For the first but by no means last time, Mel was getting politically active . . .

Having read the script of *Living Dangerously* (as it was titled in the US) Mel became convinced that it had the same sort of romantic drama undertones as the classic movie *Casablanca*, one of his all-time favourites, with his boyhood hero Humphrey Bogart.

Living Dangerously is set in Indonesia during the

downfall of dictator Sukarno, seventeen years earlier. Weir and his production team chose Manila because its vast crowds would give the project a more realistic feel.

Mel portrayed Australian Broadcasting Service reporter Guy Hamilton, arriving in Djakarta in 1965 ready at all costs to make a name for himself on his first overseas assignment. Indonesia at the time was a tinderbox threatening to ignite into a bloody civil war.

Hamilton becomes increasingly involved with the political turmoil of the country, and meets elegant British embassy attachée Jill Bryant (played by American actress Sigourney Weaver). The two fall in love but Hamilton must choose between swashbuckling journalistic adventures and his passionate relationship with Jill.

The third major character in the film is a diminutive Chinese-Australian photographer, Billy Kwan, who provides Guy with many local contacts, helping him scoop the opposition.

Kwan was played by tiny American actress Linda Hunt (just four foot nine), who went on to win an Academy Award for best supporting actress in the part. It was the first time a 'crossover' performer won an Oscar.

Mel has always been warm in his praise of Linda Hunt and Sigourney Weaver – though not for the film in general. It was a classy picture in Hollywood terms, but made little money at the all-important box office.

To Gibson, Hamilton is "a hybrid like me, belonging to two cultures but really belonging to none. He's the sort of fellow who goes in boots and all. He takes chances. He gets off living dangerously. He is like a person taking a journey – things happen to him. He's involved but he's got that love, I think, which I can understand. I was like that for years until all of a sudden I snapped out of it – that's what made me get married . . ."

However, Mel's opinion of the role changed considerably. His initial enthusiasm may have been tainted by the practical realities.

"Dimension-wise, Guy Hamilton provided a very limited framework for an actor. He really was just a puppet, though not such a dud as he was in the book. He seldom initiated anything. For an actor it was a question of filling up the role as much as possible to make it interesting."

Mel had gone through all the usual detailed research before starting filming in Manila. He met some of the war correspondents roaming South East Asia at the time and saw a little bit of himself in those gung-ho characters.

"Those guys I talked to who were stationed in Djakarta during the rebellion were a fearless bunch, living on the edge all the time. They were fun guys, good drinkers, ratty as hell, and would stop at nothing to get a story. Really ruthless bastards. No ethics at all. Their god was the story. That was everything. They admitted it. These guys weren't afraid of anything."

Death threats he received in Manila meant that Mel *was* understandably fearful about losing his own life. It made it difficult for him to convey the risk-taking attitude of the character he was playing.

Mel found himself working with three American performers who did not come from the same school of acting: Sigourney Weaver, fresh from spectacular success in *Alien*; Linda Hunt, giving a *tour de force* performance; and lesser-known but equally adept Michael Murphy.

Mel admitted he was put on his mettle by the talent surrounding him.

"I did stand off and watch. And I found that each of the American actors had their own, totally different way of getting into what they did. One thing all three of them had was this greater degree of energy. They had tons of energy. It was as if they got charged up a bit more than I'd ever seen somebody do in Australia. That's their way, the American way, of doing things."

Mel knew that Linda Hunt, although delivering an extraordinary performance, was nervy about the effect playing a man was having on her. She reported being "freaked out" when a waiter at their hotel kept calling her "sir" and she frequently doubted the validity of what she was doing.

But Mel was full of admiration for Linda, and as in his previous movies, made absolutely no attempt to grab the limelight from his co-star. *Living Dangerously* was the first Mel Gibson movie where his performance did not dominate. But he never objected.

"Most Hollywood stars are so insecure they would have tried to instigate script changes to ensure that Linda's role was not too dominant," explained one Los Angeles producer. That was not Mel's way. He regarded the role of Billy Kwan as the toughest in the film and would happily tell everyone on the set what great work Linda Hunt was doing.

And Linda needed supportiveness . . .

"When I hit Manila, I went into gender shock as well as culture shock. A lot of Filipinos assumed I was a man," she later explained.

On the set, Weir ordered cast and crew to call Linda by her middle name, Phipps, because he felt this would cause the other actors less confusion in scenes with a woman who was supposed to be a man.

Linda analysed Mel as "the type of actor who's not there before a scene. His attention is somewhere else. He's deliberately uninvolved, absent. It's a macho thing – 'movies aren't work'. But when he gets in front of the camera, his attention is forceful and total. He controls the camera. It's how they say the early Brando acted – saving himself, marshalling his energy for the performance. Watch Mel on screen; it shows. There's absolutely no waste."

It was Mel's eyes that, according to Linda, said it all about the man behind the mask.

"Those great blue eyes take you in but erect a barrier and push you away."

But the onscreen relationship expected to cause a spark was between Mel and Sigourney Weaver. She was the tall (over six feet), red-haired actress, five years Mel's senior, who – physically at least – topped her handsome co-star.

Again, Mel's overt lack of vanity is worth examining. He did not seem to give two hoots about looking like a midget alongside the New York actress. When the producers insisted he wear built-up shoes he obliged them, and has laughed about it ever since. Even at a premiere for the film more than a year later, Sigourney Weaver was amazed that Mel did not mind wandering around the party afterwards alongside her as she wore high heels that boosted her height to almost six feet four inches.

And Sigourney's background might also have been expected to prove a little daunting for railman's son Mel. She was the daughter of former NBC President Pat Weaver, innovator of the "Today" programme and other top-quality news shows in the US, and actress Elizabeth Inglis. She had won a bachelor's degree at Stanford and a master's at Yale before embarking on a theatrical career. Appearances in a number of very serious off-Broadway productions followed, then *Alien* and *Eyewitness* turned her into a Hollywood name.

Mel took Sigourney's status in his stride, although he did feel a trifle wary, especially since she was only his second leading lady.

He started rumours of a bad working relationship with the actress after telling one reporter that she had "really rotten breath" (later, he explained it was a joke and Sigourney accepted his humble apologies, graciously). For whatever reason, it was onscreen love scenes that he found difficult to handle.

"That kind of thing is always a touchy area with actors. It requires a lot more simplicity than anything else. Man . . . woman . . . attraction . . . it's animal stuff, an instinctive type of behaviour," he recalled later.

Mel felt like a teenager out on a first date during those early days shooting scenes with Sigourney – and he confessed he was terrified, to Peter Weir.

Weir helped him overcome shyness by going to a film library and picking out some movies with the most famous kisses of all time. Then he showed Mel the scenes and they both picked out Ingrid Bergman and Cary Grant's lingering embrace in the Hitchcock classic *Notorious*. Seeing it inspired Mel and gave him the courage to start approaching his role from a romantic standpoint.

Gradually the leading man and leading lady became closer and began to feel confident in each other's company. It led to inevitable gossip over a romance, but in fact Mel and his attractive co-star simply respected each other as actors.

That was all, really.

"We had a close friendship," he volunteered. "It's very difficult to work with someone you don't get on with."

Sigourney was full of praise for her co-star – "The most gorgeous man I have ever seen. But people focus too much on his looks. He's also shy, and a very devoted family man. And as an actor, he is extraordinarily good."

This was before the most talked-about scene in the film, in which Sigourney, passionately attracted to Mel, mysteriously refuses to see him again after a single night of love. He goes to an embassy party that he knows she will attend, strides purposefully to her side, grabs her by the arm roughly, backs her into a corner, and demands: "What do you mean, not taking my calls?" Smothering her with kisses, he makes her leave the party with him.

She refuses, despite being obviously aroused. Then he kisses her once more, pulls back, turns abruptly and walks away. She is both alarmed and excited, and surrenders by leaping into a car as he is about to drive away. She devours him with kisses and they roar off into the night, laughing ecstatically, and just for the hell of it, crash through a heavily-armed road-block – military police shoot out their tail-lights.

It was a highly charged, erotic scene and renowned New York film critic Pauline Kael's summary was that "the gun bursts are like applause for their sexiness".

But life in Manila was getting far too hot to handle. Death threats were being made to virtually everyone on the production. Hollywood backers were genuinely fearful that their carefully invested millions might go up in smoke if they did not complete filming in some other, safer location.

So it was that the final week of shooting saw cast and crew reassemble in the dead of winter in Sydney to secure some of the most crucial scenes, not least a swimming pool sequence that looked as if it had been shot in Manila . . . though all the actors had goose pimples.

But Mel had other things on his mind. Robyn was days from giving birth to their second child and he was stressed by the impending birth and that age-old actor's problem – where would he get his next job once *Living Dangerously* wrapped?

Partly as a response to these worries and also because he was in need of a good night out with old friends, Mel ended up taking co-star Michael Murphy on a pub crawl around his favourite taverns in Sydney. It was an eye-opener for Murphy, who had never seen party animal Gibson before.

"He likes to have a good time. We stayed out drinking later than we should have, and had to be on the set at the crack of dawn. Sydney, you see, is a lot different from Hollywood. All the guys hang out together and Mel was always smack in the middle of the fun. It's extraordinary for a guy who's coming along as strong and hot as he is, but he has absolutely no vanity, no ego."

On June 2, 1982, Robyn gave birth to twins at the Women's Hospital in Crown Street, Sydney and this time Mel was there to see the whole proceedings.

Mel treasures witnessing the birth of twins Christian and Edward as "one of the happiest days of my life. I was right there with her through the entire delivery and it just knocked the stuffing out of me. I wouldn't have missed that experience for anything."

Sigourney Weaver was full of praise for Mel's professionalism. He had been up all night with Robyn as she gave birth to the twins. "Yet he turned up right on time early next morning."

All three of his children so far had been born while he was making movies for Peter Weir. Robyn joked just after the birth that he had better not work for Weir any more.

Reviews of *Living Dangerously* were good.

One critic wrote that the movie was "genuinely underrated and Mel and Sigourney Weaver worked well together".

Praise or no, Mel still could not conquer his distaste for the press. At one Sydney conference to promote *Living Dangerously*, assembled journalists noticed how he smoked jerkily and heavily, jumped and clenched his fists every time a flashlight popped.

Then he startled the reporters by complaining: "The very fact I'm doing this interview is killing my credibility as an actor. I'm letting something slip, I'm talking about myself . . ."

And to another assembly of journalists he insisted: "I don't like doing interviews because they reduce my potential to surprise an audience. Doing this interview with you is a contradiction to that, but I've got pretty good defences. When this interview is finished, you won't know much more about the personal side of my life than you do now."

Producer Jim McElroy was not best pleased by the way Mel handled press conferences after the release of *Living Dangerously*. "Mel is two different people, you see. He's Mel the confident and articulate actor. Then he's Mel, the ordinary guy."

Mel's first trip to the annual film festival at Cannes, for a showing of *Living Dangerously* in May, 1983, left the young actor with a definite taste for the good life. This would resurface on a subsequent trip to Cannes, four years later.

Writer/director Scott Murray was shooting a documentary about the resurgence of the Australian film industry when he encountered Mel. "We filmed him at a press conference and then at a party on the beach at Cannes that night. He seemed completely hyped up with nervous energy and was hugging and squeezing Sigourney Weaver all night. He had the most amazing energy. He really cut loose with people. In the end he spotted my camera and put his hands right in front of the lens and said directly into the cameras, 'With these hands I could kill.' It was certainly a bit unnerving."

In France, Mel was hailed as the "new John Wayne" in a cover story on the mass-circulation *France Soir* magazine. A caption under a photo of the actor proclaimed: "Mel Gibson nouveau John Wayne."

The article went on to suggest that Mel was at the forefront of a new breed of male movie heroes including Tom Selleck and Harrison Ford.

The new John Wayne, unlike publicity-hardened Duke,

was still insisting in press interviews that "I don't want anyone to know everything about me. I've got to keep something back for myself. I like being an enigma."

He rationalised this obsession by saying: "Other actors get right in and become a character. I have to stand a little bit apart. I find out what it's all about, store it away, and fake it. My mind is outside that part a little, watching. I'd like to try and avoid playing myself." He hesitated for a moment as if considering the validity of what he just said. "That's pretty scary. I'd blow my cover for ever."

Mel also insisted that typecast roles akin to Mad Max were not for him.

"The important thing is to have job satisfaction. I want to keep doing different things. I want to keep growing and getting better at what I do. It's what keeps me going." And he told agent Bill Shannahan that he would not do any more television. "You just do the same stuff all the time. It wears you out."

Within weeks of finishing *Living Dangerously*, Mel was breathing down Bill Shannahan's neck for a theatre role. He was determined not to be another jobbing movie star. He wanted to refresh his instinct by treading the boards. Shannahan could have tried to dissuade Mel; scripts from Hollywood were literally piling up in his office. And there was a huge offer to play a Prince Charles-type character in an American film entitled *Myerson and the Prince of Wales* about a Jewish girl from the Bronx who falls for a British royal. Mel never seriously contemplated the role. Playing a member of the British royal family was not his lifetime's ambition . . .

Shannahan felt sure that the only way to keep Mel safe was to keep him in Australia. He was also well aware that Hollywood sharks were circling, looking for a piece of Mel to take home to Tinseltown. William Morris Agency top gun Ed

Limato had already signed Mel as his Hollywood client and he would be putting Mel under pressure to accept fat paychecks.

Limato was as stunned as Mel was delighted when the actor landed the $250-a-week role of Biff, disaffected son of Willy Loman, in a two-month run of *Death of a Salesman* at Sydney's Nimrod Theatre. Director George Ogilvie, who would go on to co-direct *Mad Max III* with George Miller, was in no doubt that if the young actor had been around in the thirties "he would have been a Cary Grant – although underneath it he is really a character actor".

And Mel must have further infuriated Hollywood by claiming that: "Sometimes it's a lot better to do a little stage play somewhere than a big-budget movie – you can get an excellent chance to polish up your craft."

Ed Limato had other grander, much richer plans for his fledgling film star – now to be put on ice. Playing the son of the quintessential American dreamer and symbolic father (wonderfully portrayed in this version by "Alf Garnett" Warren Mitchell) in *Death of a Salesman* is a difficult task, greatly prized by actors across the world. Mel sought to capture every shade of the complex character.

He was enjoying every minute on the stage and did not regret turning down a lucrative offer to star in a US film called *The Lords of Discipline*. Shannahan was taken aback when Mel also rejected *Once Upon a Time in America*, with Robert De Niro, after much procrastination. Mel assents that his biggest professional fault is taking too long to make up his mind about movie offers. But his decision turned out to be a wise one – the $38 million film was dismissed as twaddle by many critics and failed miserably at the box office.

Mel believed that for the time being he could continue to combine stage and film work. The fact that one day he would be staying in a luxurious hotel suite and the next, rehearsing in a cold, damp hall for a stage run did not bother him. He prided himself on the fact that he brought home-made fruit and date loaf complete with two health-giving apples in his lunchbox from home every day during theatrical appearances.

For an interview with Susan Molloy of *The Australian*, Mel was photographed sitting on the steps of the rehearsal hall smoking a butt end and wearing tatty slippers as he explained his love of the theatre. It was a photo opportunity that would horrify his new agent back in Hollywood, but Mel did not care.

"I started in theatre and it gives me a lot. I like it. There is nothing that replaces that kind of empty feeling you can get in films. You really have to trust the director. He is your audience.

"What I plan to do is find a happy mix of both, to intersperse my stage work with films. But for me stage work is far more exhilarating than any other form of acting. It just doesn't pay as well.

"I've been very lucky in working with good people on stage, like Warren Mitchell. He is a bloody good actor and he draws a lot of his acting just from having been around so long. As an actor, the older you get, the better you get, just through having lived more."

And Mel Gibson certainly had a lot more living to do . . .

Much of Mel's appeal as an actor at this time had to do with the fact that he was the man from Down Under who was starting to make it in Hollywood.

Mel had never concealed the spending of the first twelve years of his life in the United States, but then some Sydney newspapers decided to reveal his "shocking secret".

The Australian announced with horror: "MAD MAX STAR NOT AUSSIE AFTER ALL" and went on to tell its readers: "Australia might have claimed actor Mel Gibson as its own, but Gibson sees himself as an American . . ."

Mel was stunned. Bill Shannahan had always advised him, with great foresight, not to take out Australian citizenship because it would make working in Hollywood all the more difficult. Mel's outlook is more "'Aussie" than "Yank" but there is no getting away from the fact he is American by birth.

A slightly defensive Mel told New York's *Interview* magazine: "American citizenship . . . despite all the cynicism in the world today, I'm proud of it. You have to be. The United States is not a bad place, they're great people."

The harder-hitting *Sydney Sun* took the would-be controversy a stage further by grilling Mel to explain his love of Australia even though he might always be officially American.

"It's not that I don't love Australia and Australians. I do. I married one and I've fathered three," the harassed actor told the *Sun*.

"I regard Australia as my home. My work may take me around the world, but when I'm not working this is where I want to be," he added. Secretly, he knew full well that his career could depend on his ability to make an accent switch back and forth. "It's not hard to turn it on and turn it off again," he pointed out.

Director Peter Weir confirmed that Mel was "unpigeonholable".

"When I was working with him in Australia, I sometimes thought of Mel as an American, but when we were in New York he seemed totally Australian. This gives him an extra cutting edge as an actor. An interesting tension is set up – a sort of who-am-I-where-do-I-belong? dilemma, a push-pull energy he can draw on."

Mel believes: "I'm in tune with this place. It's not a question of Australian loyalty. I just want to do interesting work. I'm not going to Hollywood just because it's Hollywood."

Sadly his pledge of allegiance to Australia did not last for ever.

Mel was at a crossroads in his career – fame and fortune in Hollywood beckoned. He said he felt like "a kid in a candy store. I just cannot make up my mind."

In November, 1982, just a few weeks after finishing his highly acclaimed run in *Death of a Salesman*, Mel got his first real taste of what it is to be a film star.

MGM chief Freddie Fields hosted an informal gathering at Elaine's restaurant in New York. It was billed as a getting-to-know-Mel Gibson event. But Mel found it a terrible strain.

"I start conversation with one person and just when it gets interesting, someone else nudges in and I have to turn away and begin a new conversation," he moaned.

When a tall woman swooned over Mel, waving a book of matches and trying to get him to light her a cigarette, he casually took the matches and lit his own.

Now a question was asked, and it would come to haunt him in the following years. *Would you consider living in California?*

"Never. I have to return to Australia to clear my head and think things out, like this party."

Many film industry figures present at that party and another held a couple of weeks earlier at agent Ed Limato's home in the Hollywood Hills mistook Mel's humour for rudeness. They just could not understand why the boy from Peekskill was not more grateful for being a hot property.

But at least at Limato's, Mel spotted fellow Aussie Fred Schepisi, recently arrived in Tinseltown and about to direct a big feature. The two men raised eyebrows, looked skywards and promised to hit the town together at the next possible opportunity. Both knew they just did not belong.

Months later Mel summed up a difference between the

Australian and Hollywood film industries when he said: "In Australian film-making, everybody sort of pitches in. There are no unions. I carried camera gear up the pyramids in *Gallipoli*. On American film sets someone runs to get you a drink and shoves a chair under your backside every five minutes – that can get on your nerves. I like to be comfortable . . . but you can go too far."

Although he did not realise it, he had already waved goodbye to those relaxed times and was about to embark on a trip to megastardom . . . The ticket, natch, being a Major Movie.

The first of those was to be *The Running Man*. But Mel pulled out as it started pre-production, to go for a movie that Ed Limato promised would make him a truly international star – *The Bounty*.

I'd go into a bar, pull up a few beers and put some scotch in like a depth charge...

"The sweet and troublesome smell of success hung like a huge fluffy cloud waiting to turn black and rain on everyone's parade . . ." So read a quotation in an American magazine, and contrived though it was, it applied to what was going on in Mel Gibson's life in 1983.

He was already being hailed as the latest contemporary film hero, and the attendant circus had him in a state of almost constant bewilderment.

He had been to war, epically, in *Gallipoli*; behaved with care and courtesy in *The Year of Living Dangerously*; fought futuristic villains in *Mad Max I* and *II*, and his latest mission was to portray the clean-cut and caring super-hero Fletcher Christian in *The Bounty*.

A nine-week shoot on the island on Moorea, near Tahiti, sounded idyllic with its lagoons, coral sand beaches, lush green vegetation and palm trees. In reality it turned into a painful experience that put Mel off location filming for many years to come and probably marks the period when his drinking and off-set behaviour reached an all-time low.

Even his co-star, the recently knighted Sir Anthony Hopkins, grumbled: "Paradise can wear a bit thin after a while. If you're on Moorea for more than two weeks you can go stark raving crazy. There's a feeling of confinement on the island. There's also heat – terribly enervating. After a while you see the same faces at breakfast and it starts to get to you . . ."

Twenty years earlier, the cast and crew of the previous Hollywood star vehicle, *Mutiny on the Bounty*, had suffered the same ordeal by heat and tedium – and found an answer by consuming vast quantities of alcohol. Trevor Howard spent a night in the local police station after a drunken brawl; Richard Harris picked regular fights in local taverns; Welsh actor Hugh Griffith drank so much he was kicked off the island by its authorities and Australian actor Chips Rafferty became famous for his dog impersonations at dawn.

In the middle of 1984, Mel and many of the cast and crew of *The Bounty* revived those traditions by embarking on massive drinking bouts and, inevitably, bar-room battles.

"Mel liked to drink the whole time," alleges Hare Salmon, a costume designer who became a drinking pal of Mel's throughout his stay on Moorea.

Hare broke a ten-year silence to speak about his friend. He said that the actor's behaviour in the bars on the island endeared him to the locals if not *The Bounty*'s producers. And he chuckled over the night that Mel got knocked to the ground after interrupting two Tahitians arguing during a mammoth liquor session at the Tattoo nightclub.

"I was with him. I told him to keep out of it. The Tahitians were fighting over a girl. He said to me: 'I am Mel Gibson, I will go over there and stop them. They will respect my work, you watch.'"

But the two locals took absolutely no notice of Mel, beyond smashing him to the ground.

"They hit him in the head with a Coke bottle. Mel just loves to brawl."

Staggering to his feet, Mel was taken back to his hotel where a very worried unit production manager quickly contacted a hospital in the capital city of Papeete, five minutes' flight from Moorea. The whole of one side of Mel's face was cut and bruised. The filming schedule was hastily juggled so that scenes without him could be shot while he spent a day in the hospital having his face fixed.

A shamefaced Mel admitted to friends that he had gone "stir-crazy"; hence the incident. "Those Tahitians are big – six feet across. I tried to get our guys out of there but suddenly this huge gorilla hit me on the side of the head. When one of them hits you, you stay down. Let's just say there was a serious lack of communication for a while."

Even some of Mel's closest pals were astonished by his bravado. "He seemed to be so proud of what had happened," said one old friend.

And as Hare Salmon recalled, he was soon back to his old tricks once he returned to Moorea.

"One night we went to the Club Mediterranean and he got very drunk. There were lots of women surrounding us the whole time and Mel was happy to talk to them all – but nothing more. He was such an unsnobbish person, very honest and straightforward. We liked him a lot and he seemed to love Tahitians."

Once again, Mel's drinking had got out of control because Robyn and the children were not staying with him on the island. It was as if their presence was needed to remind him of his responsibilities as father and husband. It was a recurring problem through many of the films he made during this period.

Bar-room brawls were simply Mel's reaction to a very difficult series of circumstances on the set of *The Bounty*. He had taken to the bottle in an effort to forget that the film was feeling like an unmitigated disaster. Showings of the rushes each evening gave the distinct impression of an episode of "The Onedin Line" rather than a $20 million Hollywood movie.

The Bounty was the fifth version of the saga to be brought to the cinema. The first was an Australian silent film made in 1916, then came *The Wake of the Bounty*, featuring Australia's only other romantic Hollywood star, Errol Flynn. There followed a 1935 version starring Clark Gable and Charles Laughton, before the Trevor Howard and Marlon Brando edition in 1962.

Originally, legendary director David Lean (*Lawrence of Arabia*, *Bridge Over the River Kwai*, *Ryan's Daughter* and *Passage to India*) was set to make *The Bounty*. Five years earlier he arrived in Tahiti with the intention of filming the story of Captain Cook, but soon decided the raunchy story of *The Bounty* would be much more rewarding. Lean got Warner Brothers to back his development of the project and briefed old friend Robert Bolt to start a script. Eventually – and this is par for the Hollywood course – the studio withdrew from the project, to be replaced by top producer Dino De Laurentiis, complete with an open chequebook.

The outspoken Italian immediately paid $2.5 million t a New Zealand company, Whangerei Engineering, to build an exact replica of the *Bounty* from original plans held at the Maritime Museum in Greenwich, London. This "little shitpot", as Mel later described it, was a 380-ton vessel built of steel then planked with wood, her ropes and sails virtually identical to those of the original ship. Above deck she was a copy of the *Bounty*. Below, she was a modern cruiser with luxury cabins, microwave ovens, automatic pilot, satellite navigation and twin 400 h.p. engines giving a range of five thousand miles.

Lean approached *Superman* star Christopher Reeve to play Fletcher Christian. Grandiose plans concerning not one but two films about *The Bounty* were revealed to the Hollywood trade press by De Laurentiis. Later Lean referred to the project as "the saddest dead duck in my career". His dream project was far too expensive, and he eventually abandoned *The Bounty*.

For a while it floundered around as a possible TV mini-series, then Orion Pictures in Hollywood agreed to finance it and recruited young New Zealand director Roger Donaldson to the project. Reeve, upset by all the changes, pulled out of the film just six weeks before shooting was scheduled to commence. Belatedly, he claimed, "I must confess to twinges of remorse."

Anthony Hopkins had already been signed up to play Bligh, but actors in line for Fletcher Christian ranged from Jeremy Irons and Anthony Andrews to rock star Sting. For various reasons they all passed on the project. Mel Gibson was approached almost as an afterthought.

At first he was not at all keen. "I thought Christian was made to look too weak. Besides, he was hardly in the picture. And I didn't want to get involved in the remake of a film which had been done a couple of times before."

But agent Ed Limato assured him it was a good project. He reminded Mel that he had by now turned down *An Officer and a Gentleman* – a role that helped elevate Richard Gere to international stardom. Roger Donaldson, who had made just two films – *Sleeping Dogs* and *Smash Palace* – also appealed to Mel to consider the "richness" of Bolt's script and the more Mel researched the subject, the more he was intrigued. As an often-misunderstood maverick himself, he liked the fact that Captain Bligh was not being made out to be such a monster as he had been in previous versions. Mel signed on, and cleverly, asked a London psychiatrist to assess different aspects of Christian's life. Then he made a pilgrimage to the house in the Lake District of Cumbria where Christian was born.

"I discovered he had left his footprint in the lead guttering on the roof and scratched his initials in metal. I put my foot inside his imprint and discovered it fitted perfectly." Mel thought that alone was worth the journey.

But when cast and crew arrived in Tahiti, they discovered that producer De Laurentiis had taken it upon himself to cast a Tahitian first-time actress as the Princess Mauatua, with whom Fletcher Christian falls in love. Beautiful 18-year-old Tevaite Vernette had been plucked out of a local high school and made to feel she was on the verge of international stardom. At first there was talk that Tevaite might have broken strict local employment laws by leaving school to make the movie. Shooting was eventually rearranged to make sure she was free to study – while taking a role that would make her the envy of women around the world.

She would get Mel. As his romantic interest, the script called for some very passionate scenes between the actor and Tevaite. It was a lot for a young girl to cope with; Tevaite admitted she did not want to do the film.

"I was a law student, not an aspiring actress. All I really wanted to do was continue my studies – they were much more important to me."

Director Donaldson and co-producer Bernard Williams were at first astounded by the girl's reluctance to be turned into an overnight star. Back in Hollywood, thousands of actresses would have killed to get a role opposite Mel Gibson.

Then there were the topless scenes involving her and Mel in the lagoon. Local women claimed they degraded the good name of Tahitian women but it turned out to be little more than a storm in a b-cup. However Tevaite – essentially a shy girl – dreaded stripping. Mainly because she had developed quite a schoolgirl crush on her handsome co-star. "I liked kissing him. It was very easy!"

Ten years later, she candidly recalled: "It was funny to kiss him. It was funny for him too. It was embarrassing. We were both shy. When we were swimming naked it was very difficult. He told jokes to relax me."

But one of her oldest friends on Tahiti recently explained why the young actress found the entire shoot so stressful: "Tavaite just couldn't cope with her emotions. One minute she was expected to be kissing Mel passionately and the next he would walk past her without so much as a glance."

(Ironically, at around this time Mel was named the man with America's most kissable lips when yet another magazine survey proved what a vast female following the actor had built up over the previous couple of years.)

Unit driver Irene Fuller – who still lives on Moorea – said: "Tevaite was absolutely besotted by Mel. But she was so shy. She was not an actress and it was difficult for her. Mind you, all the other women were very jealous of her."

Interviewed in March, 1993, Tevaite disclosed that her experiences during the making of *The Bounty* were so distressing that she never wanted to act again. Now working as a nurse in post-operative care at the same hospital where Mel was taken after his drunken brawl on Moorea, she said:

"I do not want to act ever again because I did not find it enjoyable. The other actors did not really help me much. Acting was very difficult and that movie was emotionally draining. I was just a child. It seems like a dream now. It was all so unreal."

Tevaite was offered millions of dollars' worth of work after her debut with Mel but says now: "I decided I did not want to carry on acting. There is more to life than just being in films."

When asked if she had felt just a little in love with Mel, as some of her friends claimed, Tevaite blushed.

"I do not want to answer that question. I find it embarrassing. I do not know how to respond." She did add that it was "a shame that Mel was married. But that's the way it goes, I guess."

She also said of Mel: "He helped me relax. He was very Tahitian in his outlook. He liked to have fun and some of the other actresses did seem a little jealous of me."

Did he break her heart? Tevaite looked embarrassed and refused to answer.

Mel stayed at a luxury hotel near the island's tiny airport while Tevaite and most of the other Tahitian women employed in the movie lived in rented bungalows overlooking the Pacific near Cook's Bay.

But at one stage, Tevaite "ran away" from the movie location and a producer had to be dispatched to the main island to persuade her to return to the set.

"She did not want to come back. She just could not cope with it. Maybe it was because she did fall in love with Mel," said Maimiti Kinnander, who appeared in the movie as a topless Tahitian dancer and became close friends with Tevaite during the shoot. "Tevaite did not do well because of Mel."

Tevaite now says that working as a nurse is far more satisfying than acting. "I am happiest here in Tahiti being a nurse. It is much more fulfilling. Much more satisfying." With a definite twinge of sadness, Tevaite added: "I have never heard from Mel again."

Many of the locals of Moorea still talk about the four months when *The Bounty* carnival invaded their little piece of paradise. It was a big event for them, but some of the vast number of extras were not so taken with Mel.

Maimiti Kinnander sniffs: "Mel Gibson is not a very responsible person. His fighting caused the film to be held up and he was a bit of a Jekyll and Hyde figure, typically Australian; in the day all solemn while at night he got drunk and did wild and crazy things.

"Mel broke a lot of hearts even though he was very moody. When he did not have any alcohol inside him on the set during the daytime he did not even say hello to anyone."

The first few weeks on Moorea, a pretty island, went reasonably well. But then bad weather set in and tempers frayed. Hurricane-force winds swept across the bay where *The Bounty* was anchored – Mel was knocked and washed to the other end of the vessel by a huge wave. Even the usually quiet and reserved Anthony Hopkins started arguing with director Donaldson; conditions were getting to the team.

And Mel's intake of alcohol appeared to increase by the day. He developed a disturbing habit of mixing a double scotch with his beer; he called the drink "liquid violence".

Mel felt uncomfortable about Anthony Hopkins, a reformed alcoholic who restricted himself to mineral water. It was as if Hopkins's ability to give up the demon drink in some way intimidated him.

The movie's producers held their breath every time Mel wandered off to local taverns with his new best friends. They feared – with much justification – that he might not get back in one piece for the following day's filming.

And then there was Mel's habit of improvising all the time. He loved to find a hole in a script and "improve" it himself, often arriving on the set having decided completely to rewrite a few lines of dialogue.

One of the most important scenes in the film was where Christian tells Bligh he is taking over the ship. Mel felt, as actors will, that his role needed a little "spicing up". Neither

Donaldson nor Hopkins had any idea what the star had in store for them.

"I only wrote the scene that morning . . . the character was lacking and the only place to do something was in the mutiny scene when he flips out. I thought the only way he can do it is by being like a loyal office boy, which is what he was – a loyal public servant. He knew what job he had to do and got fed up with it one day. The only real threat he could make, as I saw it, was to knock himself off and leave them without a navigator. If they knocked Bligh off, then he'd threaten to kill himself. It was in the nature of the Christian character. He went schizophrenic one day. Wacko!"

Donaldson and Hopkins were, well . . . astonished by Mel's interpretation.

"It was totally unpredictable. Mel just exploded and it caught everyone off guard. It was brilliant," said Hopkins tactfully. Mel took heart from the crew bursting into applause after his improvisation. Their motives were not entirely clear . . .

He gave a little clue to his true feelings about the British cast and crew, reflecting his opinion of the English. "It was a big film, shooting a lot at sea and with a lot of whingeing Poms on the cast and crew."

But he excused Anthony Hopkins from the brand of a "whingeing Pom". Mel said: "He was terrific. He was good to work with because he was open and he was willing to give. He's a moral man and you could see this. I think we had the same attitudes."

Other rumours emanating from the set included the bizarre one that Mel had real tattoos imprinted on his buttocks during a painful-looking sequence of actual film.

Hare Salmon, as well as being involved in costume design, designed and put the tattoos on the star. He agrees that Mel was "desperate" to have a real one. "But the producers would not allow it so we used paints instead," explained Hare, who also "starred" in the tattooing scene in the film.

Other Tahitians have fond memories of Mel. They appreciated that he behaved "more like a Tahitian than a white man".

"He had a real sense of fun. He liked to party and have a good time. It's a very Tahitian outlook on life," said production unit driver Daphne Fuller.

And while he was bouncing around Moorea's nightclubs and bars, some crew members were behaving more like the real crew of *The Bounty*, hundreds of years before them.

"Many of them fell in love with local girls and have ended up with part-time wives here on the island whom they come and see now and again," discloses one woman who worked on the film.

Local hotel owner George Logue said that many of the cast and crew members' wives insisted on staying with their partners on Moorea for fear of such developments.

"All these wives were very worried about their husbands going off with the Tahitian women. Those guys would have been much more relaxed if their wives had not been there," he recalled.

Dancer Maimiti Kinnander affirmed: "The crew had their wives staying, keeping an eye on them. It did not help. When the wives saw all of us topless girls they seemed very upset. One wife used to even hang around the set the whole time just to see what her husband was up to."

Mel's own driver was an elderly man who happened to have one of the few American limousines on the island – a 1975 blue Oldsmobile.

His daughter Irene Fuller – sister of Daphne – said that the star "obviously loved it here". She said, "We all fell in love with Mel," adding with a note of disappointment, "but nothing serious happened between him and the women here."

Irene Fuller now owns a successful bar and restaurant on Moorea, bought with her earnings from working for *The Bounty* during four long months in 1983.

The Bounty was given a lavish royal premiere in London where Mel and his co-stars were presented to the Duke and Duchess of Kent for a fund-raising gala that helped add $30,000 to the coffers of the Variety Club, which helps handicapped and deprived youngsters. Mel may have been unaware that the rest of the proceeds from the event went to the Press Fund, founded in 1864, to assist families of needy journalists!

One historical sidelight never referred to in *The Bounty* is that Fletcher Christian suffered from syphilis. When the film finally arrived in movie theatres in the spring of 1984, audiences avoided it as if they feared catching the disease.

In a seven-week run in the US it took just £3.5 million, a pathetic showing considering final estimates of the cost were in the region of $40 million. Meanwhile *Ghostbusters*, starring Dan Aykroyd, Bill Murray and Mel's one-time leading lady Sigourney Weaver, became that year's highest earner with takings of $127 million.

Unfortunately the finger was pointed fairly and squarely at Mel as the actor most to blame for the film's disastrous performance.

The *Sydney Sunday Telegraph* wrote: "The only problem with an otherwise fine movie is the casting of Gibson as Fletcher Christian. He is lost at sea. It is not so much that he's outclassed by Hopkins, it's that he's in a different league. It's a large weakness."

And respected film critic Julie Salamon cruelly pointed out in the *Wall Street Journal*: "For a thrill, keep a lookout for late-night television listings so you can watch the original."

Philippa Hawker, writing in Australia's prestigious *Cinema Papers* magazine, accused him of giving one of his "least convincing performances". She went on: "Just before Mel puts Bligh into the lifeboat, he erupts into a raving frenzy, an outpouring of hysteria that breaks his voice and gives us precisely – nothing."

Hollywood columnist Frank Osbourne was a little less blunt. "There's hope for Gibson but if he is to go the distance he'll need not only to be talented and lucky; he will need to be attracted to the idea of stardom and frankly I don't think he is."

Mel Gibson's assessment was, for once, a shade evasive instead of all-or-nothing trenchant. "I liked the film, but it had its flaws. It was a difficult film to make. It took a long time, and the weather was terrible."

*I am being packaged here as if I were
a hamburger – fat and tasty.
The new sex symbol.*

Before sailing off to Tahiti on the *Bounty*, Mel met leading Hollywood director Mark Rydell to discuss the possibility of him casting the young actor in the lead role of a movie that Mel envisaged as his biggest breakthrough in Hollywood. Rydell's reputation was riding high on the back of the multi-Oscar-nominated *On Golden Pond* starring Henry Fonda, his daughter Jane and Katherine Hepburn. So Mel implored his Los Angeles agent Ed Limato to put him up for the lead role of a farmer in *The River*, which Rydell planned to shoot in the mountains of Tennessee the following year.

At first Rydell was reluctant to consider him seriously. Mainly because he believed that an Australian background would make it difficult for Mel to convince, in the role of a hard-working, God-fearing Tennessee farmer trying to stop the government taking his land. Mel – whose happiest childhood years were spent in those country houses in

Upstate New York, felt differently. And he was absolutely determined to get the role.

"All I ask is that you wait until I get back from *The Bounty* before casting anyone else," he implored Rydell.

Within hours of reaching London to start shooting some of *The Bounty*'s interior scenes, Mel was hard at work on his Tennessee accent with dialogue director Julie Harris. She discovered that he had a truly amazing ear for accents, no doubt helped by those early days in Australia as a "Yank" when he learnt to adjust to the local sound or face non-stop ribbing in the classroom.

Three months later, Mel turned up at Rydell's house in Los Angeles. The director was flabbergasted. "He started reading the script, talking, reading the newspaper, in this perfect Tennessee accent. I was really impressed."

Then Rydell introduced Mel to actress Sissy Spacek, already cast as the farmer's wife in *The River*. And she was just as impressed. "When he stood next to Sissy, who's like a tuning fork when it comes to accents, I knew he had damn well done it."

The only slight damper was that Mel – staying at the exclusive Chateau Marmount Hotel in West Hollywood – had left his passport, travellers' cheques and cash all in his room while at the audition.

They were stolen by an intruder, but that didn't stop Mel making exactly the same mistake at a hotel in Cannes four years later.

As Mae and Tom Garvey, parents of a young boy and girl, Mel and Sissy Spacek played small-time farmers struggling desperately to hold on to their farm despite economic depression, mounting debts at the bank, and ravages of nature. The worst being heavy rains making the river near their home flood their crop fields, often wiping out livestock as well as threatening the family's lives.

For Mel, *The River* was a vitally important stepping stone into Hollywood acceptability. It was the first time he would play an American, his first experience under an American director and the first time he had acted on American soil.

Soon the beautiful mountains of eastern Tennessee were providing the backdrop for a movie that was probably his most enjoyable experience on location, until then. For much of the gruelling nine-week shoot, Mel had Robyn and Hannah and the twins with him at a picturesque farmhouse rented for the duration of the film, in Kingsport. He had seen at first hand the temptations that can weaken cast and crew members through the long months of a difficult shoot and he was determined to have his family as near to him as possible. They were a calming influence. They provided him with that little piece of sanity to return home to each evening, and represented a sheet-anchor while he was at work.

As a child, Mel had never travelled outside New York State, so his stay in Tennessee also provided him with an insight into one of the most rural areas of the United States. It was to have a lasting, long-term effect, and ultimately convince him to enter the world of livestock farming – and another, albeit part-time, career.

In September, 1983, shortly after beginning filming of *The River*, newspaper headlines around the world reported that Mel Gibson had died in a plane crash. Sydney agent Bill Shannahan found himself being woken in the middle of the night by an anxious journalist asking him to contribute to an obituary of the star "who had died at the tragically young age of 27".

The veteran agent who had nursed Mel's career so carefully in Australia was close to tears as he put the phone down.

He could not believe that Mel was gone. For an hour he paced the floor of his bedroom, unsure how to deal with the tragedy. Finally, he rang Mel's house on location in Tennessee and breathed a huge sigh of relief when the star answered, sounding perfectly healthy.

Very much alive and well in Kingsport, Mel was proving a reluctant hero to the locals, obviously impressed at having a real live movie star as their neighbour.

One local commented: "A lot of people, at first, just thought he was a real smartass because he kinda kept his distance. But, as time wore on, he made friends, quite a lot of 'em, on his terms."

Familiar pattern: natural reserve was being mis-interpreted. *The River* co-star Sissy Spacek put it perfectly when she said: "There's not a lot of bullshit about Mel. He's kinda shy and has a certain reserve that I think is nice."

Even with Sissy, Mel was reluctant to talk about himself or his career, preferring to hide behind a stream of wisecracks and innocuous pleasantries, but the actress grew accustomed to his ways and told friends that it was part of Mel's charm.

In any case, he saw the role of Tom Garvey in *The River* as far more important than the impression he left with either the locals or his colleagues. In many ways he related strongly to a character whom he later described as being "rooted in the land; he's like a tree, earthbound, enduring, very basic. There's lots of guys like him; very hard-working, staunch, God-fearing men."

To any of Mel's closest family and friends he could well have been describing himself.

Mark Rydell intended *The River* to be "a tribute to a vanishing America, the America of the independent farm family". In other words, it was to be about the American Dream. And in Vilmos Zsigmond, he also had one of the world's finest directors of photography on board, to evoke it.

But this was an expensive dream; production estimates put it in the $20 million range. Another first in his career: Mel was the star of a movie in which everyone around treated him as such. It was a strange experience; someone was at his beck and call the whole time. If he so much as attempted to help a camera assistant with his gear that crew member would be severely reprimanded by superiors. Lines had been drawn long before, between cast and crew, and they were not to be crossed. Although Mel, to his credit, would continue breaking those rules right throughout his career.

He brought his own stamp to the production by encouraging his children to accompany him to the set, where they played with Sissy Spacek's sixteen-month-old daughter Schuyler as well as co-star Scott Glenn's young daughters Dakota and Rio.

Director Rydell's patience was severely tested when the children started demanding non-stop attention from their parents. Sissy Spacek explained:

"Both of us found our children were just so noisy and demanding that everything was taking twice as long as it should. Mel's little ones and my daughter were all great pals but were too young to understand the word silence. So we had to keep doing retakes."

Sometimes Mel – whose trailer had the name "Frank Lyons" chalked on a blackboard on the door – would take off for an evening with colleagues, often ending up singing "Clementine" at the local hotel.

For this was like no other film Mel had ever worked on before, and the family mood continued with cast and crew lunching together most days at picnic tables, and Rydell hosting informal Sunday lunch parties for everyone, including children, at his rented house in Kingsport.

Rydell later conceded that Mel was not an easy person to get to know.

"He's very careful about offering friendship. It takes a long time for him to allow you into his world. Mel was always there at these Sunday brunches though I knew it was difficult for him. Originally he did it out of respect, but he also came to develop a relationship with me. He doesn't make friends easily, but when he does, it's an honour."

The same might be said of Robyn. Concerned by those long, enforced separations she had already suffered during just a couple of years of marriage, she was happy to stay on location with Mel. But there was an inevitable shyness on her part over getting involved with the actual production. She often stayed back at the house in Kingsport while a nanny accompanied the three children to the set. It surprised some that she did not want to go on the set, but there was little doubting that her husband preferred it that way. As he has said many times since, he never wanted to marry an actress . . .

Wayne Bailey, local resident and production assistant on the movie, recalled: "I only saw Mel's wife visiting on the set about three or four times. But his kids were on the set a lot, in Mel's mobile home, with a woman who was there to look after them."

His thumbnail portrait of Robyn Gibson was, "My impression of her was that she was kind of backward."

But Robyn should not take offence at this description, as it is purely a Southern States alternative word for "shy". Backward she ain't!

Others on the set of *The River* noted that whenever Robyn did appear there or at the Rydell Sunday lunch parties, she had a strong presence. Her role in Mel's life is pivotal.

"You knew who was in charge when Robyn was around," said one crew member.

Even when two stunt men were injured in accidents and a union demarcation row led to unpleasant incidents in which cars and film vans were vandalised, Mel remained unruffled. Having his family close made it so much easier to handle the glitches and hassles . . .

His fee on *The River* was $500,000; director Rydell was convinced he would have been a bargain at twice that price. As the movie-maker edited *The River* back at Universal Studios in Los Angeles, he gloated that Mel had "the roughness of McQueen, the gentleness of Montgomery Clift and he's going to turn this town upside down".

Ironically, *The River* was sneak previewed at the first annual benefit of the Lee Strasberg Actor's Studio, the home of method acting in the United States. Mel – who has already vigorously denied any interest in Method acting – attended the screening and formal dinner at the Pierre Hotel with some of Hollywood's most dedicated Method actors and actresses, including Paul Newman, Joanne Woodward, Ellen Burstyn, Robert De Niro and Shelley Winters. She said after seeing *The River*: "There was so much water I had to keep going to the john."

When *The River* opened theatrically in New York, it was to mixed reactions and verdicts.

One reviewer described Mel's performance as "less than convincing, not for lack of trying but because he is just too clean-shaven, too well coiffed and too obviously handsome by half for someone with as hard a row to hoe as farmer Garvey".

And noted Australian critic Scott Murray, of *Cinema Papers*, rated the film as "only okay. Mel is quite good in it and he puts a lot of energy into his performance."

But the *Sydney Sun*'s John Hanrahan wrote of Mel: "Gibson, in particular, displays for the first time subtleties in his performance that enhance his watchability."

Yet it was Sissy Spacek – already an Academy Award winner for her portrayal of the *Coalminer's Daughter* – who got the most praise, and yet another Oscar nomination.

Almost ten years later, Mel accused himself of doing an inferior job on *The River*, telling one associate: "I think I did a really bad job on that film. When I look at it, I was young and stupid. And I was trying to phone it in, maybe." (Hollywood jargon for walking through a role, without commitment.)

A few weeks before completion of *The River*, the first in a series of newspaper tales that would irk Mel for the following ten years appeared in the *Sunday Telegraph*, in Sydney: "007 OFFER TO MEL GIBSON," ran the headline.

His Sydney agent, ever-dependable Bill Shannahan, confirmed that Bond producer Cubby Broccoli had made an offer to Mel to step into the slot made so famous by Sean Connery and then Roger Moore.

However, the most significant paragraph in the article appeared next. It read:

"The spokesman says Gibson originally rejected the offer as he would find the inevitable typecasting too limiting and there were too many other projects in the offing."

The paper went on to claim that the Bond producers were planning to offer him the role again with even more money attached. Three months later, the same newspaper quoted Sean Connery – ever the mickey-taker – quipping: "As a replacement, I think the Australian actor Mel Gibson would be ideal – then Roger could play Q and I could play M."

The truth was that Mel quashed any possibility of playing the next Bond, within minutes of hearing about it, first time round. He was absolutely set against the role but newspapers across the world have speculated ever since that he will one day take the part. But as Mel himself has frequently told friends: "Why take the Bond role when I already have the 1990s version in *Lethal Weapon*?"

Also, Mel had decided long before that first Bond offer that he would only take roles that stretched his abilities. He saw Bond as "dead and buried".

Even before shooting *The River*, Mel had committed to

another picture to be helmed by Australian director Gillian Armstrong. He had surprised his Los Angeles agent Ed Limato by continuing to pass on *The Running Man* in order to make this film, entitled *Mrs Soffel*.

"Everyone in town's chasing Mel. You should be grateful. He likes Gillian, he likes the role. Just find a new goddamn title, okay?" Limato told MGM's Freddie Fields when he turned up in his Hollywood office one day.

As a result, Mel, Robyn and the children headed straight for Toronto, Canada, for *Mrs Soffel*. This movie almost killed his enthusiasm for Hollywood and movie-making before his career got into second gear. It also earmarked him unfairly as a "wild, unpredictable actor", in the eyes of certain strait-laced studio chiefs.

Before shooting got under way, Mel was invited to fly down to Los Angeles to be a presenter at the Academy Awards in April, 1984. It was a trip he sensed he should not have made the moment he stepped inside the Dorothy Chandler Pavilion.

Linda Hunt's much-deserved award as best supporting actress was greeted with delight by Mel; his own performance as one of the hosts was widely condemned by the media.

"On the Oscar show, Gibson radiated all the warmth, sincerity and charm of a doorstep, and for good reason, he was terrified," sniped one showbusiness reporter the next day.

Mel agreed that he *was* very nervous on the big night. He told a fellow actor: "Skid marks. It was nerve-racking. I just can't be relaxed on television, unless I'm playing a role. It's the only way to get through it."

Mel had taken a few shots of Dutch courage but they had simply accentuated his nervousness. It was an unmitigated disaster and Mel steered clear of the Oscars for many years thereafter.

Mrs Soffel – or "Mrs Whatchamacallit" as it was known to

certain MGM execs who loathed the title – started shooting in Canada at that time. Mel settled into the cold north with his family and formed a reasonable on-screen relationship with co-star Diane Keaton and director Gillian Armstrong, whose Australian film *My Brilliant Career* had created quite a stir in Hollywood. Although it would not, unfortunately, turn out to be a prophetic description of the way Ms Armstrong's own career proceeded.

Back in Tinseltown, there had been problems before the film even began production. Executives at MGM – the studio backing the project – were split as to the potential of the movie and they were weary of Gillian Armstrong, a Hollywood first-timer who demanded complete and utter independence from her paymasters at MGM. One of the project's biggest backers was Freddie Fields, the same studio executive who had nurtured *The Year of Living Dangerously* so adroitly. He looked on Mel as his protégé and backed any project that the young star might support.

"In Fields's view, Mel Gibson's charisma would carry the film. He had seen it happen on his previous movie, *The Year of Living Dangerously*, and it would happen again on *Mrs Soffel*," wrote former MGM-UA executive Peter Bart in his book *Fade Out – The Calamitous Final Days of MGM*.

Mel endured sub-zero temperatures and painfully slow set-ups for each scene because he truly believed that this bittersweet Gothic love story about the wife of a prison warder (Diane Keaton) who falls in love with one of the prisoners (played by Mel) was a dark and brooding non-traditional project that would greatly stretch his acting talents and therefore further his career. He said later he knew it was going to be tough, but he was prepared for all that – and did have his family with him to keep him on the straight and narrow. They would, as always, provide him with that source of security he needed to stay on the rails.

However, Robyn and the children soon decided that life at home Down Under was far preferable to winter in Canada. She spent many lonely days in Toronto while Mel was a four-hour drive away in the countryside, returning at weekends. Also, Robyn was expecting the couple's fourth child and wanted to be back at their Coogee beach house with her relatives and friends. Mel was devastated by Robyn's decision. It would be selfish of him to make his family suffer the unfamiliar surroundings a moment longer – but he knew his own weaknesses and feared that Robyn's departure would spark a lot of problems. And he was absolutely right.

"I like Robyn to be there because then I don't forget, we don't all forget, what's reality. It could be so easy. Otherwise what's the point of getting hitched in the first place," he said a few months after *Mrs Soffel*.

According to those close to the star, Mel became "restless" and "unhappy" both on and off the set, as soon as Robyn departed for Australia.

"They've scheduled it so I work only every fifth or sixth day because they think I might run off to Australia and never come back," he told one visitor to the set.

Shooting take after take in difficult conditions, along with the constant studio-politics problems on the production sank Mel into the depths of despair. Unhappiness was pushing him close to a nervous breakdown, as he recognised in an interview with journalist Melinda Newman.

"You just have to get your mind right. You say to yourself, 'Relax, don't be upset by this. Roll with it and see if you can master it.' Happiness is a state of being, isn't it? You can be happy with a little or a lot. Mel Gibson can be happy with anything if he gets his mind right."

Around him raged a feud. Points-scoring MGM bosses started accusing Mel and Diane Keaton of making their lovemaking scenes too sexy, at the insistence of director Armstrong. As so often happens, the actors were getting caught in the crossfire of a boardroom vendetta.

At one stage, both performers virtually collapsed from exhaustion after Armstrong had them kissing non-stop for hours in a scene requiring Mel and Diane Keaton to embrace passionately through prison bars.

The Oscar-winning actress eventually took a breather, sipped tea and applied Blistex to her parched lips, obviously frustrated by her director's obstinacy. Bravely, she continued the scene after whispering to Mel: "Thank God you're the world's best kisser." Witnesses say that Mel looked just as pissed off as his co-star.

Ironically, rumours were rife that Mel and Keaton were not enjoying a warm relationship. She was deemed to be slightly aloof because she tended to withdraw into her shell the moment the director shouted "Cut". Not hauteur, it was only her way of intensifying her performance.

"She spent many days between takes listening to her Walkman and saying very, very little," said one member of the crew.

Mel, frantic to dispel his gloom, made admirable attempts to improve the atmosphere on the set. On one occasion, following the end of a particularly passionate bedroom scene, he suddenly dropped on all fours, crouched like an ape and then chased Diane Keaton, growling ferociously. The actress darted away from Mel squealing; it was a rare moment when she could truly shrug off the intensity of her role.

Mel continued bottling up his frustrations over what was happening on the set, and his loneliness in the evenings since Robyn and the children had left.

A tell-tale symptom came when in one scene Mel was called upon to hurl himself on top of a fire in his prison cell.

He refused to let a stunt man intervene. By this time he was so patently fed up that no-one dared argue when he insisted on doing the stunt himself. As if he wanted to vent his frustrations by letting studio executives watch him coat his body in gel before being set alight – just to make them that little bit more anxious. Luckily he was not injured, but everyone on the set that evening could predict that Mel was heading for serious trouble.

At 8.30 p.m. on Wednesday, April 25, 1984, just a few days after Robyn and the children returned to Australia, Mel's rented Pontiac failed to stop at a red light on Yonge Street, Toronto, smashing into the back of unsuspecting 23-year-old Randy Caddell's car.

Seconds later the young mechanic snatched the keys out of the Pontiac's dashboard and started screaming and yelling at the drunken figure behind the wheel.

Mel emerged smiling from the car and held up a hand to make peace with the guy whose car had just hit, exclaiming: "Hey, I'm for love, not war. How about we have a beer?"

Randy Caddell recalled: "I was so mad I was doing a little dance in the street and using some terrible language. I mean, I was dangerous." Fortunately, he was no Lethal Weapon . . .

It took a few minutes before he realised he had been hit by a car driven by Hollywood star Mel Gibson. When the police arrived Mel was taken to the Five District traffic station where breath tests showed he was over the legal limit of alcohol allowed for drivers. He had between 0.12 and 0.13 per cent alcohol in his bloodstream. The legal limit in Canada is 0.08.

"MEL GIBSON JAILED!" and "MEL GIBSON ARREST" were just two of the headlines that appeared in newspapers around the world the next day. Articles gleefully reported that Mel "could face six months in jail and fines of $2,000 if convicted".

In Australia and Hollywood alike there were fears that Mel might have blown his career. Any hopes of covering up the arrest were dashed by those headlines. Mel's agents were trying to do everything possible to "damage control" the whole incident in their own inimitable fashion, but in the end they all realised that it would either blow over and become yesterday's news or his career had just taken a huge backward step. Or lurch.

Back at MGM/UA, studio chiefs already split down the middle over backing *Mrs Soffel* were now petrified that their $15 million movie might have to be scrapped if the actor was jailed. They despatched a trouble-shooting lawyer and two minders to keep an eye on Mel.

One week later, while other members of the Gibson family were celebrating his parents' fortieth wedding anniversary in Australia, Mel kept a court date in Canada.

Hair slicked back and dressed in a dark, double-breasted blazer complete with tie and grey slacks, Mel managed, typically, to turn up late for the opening of court. His luck held out because his case was not the first one to be heard.

Hordes of female fans filled the public gallery of the court at the Old City Hall in Toronto. Many tried to pass him scraps of paper with their names and phone numbers. Resignedly, Mel told his lawyer William Trudel, "It happens every week."

Mel then pleaded guilty to the charge. His lawyer told Judge George Carter that his client wanted to record an apology "to the court and the Toronto community and would like to thank the police officers who dealt with him . . . in a professional and courteous manner".

Judge Carter banned Mel from driving in Canada for three months, fined him $300 and then, provoking a wave of laughter from his fans, warned that the star would get "thirty days in jail if he doesn't pay".

Before banging his gavel and declaring the case closed, Judge Carter said warmly to Mel: "I hope your stay in Canada is otherwise pleasant."

The actor dashed from the court and through a vast crowd of mainly female onlookers towards a waiting gold Lincoln. Somebody shouted: "We love you Mel!" Beaming back he said: "I like you too." Note the distinction between love and liking, even under pressure . . . Flashbulbs popped and he even patiently signed a few autographs. One woman, close to tears, whimpered, "I don't care if he is a drunk, he's still Mel Gibson and I just love the man."

But that court appearance provided further evidence of Mel's increasing reliance on alcohol. The stresses and strains of being away from his family on *The Bounty*, then the gruelling schedule on *The River* followed by weeks away from his family on *Mrs Soffel* had taken their toll.

Robyn was unsympathetic when Mel rang to tell her the news about his arrest. "What the hell's the matter with you?" came her uncompromising reply.

It was bracing and abrasive – and he had to admit that she was absolutely right. Patience and understanding would only make him feel he could keep getting away with it.

Mel's mother Anne believed that her son's arrest for drunken driving in Toronto marked his moment of realisation that alcohol was taking over his life. "That really woke Mel up. He realised he'd let the beer take hold. The boy changed after that. I was particularly happy no one got hurt in the transition. It could have been tragic," she said later.

During that time alone in Canada, Mel's drinking capacity increased enormously. He sought solace in endless bottles of beer, where before he could have read the kids a bedtime story or enjoyed a quiet dinner with just Robyn for company. He was also painfully aware of behind-the-scenes problems, bad vibes, that were becoming an everyday part of life on *Mrs Soffel*. Director Gillian Armstrong felt persecuted by bullying studio executives angry at the way the shooting schedule had slowed to a snail's pace. She confessed that there were times "when I wish I'd stayed home in Australia".

Merchants in at least two vital locations refused to co-operate with the film unit unless "donations" were made to various local causes. The studio wanted to cut costs and prohibit Armstrong from shooting a death row scene in the gloomy confines of the Pittsburgh prison where the real characters, upon whom Mel and Diane Keaton's roles were based, had met.

"Just find any nice empty prison in Canada," they implored (Armstrong stood firm and they eventually backed down).

Loyally, Mel and Diane Keaton sided with Armstrong throughout all those problems. But he was forced to question if it was all worth the stress. The freezing cold, the extraordinarily long hours, constant on-set tensions, the loneliness combined with the shame and embarrassment of that drinking driving incident (which provoked the studio into insisting he had those two minders with him the entire time). Mel was, he admitted eventually, at his lowest ebb. He could not see any light at the end of the tunnel. He and the rest of the cast half-expected the studio to pull the plug.

Back at his rented house in Toronto, Mel shunned the concerned colleagues whom he had befriended during the earlier, happier stages of the shoot, succumbing to deep bitterness and resentment.

During *The River* he had truly thought he had found happiness and contentment throughout the film-making process. *Mrs Soffel* had destroyed all those hopes and illusions. He was back at square one.

Both films opened in America just seven days apart, but the memories they held for Mel cold not have been more different. *Mrs Soffel* had its premiere just in time to qualify for Academy Award nominations, not one of which it received.

And still Mel was claiming that he had no special ambitions. In a sparse four-page publicity biography to help publicise *Mrs Soffel*, he insisted: "I never planned a career. I still don't. It kills people when I tell them this, but I don't have a master plan. I don't plot my movies. I just take things as they come, flow with it, go with my gut instincts. You have to know when to do that."

Reviews of *Mrs Soffel* were astonishingly varied.

Bill Collins of the *Sydney Daily Mirror* wrote: "Like all great movies *Mrs Soffel* lives on in the heart and in the mind for those moviegoers sensitive to the film's content as much as its sometimes casual, rarely obvious artistry."

And he registered Mel's performance as "thoughtful and understanding. His characterisation is a personal triumph." The *Sydney Morning Herald*'s Paul Byrnes acclaimed Mel as "demonstrating more ability as an actor in this part than I have seen before".

But fellow Aussie critic Scott Murray says that *Mrs Soffel* "is a very strange film and the love story does not work. Diane Keaton is miscast and the film never recovers. It was a failed project."

New York critics were even more blunt. The *New York Daily News* said Mel "could be in danger of becoming movies' incredible hunk; he's a real actor and he needs real parts to play".

And *New York Times* reviewer Vincent Canby blamed much of the failure of the film on Gillian Armstrong, saying that "it more or less plods to its conclusion".

Armstrong herself has remained strongly loyal to Mel even after the traumas of *Mrs Soffel* and passionately defends the actor against criticism that sometimes he "doesn't care about his performances".

"He certainly does care. I think people would be surprised to know how committed Mel is to his craft. He isn't just a pretty face. He's also a great actor. I've see his theatre work in Australia, so I have a good idea of his range. He's unique, and his charisma – I don't think it is prettiness at all – his charisma draws your eyes to him even in a fray. In Toronto he became very involved on the set with Diane Keaton and Matthew Modine, who plays his brother. The extra spark is his generosity – there is love and respect among them."

Mel theorised that the film was misunderstood by its critics. "*Mrs Soffel* is a beautiful feeling mood piece. I think it is a brilliant film," he said shortly after the movie's release.

Besides being relieved that the *Mrs Soffel* shoot was over, Mel could not wait to get back to Australia for the birth of baby number four, named William, born in the middle of June, only days after Mel's return to the peace and relative sanity of Sydney.

But the three-month break changing nappies, recharging his batteries and catching up with his parents and his children, just wasn't long enough. He had already committed to play Max Rockatansky one last time for *Mad Max III*. It sent him over the edge and rapidly heading for what he termed "burn out".

In a remarkably candid outburst, Mel told one reporter: "I'll probably be washed out in a couple of years. People get tired of seeing your face. They want to see another face. And there are faces better and there are talents better – or as good."

When I was 22 I was a right idiot. I guess when I'm 35 I'll think I was an idiot at 28.

While *Mad Max – Beyond Thunderdome* may well have done more than any other film to maintain Mel's reputation as an up-and-coming Hollywood star, it also sent him spiralling into an alcoholic haze threatening to destroy him.

His ordeal began the moment he turned up at the movie's isolated location, a dusty old mining town called Coober Pedy, some 500 miles north-west of Adelaide, but it could have been a million miles from civilisation as far as Mel was concerned. He had just done three movies, *The Bounty*, *The River* and *Mrs Soffel*, back-to-back and a twelve-week break at the family home on the beach at Coogee could not offset that. Mel knew in his heart he should have taken six months, maybe even a year off.

But when Hollywood wants to make the third in a series of movies as phenomenally successful as *Mad Max*, they do not tend to take anyone's feelings or state of mind into consideration. Warner Brothers were willing to pay him $1 million and Mel, ever the insecure freelance artist terrified that it might be his last job, took the money on the basis that it would provide his family with the security they deserved.

In Coober Pedy, with temperatures regularly topping the hundred-degree mark, he was forced to doubt the wisdom of that decision. Conditions were appalling. Within days of setting up camp, seven crew members were taken to hospital suffering from heat exhaustion. Tempers were tested; people started taking their frustrations out on one another.

The matter of stunts screwed tension a notch tighter, too. Director George Miller was aware that Warners were expecting something really spectacular for their money and, after one particularly outrageous sequence, two stunt men threatened to walk off the film.

Caught in the middle of all this was Mel. Already mentally and physically exhausted, worried about his career, anxious about his wife and children, no wonder he turned to the only immediate source of comfort – alcohol. Mel knew what happened when he drank too much but he could not stop himself. His drink-driving disgrace during the making of *Mrs Soffel* was only just behind him but he had no other way to turn.

Years later he reflected on his excessive drinking in the course of *Mad Max – Beyond Thunderdome*, admitting that life at that time had darkened into nothing much more than a blur.

"Not drinking certainly does make a difference to the tenor of my work. When you stop your mind clears up a little, you're able to see things a little more clearly. Even one drink stays in your spine for months . . . it's amazing how it can affect you . . . you don't realise it."

Deep inside Mel saw precisely what was going on. He had reached another crossroads and it was up to him which direction he took. "I felt as if I was a juggernaut, hurtling down a steep hill, with the brakes not working and the controls all screwed up. Everyone expected me to live like a hard-livin', tough guy in real life, so I did.

"Sometimes I fought so hard and drank so much that I surprised even myself. But there were so many people hanging around me, assuring me I could do anything I wanted, that I believed them. I'd wake up in the morning with no idea where the hell I'd been the night before. And then I'd get dressed, stagger out and not know where the hell I was gonna finish up.

"I tell you, I've got to know so many gutters in my time."

Mel blamed much of his boozing on his youth in Australia.

"I'd been a heavy boozer since I was 16. In Australia you're not considered a proper man unless you drink yourself stupid. I was a real hard case, a wild boy, knocking liquor back like there was no tomorrow. Then I'd get into fights because I was always shooting my mouth off."

Adding fuel to the fires already banked within him, *People* magazine proceeded to dub him The Sexiest Man Alive. It infuriated Mel. His self-esteem was at its lowest-ever ebb and here was some magazine trying to turn him into the world's leading sex-symbol. He told friends the title was "a joke" and steered journalists away from the subject if they were unwise enough to raise it.

By now Mel was openly consuming five bottles of beer even *before* getting on to the *Beyond Thunderdome* set each morning. Uncannily – was it willpower or vitamins? – he still managed to give director George Miller one hundred per cent effort when required. The problems were chiefly caused by huge lulls between set-ups when Mel would sit around playing cards, drinking more beer, smoking cigarettes, talking, cracking childish gags and swilling yet more beer. And this was only a few weeks into what was to be a gruelling four-month shoot.

The movie's producers – alerted by Mel's drink-driving

offence – provided him with a driver and a minder so that their star would not end up in some small-town jail cell when he was supposed to be shooting a $10 million movie. But the actor's "companions" could only keep an eye on him – they were powerless actually to take the endless bottles of booze away. In any case, he had no intention of stopping his drinking. It was, after all, his only means of escape.

Back home in Sydney, Robyn immediately sensed that Mel was in trouble. She told him to give up alcohol. But it wasn't as easy as that. He was stuck on a movie he did not want to be on.

"I was coming to the end of my rope. I needed help but I wouldn't admit it. My family went through hell," admitted Mel, years later.

Sapped of energy and enthusiasm, he felt as if his career was about to collapse and dreaded that his marriage also faced destruction.

"I was about to lose all the important things in my life."

Sound technicians on *Beyond Thunderdome* began to notice that Mel's voice was getting raspier from such vast quantities of beer and cigarettes. However, throughout the entire shoot, he epitomised the perfect professional in other ways – always on time, acting with great competence and knowing every word of his dialogue.

Part of his unease was that Mel was daunted by his prospects. Those three films, just completed, had not turned out to be box office successes and he knew that if he made another three flops then he might as well wave goodbye to a Hollywood career. His fears manifested themselves in his increased need to drink. What made it worse was that he had no one to share his problems. He may have had many drinking buddies on the film, but there was no way he would tell any of them his troubles. Again he bottled it all up.

His fuse became shorter and shorter as the film

progressed. He started to snap at virtually anyone who came near him on the set. He clammed up completely during interviews with journalists and soon inevitable rumours about his well-being permeated the Australian film industry. It would only be a matter of time before word got back to Hollywood.

"The desert heat has got to him," said one journalist. "He's a different guy. I don't think he even knows himself now."

But Mel's attitude towards the press was not just a result of his own unhappiness at that time. While he had avoided any actual scandals, reports of his drinking were being openly published and he was especially sensitive towards his parents' feelings on the subject. After all, Hutton Gibson had never even allowed alcohol in the house throughout Mel's childhood. And then there was Anne Gibson – like any mother she was increasingly concerned by stories of her son's hellraising.

"I never chastised him about it but he knew how I felt," she said afterwards. "Mel was tired and confused and missed the family. It was a matter of priorities."

Mel was heading for a very bad case of extreme burn-out during the shooting of *Beyond Thunderdome* – and he was in a grandstand seat for the imminent crash. Nobody had a better view, so he could not have shut his eyes to it. Sometimes his desperation was there for all to see. Like the time he asked one astonished journalist how he could earn better press coverage. "These latest incidents really hurt my ladies. Robyn knows me too well, and she's a big help. But poor old Mum freaks out and really suffers when she reads anything I've done, whether it's true or not. I'm not really like I'm made out to be, am I?"

It was a plea from the heart of a very jaded character.

Stunt men on *Beyond Thunderdome* were the true barometer of his welfare at that time. Many of them had worked with him on the previous two *Mad Max* films and they were disturbed by his drinking and temper tantrums.

"He's usually like a brother, but lately, man, the booze has got to him. It's like he's too much into the Mad Max character," said one stunt man on the set.

Another told the star: "You look bloody ancient."

"It's part of my character for the movie," came Mel's reply.

He had always assumed that he was nothing like the characters he portrayed on screen. But he was starting to understand that his own complexity of character was shown in the fact that every role defined an element of him.

"The characters are not like me, and yet at the same time they are, because I've only got myself to draw from. You kill your own dominant aspects and try and bring out some of the recessive and make them more dominant. It's a reshuffle I guess."

By the time *Beyond Thunderdome* ended, Mel had made up his mind; this time he was going to take a complete rest from film-making for as long as it would take to recharge his batteries and get to know his family again. His newest child William was more than six months old. Yet William's father had seen him for less than half his life.

Even a big-money offer from his Hollywood agent Ed Limato to star with rock legend David Bowie in *Burton and Speke* fell on deaf ears. As it happened it was a sensible decision, for the movie – to be directed by American veteran Bob Rafelson – never got off the ground.

Mel had no idea – possibly he hardly cared – whether *Mad Max III* would be a hit movie or not. He certainly knew he was burnt out and on the edge of a nervous breakdown. As it turned out, the film became a huge box office success and his gamble paid off.

He promised himself then that he would never again make so many films in such a short space of time. But he managed to repeat that dangerous marathon on at least two more occasions, with even more dramatic results.

For the moment, Mel was happier. He had waved farewell to Hollywood, albeit temporarily.

"It was too much work. I just wanted to say goodbye and try something else. I felt I had to clear my head. It took nearly a year for me to get my straitjacket off. I didn't know what to do with all the attention I had been getting. It was confusing and I needed time to see where I went wrong. I was starting to slip, I had to learn to relax and not take things in Hollywood too seriously. I realised you had to put on the brakes or go away and return to the fray with new armour."

Mel rued the price of those three back-to-back movies. "You can't do that much work and remain sane. You get off a plane somewhere and suddenly you're being steered towards this red carpet. Someone's handing you flowers, offering you a drink, telling you to relax . . . it's really jarring, and you're sort of cringing, hiding.

"But then you realise that if you don't go along with it then they resent you for it. And if you went the other way, became a big asshole and made a big hoot and holler about how important you were, they'd still do it anyway. So what can you do? You're fucked no matter which way you jump."

Most important of all was Mel's reunion with his family back in Sydney. He and Robyn wanted to bring the children up on a farm in the countryside. They began looking at suitable properties. Besides swimming in the sea near their existing Coogee home, his only real exercise was "lifting babies".

As *The River* director Mark Rydell commented: "He seems to revere his wife and children. He's a wonderful father, and the kids are hanging on him all the time . . . "

Mel has always remained devotedly, *hair-trigger* protective of his family. During his break from the limelight, he went out of his way to make sure they did not come under the public gaze.

"I've got a red light that goes on inside me . . . I don't even like to say I go to the beach. If you don't say what you're doing, nobody knows where you're coming from!"

When one reporter came knocking at the door of the house in Coogee, an infuriated Robyn "told him to get lost in less than polite language", said Mel, proudly.

He even persuaded Robyn – a very traditional, self-sufficient kind of mother – to employ a nanny to help her with the four young children, and also give her and Mel a chance to get to know each other again.

Inside the Coogee house, Mel used tools that Robyn had bought him for Christmas and birthdays over the years to put finishing touches to the property. Visitors recall that the interior was like a huge football field with children running in all directions on the vast, open-plan ground floor.

Within months of starting his "lay-off" Mel and Robyn paid $350,000 for a beautiful farm with 6,000 acres in the picturesque Kiewa Valley district of northern Victoria.

Mel saw the purchase of the farm called Carinya – which means "happy home" – in Tangambalanga as a key move in his recovery from the stress of making those four films. Strolling between gum and willow trees lining the driveway, Mel trusted that he and his family could lead the ordinary sort of life they all longed for.

"I think everyone needs an interest apart from his work; another avenue of experience, something to be enthusiastic about.

"Working on my farm made me normal again. I looked after my cattle, ate snake pies and raw vegetables and got closer to my wife and kids again. I cut out the heavy boozing, although I wasn't teetotal, and I realised that I had used alcohol as a prop but it made me a bastard. I'd missed out on kids, family, all the joys of being a parent."

Hutton and Anne Gibson joined Mel and his family for long weekends. For the first time in his adult life, Mel had an opportunity to rebond with his father. Together they tore down a cottage on the farm estate and rebuilt it brick by brick. Hollywood must have seemed a million miles away, even if the father–son scene cried out for cameras.

And Robyn insisted that Mel do his bit around the house like any other husband. Often she would stick a message above the telephone in the kitchen reminding Mel, "Do the dishes."

A thankful, mellowed Mel even tried to re-evaluate his relationship with the media. He acknowledged that they came with the job. He even started to relax in the company of journalists.

"I used to be afraid of this," he said to one reporter. "Now it's not worth getting worried about."

To another he said: "This time last year I could never sit down and talk to complete strangers about myself the way I'm doing now. But I've emerged as a new, bold me. I've decided that life's too short."

As much for his own benefit as any listener's, he justified putting his career on hold. "When you're just living your life as normal and you walk down the street and nobody notices, and then all of a sudden that [being noticed] begins to happen, it's not a natural way to exist. You are not used to it and you think it's going to be great. But it's not . . . And then when that happens you can go two ways. You can kind of try and kill it. It becomes a problem that you can try and wrestle and fight with, right, just fight it, just be ill at ease with it, and you usually end up in a lot of trouble that way. So what you've got to do is ignore it, in a way, but not be fighting it and it'll just be water off a duck's back. I think it's something that you have got to get to, it's stages of . . . it's hard to explain."

In this self-revealing mood, he explored personal fears – like talking to the press.

"True. I suppose I thought I'd make an idiot of myself. I used to build up a lot of negative energy about doing interviews. I guess it's like cheesecake. If somebody told you about a cake made out of cheese and you'd never had it, you'd think it was terrible. Now, I've been doing this for a while and I've got used to it."

But the life-saving aspect of his long "sabbatical" was that he tapered off the booze.

"When my doctor told me my liver was shot to hell, I decided it was time to cut down on my drinking. The first month was awful, but now I'm happy to drink just soda water," he told a reporter.

Mel looks back on that eighteen-month period as the time he improved his entire existence – and entered the world of farming.

"I didn't know anything about farming when I went down there [to the farm], which means you get ripped off a few times, but gradually you get this little stockpile of knowledge and it's just like learning any skill.

"Even after a year of taking a crack at it, I wouldn't be what you'd call a good beef cattle manager. I've still got a long way to go, but the experience has made me feel replenished. The spark is back.

"We all found so much happiness that I get tears in my eyes when I think how I nearly blew it."

Not even a court summons to appear before a magistrate for failing to lodge his 1984 tax returns ruffled the newly relaxed star. He was fined A$100 and ordered to pay $18 costs. Only a year earlier he had been find $60 for an identical offence involving his 1983 returns. Back at his Sydney office, Mel's Australian agent Bill Shannahan was hardly surprised. His best client treated tax returns in the same way he used to treat parking tickets.

When Mel was asked to select his favourite paintings for the New South Wales Art Gallery's Celebrity Choice Exhibition, he light-heartedly hid behind a false moustache –

because he was embarrassed at his choice of works.

"This is an exercise in honing my appreciation. To try and take it all in, and I mean all in, is just impossible. Your head just falls off," he told a local newspaper reporter before posing for a fun photo complete with false moustache.

Then Mel joined a consortium of actors, writers and artists resisting closure of Sydney's Nimrod Theatre, where he had so successfully portrayed Romeo just a few years earlier. Mel was regaining his appetite for life by doing the things he had missed out on for three or four years.

Naturally, it wasn't all play and no work. He was swamped with screenplays sent over by agent Ed Limato from Hollywood. Among the movie projects that caught his eye was one about wayward soccer star George Best. The rags to riches and back to rags story of the talented Manchester United player seemed tailor-made for Mel. After all, Best's life of excessive drinking was not that different from some of the trials and tribulations that Mel had experienced. But the Best movie never happened and Mel pledged that the next project he joined would be in the traditional Hollywood action genre. Something very special indeed was called for, to maintain his career in Tinseltown.

Pressures of life as one of the world's top box office attractions would eventually push Mel back towards alcohol. But for the moment he was content.

I used to misbehave a lot. I didn't have any direction. Does anyone?

13

In April 1985, Mel met his Australian agent and mentor Bill Shannahan in Sydney to discuss the actor's future. He was slowly recovering from the burn-out suffered after those three back-to-back movies and once more his career was at a vital crossroads. Stardom had beckoned and proved disastrous. Now Mel wanted guidance on what to do next. Hollywood was the last place on earth he wanted to end up in, and he had even at one stage seriously considered quitting the acting profession altogether.

He also turned down the lead in *The Running Man* after being pursued for three years for the part. So it went to Arnold Schwarzenegger and is credited with having launched the former Mr Universe on to an even more successful movie career than Mel's. The project's producers let it be known that Arnold came at about half the price of Mel – a situation reversed within four short years.

Mel trusted Bill Shannahan more than anyone in the

business and this fatherly figure rewarded that loyalty by advising him to keep his roots in Australia. After all, the film industry Down Under had been enjoying a renaissance of sorts since the late 1970s. It seemed a perfect time for Mel to expand his interests and set up a company to make films in his homeland. It would also help keep him closer to Robyn and the children, whom he considered some of the few sane people in a very crazy world.

"Bill Shannahan was a wonderful influence on Mel. He really cared about what Mel did and he, more than anybody other than Robyn, realised that Hollywood was not a very nice place," says one close friend from Sydney.

Shannahan suggested that Mel link up with Australia's leading woman producer, Pat Lovell, and form a company to develop feature projects. The two had met and worked together five years earlier on *Gallipoli*, when Pat had been a second mother to Mel and his young co-star Mark Lee.

On a rainy day in May 1985, Pat visited Mel, Robyn and the children at their home in Coogee. The reunion was with a very different fellow from the fresh-faced actor of half a decade before.

Mel later told Pat Lovell that what saved him was reading Hollywood screenwriter William Goldman's book *Adventures in the Screen Trade*, considered by many to be the finest account of life inside the movie industry ever written. Evidently he took the inside stuff of the book as a warning.

Pat Lovell was as well aware of the stories of Mel's excesses as anyone else, but she also recognised that the actor had made a conscious effort to turn himself around, escape the trials and temptations of Tinseltown. Setting up a production company with Mel in Australia could only be good for all concerned. So, with Mel rocking youngest child Will in his arms (Pat says he is a clone of his father) in the garden of that rambling Coogee house, the two agreed to form a company called Lovell Gibson.

As Pat – a grandmotherly figure in her fifties – explains, "Mel told me that the eldest came first."

Soon they were working on a project entitled *Clean Straw*, about three Australians who go to Britain to seek fame and fortune and end up on a Greek island instead. Gillian Armstrong – who had worked with Mel on *Mrs Soffel* – was slated to direct. The idea was to keep the company small and run it like a family.

But then Hollywood producer Jerry Weintraub came on the scene. He calculated that if he could get Lovell Gibson to commit to giving him a first-look deal on all their projects then he must gain immense influence over Mel, one of the most exciting new stars in Hollywood. Pat and Mel were impressed by Weintraub's enthusiasm and soon struck a development deal that, on the face of it, seemed the perfect springboard for Lovell Gibson.

Mel was excited as a schoolboy over Lovell Gibson's partnership with Weintraub. He enthusiastically told Hollywood trade paper *Variety*: "It's a tremendous opportunity to work hand-in-hand with them. I've been presented a lot of development deals before and Jerry has taken us on as a production company, not me as an actor."

Headlines in Australian and US newspapers shouted about Mel's "Ten Million Dollar Deal". However, like most Hollywood deals, it was not quite what it appeared: $200,000 a year for developing projects, a salary of just $50,000 a year plus $150,000 a year to run an office. And most of that had to come from the budgets of any films that actually got made. The $10 million figure was simply a "projection" of what he could earn if all the company's projects actually went into production. In reality, they would be lucky if just one left the pitfalls-strewn runway . . .

As Pat Lovell agrees, ruefully: "It was not the richest deal in Hollywood history."

She also discovered the Sting; those notional millions of bucks were conditional on Mel starring in every single movie developed – exactly the opposite of what the actor had intended when launching himself as a serious producer.

The first instalment of money took four months coming through and Mel had to loan $6,000 of his own money to Pat to start up the office. Only a few months earlier she had remortgaged her own house just to keep her business running.

Pat was also concerned by Mel's condition at that time. He admitted he had been drinking beer and blacking out. His tapering-off during the family sabbatical was over.

(Interestingly, Mel's friend from his NIDA days, Linda Newton, recalled the actor doing exactly the same blacking out after consuming large amounts of beer during his three years in college.)

"He said he had been keeling over and had very low blood pressure. The whites of his eyes were yellow. I was quite worried about him," Pat Lovell recalled.

After a visit to a homoeopathic doctor in Sydney for treatment, Mel headed to Hollywood to star in *Lethal Weapon*. Lovell Gibson had not got off to an impressive start.

When Pat went to Los Angeles to discuss projects she had in development, she had to pay her own airfare and get it reimbursed by the company later. Pat was met at the airport by Robyn and whisked straight to their rented house in Beverly Hills. She found a completely different Mel Gibson from the exhausted man encountered in Sydney only a few months earlier.

"I did not recognise him when I saw him. He was tanned. His blue eyes were sparkling. The change in him was quite extraordinary. He looked absolutely glorious."

It emerged that Mel had been to a nutritionist in Los Angeles who had discovered he was suffering from a yeast deficiency illness, Candida.

"The yeast in beer was doing particular damage to him," says Pat, who insists that the strongest thing Mel ever drank in front of her was either a natural fruit cocktail or mineral water.

Mel had turned his back, it seemed, on late nights with a beer bottle for company. He announced his newest favourite drink was carrots, celery, raw beetroot, red capsicum, raw garlic and ginger, all combined and strained through a juice extractor.

"You drink a couple of pints a day and you have all this energy," he told Pat Lovell enthusiastically.

During a later trip to Hollywood in September 1987, Jerry Weintraub laid on a stretch limo to take Mel and Pat to numerous development meetings. The meetings were intended to introduce Mel and Pat to writers with interesting projects that might be worth pursuing.

Before each meeting Mel would hold a competition with Pat to see who could throw the most peanuts in the air and try to catch them in their mouths which was most disconcerting for the writers they met at that first gathering. Pat insisted that Mel was breaking the ice in Hollywood terms.

By this time, Robyn and the children had returned to Australia, leaving Mel staying alone at his apartment in Santa Monica. Unbeknown to Pat Lovell, he resumed drinking heavily and enjoyed at least one encounter with a woman during the trip. He was also driving around in a gleaming, very noticeable turquoise Thunderbird classic automobile.

Some of the more important meetings with writers were held in the famous deal-making arena of the Polo Lounge of the Beverly Hills Hotel. Mel renamed it the Polio

Lounge. But, despite all their efforts, not one real project could be found during that trip to LA. Mel's agent Ed Limato was hunting for a deal to be set up with Mel that would be far more lucrative. Warner Brothers, for example, were desperate to seal their relationship with the young star of their phenomenally successful *Lethal Weapon*.

Pat Lovell has an interesting opinion of Mel's ability to judge the quality of scripts.

"Mel could be very intelligent about the structure and character and all those things. He is a highly intelligent boy. But he did have a weak spot and would say something was fabulous when all it had was a good part for him. Often the rest of the script did not gel at all," recalled Pat.

Vague projects like an Aussie television mini-series called "My Brother Jack" surfaced at Lovell Gibson with Mel's old NIDA tutor George Whaley attached as director. Then there was talk of a so-called "high-class soap" called "Hot Air" but in the end that was all it turned out to be. Regular press releases to the trade papers gave the very clear impression that things were bubbling at Lovell Gibson; unfortunately the majority of projects did not get beyond the development stage.

However, in the back of Mel's mind was the notion that just so long as he eventually found the right sort of comedy vehicle, he could remain in Australia. His aim was to succeed *Crocodile Dundee* star Paul Hogan as the most successful (and richest) actor Down Under. *Crocodile* had just outstripped Mel's *Mad Max* series as Australia's most successful film ever. In the Sydney press, invented rivalry between the two men was being projected as some sort of movie duel.

And Mel, ignoring the reality, was still high on Lovell Gibson's promise. "I want to get familiar with the financial aspects. It's my weak spot, making deals. It's really been an eye-opener. I'll soon be able to understand my own contracts!"

He assured one journalist that he would definitely not direct any films "yet", admitting that he hoped to helm a movie in the foreseeable future. It would be another five years before he actually got to direct his own project.

Mel wasn't bluffing. He believed that his company could make "classy" films and television programmes. In fact, all the projects at Lovell Gibson had a distinctly un-American feel to them, and were all the less likely to tempt Hollywood-based Jerry Weintraub.

One of the more interesting projects to float up on all this hot air was a treatment about a petty villain with an absurdly hapless streak, "Tetley". The idea came from the pen of talented British writer Linda LaPlante, "an old mate" of Pat Lovell, well known in the UK for her television series "Widows".

Mel saw it as the perfect vehicle to expand his talents as a comedy star and catapult him above Paul Hogan, and when he summed up the character it sounded suspiciously like himself.

"He goes from bad to worse – and worse and worse. The man is always getting himself into sticky situations but this one is way out of his league. At the end he has to extricate himself from it."

As part of their development of "Tetley", Pat and Mel paid a very low-key visit to London just before the 1987 Cannes Film Festival. The couple stayed at writer LaPlante's home in Kingston, on the outskirts of London, giving Pat a rare glimpse of Mel off-duty and among friends. She noted that the actor who claims to do no physical exercise went on long jogs around nearby Richmond Park every morning as well as doing fifty lengths in the LaPlantes' pool, immediately after his run. Mel even taught the bubbly, attractive writer how to bake his favourite soda bread during the five-day stay.

Mel filmed the entire trip on a newly-acquired video camera that he turned on whenever he felt like shooting some embarrassing scene or other. Pat said there were times when he behaved like an overgrown schoolboy. For Mel it was a rare opportunity actually to sit with a writer and help develop characters and scenes – something that most actors crave without attaining.

Most nights Mel, Pat, Linda and her husband Richard ate out at modest local restaurants. On one occasion Mel and Linda went out alone to the theatre to see the play *Les Liaisons Dangeureuses*. Mel was delighted because his trip received absolutely no coverage in British newspapers.

Before going to England, Mel and Pat had both decided to go to the Cannes Film Festival mainly to help promote their company. They also wanted to try and get some major financial backing for "Tetley".

Pat Lovell remembers: "We arrived at the Carlton Hotel in Cannes and all hell broke loose. There were hundreds of screaming fans. *Lethal Weapon* was about to come out and Mel was immediately cornered in the foyer, signing autographs. In the end the manager had to escort him to his room."

Mel was also angry that he did not get a full sized suite at the hotel.

Pat went on: "He was upset he did not have a larger room. He said it wasn't comfortable and then I had to smuggle him out of the trade entrance every time we left the hotel because of the fans."

That first evening Pat and Mel went to a party for Paul Newman at a restaurant in the hills behind Cannes. They were seated at a table which included such film notables as British producer and short-lived Columbia studio chief David Puttnam and highly respected actor John Malkovich. Intriguingly, Mil rejected an offer of an introduction to Paul

Newman by his Tinseltown agent Ed Limato. Ultimately Malkovich, a renowned raconteur, entertained everyone by telling some very funny Hollywood stories, but Mel kept uncharacteristically quiet throughout the entire evening.

The next day, Mel was turned away from the British film industry's pavilion near the hotel, because he and Pat did not have tickets. It was the year of Prince Charles and Princess Diana's special dinner at the pavilion. Black market prices for tickets to that event were said to be upwards of $1,500. Demand for the 800 seats was so high that the organisers had deliberately avoided releasing the tickets until the day of the event, to foil forgeries.

A trip to the beach at Cap D'Antibe followed the next day, but Mel was getting increasingly restive and displeased. At a typical film industry ceremony for fifty movie stars to provide hand prints, he pressed his palm into wet cement at the beachfront event and photographers caught him yawning. It was a broad hint of what Mel thought of being there in the first place.

Also at Cannes that year, besides his agent Ed Limato was producer Weintraub, who chartered a yacht called the *Galu* at $30,000 a week to launch his own new company. Four days after arrival in the south of France, Mel took up Weintraub's offer to let him sleep aboard the yacht instead of that cramped, cheapo, only $300-a-night room in the Carlton Hotel.

"Mel was so much happier on that boat. He was in the lap of luxury and everyone was treating him well," comments Pat Lovell.

But Mel – who admits he cannot pack a suitcase properly – had managed to leave his passport and wallet behind when he checked out of the Carlton and headed for the Weintraub yacht in such a hurry.

"It was typical of Mel. He had not even noticed that the passport and wallet were missing," Pat sighed.

Mel's contentment on the yacht manifested itself in a series of incidents sparking memories of those drunken, hazy Hollywood days a few years earlier.

The morning after one particularly alcohol-deluged night, Pat Lovell appeared on the yacht for a meeting with Mel, to be greeted by a grim-faced Jerry Weintraub, who said: "I think you better go down and see your boy."

Pat gingerly opened the door to Mel's cabin to find the star suffering from "some sort of ailment" and swigging water from an Evian bottle.

"I had never seen anyone look as ill as he did," she says.

Mel asked Pat to put him on a plane back to Sydney that night. He wanted to get home to Robyn as quickly as possible. He needed to get away from the glitz.

Pat packed his bags and pushed him into a shower before taking him to the airport. There he discovered he had no cash on him so she gave him $100. It was never paid back. She even felt obliged to arrange for someone to meet him at London's Heathrow Airport, to make sure he caught the connecting flight to Sydney. Sometimes movie stars really do act like children.

"He was so desperate to see Robyn again after all that fuss at Cannes," said Pat.

Another person present on the yacht revealed that there was an altogether different reason for "the errant son" to leave town in such a hurry. Mel had rejected the advances of the wife of one of Hollywood's most powerful players during a party on the Weintraub yacht. Pat Lovell was not present at the time, but the other informant said that this woman forced herself on Mel and made it clear that she would make trouble for him with her very powerful husband if Mel did not slake her lust.

"To his credit, Mel totally rejected this woman," said the source.

"He was fed up with this woman coming on to him the whole time," added the source.

But Mel's rejection of the would-be bedmate sparked a furious exchange of words between the actor and that Hollywood executive. To make matters worse, another Hollywood executive was on board who had been one of Mel's fiercest defenders up until that time.

Yet more disapproval of the actor was voiced when he went off alone one evening to a party hosted by Britain's Monty Python crowd, on a neighbouring yacht. He followed this up with a visit to the biggest yacht in the harbour, where an Arab prince was hosting a cocktail party. No sooner had Mel got aboard than the prince's sister made an outrageous pass at him. Mel beat a hasty retreat and, armed with $3,000 in cash, moved on to a nearby casino where he proceeded to lose the lot at a roulette table.

Film industry writer Andrew Urban interviewed Mel on board Weintraub's yacht after his drinking, gambling and female encounters. He recalled for the first time some of the details about the interview that did not appear in the article he wrote at the time.

"It was eleven in the morning when I climbed aboard and someone was sent off to search for Mel. He eventually appeared with a good growth of stubble. He was very bleary-eyed and extremely hungover after drinking considerable amounts of Cognac at the casino. He proudly told me all about it," said Urban.

Mel even admitted to Urban: "I'm sorry, I'm completely out of it. Jesus, have you got some headache pills?"

Urban went on: "He looked pretty shocking and wasn't really in the mood to be interviewed about anything. The only thing I remember clearly about the actual interview, apart from his dreadful state, was that he was anxious to get involved in the other side of business; behind the cameras."

What surprised Urban was that Mel – barefoot in just jeans and a T-shirt – openly admitted he had lost "a lot of money" at the casino. "He also said how much he liked Cognac."

Urban's interview with the obviously still inebriated Mel only lasted thirty minutes although the Sydney-based writer says that the actor was in good spirits and obviously "on a hangover high" that morning. But he said the actor was "very deferential" to Pat Lovell, whom he looked on as a mother-figure.

Mel became increasingly obsessed with a role that he considered tailor-made – Captain Hook in Peter Pan. Weintraub had the rights to the classic J.M. Barrie work and Mel tried very hard to convince Weintraub that he was the man for the job.

But Weintraub eventually passed the project to Steven Spielberg and Mel's incredibly successful role in *Lethal Weapon* pushed Pan into the shadows. He was, by all accounts, positively heartbroken when the coveted Hook role went to Dustin Hoffman in the movie *Hook*, that eventually hit the screens in 1991.

Pat Lovell also said that Bruce Davey (later to become president of his production company and sole producer on some of his biggest grossing films) admitted he did not approve of the way she and Mel often argued, quite sharply, often enjoyably, with each other. Pat regarded it as part of the creative process and never took it personally until Davey warned: "I would be very careful. Mel hates being told he is in the wrong."

Then there was Ed Limato, Mel's Hollywood agent. He had recently moved to the giant ICM organisation and he was, naturally, anxious to keep Mel in Hollywood on a virtually permanent basis. One day Pat picked up a film industry magazine and read, to her surprise, that he had formed an LA based production company.

"I could sense that Mel was not happy. We were getting loads of no's on projects," recalled Pat. Even so, she was stunned to read that Mel had even appointed a development person at his company in Los Angeles.

"I was so relieved that it had come to an end. I was basically being buffeted by all these people who wanted a piece of him," said Pat.

At a meeting after the announcement, Mel took all phone calls in a next-door office, carefully shutting the door behind him as he went. Pat, close to tears, left the building. She never saw Mel again and was left to deal with Bruce Davey as lawyers tried to unravel their complicated business partnership.

She is not bitter about what happened with Mel because it gave her "an incredible insight into Hollywood".

But she says her biggest sadness has been caused by the end of their friendship. "It was more than just a working relationship. I miss Robyn and the children very much. She was such a sensible influence on him."

After months of negotiation with Davey to close Lovell Gibson, she received a cheque for one dollar as her share in the company. It was merely a legal formality as the company had been effectively worthless – no projects had actually been made. And to Pat it seemed a hilarious way to end a partnership.

Pat says that Bill Shannahan's death in 1990 marked the final cutting of Mel's umbilical cord with Australia and the people she believes truly cared for him.

"He was very truthful to Mel. Mel was very upset when Bill died. It was a turning-point for him."

Lovell Gibson officially folded with that low-key

announcement in the film industry trade papers on January 14, 1989.

In a carefully-worded statement, Pat Lovell told reporters: "Mel is a very fine actor with boundless potential so his acting career should take priority."

Behind the scenes, Pat's lawyer Michael Frankel dealt with Bruce Davey – who just three years earlier had been a run-of-the-mill accountant – on winding up Lovell Gibson.

Another friend described Bruce Davey as an "astute businessman who lives, breathes and eats for Mel".

The source said: "He got on well with the Warners people".

A few months later Mel was nothing if not philosophical about his experiences at Lovell Gibson.

"It's disappointing. I tried to get projects up in Australia, and it's impossible. So I decided I'd rather be rich, and I plan to have fun for a change."

"Being rich" meant that in Hollywood, Mel's LA-based company Icon Productions was already gearing itself up to start seriously developing big-budget vehicles for him. He had gradually come around to agreeing that if you can't beat 'em, join 'em.

Hollywood is a factory. You have to realise that you're working in a factory and you're part of the mechanism. If you break down, you'll be replaced.

14

Mel had just walked in from castrating a bull at his farm in the Kiewa Valley when the screenplay that would change his life arrived by courier from Los Angeles. He had spent eighteen months seriously reconsidering his entire future. He wondered if movies were worth all the emotional upheavals he had been through during the previous five years. He had already decided that unless the right sort of projects were offered he might as well stay on the farm with Robyn and the children. He had the resources to do it. Why get back under brutal pressure – and risk going off the rails again?

But within minutes of picking up that script – entitled *Lethal Weapon* – Mel recovered his appetite for work. He was hooked by the project, after the first five pages. It had action, humour and a leading character strikingly similar to Mel. In many ways it *was* Mel. The more he read, the surer he was that this was the movie to revive his career.

LA cop Martin Riggs: Vietnam vet, suicidal following

the death of his wife, on a fuse so short it would take a split-second to ignite – this was Mel's speed, all right. Riggs was merciless in his pursuit of the bad guys but able to weep at the memory of his dead wife. He was a hero given extra dimensions of pathos and tragedy.

Within days, Mel was bound for Los Angeles – a city he continually cursed and swore he would never live in, the city that was the key to his success whether he liked it or not. On arrival at LAX airport, Mel went straight to the impressive Hollywood Hills home of director Richard Donner, already attached to *Lethal Weapon*. A film-maker whose best-known project to date had been *Superman*, starring Christopher Reeve, Donner had been recommended to Gibson and Danny Glover as the unlikely pair of hero cops by casting director Marion Dougherty.

At Donner's house, Mel was introduced to Glover. Contrary to popular opinion, the two stars had a few creative problems to begin with. They came from completely different schools of acting.

Glover – the quietly-spoken, San Francisco-born one-time economics student – had not even decided to become an actor until he was 30. He also had a partial affliction from the learning disability dyslexia. But once the decision had been made he threw himself into studying every aspect of the art and a steady stream of very respectable movie roles followed. Now – fresh from his success as Mister in *The Color Purple* – he was being offered a buddy-buddy role in a cop film.

But Glover saw the role slightly differently.

"I jumped at the chance to play the intricate relationships and subtle humour that exist in every close family group. It was an intriguing challenge," he said.

Glover was a Method actor and for Mel that took getting used to. Glover's movement classes at acting school ran parallel to his reading and study. Among his books was one on the life and work of Konstantin Stanislavsky, the guru of Method actors such as Marlon Brando, James Dean and Rod Steiger. Glover was a product of exact, meticulous training – the opposite of Mel, who tactfully commented on such Methodical American actors thus:

"I find that each one has their own, totally different way of getting into what they do. It's sort of a hard sell – sort of get yourself up to a higher pitch and be really positive. Australians, I think, do tend to come underneath that a bit."

Mel believed firmly that "the only way to get there is to be relaxed and happy. There can't be a conflicting attitude that's in there already for me. Otherwise you have to rip that down and just be open and accessible and be an instrument."

He also confided to one associate that he believed he could "fake it" if necessary – something that purists like Danny Glover wince at hearing.

"I think it is possible to fake it – to go into something you don't know about and get away with it – provided you do your groundwork."

Mel has acknowledged, privately, that he and Glover did not hit it off immediately. It was to be a gradually improving relationship that reached the height of familiarity only in the *Lethal Weapon* sequels. And it wasn't helped by Mel's honesty about his attitudes towards Method acting.

"Some actors – Method actors – remain as the person they are playing during the whole working day. For me, the Method is to get away from it. If you're enjoying yourself, even showing grief, then it comes across better in acting."

Yet Mel – with his background on the stage – could be fairly impressive in a rehearsal situation.

"One of the first things about Mel is the visual thing. I also liked the way he spoke. He was very good at dialogue. His delivery was good and very comfortable. He spoke trippingly off the tongue, much more than most Americans, who cannot get their mouth wrapped around a lot of dialogue," enthused actor John Philip Law, who starred with Mel in the earlier *Attack Force Z*.

Although Donner knew after a couple of hours of rehearsal at his house that Mel and Glover were perfect for the key roles, he also knew that their professional conflicts might send either of them over the edge at any time.

Director Donner had been harbouring exactly those types of fears – about Mel rather than Danny Glover.

"I was expecting to have problems with him. I thought he was going to be a Method actor, somebody who wanted to know where everything came from and why. But give him one word and he runs with it. Half the time he doesn't even need that."

But this was a different Mel. He was refreshed and invigorated by his lay-off. He had a new appetite for work and he believed that *Lethal Weapon* was going to be "something very special". He had also just celebrated his thirtieth birthday. It was time to consolidate his considerable gains, take a grip of his responsibilities.

"I noticed that things aren't what they used to be; after that third decade you've got to be careful," he mused on the set of *Lethal Weapon*.

Robyn and the children settled into a rented home in Beverly Hills within days of Mel signing contracts with Warner Brothers – his fee was a very healthy $1.2 million. His human sheet-anchor mattered more, though.

During the preparations for *Lethal Weapon*, Mel and Danny Glover wanted to get the feel of what it was really like to be LA cops by going out on patrol with the real thing. The naked truth about being a police officer in a crime-riddled city is that it is a tough, dangerous and exhausting profession in which you go to work every day wondering if this could be the last day of your life.

"It's hard to imagine what it's like to be a policeman until you find yourself in that situation," said Mel. "You feel very vulnerable. I was never involved in anything big. They obviously weren't going to throw me into the middle of a hotspot in LA. But it's just your whole perception – and your imagination starts to get to you. You even start to look at little old ladies walking along the street in a different way.

"You can see why these guys are wired up and ready for action all the time. You can also see why they have a lot of problems in the police force. There are many marriage break-ups, a high suicide rate. I gained a lot of respect for them . . . I'd hate to do it. It must be terribly hard and you don't get many rewards for it."

Despite initial problems over Method acting, Mel and Danny Glover forged a partnership that had all the ingredients for a buddy-buddy cop movie, which is exactly what they turned it into. Early difficulties were perfectly reflected in the way that Glover's structured, uptight character in the film starts by completely mistrusting Mel's wilder figure, Riggs. Once again real life had spilled over on to celluloid and provided Donner with the love-hate chemistry he sought.

Mel granted that the character he was playing was "fairly unbalanced. Now I'm not as unbalanced as him. I would not try and shoot myself. I would not jump off buildings." But . . .

His intensive martial arts training before shooting began, and the very physical aspects of the character he was playing, menaced his life at one stage during filming. For it is little known that by shooting ten, sometimes twenty takes on difficult chase sequences, the actor – still smoking two packs of Marlboro a day – was running up to ten miles daily. Once he was so exhausted that he collapsed on the set and had to be given oxygen. Paranoid studio executives ordered a cover-up of the incident, fearful that any shadow over Mel's health might seriously affect the image of the movie – which was about a super-fit ex-soldier, after all. From that moment on, Mel sustained his high-energy antics by being administered oxygen between most takes.

Just a few months earlier, he had visited an iridologist in Sydney who had told him to stop ingesting certain meats and beer and too much coffee. He lost twenty pounds and began yet another new lease of life.

Mel was convinced the appeal of *Lethal Weapon* lay in the relationship between the cops played by him and Glover.

"This thing is going to work simply because it has a strong basis, a strong foundation. You are going to care about all the action because you care about the characters, that's what I like about the script – those two guys are great," he explained enthusiastically.

According to cast and crew on the first *Lethal Weapon*, it was an exhilarating, happy shoot – something which Mel had rarely experienced in his previous movie outings. It was also reflected in Mel's willingness to expand his character of Marty Riggs. He wanted to put a personal stamp on the role and director Donner was more than happy to permit that.

In fact, Donner recognises that Mel rapidly became more than just another actor doing a job of work. He found the star prepared to add nuances to his character that were not even touched upon in the script. It was something which can mean the difference between a satisfactory performance and one that lights up the screen. Mel added little touches of humour here and there, but it was the movie's most emotional scene that probably did more for his career than any other sequence.

A despondent Riggs decides to end it all, puts his police

revolver in his mouth and starts to squeeze the trigger. It was a familiar set-up, repeated many times over on the big screen. But Mel decided to take it one stage further, with literally dramatic results, as Donner confirms.

"Because the scene was so intense, and shot under extremely difficult, cramped conditions inside a trailer van, only the camera operator was in there with Mel as he went through his paces. I checked the revolver myself before it was handed to him by the unit's official armourer."

Even a blank would inflict terrible damage if it went off when the barrel was near the mouth (wadding from a blank killed actors Jon Erik Hexum and Brandon Lee in separate incidents on movie sets in recent years).

Mel gripped the pistol tightly and rammed the muzzle into his mouth. Donner and his crew gasped. This was definitely not in the script.

"I watched the scene on a video monitor outside the van. I watched . . . I couldn't believe what Mel was doing. It was so real. I thought, hell, he might have put a shell in the gun . . . things rushed through my head. Did Mel ask the armourer or special effects guy to 'put one in there to give me motivation'? I tell you, I was terrified as Mel started to choke on the barrel, his finger tightening on the trigger. I was torn between rushing in and stopping the scene in case there was a shell in the gun and getting this amazing performance. I was glued to watching the video screen. The crew was spellbound. A couple of girls were choking, beginning to cry behind me.

"I figured we had what we wanted and was about to call Cut into the radio mike that went to the cameraman's earphones. But Mel kept it going, adding a final few tears of frustration and mental anguish as he wept, apologising to a photo of his dead wife. I can tell you I breathed out loud when he stopped the performance and I called a meek Cut to the operator.

"I rushed into the van and hugged Mel. Told him it was great, fantastic. He looked around, shook his head. 'Want to try another one, for safety?' he said to me quite innocently, wiping a real tear from his eye.

"I gave him another hug and said, 'You were perfect, the film gate is clear. We've got it.'

"I could never have gone through that again. But Mel would have done it again, gladly. When I saw the scene intact as part of the finished film it still took my breath away. My hair stood on end. This sort of thing rarely happens. With Mel I guess anything is possible. He's one of the greats and he seems to be cruising most of the time."

What Donner failed to mention is that after that sequence Mel sat down, blew his nose, took a breath, reached into his pocket – and pulled out a red clown's nose and put it on . . .

When the actual gun-in-the-mouth scene appeared during screenings of the movie in cinemas, voices would erupt from the audience: "No, don't . . . don't do it."

One person who saw that scene and was deeply moved by it was eminent Italian director Franco Zeffirelli. He made a mental note to approach the actor about a special project he had been trying to get off the ground for years.

"It was a scene in which he has a kind of 'to be or not to be' speech with a gun. But he's not able to pull the trigger. When I saw that I said: 'This is Hamlet. This boy is Hamlet!'"

The essence of Lethal Weapon is that it is a violent film and there can be little doubt that Marty Riggs is a violent character. As his partner Roger Murtaugh (Danny Glover) asks: "Have you ever met anyone you haven't killed?"

Mel later explained that this underlying current of violence was one of the main reasons for injecting his own throw-away lines into the dialogue.

"I wanted to give the character a bit of life. I thought that to give a man who was in so much pain a bit of light relief would be interesting. I got that idea from a Shakespearean play," he explained.

At the time, this injection of humour was revolutionary because the characters Mel had portrayed up until that point tended to be stern, distinctly unfunny people like Mad Max or Fletcher Christian.

But, as Mel's confidence grew during the making of *Lethal Weapon*, so did his comedic talents. Eventually those awful one-liners and constant bad jokes became his stock in trade.

"He could have been a Marx brother, there's something undeniably zany about the man," says Robert Towne, who later directed Mel in *Tequila Sunrise*. "Beneath the romantic exterior, there is this preposterous farceur longing to get out."

Richard Donner had a slightly different take on Mel's humour level. "He is God's gift to a director. But he tells the worst jokes in the world."

A higher opinion is held by *Living Dangerously* co-star Sigourney Weaver: "He can sing and dance and he's all over the place, and he's very funny. Mel is all the Three Stooges rolled into one."

Certainly he has confessed to enjoying "horsing around".

"I figure if you have to work for a living, you might as well make fun of it. What I do certainly isn't a cure for cancer. And one of the best things about this job is that you can enjoy yourself at it almost all the time."

The "new" Mel had secretly got himself into shape before *Lethal Weapon* began by lifting weights in preparation for those martial arts. It was a fascinating about-turn in his attitude towards keeping fit. Previously, his most strenuous exercise had been lifting babies. He kept his painstaking fitness routine out of the public eye because it worried him that his fans might think he had completely abandoned all those Hollywood-won't-get-me statements from earlier in his career.

But Mel needed no telling that *Lethal Weapon* was his biggest and best movie opportunity to date and he did not intend to blow it. He was only too well aware that if the project had landed on his lap two years earlier then he might well never have coped with it because of the disarray of his life then.

Yet probably the most significant evidence of the change in him came when two young fans approached him for an autograph on the set of *Lethal Weapon*. The old Mel would have gruffly refused to oblige. The new version smiled warmly and wrote: "*To Michelle and Karen – Mel.*" Then, pondering for a minute, he inserted the word "*love*" as if afraid to seem cold, but reluctant to appear too demonstrative.

Lethal Weapon represented another important first for Mel. It was the first time he had actually based himself in Los Angeles, instead of flying in for two- or three-week bursts of meetings. It had a profound effect on the actor; his attitude towards Hollywood as a place, if not its society, began to soften.

"You see when I first went there you'd go over and you'd talk to guys in studios about deals and you'd feel uncomfortable because you didn't know how the place worked, you were somewhere else and you'd get a very slanted idea of it. You'd be staying at a hotel somewhere in Beverly Hills and you'd have these kind of 'dying to meet you' lunches.

"It's not a natural sort of environment at all, so that you can get very sort of uptight and you can find it repulsive, you know you want to get away from it. But when I was there to work and do a job it was a total joy. I really enjoyed it. I lived there, I got up in the morning, I went to work, came home, had dinner, it was . . . you know, fantastic."

With Mel's agent Ed Limato constantly reminding him that it was impractical to live anywhere else but Los Angeles, Mel conceded that he might have to end up eating all those angry, bitter words about Tinseltown . . .

His fitness became a vital factor in the original *Lethal Weapon*, especially the climactic scene in which he ends up in a life-or-death struggle with the villain, played by Gary Busey, on the front lawn of partner Roger Murtaugh's house.

"Yeah. That was a hell of a scene," said Mel afterwards. "Water pouring from a burst main, hovering helicopter with its blinding light, cop cars and uniformed cops everywhere, chanting for Riggs to 'kill the bastard'. When we finished the scene, after four days of being so wet, I could feel every sore bone in my body. It was like I'd been run over by a bus. But when I watched the rushes the next night I knew it would all come together as a great final piece. I felt it was all worth it, even though the bones still creak."

The most extraordinary thing about the first *Lethal Weapon* movie was that it had no romantic interest. In fact, as Australian film critic Scott Murray pointed out:

"It was all about the relationship between Mel and Danny's characters. There is such a fusion between them despite the fact they came from two completely different schools of acting. It is almost a love story between them."

Before shooting was completed, Warner Brothers executives had decided that a sequel had to be made. There was a constant buzz on the set that "this is going to be a big one". The first *Lethal Weapon* eventually grossed around $120 million world-wide, making Mel Gibson what everyone had been expecting – a box office star who could write his own ticket. He even started taking Robyn out in Tinseltown, to movie premieres like the new Bette Midler/Danny DeVito comedy *Ruthless People*. The town he said he would never become a part of was starting to suck him in.

'Going Hollywood' is an insidious malady, and industry cynics sneer that it melts the toughest armour, eventually.

Mel's relationship with Donner was so good that the director allowed him time off a tight shooting schedule to tape the presentation of the best director award for the Australian Film Institute. Mel recorded all four nominees, separately, as the winner so that the correct contender could be announced on the day of the ceremony. By a pleasant chance, Mel did his taping on the Hollywood Boulevard Walk of Fame star for Tasmania's Errol Flynn, the only Australian to make any real impact in movieland.

Critics in the US did not really know what to make of *Lethal Weapon*.

But in Mel's adopted homeland of Australia there was no such confusion about it.

"Gibson clearly relishes a role that gives him a chance to show that he's more than just a pretty face," wrote Bev Tivey in the *Sydney Telegraph* in June, 1987.

And in the *Sydney Sun*, critic Peter Holder wrote: "Mel proves once and for all he is an accomplished actor first, with the 'sex-symbol' tag running second."

However, controversy erupted in August 1987, when the movie was released in Britain just after the tragic massacre of sixteen people by a gun-toting man in the quiet Berkshire town of Hungerford. The movie – with its virtually non-stop depiction of trigger-happy cops and robbers – was withdrawn from a cinema near the scene of the killings. A local vicar attacked a London newspaper for carrying a full-page colour photograph of Mel pointing a gun, in the same issue that reported church services mourning the victims of the massacre the previous week.

Just after the release of *Lethal Weapon*, Robyn weighed in with her own production, giving birth to the couple's fifth child – a boy called Louis. Hollywood noted with glee that

Mel was proving very different from their traditional multi-divorced megastars.

Mel had so enjoyed the happy-families atmosphere of the first *Lethal Weapon* that he was delighted to make a sequel less than eighteen months later. Hollywood was much more surprised by director Donner's decision to take charge of it. He had never before agreed to direct a sequel, despite the fact that five of his previous films had been turned into series.

The sequel proved an even bigger money-spinner than the original – which is virtually unheard-of in Hollywood – by grossing $147 million in the US alone. Marty Riggs was on his way to becoming one of the biggest-earning creations in movie history.

"It was Donner and the boys again. There's a great sense of freedom on these sets with this crew and it's pretty familiar territory, so it's easy to just step into it and feel free to experiment and push it to the edge," is Mel's tribute. He'd been pleased to settle Robyn and the children in another rented house, this time in Malibu, for the duration of the shoot (its $23,000-a-month rent was picked up by Warner Brothers).

Lethal Weapon's original creator – a shy ex-film school student, Shane Black – refused to help write a sequel because he felt he had taken the characters as far as he could. Donner turned to writer Jeffrey Boam for some new ideas. He came up with a ludicrous plot concerning evil South African diplomats running a drug cartel which predictably sparked mild outrage from non-fiction South African officials, who claimed the film was yet another sample of "the villainisation of South Africa in films".

But this time, the film had a definite love interest in the shape of young British star Patsy Kensit. It looked like a match made in heaven, to the British tabloids, determined to create a romance between Mel and his blonde, 21-year-old co-star. But her presence was much more significant for Detective Marty

Riggs. Jeffrey Boam had – by introducing love interest – changed the perceptions of *Lethal Weapon* and in the process set up the formula for the series. Sexuality had been virtually non-existent as far as Riggs was concerned in the first *Weapon*.

Mel reacted to this new situation with a measure of reluctant pleasure. His character had to have romantic touches if the *Weapon* series was to remain fresh and appealing. It also enabled Mel to add another dimension to the role.

And Patsy Kensit – herself only recently married (and only a year off divorce) – proved the perfect female lead. Though she confirmed coyly that her passionate love scenes with Mel were not the real thing.

"We are both married, both Catholics, so it was a little weird. He was as uncomfortable as I was, but he was a real gentleman about it. He was very delicate."

During the kissing scene, impish Kensit said she mouthed the word "vomit" to her handsome co-star. He in turn told her dirty jokes. Their most physical moment was, according to the blonde actress, "when I had cold feet and warmed them up on him. But apart from that, I just lay there with my legs open . . . " (Maybe she ought to have rephrased that, but it guaranteed attention!)

The rest of the time on set, Mel kept up a constant stream of antics and gags, entertaining anyone who happened to be within earshot.

He would appear wearing a coffee filter on his head like a Jewish yarmulke. He bellowed never-ending renditions of "Edelweiss" from *The Sound of Music*. And he had the set in stitches as he would criticise himself out loud: "What! Oh, no, you're terrible. Gibson! Lighten up. Stop twitching."

Director Richard Donner explained: "He's crazy. He lives on the edge, full of energy and excitement. If Hollywood was still doing drugs, I'd say Mel was taking lots of drugs; but the truth is that he is crazy naturally."

That led to the oddest scene in the entire movie, when Danny Glover's character is sitting on the toilet and discovers it is rigged to explode, so he cannot leave the throne. The whole sequence was created the day before, much of it by a very amused Mel who thought "it would be a gas" to have his partner "stuck on the john with his trousers round his ankles".

Critics were just as bemused as before, afraid to condemn the film completely but remaining patronising.

"It's a potentially interesting film, but it leaves a bad taste in the mouth because it pretends to treat us as a mature audience capable of judging difficult moral dilemmas while leaving little doubt that Gibson's line is the one we are supposed to agree with," wrote Lynden Barber in the *Sydney Morning Herald*. "This is the eighties, is the message. No-one cares any more. Help yourself."

But the authoritative *New York Times* positively glowed in its praise. "Gibson, Donner and Glover have concocted the best action-buddy-comedy formula since *Butch Cassidy and the Sundance Kid*."

After it was released, Mel announced he would never make another *Lethal Weapon* film. His commitment to the sequel had meant having to turn down the lead role in *The Untouchables* – a part which springboarded the lesser-known Kevin Costner to even greater fame and fortune than Mel.

In any case, he was excited by the prospect of playing opposite a young actress dominating Hollywood's female marketplace – Julia Roberts. The two were slated to star together in *Renegades*, a western told from the woman's point of view. Mel's first meeting with the still shy (and very young) Roberts occurred at Hollywood agents' ICM, in Beverly Hills. He and the actress exchanged few words but Hollywood remained convinced that they would make a lethal box office combination. Mel, on the other hand, thought otherwise.

Without any explanation he pulled out of *Renegades* within days of that meeting.

It took just one phone call to his farm, where he had immediately retreated, from larger-than-life Hollywood producer Joel Silver to get Mel to change his mind about making *Lethal Weapon 3*.

In this film, Murtagh is seven days away from retirement when the pair investigate the disappearance of firearms from a police lock-up, finding a trail leading to a crooked cop.

Trying to do their job despite interference from a beautiful martial-arts-trained Internal Affairs detective played by Rene Russo, and the egregious informer, Leo Getz (Joe Pesci), still keen as ever to play amateur cop, Mel and Danny take their audience on yet another action-packed adventure, considered by many critics to be vastly superior to its predecessor's plodding, unbelievably plotted progress.

Pesci and Mel became good pals on and off the set. Mel had lobbied hard for Pesci to return in the role he played in *Lethal Weapon 2*. Just after release of the third film, the two actors narrowly avoided being victims of a punch-up in the Hollywood nightclub Roxbury's, following some pushing and shoving involving a dozen well-built weight-lifter types.

After three *Lethal Weapons*, even Mel admitted that there were a few flaws in the movies. A rumoured $10 million fee probably helped allay any creative fears he might have had about the latest instalment.

"I'm the first to admit the plot's got huge holes in it, you know. But it's interesting to watch. It's full of humour and warmth and it talks about things that maybe in society need talking about – like the firearms issue or little jabs here and there about cruelty to animals, or save the whales, or something."

Interestingly, Mel persuaded Donner to let him repeat his dogfood-eating antics from *Mad Max II*. (He also did the same thing when he visited the home of three young college students in Modesto, California.)

There were rumours that Robyn was concerned that Mel was taking too many risks by doing many of his own stunts. One source even claimed that Mel had been told to "go away" by his wife and think about his actions and not come back to his family until he had agreed to stop taking such risks.

She had never forgotten how Mel's hyperactivity on the set of *Lethal Weapon 2* nearly cost him his life, when a stunt went horribly wrong. The actor had insisted he could handle a sequence where he was tied up in a sack and dumped in a water tank. In theory he was supposed to unravel the rope with ease and come to the surface. But Mel stayed under the water for a dangerously long period. Professional stunt divers were poised to plunge in to the tank and rescue him when he finally emerged.

"His cheeks had ballooned up and his eyes were popping out of his skull. We thought he was goner," said one shaken member of the crew.

Obviously well aware of the concern, Mel looked at all the anguished faces, smiled and moved on to the next scene as if nothing had happened.

All the *Lethal Weapon* films did get a lot of criticism for their high violence quota. However, Mel – who sees the series as being comic-strip-comes-to-life – defended them stoutly at a press conference just before release of *Lethal Weapon 3*.

"It drives me nuts when people say it's violent and offensive and going to scar people's minds. It's entertainment. There are a lot of problems in society and they like to lay blame on things like this. But I don't think that's fair. If there is anything harmful in a movie, it's wrong. But who's going to be a judge of that? In my case, it's me."

When the film was released just after the LA riots erupted – the worst civil unrest in US history – he refuted suggestions that his movie might incite more violence by saying: "What happened in Los Angeles is lamentable. But I don't think a film like this threatens to incite anything. When John Wayne got hit on the head with a shovel in *Legend of the Lost* in 1957, I can't recall a rash of shovel-hittings."

But Mel is nothing if not inconsistent. In an interview with *Cleo* magazine in Australia, he admitted: "I loved violence in films as a kid, especially when you realise it's not really happening. It depends on how it's put out. Every cartoon I saw as a kid had cats and dogs blowing each other up and shooting each other – hilarious fun. Knowing that violence exists is a necessary part of your education."

(Mel did later insist that he would never let his own children watch the *Lethal Weapon* films.)

The media continued heavily to criticise violent aspects of all three films. The *Sydney Telegraph Mirror* even went so far as to publish a tally of comparative totals for everything from car wrecks to killings in the *Lethal Weapon* series:

Numbers of cars wrecked: 7, 14, 5
Number of people killed: 24, 29, 16
Number of explosions: 3, 7, 4

Interestingly, there had been a definite effort to cut down on mayhem in the third instalment, but by then perhaps it was too late.

In an effort to defuse the criticism, Warner Brothers gave proceeds from the first few Hollywood screenings to help the victims of those same LA riots that tore the city apart in the final days of April, 1992.

Prophetically, in one interview to help publicise *Lethal Weapon 3*, Mel compared the phenomenally successful series with that supposedly dying breed of movie – the western. Just a few months later he was persuaded by director Donner to play the lead in a western that, if successful, could once again alter the course of his career.

Mel with Goldie Hawn, his co-star in *Bird On A Wire*.

Top: Mel and *Mad Max III* co-star, Tina Turner.

Below: Mad Max Mel in a scene with young road warrior co-star, Emil Minty, whom some critics said stole the film from Mel.

Top: Mel with *Mad Max I* co-star Joanne Samuel.
Below: Mel with *Living Dangerously* co-star Sigourney Weaver.

Top: Mel's British friend, Miranda Brewin, who enjoyed bar hopping with the actor in Sydney's red light district.

Below left: The drinking club where Miranda Brewin first met Mel.

Below right: The late night bar in Sydney that Mel and Miranda stumbled out of in the early hours.

Mel in a typical pose from *Lethal Weapon*.

Top: Mel with *Lethal Weapon II* co-star Patsy Kensit, whom many newspapers tried – without success – to link romantically with Mel.

Below left: The apartment block in Santa Monica, California, where Mel entertained his friend, Cassandra Kirton.

Below right: Cassandra Kirton, the Los Angeles based British girl who enjoyed a candle-lit meal with Mel.

Mel with *Lethal Weapon* co-star Danny Glover, whose
relationship with the star only improved after they resolved their
acting differences.

Top and Inset: Mel's empty chair during this production photo on *Air America* reminded the film's producers of how upset he was over missing the birth of one of his children.

Below: Mel, complete with receding hairline, on *Air America*.

Top: Mel in action during *Air America*.

Below left: Thai wardrobe girl Micky Bacon, who fended off prostitutes during the filming of *Air America*.

Below right: Thai wardrobe girl Juh, who also helped protect Mel from numerous prostitutes who tried to tout for business with the star during the making of *Air America* in Thailand.

Top: Mel with Oscar winning co-star, Sissy Spacek, filming *The River*.

Below: Mel appears the same height as six foot *Living Dangerously* co-star Sigourney Weaver, but he was actually wearing specially built shoes to give him extra height for the entire film.

Top: Michelle Pfeiffer stood between Kurt Russell and Mel in every sense of the word during their appearance together in *Tequila Sunrise*.

Below: Mel with probably his most unusual co-star, actress Linda Hunt who portrayed a Chinese photographer in *Living Dangerously* and went on to win an Oscar for her performance.

Mel with Diana Keaton on *Mrs. Soffel*.

Mel, in a rare public appearance with wife Robyn at a film premiere.

Top: Mel and British *Hamlet* co-star, Helen Bonham-Carter, who created a stir with her very personal remarks about Mel.

Below: Mel and *Hamlet* co-star, Glenn Close, during one of the film's many highly emotional scenes.

Mel's ultimate role as *Hamlet*.

Mel made his dream come true by playing a cowboy in his latest film, *Maverick*.

True to form, reviews for *Lethal Weapon 3* were just as mixed as for the previous two films.

Hollywood's *Entertainment Weekly* magazine claimed: "*Lethal Weapon 3* is like a pile of odds and ends that never made it into the first two movies. It zips around without any true forward momentum."

And the *New York Times* could have spotted a recurring theme in Mel's life when their critic wrote: "Gibson looks tired – and has every right to. The movie isn't going anywhere but it goes in circles at top speed." But the *Hollywood Reporter* said that Mel's performance was "a bullseye".

Lethal Weapon 3 – which cost $40 million to make – grossed more than $300 million world-wide during the summer and autumn of 1992. Yet again, it outdid its predecessor, just as that movie did better than the original. Warner Brothers were so happy they presented Mel, Danny Glover, Richard Donner and Joel Silver with brand-new four-wheel-drive Range Rovers as a token of appreciation. Silver immediately commissioned *two* separate writing teams to prepare *Lethal Weapon 4* screenplays at a cost of more than a million dollars, despite the fact that neither star was prepared to commit to another sequel.

Mel's company produced a Home Box Office documentary for TV, on the making of *Lethal Weapon 3*, with the actor playing host and singing a dreadfully out-of-tune version of "King of the Road". At one stage he takes on his favourite Three Stooges guise and proclaims: "You know human nature is a very telling thing and you can tell a lot about a man or a woman by the tone of their voice." Just then the entire crew joins in yet another chorus of "King of the Road" before Mel signs off by talking about "putting my feet up, counting the money. Hope you had fun." Another way of saying it was time to take his next break.

Having completed *Lethal Weapon 3*, both Mel and Danny

Glover agreed that it was getting hard to keep up enthusiasm for the series. Ironcially, the third film marked was the first time Danny Glover had truly sat down and talked on a proper personal level with Mel.

On the Arsenio Hall show on US television in May, 1993, co-star Glover made it absolutely clear that he had no wish to make a fourth film. "It's time for us all to go on to other things," he told Hall. It remains to be seen whether money will once again speak louder than words.

If I've still got my pants on in the second scene, I think they've sent me the wrong script.

15

After the incredible $30 million plus opening weekend at the US box office for *Lethal Weapon 3*, rumours swept Hollywood that Mel was paid an extra $5 million to bare that famous bottom in the movie. Industry experts estimated that the sight of the actor's rear would automatically add $20 million to overall takings of any film.

He made light of the tales with: "I haven't got anything that no one else has."

But the truth was that every time he showed his naked backside, women wanted him to turn around and then went home from the movie and told all their friends what wonderful shape Mel was in.

Although he doesn't like to admit it, he bared all (very briefly) during a mooning scene in his first film *Summer City*. That should have provided him with a taste of what was to come. Then there was a brief glimpse of that famous rear in *Gallipoli*. A four-year hiatus followed. Mel's bottom came back with a vengeance, as it were, in the original *Lethal Weapon* – and it has rarely looked back since!

Initially, Mel's family were "very concerned" about the embarrassment caused by his nude scenes, but when he continued to do them if they were part of the story, they reluctantly approved.

He is also well aware of the financial value of his best-known asset, not counting those eyes.

One Hollywood producer said: "You've heard of the $6 million man? Well, this is the $20 million bottom!"

There is a nudity clause in every movie contract Mel signs, and though $20 million may be nonsense, his fee does increase if there is a scene in which he shows a lot of skin.

"People want you to take your clothes off," says Mel with feigned bewilderment. He even sneaked into a movie theatre one night to see *Lethal Weapon* only to flee by the back exit in embarrassment when that famous nude scene flashed on the screen.

Hollywood gossip had it that an indignant Mel refused to strip for any of his naked scenes – and that a lookalike bottom was used on each occasion. That is patently untrue. He confessed to one producer that he was surprised by the sight of his bottom on the screen because "my bum's got a fair carpet. I didn't realise I was so furry on my back end."

And in August 1992, American magazine *Women on Top* even went so far as to claim that Mel had bared his bottom more times than any other Hollywood star.

In *Bird on a Wire*, a comedy in which he starred with Goldie Hawn, he even had a bullet sliced out of his rear by a beautiful vet. And by the time his slushy romantic comedy *Forever Young* hit the screen in late 1992, Mel's naked rear caused nothing more than a ripple of excitement, after his earlier stripteases.

But there is absolutely no question of upping the ante, by

trying full-frontal nudity in the future. "He draws the line at that for the sake of his family and his pride!" said one Hollywood associate.

Proof of this came when he refused point blank to strip naked for a centrefold in the Australian women's magazine *Cleo*. Irritated by the star's decision, the magazine brazenly ran a composite photo of Mel's head on the 1972 photo of fellow Aussie actor Jack Thompson. The shot outraged Mel's Sydney agents and they immediately posted a rebuke to the editor of *Cleo*, who gleefully reproduced the rather pompous letter in its following issue. The letter's style was Victorian.

"Every person, whether in the public eye or not, has a right to be represented with a minimum degree of fairness and dignity," it droned. Shannahan Mangement refused to confirm if they had acted on a direct complaint from Mel.

Interestingly, Mel's chief rival for the Hollywood heart-throb title, Kevin Costner, got on to much the same bandwagon in the early Nineties. Hollywood could not fail to notice his pants coming off much easier than his shirt in films like *Revenge*, *Dances with Wolves* and *Robin Hood: Prince of Thieves*. The box office pull of a male star's bare buttocks is now unquestioned.

However Mel's continual exposure in movies did foster another line of thought among more cynical members of the Hollywood establishment – that this very heterosexual star was unintentionally attracting a large number of gay men to his films.

"It seems ironic but this certainly appears to be the situation in some of the bigger US cities like New York and Los Angeles," said one well-known Hollywood producer.

The irony cannot be lost on members of US gay groups such as Queer Nation, which selected Mel as its *bête noire* of the season after he made a number of controversial comments to the Spanish magazine *El Pais* in December 1991.

In the article, Mel said that when he first took up acting he assumed many people would think he was gay.

"When you are an actor they stick a label on you. I went from playing rugby one day to taking dance classes in black leotards the next. Many of the girls I met in school took it for granted that I was gay," he told journalist Koro Castellano.

"But I did it. I became an actor despite that. But with this look, who's going to think I am gay? It would be hard to take me for someone like that.

"Do I look homosexual? Do I talk like them? Do I move like them?" he was reported as saying before going into a graphic description of sexual activity which included getting up from his chair, bending over, pointing to his posterior and saying it was for use only in the smallest room in the house. Those gestures were described as being "crude and disgusting".

The comments caused an outcry across the US and *The Advocate*, a gay and lesbian weekly newspaper, took waspish revenge by naming him Sissy of the Year, in its annual Sissy Awards for allegedly homophobic, anti-gay actions. They had been looking for ammunition to fire at Mel ever since his "mincing portrayal" of a supposedly effeminate hairdresser in *Bird on a Wire* had enraged many members.

A spokesman for the powerful Gay and Lesbian Alliance Against Defamation (GLAAD), the media organisation that "watchdogs" the press for derogatory remarks about gays, said: "If Mel Gibson has such deep religious views, he should be using his status to educate and not to spread hate. There are many people of deeply religious views who certainly are very tolerant of gay people and who don't find it necessary to insult or degrade. Mr Gibson seems to be hung up on some stereotype of how gay men are supposed to look or behave. If, as he says, he knew gay people in drama school, then he would know that there is no particular way in which gay men look or behave."

(Mel's remarks haunted him, even as recently as August, 1993, when gay protesters tried to prevent him becoming the 158th star to set his handprints in concrete on Hollywood Boulevard's famous walk of fame. He ignored dozens of placards to go ahead with the ceremony, but was clearly shaken by the continued controversy.)

Even top US syndicated columnist Liz Smith joined in the row shortly after the Spanish interview occurred by snapping that "Mel Gibson lives in the dark ages".

Refusing to reprint any tangy excerpts from his original "bigoted" interview, she said: "Mel Gibson is so divine on the screen, it is awful to discover he thinks this way. I find his remarks astounding."

Privately, Mel was stunned by the reaction to what he considered perfectly reasonable comments. After all, he had never hidden his feelings about homosexuals, even back in the days when he was at drama school.

Nearly a year earlier in an off-the-cuff remark to Australian journalist Matt White, Mel referred to homosexuals as "faggots" without causing so much as a flurry of reproof.

And his brother Donal – the only other member of the family who was also an actor – proved that homophobia ran in the family when he referred to homosexuals as "poofters" during an interview with a Sydney newspaper.

In Hollywood – where a high percentage of people inside the industry are homosexual – a vicious verbal hate campaign was launched against the star. Two muscle-bound bodyguards were hired to keep an eye on Mel, prompted by serious fears of physical attacks being launched by members of Queer Nation.

Mel's Los Angeles agent Ed Limato ordered an immediate "damage-control" operation. But by trying to dampen the flames of a crisis, he unleashed even more publicity through calling Liz Smith (presumably after consultation with Mel) and insisting that the actor had never even had an interview with *El Pais*. It was a disastrous move because Mel then did a movie promotional interview on TV's "Good Morning America" and immediately confessed that he did make the comments, before accusing Liz Smith of "violating my right to have an opinion".

Smith – whose column is read avidly in Hollywood – then ran an interview with GLAAD spokesman Robert Bray, hitting back: "He can't defame gays and then try to wriggle out of it by blaming the translation. Gay fans of Mel Gibson need to throw out their *Mad Max* tapes and stop going to his movies until he stops defaming gay people."

As all the flak over his gay remarks was reported across the world, other details of this indiscreet interview in *El Pais* were overlooked, especially his comments about religion. They indicated that he was as committed as ever to his father's cause.

"We Catholics are being cheated. The Church has abandoned me," he stated in an echo of Hutton Gibson's extremist views.

A few weeks later, a bewildered Mel still could not quite understand what all the fuss was about, although he certainly was not going to back down from what was his honest opinion.

"If someone wants my opinion, I'll give it. What am I supposed to do, lie to them?"

About the only thing Mel did not touch upon in the *El Pais* article was his attitude towards feminism. But it is worth examining because it helps complete a picture of Mel's outlook, and also shows that his black-or-white philosophy is rapidly reaching his father's inflexible levels.

Asked by *Cosmopolitan* magazine for his thoughts on feminism in Australia, Mel uttered a classic, 'Mel-ism' lecturette.

"Women's Lib? It exists there, but for someone like me,

it's an altogether unnecessary thing. I mean, it's simple – women are people, just like you and me. If they do the same job we do, they should be paid the same salary. Women may not always be rational, but they are . . . mysterious. They have powers you and I don't possess."

But it was Mel's views on a woman's role in the home that raised hackles, set teeth on edge.

"Most wives who stay home while their husbands go out and work don't get ruffled by household chores. It's the militant stance[of women's lib] that gives me a severe case of the runs – that reactionary, hostile attitude towards men."

His most brutal attack on feminists came in the *Sunday Telegraph* in May 1984, when Mel was quoted as saying: "I think that word feminism is bull – it's a term invented by some woman who got jilted."

And then there was: "I think that whole women's superior thing is really contrived. If I were trying to fit in with it, I would be really sick in myself."

Mel's comments were starting to grate on some studio executives and publicity chiefs. They concluded that more had to be done to "protect" the star . . . from himself. Access to Mel became difficult and whereas he had spent some years booking in and out of hotels under assumed names, now his actual travel movements started to become shrouded in mystery. Ed Limato – who knew just how plain-speaking Mel could be on occasions – suggested that his client enter restaurants by back entrances to avoid "problems".

Reporters trying to arrange legitimate interviews were coming up against corporate brick walls that the star himself usually knew nothing about.

Paul Mansfield, a Melbourne reporter, negotiated for almost two months to get a meeting. But all he obtained was a constant stream of studio secretaries, public relations firms and personal assistants. While most of them referred to Mel by his first name, as if members of some inner circle, none of them would give a straight answer to Mansfield's request for an interview.

Finally Mansfield tracked Mel down to an isolated film location only to be told by a flunkey precisely what questions he could and could not ask.

"Mel gets sick of people asking him about politics and stuff. After all, why does he have to have an opinion on anything?"

Mansfield was starting to doubt if Mel even had a brain by this stage. When he met the star, Mel showed amazement at the barrier that apparently protected him.

"I don't understand it," said he, before giving Mansfield outspoken quotes on just about every subject under the sun.

His army of advisers was to learn that keeping control of a character like Mel Gibson was not as easy as they thought it would be.

In 1988, Mel received what was for him probably the most offensive role offer anyone could make. As his career bloomed, his commitment to God and the Catholic Church had deepened, even though – under Papa Hutton's strict instructions – none of the Gibson offspring attended church any more, due to modernisation of Catholic observances.

However, when Ed Limato contacted Mel in Australia to say that foremost director Martin Scorsese wanted him to play Jesus in the *The Last Temptation of Christ*, Mel was outraged and told Limato, "I would not touch that one."

Further, he did not think *any* actor was capable of portraying Him.

At home in Australia, Mel's new-found confidence manifested itself in many different ways. Gone was the shy, reluctant star who dreaded every press interview. In his place was a determined character who had finally found his place in the world – and, like his father before him, had some fairly rigid views to lay on the community.

Mel the farmer was as determined as any family man to make sure the wholesome values that come with living in such a rural area were kept up. Working in Hollywood had made him all the more determined to avoid becoming another multi-millionaire star with a string of broken marriages and a worthless private life. He had long since seen past the tinsel and come to the conclusion that La La Land had a lot of problems he hoped would never emigrate to his beef farm near Tangambalanga.

In 1987, with his box office presence confirmed by the success of the first *Lethal Weapon*, Mel took a step that disturbed many of his advisers and fans. He hooked up with Australian right-wing politician Robert Taylor and actively campaigned for the return of what Mel called "old-fashioned values and traditional family values". It was a dangerous move.

In the week that a poll carried out in singles' bars in the US found that Mel was the man with whom most American women would like to be marooned on a desert island, he was out voicing his support for a return to a puritan lifestyle, in the outback town of Albury-Wodonga.

Taylor never had a bigger audience. As an independent candidate in the 1987 Australian federal elections, he was more used to addressing tiny groups in roomy halls or from the back of a truck in a dusty township. Most voters tended to ignore people like Taylor because they were not aligned with the three major parties. He was also against many of the products of democracy like unions and support for the needy. His dislike for government bureaucracy, heavy taxation, Fabian socialism and humanism had been heard a thousand times before. But to Mel, Robert Taylor represented all the values he believed in – and he was determined to help him get elected.

Taylor was a 27-year-old truck driver from the town of

Yarrawonga on the New South Wales–Victoria border. He believed that with the right backing he could get elected by exploiting voters' apathy concerning the three major parties – Labour, Liberal and National. When Mel approached Taylor and asked him if he could share his platform with him, it was like a gift from heaven for the young Aussie politician. Soon crowds of at least a few thousand were gathering wherever Taylor and Mel appeared. The fact that much of their audience was made up of teenage girls clutching autograph books did not seem to matter.

Mel was exposing his political beliefs to the world – and he got an understandably mixed reaction. After all this was the movie hero who had shot dead countless villains and punched out hundreds more – not to mention baring his bottom to his adoring female audience on quite a number of occasions.

Now here was the real Mel Gibson taking a political stance that could only be described as so right-wing it made people like Ronald Reagan look mildly liberal in comparison. The Australian media were sardonically amused.

One local paper seemed to sum up feelings in the area with a headline: "MAD MAX WEIGHS IN FOR A TRUCKIE". It must have made Mel cringe.

But none of that deterred him. At every gathering he voiced his support for Taylor, often standing next to him on the platform as he ranted about "the evil vices plaguing today's society".

"Our nation today is suffering a massive increase in child abuse, drug abuse, suicide, pornography and the AIDS thing," thundered Taylor as Mel led the applause.

"Our nation is in the grip of hopelessness. That's why you're here today, because you're dissatisfied."

The truth was that much of the audience of teenage girls were only there for a glimpse of Mel.

"Abortion is legalised mass murder," continued Taylor.

And Mel backed his candidate to the hilt.

"Robert Taylor speaks more sense than anyone I've talked to for a long time," he exclaimed.

Everything Taylor said brought a nod of approval from the film star. These were the beliefs instilled in him by his father, Hutton. Taylor even suggested a return to the old values of the Ten Commandments, going so far as to say they should be enshrined in the Australian Constitution. It was music to Mel's ears. This was the creed that Hutton Gibson had preached to him and his brothers and sisters.

The brief temptations that Hollywood and stardom put in his path merely served to remind him that the old ways were best.

Mel recognised that he was Taylor's only chance of being successful in those elections. Newspapers, television were all giving him the sort of coverage he could never have dreamed of before a star came on board.

"I couldn't even get my press releases in the paper before Mel came along," enthused the young politician.

Mel turned to Taylor because in the couple of years since buying his farm, he had seen at first hand all the problems and frustrations attached to trying to earn an honest living from the land. "People think these guys sit in their properties in front of their fire and it all just happens. That's crazy. I've never met such hard-working people in my life as I have in the country areas of Australia."

He considered himself one of them. In the area near the farm, Mel went to great pains to be just another farmer. Instead of displaying his wealth with pride, as has always been the American way, he drove around in a scruffy Volvo estate, chewing bits of straw and talking about the cost of cattle.

But there was one aspect of his involvement in local politics that was bizarre, to say the least – he could not vote in Australia because he still carried his American passport. In fact, that explained in many ways why he exposed his views so publicly. It was the only method he had to give his beliefs any influence.

"I haven't got a vote, but I certainly give a hoot about what's happening to this country, because I'm responsible for bringing six Australians into the world. I can't think of anything more challenging or important than making sure we guarantee the future of our young ones," stated Mel.

His somewhat surprising foray into politics began after chatting to a neighbouring farmer, Ed Jacobs, who happened to be an adviser and long-time family friend of Taylor. But then Mel did not take much persuading that the young politician was "on the right track".

Within days of hearing of the actor's interest in backing him, Taylor flew to Sydney for a meeting, then stayed at his Coogee home. Also there was his brother Donal. Soon the three men were deep in discussion of how they all wanted right-wing conservative values to return to the political arena. Thick clouds of cigarette smoke wafted across Mel's study as they talked into the night, supping cold beers and hot coffee when the fancy took them. The only interruption came when they walked to a nearby Chinese restaurant to bring back a meal for the family and themselves.

"Mel was committed to helping me," Taylor said. The Hollywood star also reckoned he could help the small-town politician's "stage performance". He began secretly coaching him on speech delivery, using all the tricks of the stage and screen, learned so carefully over the previous ten years.

"There were little hints about my wording in speeches, my delivery . . . Mel was great at helping without interfering or treading on toes. I was so lucky having a famous person supporting my own long-held beliefs," continued Taylor.

Mel threw himself into the thick of the battle. Opposition politicians were ridiculing Taylor for needing a film star to get sufficient attention. But the actor ignored the criticism and stuck by his man throughout the campaign. He not only attended meetings, he also drove Taylor's truck around the constituency.

In the middle of all this he also found time to visit the inmates at the Children's Hospital, in Camperdown, Sydney. Many of the young patients were victims of brain tumours and Mel showered them with attention, oblivious to long, adoring stares from nurses and parents alike. Mel, unusually, endured all that and willingly signed autographs on anything thrust under his nose.

"It's five minutes of magic. If they saw me for an hour they would find it boring," he said to a reporter at the hospital.

But the newly-politically-charged Mel managed to turn his goodwill visit to the hospital into electioneering, when he publicly accused the Australian government of failing to give sufficient funds for the running of the hospital. According to newspaper reports, he was "sickened" by the state of the unit and made a "sizeable" donation towards the hospital funds.

With him during the visit had been *Lethal Weapon* director Richard Donner, who was also shocked by the conditions.

"We were terribly disheartened to see the city ripping up streets and putting up new buildings for the bicentenary celebrations when the hospital is struggling to save little kids' lives. It is the most frightening, sickening thing I have ever seen, these little kids with brain tumours who don't have a chance unless they can raise the millions of dollars needed to get these machines."

Mel even persuaded Warner Brothers and the Australian distributors of *Lethal Weapon* each to give $5,000 to the hospital's fund-raising body. Mel and co-star Gary Busey also signed a poster to be raffled to raise further cash for the ill-equipped hospital.

Some Australian politicians were outraged by what they saw as an actor sticking his nose into something that was none of his business.

Australian MP Peter Anderson, during Question Time in the State Parliament, jeered at the actor as "mistaken Mel" and went on to say: "He may well be beyond the Thunderdome, but in this case he is off the planet in regard to the things he had to say."

Anderson – a former policeman – went on to promise that he would stay out of the film industry if Mel would stay out of the New South Wales health-care system. What angered him most were Mel's claims of negligence by the government. He claimed that funding to the hospital had been substantially increased and the government also had plans to redevelop it at a total cost of $72 million. Even the hospital's administration department contradicted Mel when they said: "The government is extremely generous."

The bottom line was that his emotive outburst had been completely off the cuff.

"He had not checked his facts out beforehand like any good politician," said one government spokesman.

(Mel kept in touch with the hospital and even became chairman of their Christmas appeal the following year, during which they managed to raise $360,000 for specialist equipment.)

Later, he let slip another of his strong-willed opinions – no doubt passed on by father Hutton. This time the subject was capital punishment.

"I think capital punishment is a valid issue. In today's world I support it. I back it 100 per cent."

In a typical Mel comment, he informed one reporter that executions were "no different from when they hooted and cheered John Wayne when he shot the bad guy".

He was even more blunt a few months later: "It's a sick violent world out there and a humane form of capital punishment is a valid way of dealing with that sickness."

Gradually, his fans were being shown an entirely different picture of their hero.

On federation election night, Mel and Robert Taylor sat together to watch the results, but as it turned out, not even a famous face and all his efforts could help Taylor to victory. His final share of the vote turned out to be just 9 per cent.

Taylor claimed after his defeat that "big bucks and the system beat us in the end". Cynical observers insisted that Mel's involvement had cheapened Taylor's campaign and exposure of his fiercely right-wing beliefs had come as quite a shock to his previously unquestioning public. For someone who only a few years earlier had complained bitterly about having to talk to the press, Mel had gone to the other extreme and his fans did not necessarily approve.

Reflective after that defeat, Taylor was unswerving in his loyalty to Mel.

"I learned a lot from that plunge into politics. And quite a lot of it came from watching Mel in action. It wasn't like watching him on screen playing a character. He was speaking from the heart. Mel Gibson the Aussie . . . Mel the father, the family man. He wasn't acting, and the people who came to our campaign meetings knew it too."

Taylor soon disappeared from the political scene and took up a new career selling office supplies. But he gained an insight into Mel that few outside his family have ever been afforded. And he predicted, accurately, that Gibson would return to the political arena some day.

"I would love to think that Mel would be back again. He gave me valuable exposure with solid campaign backing and a grand show of loyalty and convictions."

Back in Hollywood, Mel's extreme right-wing views did

not go unnoticed. In one camp there was delight that he was proving such a traditionalist – it would obviously do nothing but enhance his reputation as a straitlaced action hero. But there were others who were muttering jibes like "redneck" and "right-wing extremist". He was treading a very thin line ...

Two years later, Mel proved that once you get a taste for politics it is hard to resist the temptation to get involved. It was federal election time once more in Australia and this time he was throwing his weight, influence, charisma and wallet behind another independent candidate, Barry Tattersall.

Mel was even more sure of himself than on his previous political outing. He appeared in television advertisements for Tattersall, championing the value of independents in politics. Some of his friends and advisers believed that his first outing with Taylor could hardly be described as a public relations triumph, but Mel was his own man and no one could stop him standing up for what he believed in.

If anything, in the two years between campaigns he had become farther right-wing in his beliefs. Just like Hutton Gibson, he saw things in purely black-or-white terms. There was no centre ground. Mel seemed to be preparing himself to take on his father's mantle in every sense. Already he was financially aiding many of his family. That was fine with Mel. Keeping the Gibson clan intact was his number-one priority.

Independent candidate Tattersall insisted that his famous backer was "talking straight from the heart. The value of the individual is important to us and I want to serve the electorate, not dictate to it."

But once again, Mel's ability at getting his candidates publicity was not enough to persuade a very cautious electorate to vote for such a radical change in power.

However, none of this altered his political standpoint. He still believed that Australia, along with most of the Western world, was going downhill fast. It was an attitude that had made his father up-sticks and abandon the United States twenty years earlier. But this time, there was nowhere to escape. Mel just had to keep preaching what he believed when the opportunity arose. For the first time in his professional career, he had discovered that his stardom provided a very useful platform from which he could seek to influence others. He was determined to spread the word about right-wing conservatism, but his experiences during those two elections persuaded him that politicians were the lowest of the low. Along with journalists, naturally.

During an extraordinary outburst while being interviewed on Australian television's Channel Nine "The Midday Show" by Ray Martin in 1990, he showed frustration when asked what he thought about high interest rates and taxation.

"I suppose they're going to have a nose-picking tax next. I just don't think the people in power in the government have in their hearts anything good for the country. I think it's nothing short of traitorous what they're doing."

But he invited criticism about where his loyalties really lay when he also admitted: "I haven't been home in a long time but I keep getting reports that there's a recession."

Privately, he was voicing his disillusion and reactionary aspirations even more bluntly. He believed that he really had something to offer the world of politics. With that in mind – plus the runaway success of the *Lethal Weapon* series – he surprised (and delighted) his Hollywood agent Ed Limato in 1989 by deciding to splash out $2.4 million on buying pop star Rick Springfield's luxurious Malibu mansion.

The town he had once said he would never ever live in had transformed into a much more attractive proposition. The financial incentives of living "nearer to the office" were growing into the tens of millions of dollars zone and there was also a germ of an idea about one day putting all those political ideals to the test.

On his less frequent trips back to the farm in Australia, he continued the political rhetoric. In February 1993, Mel told Sydney's "A Current Affair" programme that he was deeply saddened by a federal government he described as being "like a liability".

"Australia was the greatest country, the most affluent, with the highest credit rating in the world, with the most natural resources, with the least amount of people in it . . . "

Then he lashed out at former Labour prime minister Bob Hawke, who had told the star to "stick to acting" and keep his nose out of politics.

"I was very offended. To actually say that I have no say in what is happening is a very scary thing to say. A very fascist thing to say," Mel struck back angrily.

The sub-text might have been readiness to distance himself from Australia in preparation for a US political move. Many friends believe he will take that step, one day. And he also grew increasingly edgy whenever cornered about where his Australia-versus-America allegiance lay.

On the American NBC network's highly-rated "Today" show, interviewer Jane Pauley asked Mel whether he considered himself more American . . . or Australian? She went on and on, trying to tempt him to say something more patriotic about America than Australia. A few years earlier, Mel's answer would have been pro-Aussie, but the tide was turning and so was he. Politely guarded, he squirmed in his seat when Pauley's questioning continued unabated. In the end she switched to an easier topic.

But Mel's opinions on a whole variety of topics have startled many people. While many like him in person, they do not agree with any of his outlandish opinions.

"Mel is a great guy in many ways. He has a superb sense of humour, a deep commitment to his family, but there is another side to him. It is almost as if part of his personality is still back there knocking back beers in a neighbourhood bar in his teens. His bluntness is sometimes quite astonishing and he does tend to say the first thing that comes into his mouth," one actor acquaintance said.

Not surprisingly, Mel's more extreme opinions have not been revealed outside a small circle of his personal friends and acquaintances. But the actor friend says that in the past few years – as evidenced by his continuing interest in right-wing politics – Mel has "grown steadily more and more extreme" in his beliefs.

"It is almost as if fewer and fewer of his friends have the courage to stand up to him and tell him to cool down and take stock of some of the things he is saying," said the friend.

Many of Mel's opinions were moulded by his father Hutton, of course. Belief in the old-style Catholic Church goes hand in hand with attitudes towards race, other religions and even feminism. Hutton Gibson's writings on a so-called Communist-Masonic-Zionist conspiracy have already been disclosed in this book. But papa Gibson's continual rhetoric about the Pope has rubbed off on Mel, according to many of his friends and associates.

Even the loving son has admitted that his father was an extremist.

"People see him as an extremist. He certainly doesn't – what's the word? – compromise in any way."

But, he was asked, does he share his father's views?

"I share them because I believe them to be true," replied Mel loyally.

Back in Tinseltown, Mel and agent Ed Limato were flooded with screenplays. In fact, just about every major US film during that period was offered to Mel. It was a remarkable achievement considering that at the start of the decade he had been earning $300-a-week in theatre in Sydney.

There were also some rather eccentric proposals like the time "Dallas" star Victoria Principal begged the show's producers to sign Mel up for the Texan soap saga.

In an extraordinary move, Mel was offered a staggering $2 million a week to join the cast of the programme, once reputed to be the best-watched weekly television series in the world. But then the "Dallas" producers and Ms Principal were not aware that Mel had sworn he would never touch television again after his experiences as a young actor on a handful of dreadful Aussie shows. The offer was rejected instantly.

I'm going to channel the maniac inside me.
I'm going to get hold of it.

16

The Hollywood buzz on *Lethal Weapon* had been so good that Mel was inundated with screenplays – often poor imitations of the movie he had just made. But he and agent Ed Limato had already decided that – with a sequel already in the works – they would look for something completely different. They found it in *Tequila Sunrise*.

Mel adored the script from the moment he read it. "I was intrigued as soon as I started reading it, although I didn't understand it – 'Just be patient; eventually, it'll pay off.' It's one of those things that sucks you in slowly, but surely," he said at the time. It was also scheduled to be shot in Los Angeles and Mel had grown accustomed to going home every evening to Robyn and the kids, during *Lethal Weapon*. He did after all have a seven-month-old baby in the household, not to mention four other very active children.

The actor was still being dogged by that "Sexiest Man in the World" title bestowed on him by *People* magazine five years earlier. No matter where he turned, another publication would find an excuse either to repeat it or, worse still, give him a new label. In Britain, the tabloid newspaper *The Star* announced that Mel had been voted Mr Wonderful after nearly two-thirds of readers polled said he was their favourite actor. On this occasion, Mel beat "Magnum" star Tom Selleck to the title. Then a Los Angeles-based women's group called Man Watchers Inc. selected Mel as one of the ten most watchable men in America.

Mel laughed it off as usual when asked how he dealt with such tags.

"You deal with it by a trick of the mind. You figure: Is it worrying me that much? Does anybody else give a damn as much as I do? So you decide not to. It's easy."

But all this renewed press attention caught the eye of singing superstar Madonna, according to the *Daily Mirror* newspaper in Sydney.

An article by Rosalind Reines reported that this unlikely pair arranged to meet in a Los Angeles restaurant – with Mel almost having a punch-up with Madonna's loud-mouthed husband Sean Penn. The article stated: "Mel was a little surprised when he arrived to find mega-bore Penn had definitely consumed too much Californian champagne.

"As Mel walked up to their table and said rather unimaginatively: 'You must be Sean Penn,' Sean looked up from his glass and slurred: 'Who are you?'

"Things could have taken a turn for the worse if Madonna hadn't suddenly nudged hubby and told him: 'Sean, it's Mel Gibson the actor.'

"'Oh,' replied Sean, doing his best nerd impersonation, and continued to moodily raise the glass to his lips."

The article went on to claim that Mel had a dance with Madonna only to find himself interrupted by Penn saying: "Hey! Do you know who you're dancing with?"

The accuracy of this article is impossible to verify.

(Mel accepted a public apology on July 6, 1993, from Britain's *Daily Express* for an article in April that year which suggested he had attacked other leading movie stars including Madonna, Sharon Stone and Richard Gere for taking obscene roles and being "just like porn stars". Gibson's London lawyer told the High Court that the actor did not make the remarks, which came from "an interview" first published in an Italian magazine. The *Express* agreed to pay Gibson's legal costs.)

Back on the *Tequila Sunrise* project, there was another reason why Mel was so attracted to the project – outstanding writer/director Robert Towne, who won an Oscar for his private eye classic, *Chinatown*. Agent Ed Limato had an ulterior motive for persuading Mel to attach himself to the $25 million budgeted *Tequila*; he believed that matchmaking one of his other up-and-coming clients, Michelle Pfeiffer, with Mel would virtually guarantee the film's success. Former Miss Orange County (1976) and LA check-out girl Michelle was definitely "bubbling" in Hollywood terms after starring roles in *Scarface* and then *The Witches of Eastwick*.

But there was one snag with Dale (Mac) McKussic, the character Mel was to portray for a fee of $1.5 million. He was a former drug dealer, no longer in business, but living comfortably on the proceeds of distributing cocaine. This in itself presented Mel with a moral dilemma. How could he play a guy whose entire lifestyle was based on his earnings from drug dealing?

Seven years earlier, as his former business associate and *Gallipoli* producer Pat Lovell disclosed, he had rejected an offer to play a drug addict in *Monkey Grip*, an Australian movie. At the time, Mel felt that he could never play anyone involved in drugs. But here he was accepting just that role.

In fact, Mel thought long and hard about his role in

Tequila and, as usual, came up with his own unique piece of logic as to why the role was acceptable.

"Look, no one's perfect, and most of us have done something in life we regret or may even be ashamed of. I felt the character of McKussic was legitimate. He wasn't pushing any more; he saw the future of his son as more important than his own or his past. I mean, sure, he dealt in drugs . . . but when the story opens he's clean," Mel explained on American breakfast television during a promotional trip for *Tequila*.

"Personally, and it's well known publicly, I detest drugs, hate the damn things . . . I won't go near them, and I would hate to think my kids or anyone's kids could get hooked on them. We are the ones that make sure they don't get hit."

But then what Mel did not mention was that he had an addiction of his own. He was hooked on nicotine. He had tried everything to kick his daily intake of two packs of Marlboros but the anxiety he so successfully hid on the big screen had to be soothed by something and in his case it was cigarettes. The booze he could cut down on, sometimes even give up for a few weeks at a time. But the dreaded weed was another matter. He could not (maybe would not) give it up.

"I have to have some vice in my life," Mel would always say.

During one moving interview he even confessed that his smoking was causing endless anxiety at home.

"One of my kids came up, saw me smoking and said, 'Please don't. I don't want you to die.' They really believe that if I have another one, I could drop dead on the spot. And I could. That's a pretty strong motivation to quit."

But, even after that candid admission, it was noted that Mel immediately picked up a packet of Marlboros, took out a cigarette and lit it.

Before shooting of *Tequila* began, Mel attempted to get inside the mind of the character he was to play by talking to a real drug dealer, recently released from jail.

"I'm sure he regretted what he had done, although he never apologized for it, and never used the stuff himself," explained Mel. "He didn't consider the end result; he was just the middleman, exactly like Mac, enjoying the thrill, not to mention the money . . . He wasn't thinking about the drugs making some kid jump off a roof or shoot his sister. In the film, it's Mac's own little boy who prompts him to rethink his profession."

Mel once again saw elements of the character he was playing in himself and he rationalised: "The script doesn't deal with good and bad but shades of grey. He's retired [from drug dealing] but nobody wants him to retire."

But the question of drugs and the morality of Mel's character dogged the film. Generally the first question on every journalist's agenda.

Director Towne stoutly defended the movie. "My feeling about this is that the most dangerous thing you can do with that issue is to make *Cocaine Fiends* or *Reefer Madness* [two early anti-drug movies] because then it removes it from the world of reality, and everybody thinks, 'Well, I don't have to worry about that. It could never happen in my life.' When you show it can be in the context of our normal lives, then you can suggest the damage it does. We can't deal with Dick Tracy kinds of good and evil because it's more complicated than that."

In *Tequila Sunrise*, Mel is at odds with a high-school friend, played by Kurt Russell, who is a narcotics cop. Michelle Pfeiffer is the beauty caught between the two men.

Many of Mel's female fans who saw the film were convinced that Mel used a body double during the movie's highly charged love scene. Certainly shots of Mel's body from some angles do not look like the original, but both stars have kept a discreet silence about the subject.

The sequence involved Mel and Michelle in a hot tub for

what director Towne called a "pretty explicit" sex scene. But Mel and his beautiful co-star prevented the temperature in the bath from bursting any thermometers by playing Scrabble between takes.

While Mel enjoyed the same sort of at-a-distance working relationship with Michelle Pfeiffer that he had with Diane Keaton during *Mrs Soffel*, the actor became close pals with co-star Kurt Russell. It was a friendship that blossomed into something even more significant when Mel, and Kurt's lover Goldie Hawn, agreed to team up in *Bird on a Wire*.

When *Tequila Sunrise* came out in late 1988, Mel's performance received reasonable praise, but many of the critics questioned the drug background of the character he portrayed.

"Can you accept a cocaine dealer as a romantic, lovable, even admirable character, even if he is as handsome as Mel Gibson and is presented as a loyal friend, an ardent lover, a caring father and a connoisseur of food? I'm afraid I can't; though I'm willing when watching a romantic thriller to suspend disbelief and accept all sorts of implausibilities, coincidences and general foolishness, I won't put my moral senses on hold, too," wrote highly respected *Sydney Daily Telegraph* critic Bev Tivey.

Matt White in the *Daily Mirror* was more positive about the film: "*Tequila Sunrise* is certain to sustain Mel Gibson's regained popularity while it waits for the second *Lethal Weapon* movie." In actual fact the movie took a very modest sum at the box office and became known as one of those projects that never really lived up to its real potential.

But, for a different reason, Mel has never forgotten the launch of *Tequila Sunrise*. Shortly before a celebrity screening in Los Angeles, he had an embarrassing encounter with veteran actress Jane Wyman, former wife of President Ronald Reagan.

The two were alone in a lift together when Mel became aware that the seventysomething actress was casting seductive glances in his direction. "Hey. You're a good-looking boy. Ever considered a career in the movies?"

Mel – highly amused – replied: "Yes, ma'am. I have given it some thought."

Ms Wyman realised her mistake within minutes, when she attended the screening of *Tequila Sunrise* and saw Mel up on the screen.

During the round of meet-the-press gatherings that had become a part of Mel's staple diet in the run-up to the release of every film he was involved with, the star showed an uncharacteristic side after agreeing to be interviewed by Australian journalist Nancy Griffin.

Ten minutes after meeting Mel she found herself being driven off in his rented red Mercedes to look for a car, among the dozens of dealerships that line a two-mile stretch of Santa Monica Boulevard, near the apartment Mel had bought in 1988.

Eventually, reported an astonished Ms Griffin, Mel spotted a used navy-blue Mercedes 560SL for a bargain $52,900.

"Do you want to drive it home?" asked the starstruck dealer. Mel replied that he had forgotten his chequebook.

"We trust you," replied the dealer, handing Mel the keys and telling him to come back with a cheque when he was ready.

After *Lethal Weapon 2*, Mel headed back to Canada – for the first time since his embarrassing drink-driving run-in with the police in Toronto – to star in a "frothy piece of fun and action" called *Bird on a Wire* with Kurt Russell's live-in love Goldie Hawn. Once again, Mel had chosen something different from the Lethal Weapon series in the hope that it would help him break free of type-casting.

Before signing for the movie, he turned down a host of action-oriented projects including a film about motor racing, *Champions*, which became *Days of Thunder* starring Tom Cruise. Stories circulated in Tinseltown that Mel was offered the lead role in *Batman*, later taken by Michael Keaton. Mel denied, joking, "I think I would have felt silly in rubber." There was much speculation about how Mel's millions of women fans would have reacted to him being dressed up in a skin-tight Batsuit.

Another much steamier project he rejected out of hand was the lead role in *Final Analysis*, about a psychiatrist who falls in love with his patient. Mel found the *Fatal Attraction*-style project deeply offensive. His judgement was vindicated when the movie was released in 1991, starring Richard Gere and Kim Bassinger. It was universally slammed and did not perform well at the box office. (Gere, another Ed Limato client, remained silent on the question of taking on a role that had been first offered to Mel.)

More surprisingly, Mel rejected the role of Robin Hood that his chief rival Kevin Costner made his own – and a $100 million plus box office success. There was a suggestion that Mel "'did not fancy prancing around screen in a pair of green tights". For the second time he had passed on a project that would strengthen Costner's grip on that slot as number-one male star in Hollywood.

There was also talk of a comedy in Australia, the reality being that Mel was now such a big star that the Hollywood gossip machine attached him to just about every project in town. Mel was as choosy as ever. He was increasingly keen on doing comedy. Every time he made a movie everyone from the director down would heap praise on his comedic skills and he convinced himself that he had a long-term future doing something considerably lighter than the cops-and-robbers format of *Lethal Weapon*.

During the making of *Tequila Sunrise*, Mel, his wife Robyn and Kurt Russell and Goldie Hawn had become firm friends and inevitably conversation kept coming round to the possibility of Mel and Goldie making a movie together. But both stars agreed that it would have to be just the right project. Before meeting Goldie, Mel expected her to be "dippy and goofy". That most emphatically was not the case.

"She certainly has a vivacious quality that never lets her down. I mean it's like she's always smiling and cheery. But there's certainly more to her than the dumb blonde."

Goldie had her own reservations about Mel before they met.

"I had trepidations because I thought he'd have no sense of humour or be stuck on himself. But Mel is bursting with humour and very self-deprecating."

Goldie Hawn was, if anything, even more careful about selecting projects than Mel. She was painfully aware that it had been ten years since her last major hit, *Private Benjamin*. Other movies like *Wildcats* and *Overboard* had sunk without trace. Hence, *Bird on a Wire* became a very important project for the blonde star. Mel had no doubt it would do them both good.

"This is funny and warm," he said of *Bird on a Wire*. "I've always been afraid to try things like that, but I thought I'd just dive in and see what happened."

But Mel did expose his own lack of intensity towards the role – for which he got $3.5 million – during one interview when he said: "The title, it's an old Beatles song isn't it?" An assistant immediately corrected him. "Oh Leonard Cohen, right."

Bird on a Wire turned out to be a very basic, $20 million chase movie with Mel playing a former Sixties radical living a secret life as a government-protected witness after blowing the whistle on two corrupt drug-enforcement agents. Goldie is his former girlfriend who accidentally rediscovers him. So do the bad guys. They chase Mel and Goldie through a zoo, in cars, on motorcycles, in a plane and aboard a rollercoaster.

The movie's director was experienced Hollywood hired hand John Badham. But he had huge problems with Goldie over those rollercoaster scenes. She was so jittery that her participation was limited to a small section of the track.

"They fork-lifted me up to the rollercoaster like a jackass," she said later. "I think I risked more doing that than if I had gone on the whole rollercoaster ride. Every fear I've ever had I faced in this movie. I think I'm a new woman now. I can do anything."

Goldie's main fear was of heights. During one stunt she had to climb around the ledge of a twenty-storey building, not an easy task for anyone but especially frightening for Goldie. Vertigo took over and she completely froze as Mel and the rest of the cast and crew looked on.

Noticing her distress and just like a Saturday matinee idol, he came to his beautiful co-star's rescue.

"Mel grabbed me in his arms and hauled me back. I was shaking and crying. He saved my life."

A close and lasting friendship grew between Mel and Goldie and their respective families. Crew members say that the noise of children (Goldie has three) coming from the two stars' trailers was deafening and her caravan wall was plastered with Polaroids of her youngsters. There were champagne toasts when Robyn announced she was pregnant for the sixth time.

But the two stars infuriated director Badham by secretly agreeing to tone down the film's most important love scene during secretive late-night phone calls during shooting.

"It just wasn't right to see these two people go at it together. It would be a turn-off," Goldie admitted after the movie's release.

As the scene was rewritten, Mel and Goldie landed up in

bed together in a motel room, but their lovemaking was funny rather than sensuous.

Critics around the world dismissed *Bird on a Wire* for having a paper-thin plot and scorned Goldie Hawn's performance, but Mel's acting abilities were generally well received.

"It was an indescribably bad film but Mel came out of it okay," said Scott Murray of *Cinema Papers*, in Australia.

And Evan Williams in *The Australian* was even ruder: "The less said about *Bird on a Wire* the better. It is an ugly, witless, hyperactive film which tries pathetically hard to outdo Speilberg or George Lucas at their own game."

Despite all the criticism, *Bird on a Wire* became one of the bigger-grossing films of that year, proving that Mel had well and truly arrived as a box office star who could attract customers even when the product was sub-standard.

After two films in fast succession, Mel was feeling almost as exhausted as during that perilous period a few years earlier which threatened a nervous breakdown. He had been giving round-the-clock press interviews to promote *Lethal Weapon 2* while still shooting *Bird*. He divined that it was time to take off for Australia and a long rest on the farm.

"It's just a matter of getting back into a more sedate rhythm of life which is well needed at this time," he said, just before the end of the *Bird on a Wire* shoot in Canada.

I am attracted to other people. But I believe in absolute fidelity. Anything else would be too messy and unfair.

17

A bizarre confection of dingy lighting and muffled sound effects, the Cauldron Club reigned like a seedy street hustler over Sydney's famed King's Cross district. Inside, it resembled one of those drinking clubs from the Fifties. Outside, it was little more than a doorway with a small brass sign giving its name. But then the Cauldron's big attraction was its discretion and when Mel Gibson walked in for a beer with two friends late in 1986, he hardly even merited a second glance.

However, the shapely blonde girl in a white tube dress hugging every inch of her body certainly sparked a reaction from Mel. He just could not keep his eyes off her.

British-born Miranda Brewin was just 19 at the time and staying with friends in Sydney. She immediately noticed the movie star's attention and turned to her girlfriend, Sydney model Michelle Adamson, and laughed.

"Mel Gibson is over there. D'you think he'll remember me?"

Michelle grinned back at her friend. She knew that Miranda was a fairly up-front sort of person, but she had no idea if her claim to know Mel from a previous meeting was true or not. Miranda climbed off her stool and tottered across the bar on her four-inch-heeled stilettos. Mel watched her every move with a broad grin on his face.

"I don't know if he had any idea who she was but he was very nice and happily chatted to Miranda," explained Michelle. "And I wasn't going to say no to meeting him, so we stood and talked for a while."

(Miranda said later that she had in fact met Mel previously at Singapore Airport and he had instantly recalled their earlier encounter.)

Soon Mel, Miranda and Michelle were sharing lethal cocktails called Kamikazes and chatting away like lifelong friends. Mel talked openly about his wife Robyn and the children – even referring at one stage to the fact that she was pregnant with their fifth child Louis at the time. Intriguingly, he avoided virtually any references to his career.

Both girls were impressed by his charm. Michelle recalled thinking that he was "fabulous", while Miranda admitted she got goose pimples every time she looked at him. They knew from the look on his face that he was "out to have fun".

Mel was on a genuine work high at the time. *Lethal Weapon* had completed shooting and word-of-mouth from Warner Brothers was that the movie was a sure-fire hit that would rocket Mel to superstar status. But his drinking had reached almost epidemic proportions. Sometimes he would down five beers before breakfast and as the shoot had progressed his capacity had increased. Now, back in the security of his hometown of Sydney, he was finding it just as difficult to say no to a round or three of drinks in one of the city's most notorious drinking clubs.

That evening Mel explained to the girls that Robyn was back at their farm in Victoria and he was in Sydney for a business meeting; he admitted being "a bit sloshed" after attending "some do" before moving on to the Cauldron.

Michelle says Mel was well on the way to "getting really drunk" when the two girls announced they were adjourning to another nightspot called Rogues. The actor immediately butted in: "I'd like to come."

"So off we dragged him," recalled Michelle. Mel even brought a glass of beer with him when he slumped into the back seat of Michelle's car for the five-minute drive to Rogues. She has never forgotten finding the pint mug in her car the next morning. Michelle says he made no attempt to invite his male friends along and they made no effort to come.

Once inside Rogues – a lively yuppie type of bar/restaurant, packed out most evenings – the two girls and their brand-new superstar friend began demolishing more cocktails. Soon, each of the women was taking turns to sit on Mel's lap.

"People kept looking at us. We were sat by a piano and everyone thought I was with him. But, actually, I felt like I was sitting on my brother's lap," says Michelle, who still lives in Sydney and is now married.

But when Miranda sat on Mel's lap it was a different story altogether. She detected a definite feeling of sexuality between them and, as the drinks continued to go down at an alarming rate, a pattern that Mel has repeated on at least one occasion began to emerge.

For a while he danced with Michelle, only to return to Miranda.

Michelle reported that at one stage Mel described himself as "a real party man", although he then returned to the subject of Robyn and the children and insisted they did not lead "separate lives".

At approximately 4.30 a.m., Michelle recalls leaving

Rogues with Miranda and Mel, who was dressed casually in jeans and cowboy boots.

"I dropped them back at his rented car after he said he would give her a lift home. He was very pissed. I offered to drive him home but Miranda said, 'No, just drop us at his car.'"

Michelle says that when she saw Miranda a few days later, her friend claimed to have stayed with Mel at a house in Coogee where they continued drinking until dawn.

Miranda – who speaks with an English public school accent – says that Mel mumbled instructions on how to find the house in Coogee as the couple set off in her car.

"It had electronically operated garage doors so that you did not have to get out in the street," explained Miranda in an interview in February, 1993.

After tiptoeing in to the house – which Mel described as belonging to "my brother" – the actor opened a bottle of wine and the drinking continued.

Miranda says it was his sense of humour that she noticed the most.

"He was great fun. He laughed constantly," she recalled.

Miranda claims that she met Mel on two more occasions in Sydney but he was very careful not to give her any of his phone numbers.

The friendship faded out within weeks.

Miranda says, "There is no doubt at all that he loves his wife. He is completely crazy about her. But he is also basically a fun person."

One year later, Mel was linked by a British tabloid newspaper with another young English blonde, Cassandra Kirton, whom he was alleged to have met in a trendy Los Angeles boutique called Maxfields.

The 24-year-old Hertfordshire-born shop assistant was reported to have moved in to Mel's Santa Monica apartment, in an article headlined: "MAD MAX STAR DITCHES WIFE

FOR SHOP GIRL". There were no direct quotes from either Cassandra or Mel. Just a "close friend" confirming all the details.

The article was met with furious denials from Mel and his representatives. They dismissed it as nonsense. The actor rounded on dozens of reporters who had gathered near his home in Kiewa Valley, northern Victoria, and angrily announced the story was "absolute rubbish". He even claimed he had not been in Los Angeles for months. (But later inquiries prove that Mel was in LA in September of 1987, which is when the encounter occurred.)

Even truck driver Robert Taylor, independent candidate for the Victorian seat of Indi, whom Mel had supported so vigorously, rushed to the actor's defence.

"You can always tell when there is something wrong with a couple and there is nothing wrong there. They are happy. They are best friends," said an anxious Taylor.

He was no doubt correct because there were a number of glaring inaccuracies in the story. For instance, Mel had embarked on a casual friendship, not the live-in love affair the paper had claimed.

Mel's fury was followed up with threats of legal action against any papers that repeated the story. Ed Limato and his team launched a damage-control operation and contrived to prevent further coverage of the alleged affair. The promised legal action never materialised. But it had the required effect of scaring off scandal-hungry tabloids. There were denial stories with headlines like: "MEL SCOFFS AT REPORTS OF LOVE NEST WITH TEENAGER" and "BLAZING MEL BLASTS LOVE NEST GOSSIP".

Mel could look those reporters in the eye, with no hesitation, because there was no love nest. One Sydney paper even carried an apology, pointing out that Mel had not left his wife and family as reported.

Cassandra Kirton – who still lives in California – insists that there was a relationship although she never moved in to Mel's apartment.. She described their brief friendship in very similar terms to Miranda Brewin. She even looks similar: blonde, English and pretty.

Talking for the very first time about her friendship with Mel, she insisted: "I was nervous about it because I had never been out with a married man before."

The couple met when he walked into Maxfields to buy a shirt for his flamboyant Hollywood agent Limato. Then he decided he wanted to buy a pair of trousers and she measured him – so that they could be taken up – in a spacious rear changing room. Cassandra says that Mel "kept making flirty comments and I sensed there was an attraction between us".

Mel spent thousands of dollars on suits, shirts and ties that day. He also ended up insisting that Cassandra walk him to his rented car in the parking lot nearby, much to the amusement of the store's other assistants.

Next day, Mel called Maxfields and asked Cassandra when his trousers would be ready to be picked up.

"He was really nagging me to deliver them in person and he made a point of saying where he was staying," recalled Cassandra in an interview in November, 1992. But she refused to go to his house as the shop rules forbade that.

Mel was not deterred. He rang Cassandra back a few days later.

"This time he did not even ask me about the trousers. He just asked me out instead," says Cassandra.

The blonde shop assistant agonised, she says, about accepting his invitation to dinner, before agreeing. That night she turned up at the apartment in Santa Monica that he had bought some years earlier. (She has since pointed out the apartment and it is indeed the place where he was staying at that time.)

"Mel was already a little drunk when I got there," said Cass. But within minutes he started kissing her. After "a lot of kissing and cuddling" on a sofa, the couple went out for dinner at the nearby Chez Jay's restaurant. Cassandra was struck by the fact that the Hollywood star was so unconcerned that he might be spotted out with another woman. At one stage in the restaurant, a customer at the table next to them began taking photos of him but it did not stop Mel from smooching with his new friend.

"He just couldn't stop touching me. He did not seem to care that people were watching. He just laughed when I said I thought they had just taken our picture."

That night Cassandra drove Mel home in her car.

Cass believes that Mel "just let himself go and acted really naturally" during their brief relationship.

"He was so relaxed. Laughing and joking," she says.

But, despite wildly exaggerated claims that Cass moved in with Mel, the young store assistant never saw Mel alone again after that night. Although the actor did ring her from the airport to thank her for a great time. It was a touching gesture that Cass says she will never forget because "he did not have to bother, but he did".

However – six months later – after the dust had completely settled over his alleged affair with shop girl Cassandra, a piquant incident took place when Mel walked into Maxfields boutique – with his wife Robyn and all their kids.

"I was flabbergasted. Then she insisted I measure her up for a dress. All the time I could see how tense and un-comfortable Mel was," says Cass.

She managed to avoid embarrassing eye contact with Mel because the children were running around the shop causing chaos, but she has absolutely no doubt why they came into the shop.

"She made him come in just to see how he would react."

Despite that scene Cassandra does not show bitterness towards the actor.

"Essentially he's a good person. A very genuine person," she stresses to this day.

Cassandra believes that Mel suspects she leaked the original account of their relationship back in 1987. But the truth is that she had nothing whatsoever to do with the one and only article that saw print. Her decision to talk about it now, almost six years later, was inspired by a wish to put the record straight.

Mel's aides set up another damage-control operation in January 1993, but this ended in the biggest embarrassment of all for the actor and his family. On this occasion, Mel had gone on a bar crawl with three pretty young students in the northern Californian town of Modesto. The night of drinking, smoking and smooching ended with Mel cavorting with a blonde named Shawn.

But it wasn't until more than two years after the incident that Mel's antics reached the eyes and ears of his adoring public. Stories of his fling had become gossip fodder in Modesto ever since Mel left town following a cattle-buying trip in October 1990. But no one passed these rumours on to the notorious American tabloids and Mel must have thought that his drunken encounter would never be revealed.

However, muckraking experts on the *National Enquirer* were determined to find evidence of the much-talked-about fling in Modesto and they pulled out all the stops to unearth concrete evidence of Mel's two-timing. Eventually they tracked down the three girls concerned and unintentionally initiated a frenzied attempt by Hollywood to cover up a scandal about one of its most happily married stars.

One of the girls involved was Wendy Kain. She explained that as soon as the tabloid's inquiries reached their ears, the father of one girl called up the actor's agent "looking for a deal". Within hours one of Mel's lawyers went to Modesto. His mission: to investigate the claim that three girls were about to sell their story to the US tabloids. There was even talk about a blackmail plot by someone involved in the story who had threatened to take photos to the papers unless a six-figure sum was paid over by Mel.

The lawyer's swoop on Modesto was provoked by a genuine concern over what appeared to be a very damaging situation.

Wendy Kain explained: "I refused to talk to Mel's Lawyer. The approach made me real mad."

The college student immediately sought her own legal representation and soon Wendy's lawyer was contacted by Mel's attorney, who was concerned that Wendy should not talk to the press.

"They wanted to know what I was going to say and they were so insistent that they said we could speak to them any time of the day or night," recalled Wendy.

"Confidentiality" and "non-disclosure" agreements were drawn up for the girls to sign.

"But I did not like how aggressive they were being," added Wendy.

Furious at being pressured, Wendy eventually co-operated with the *Enquirer*'s biggest rival, the *Globe*, and supplied them with details and photographs showing Mel kissing one of the girl's high-heeled shoes, burying his head in another girl's lap, downing a vodka cocktail, and sucking one girl's fingers, with his arms round two others. Wendy claims that if Mel's lawyers had kept away from Modesto she would never have considered giving her account to the tabloids.

Lawyers also threatened to sue the *Globe* if they published an account of what happened, saying: "If you run that story, whoever writes it, the *Globe* will be the recipient of a lawsuit.

I intend suing the *Globe*."

Six months after the story appeared, no legal action had been taken. Mel's lawyers said this was because the most flagrant inaccuracies had been deleted.

Globe Los Angeles bureau chief Jim Mitteager says he was astonished by the lawyer's visit to Modesto.

"I have been in this business a long time and I have never heard of a case where lawyers have visited people who frolic with celebrities. It was very bizarre," he comments.

The articles that were eventually published gave the distinct impression that Mel's fling with Wendy's friend Shawn and his bar crawl with her and the other two girls was something that happened in a drunken moment.

However, Wendy has disclosed for the first time that Mel actually met with Shawn the previous night and arranged a date with her. Then he carefully checked out of the Holiday Inn in Modesto and booked himself into the Red Lion to cover his tracks by staying an extra night in town to have some fun with the girls.

The customary bar crawl that followed involved Mel admitting that he had a foot fetish and that he was also in love with women's high-heeled shoes. Just as on those earlier misadventures, vast quantities of cocktails were consumed between never-ending impersonations of the Three Stooges (the actor's love of their eye-poking antics that made the group famous have long been his comic, ice-breaking speciality).

Wendy recalled a boorish incident which she says completely changed her attitude towards him.

"We were in one bar when I saw Mel go over to this girl we knew at the bar and just rip her top. That girl got really mad at him but he was too drunk to work out what he had done. He seemed so male chauvinistic."

Wendy also recalled characteristics which previous

friends have commented on.

"He had such bad manners. He never opened a door for us. He never even bought us a drink all night."

At one stage during their crawl through this quiet cattle town, Mel was challenged by a local cop to prove he was the famous movie star, because no one believed him or the girls. The actor pulled out an American Express Gold Card and showed it to the cop. His name was clearly printed on it but the girls were more surprised by the fact that he never once volunteered to spend any money on them.

No question, he's a chip off papa Hutton's block when it comes to squeezing pennies . . .

All three girls plus Mel returned to Angela's father's house, later than evening. Mel continued downing hefty quantities of alcohol and at one stage, ate catfood out of two tins – something he did with dogfood in *Mad Max II* and later *Lethal Weapon 3*.

Mel and Shawn enjoyed a cuddle together and the married star was not in the slightest bit embarrassed when Wendy walked into the room.

She had already noted that the actor had an "almost exhibitionist-type habit of walking around the house stark naked".

She also said that Mel was "very sheepish" the next morning.

"He would not talk to us at all and in the end Shawn drove him back to his hotel," added Wendy.

Shawn did tell her friends that the star called his wife in Australia when they got back to the hotel and he admitted sheepishly to the student: "She's not too happy with me."

A strange twist was that Mel was extra co-operative when the girls took photos of his antics – because he had a punch-up the previous evening with a local newspaper photographer who started snapping him in a Modesto parking lot. Mel smashed the journalist's camera, only to apologise later and offer to pay for the wrecked equipment. It had the effect of calming him down and making him less neurotic about having his photo taken. He lived to regret that day . . .

Mel and his advisers are doggedly determined not to allow his image of a family-loving man to be shattered. The star frequently makes a point of talking about the importance of being faithful while married.

He has also publicly insisted that he hates women who throw themselves at him.

"I'm a romantic but I don't expect women to tear their clothes off when they meet me. That sort of thing only happens if you're nosing around asking for it – I've got everything I need at home. Some women do come on strong though."

Mel is especially prone to retell a story of how one Hollywood actress tried to chat him up at a Tinseltown gathering in front of Robyn. Mel was holding baby Will in his arms at the time. Deeply embarrassed by this flirtatious blonde, he plonked the child on the woman's lap and told her to hold him while he went to the lavatory. What he did not bother to add was that Will had just "done a present" in his nappy.

"When I came back she stood up and screamed. There was a big brown stain in the middle of her expensive white dress. She couldn't get away from me fast enough," chuckled Mel.

There is little doubt that Mel deliberately shuns women in the movie profession. He seems to feel more at home in a rough-and-tumble bar than at a swish Hollywood cocktail party.

In fairness, within months of that last serious incident in Modesto, Mel recognised that he risked losing his family and agreed to consult Alcoholics Anonymous. And according to sources inside his production company he really has calmed down, avoiding nights on the town with dangerously dizzy blondes, ever since.

In the past, he has always tried to get his family to accompany him on location shoots at least some of the time. And cast and crew on those films vividly recall how Mel pleads with Robyn and the children to stay with him as long as possible because he knows there is a very real danger he will transgress if they are not around.

Sadly, with his children getting older, Robyn has made it clear that their education must take precedence over Mel's loneliness on a movie shoot. That is believed to be one of the main reasons why he is especially keen to shoot films either in Los Angeles (like all the *Lethal Weapons*) or at least somewhere not too isolated in the United States.

Mel either completely clams up when asked about his private life or tries to turn the situation around and make it a joke. Like the occasion when one reporter pressed him about his alleged bad behaviour and he responded: "Six kids, a wife, several mistresses. I do lots of drugs, hang around bars, keep company with bad women." He was joking at the time but the magazine duly ran a headline proclaiming "SEX, DRUGS, WOMEN AND MEL".

Long-term damage control, after the Modesto revelations were published in January 1993, came in the shape of a carefully orchestrated campaign to project Mel's image as a clean-living family man.

In the notoriously inoffensive magazine *Hello!* Mel was photographed in France during the editing of his directorial debut movie, *Man without a Face*, just a few weeks after the Modesto incident was exposed. The article referred repeatedly to the actor's commitment to his family and old-fashioned morality.

"Mel Gibson may be famous for his on-screen sexuality,

but he's longing to show to the world that he's an old-fashioned romantic, who truly believes in gentlemanly behaviour," trilled the magazine.

There was also the very real and scary problem of lovesick fans. Some of them would follow Mel out of supermarkets near his Malibu home. One woman rang his doorbell and dropped her coat to the floor, revealing nothing underneath, when he answered. Another started leaving pornographic notes on his car and erotic messages on his answering machine.

Naturally, Mel and his family were irked by these weird incidents but they also helped Mel to smokescreen his own activities by claiming that women like Cassandra and Shawn were just nutty fans who had become obsessed with him.

As an actor, you're an emotional prostitute –
you get caught with your pants down.
It's like putting your dick on a chopping block
with the knowledge that no one is going
to chop it off.

Mel Gibson hates flying. He looks at aircraft with the same suspicion a desert dweller might have for a canoe. But he overcame his fear in exchange for a $4.2 million fee for *Air America*, a film in which the actor spent almost as much time in the air as on terra firma.

The star confronted his fears very simply – by taking flying lessons. Mel never got an official flying licence but he did learn to fly a helicopter.

"When I started, my instructor told me putting a helicopter down was like landing on a greased golf ball. Well, it wasn't just like landing on a greased golf ball. It was like trying to hump in a hammock. Very, very tricky"

As it turned out, flying was the least of Mel's problems on *Air America*.

The film was shot entirely on location deep in the Golden Triangle of Thailand, an area of jungle-clad mountains and almost constant steamy rain showers. Opium poppies bloom in the small clearings between the highlands and drug traders are the main employers in the region.

Mel had already discovered during a stopover in Bangkok *en route* to the jungle that any ideas he might have had about not being harrassed in such a distant land were far-fetched. Everywhere he went, a chorus of "Mad Mack!" was uttered by the locals.

"They didn't know what my name was but they knew I was Mad Max," recalled Mel. "That was the thing that really surprised me."

Air America had been pitched to Mel during earlier discussions in Hollywood, as a serious action adventure movie about the covert airline which the CIA ran out of Laos during the Vietnam War. The real Air America had been a remarkable operation, fruit of United States paranoia and run by a group of CIA operatives with fewer scruples than a ticket tout. Basically, Air America would fly literally anything across the area if they thought it would combat the spread of Communism.

"Air America flew everything from elephants to opium to monkey embryos. It was amazing. It was the world's biggest airline at one time and you could get anything, anywhere, anytime on these planes," lectured an enthusiastic Mel before he got to Thailand.

And the CIA devised some ludicrous schemes in an attempt to demoralise the enemy; they dropped vast boxes of oversized condoms behind Vietcong lines convinced that the enemy would be so overawed by the size and virility of American troops they would surrender instantly. But the Vietcong were far from impressed. They put the condoms over their rifle barrels to keep them dry, making them all the more effective for shooting American soldiers.

The pilots who worked for Air America were a law unto themselves. Although undeniably brave, tough and skilful, they were avionic cowboys – and quite a number were crazy from having lived too long in the jungle and sampled too many narcotics.

Initially, the project – which was backed by the Carolco company that created *Rambo* – was to feature Sean Connery and Kevin Costner, following their phenomenally successful pairing in *The Untouchables* (a role in which Mel had regretfully rejected two years earlier). But when their joint fee was rumoured to have risen to $15 million, the producers decided to look elsewhere for their stars.

Mel was then signed to play the younger of two Air America pilots. But he felt that at 34, he was "too wrinkly to get away with that new-kid stuff any more". So, the movie's producers cast Robert Downey Jr as the rookie and Mel played Gene Ryack, a world-weary pilot and gun-runner who finds the Laotian way of life to his liking and wants to get out of the dirty tricks business. The female interest was provided by American actress Nancy Travis.

Yet again Mel was tempted into playing a character he felt was not that far removed from his own personality. In Hollywood, scripts were now being virtually tailor-made for the star with writers casting their main role in the Mel mould before even starting a project. And, as Mel explained before setting off for deepest Thailand, those sort of parts did attract his attention.

"Ryack was born in the USA, he is Captain America but he's been so long away and has become so cynical and jaded that he's Asian on the inside. In a way, I'm a bit like that. I was born in the US, moved away and became something else, a creature not of my own creation."

Mel initially saw *Air America* as a serious project with a matching theme.

"In *Air America* we present the truth about war and business and how they are inseparable. It's a business and somebody's getting rich and it's always the wrong people," he said in the lead-up to the shoot. Unfortunately, he might as well have been talking about Hollywood instead of the CIA.

Mel landed in the Golden Triangle in early 1990 together with British director Roger Spottiswoode, a large cast, fifteen cameras, three units, five hundred crew, thirty aeroplanes and helicopters rented from the Thai military plus a physician to treat all afflictions (of which there were many).

And there was Mel's companion – a tall, well-built lady, Terri DePaolo. She had become a development executive at Mel's production company two years earlier, but to everyone else on the shoot of *Air America* she was "Mel's minder". The idea was that everywhere Mel went Terri would follow. Unfortunately, she was not very effective in her nanny role.

Terri DePaolo left Mel's company in 1991. She is very reluctant to talk about her former boss – mainly because she was forced to sign a confidentiality agreement before joining his firm.

"It's a very difficult situation. We had a kind of bitter-sweet relationship but I still care about him a great deal," Terri told me in Los Angeles in May, 1993.

"But there is a better life than being Mel's minder . . . "

Before shooting of the $35 million movie could begin there were major obstacles to overcome. Tragedy struck the project when an Israeli first assistant director died before work got under way. Talk among the cast and crew was that the technician had picked up a deadly virus while scouting for locations near a huge waste dump on the outskirts of Chiang Mai. Then there was the script. Mel decided he wanted to "lighten it up"; it became a trivial treatment of a serious subject.

Finally, there was Khun Sa, reputed to be the world's most powerful smack dealer. *Air America* was to be filmed right in the middle of his territory. And Khun Sa happened to be protected by a well-equipped private army which was in the habit of taking pot shots at any aircraft daring to fly over the region. Considering that more than 50 per cent of *Air America* was scheduled to take place in or around aircraft, the drug lord did pose something of a hazard . . .

According to production staff on the movie, fears over Khun Sa were quelled when it emerged that the drug baron was a keen "Mad Mack" fan and an autographed message of greetings from Mel would probably go a long way to promoting peace and harmony for the duration of the *Air America* shoot. Reluctantly, Mel agreed and a peace deal was struck.

Filming took place in mountainside communities that had experienced little or no contact with the outside world. Hollywood meant nothing to these people and Mel found it all very refreshing at first. It appealed to his sense of humour.

"It was fun, a great deal of fun, although it looked tough. The Thais are very hospitable. The guy who managed the place where we stayed – I won't call it a hotel because it was something else – would go down to the river, catch an eight-foot snake, come back, throw it in the pot and eat it."

At Chiang Mai, the main town in the hill country, "Mad Mack" attracted a lot of attention from the locals during a long series of night-time shoots. Crowds would gather every evening outside the Arun Rai Chinese restaurant, which had been transformed for the film into the White Rose, an establishment fondly remembered by those who frequented it during the Vietnam War. In those days, everything was available at the White Rose, from bar girls to guns to marijuana carefully rolled into cigarettes and sold in Marlboro packets. The more things alter the less they change: all the same vices were available to everyone who descended on Chiang Mai.

Mel – suffering from chronic back problems that have plagued him since he played rugby at St Leo's College twenty years earlier – surrendered his tired flesh to the ministrations of local masseusses.

With a broad smile, he enthusiastically told one visitor to the movie set: "It's the best massage I've ever come across. It's miraculous. This is a stress-free country. Everyone's cool."

In Chiang Mai, Mel was being harassed by prostitutes the whole time. Virtually every time he walked through the lobby of his hotel, lithe teenagers would approach him. Many of the hotel staff were used to Westerners ordering girls every night and they presumed Mel was no different from just about everyone else.

Even when the movie switched locations to the more isolated Mai Hong Son, many Chiang Mai prostitutes simply took a bus to where the 500-plus cast and crew were based and began bargaining for sex all over again. With only two bars in the entire town it was hard to avoid them.

One of the Thai crew – an attractive mother – took Mel under her wing and kept him on the straight and narrow.

"I wanted to protect him from the obvious temptations. Many girls would have viewed it as a feather in their cap if they slept with a movie star like Mel!"

The same source said that he was a different person when wife Robyn arrived in Thailand.

"Mel completely calmed down when she turned up with some of the children."

The woman – who became a good friend to him – said: "Mel is a troubled soul like most actors. He is always on the edge. Always looking for something more out of life."

Within a short time, the informant joined a posse of three more beautiful Thai girls from the film's wardrobe department, who took it upon themselves to protect Mel from the hordes of prostitutes.

"We did not want him to get into trouble. We were very protective towards him," one of them explained.

Thai wardrobe girl Juh was one of those who helped protect Mel from the numerous prostitutes. Helped by her Thai wardrobe friend Micky Bacon. The girls "guarded" Mel and nurtured him through the entire shoot.

At Mel's hotel in Chiang Mai, an artful tour operator organised tourist trips to point out a closed door, announcing to his customers: "And there is Mel's room." Meanwhile, the manager complained that he was completely out of beer because "the movie people drank it all".

Line producer Michael Kagan conceded that there were some local difficulties.

"We are having difficulty doing business the Western way. The Thais always say yes, but you have to interpret what that means. They're willing to help, but sometimes it's not in their means," he explained wearily.

After Mel's wife Robyn and two of his children arrived in Chiang Mai, the actor – even when he was shooting elsewhere – would join them on his days off. And he kept a generally low profile, developing his new-found love of sketching by carrying a pad of artist's paper wherever he went and drawing some very lifelike pictures of members of the cast. But Robyn did not show up until the last couple of weeks of the four-month shoot. And there were many incidents before she appeared.

Among extras used in some of the night-time scenes at the White Rose bar was United States Ambassador Charles Ray and his 13-year-old daughter.

"I did it to keep the peace in my family," he sighed when asked why on earth he was at the location in the first place. "My daughter said that if I had a chance to be in a movie with Mel Gibson and I didn't do it, she would never live under the same roof with me again. I figured it better to spend five nights out here in the streets than the next five years with an irate daughter," explained the Ambassador.

But as the boredom set in, Mel began enjoying the occasional drink with crew members after a long day's shooting. Sometimes he would wander around the town with his video camera pretending to be a television reporter. In one restaurant he approached a bemused-looking couple and asked them: "What brings you to Chiang Mai on a night like this?" They looked completely aghast when they realised the man doing the talking was a Hollywood superstar.

Mel kept the gag going for about five minutes before admitting who he was and cheerfully posing with the couple for photographs, and signing autographs. But his antics were really nothing more than a smokescreen for the fact that he had got very bored with *Air America*. He yearned to go home to Robyn, who was about to have the couple's sixth child and did not want to give birth in the middle of the jungle.

At another location, the *Air America* production benefited the local economy by paying for the construction of an entire hotel, built especially for the crew. They also brought hot water and Western toilets to all their other hotels. Even the airport runway was improved and a whole new hangar built for one important scene in the film.

The relationship between Mel and Robert Downey Jr was by all accounts "businesslike" but not close. Mel, of all people, complained that his co-star's sense of humour was "weird".

"Downey was a typical Hollywood actor, out jogging at dawn every morning and in bed early most evenings, whilst Mel just wanted to be out with the boys," said one crew member.

Probably the busiest man on the entire film was the unit doctor, a British medic from Fulham, in south west London. He was constantly warning the cast and crew about the presence of AIDS in Thailand. An estimated 80 per cent of prostitutes in the province where *Air America* was being filmed were said to be carrying the virus and it was well known that a number of people from the production had succumbed to temptation and paid for sexual services.

For that matter, plenty of non-sexual diseases are rife in the region. The doctor was working overtime with a hypodermic needle. When one scene involving a larger number of baby pigs had to be shot, he had to inoculate every single member of the crew present against some disease or other that the animals just might be carrying.

Let's not forget the mosquitoes. Vast armies of the insects were making mincemeat of most members of the cast and crew at night, as Mel recounted in his own inimitable way.

"They had mosquitoes there armed with machine guns, it was so bad. We were pumped with so many holes for inoculations I thought I would leak."

Then he decided to give up smoking. It could not have been at a worse time. He began frantically chewing gum and crew members on *Air America* swear that he became visibly more nervous. Occasionally, he would sneak a sly draw on someone else's cigarette and eventually he took up the habit again. It had been a painful experiment for all those in close proximity. With no Robyn about, he would disappear some weekends by flying to the beach resort of Phuket where he would swim and sleep on the beach away from all the rest of the all-too-familiar team.

One one occasion he shared a few beers with director Spottiswoode, confiding that what he really wanted was to die and come back as somebody whom nobody knew.

As filming progressed, events became increasingly bizarre. The crew was homesick and fed up with having to deal with the locals. And there was the rain. It didn't just shower occasionally. It came down in torrents for sometimes as long as thirty-six hours at a time. At one point, Roger Spottiswoode even consulted a village soothsayer to find out when the rain would stop.

Then an earthquake struck in the middle of the night. Although many of the film team were used to the occasional tremor back in Los Angeles, this was a big quake. It turned out to be 6.1 on the Richter scale and Mel, naturally, described the scene in graphic detail.

"You wake up at four in the morning and see the chandeliers swinging up and snapping on the ceiling and you see the top of the building touch the pavement. At 6.1 it was a big jolt, just short of the building falling over. I stood in a doorway and things were really jumping. But you can't beat the rush of adrenaline. Whoosh! With an earthquake you really know you're *alive*."

But it wasn't just the conditions that were getting Mel down during the making of *Air America*. Along with the director and producers, he had seen some of the rushes from the early days of filming and found that the film wasn't living up to its early promise. He regarded himself as "one of the boys" and became particularly close to a number of technicians as his boredom grew. He did not throw tantrums like most big stars do when they are unhappy. As *Air America* producer Daniel Melnick puts it:

"The only thing Mel demands is that he's treated like everyone else. He doesn't want star treatment. He eats in the hot sun during lunch breaks with everybody else and he's most comfortable standing around talking with cast and crew."

Mel even organised a party at the hotel in Mae Hong Son, where he was staying. Everyone was instructed to wear Blues Brothers pork-pie hats and bring a bottle of tequila. According to British crew members it was "one hell of a party".

In the same town, Mel became a regular at a bar called the Black and White – shades of his teetotal father!

One night he got involved in an incident with definite echoes of those distant days when he got in so much trouble during shooting of *The Bounty*.

"Mel turned up in the bar with a beer bottle already in his hand and came over and greeted us. He was already very drunk and he kept on about how much he was missing his wife and kids. It was really sad to see," recalled a British member of the crew.

As the night progressed and Mel and his two compatriots began swallowing quantities of the local beer, the star became more and more incoherent. Mel spoke in slurred terms about the "marvellous massages" he had received from some of the local girls.

"At first he was a bit reluctant to talk about them but he soon came out with it," said the British crew member.

Suddenly, one of the other two men made a blasphemous remark. It was enough to send Mel into a fury.

"Mel looked daggers at this guy and got up and walked out, slamming the bar door so hard that the glass broke," the British crew member told me.

Then Mel – who has always been proud of the way he used to feign headbutts on other pupils when at school – walked back in and readied himself for action.

"He went head to head with this guy. They were eyball to eyball. It was serious stuff and it was really scary. He was quite prepared to have a fight just over some throwaway remark about God.

"To make matters worse, the manager of the bar was screaming at Mel, demanding that he pay someone to clear up the glass window he had smashed. Eventually the other man paid him off to keep him quiet.

"Finally I calmed him down and he just staggered off outside with another beer in his hand," added the informant.

But the incident did not finish there. As so often with Mel, he awoke next day riddled with guilt about his actions and stumbled on to the set trying to find the man he had appeared ready to kill with his bare hands.

"But he'd gone back to England that morning. That's the thing about Mel. He gets really drunk and then the next day regrets his actions. It seems to be the story of his life."

About halfway through the shooting of *Air America*, Mel got uncharacteristically involved in a row with the film's producers. He wanted to get home to Australia for the birth of his sixth child. He had never forgiven himself for missing the birth of Hannah all those years earlier during the filming of *Gallipoli* and, in any case, he was fed up to the back teeth with being in Thailand. Excessive drinking sessions were leaving him with a sore head and a short temper most mornings. And the shoot had slowed to a crawl, thanks to continual weather problems; they were well behind schedule. Mel even suggested to producer Dan Melnick that he be allowed to fly back Down Under for a few days while Robyn had the child and return when needed. But Carolco were worried that if they let Mel go, he might never come back, and besides, he was needed on set for virtually every set-up. There was no question of him pulling out. But the producer's response sent him into a deep depression. He withdrew from most of the friendships he had made during the shoot. When Robyn did give birth to their sixth child, it should have been a time to celebrate, but Mel was in such a bad mood that most colleagues avoided anything but essential contact with him. In fact, he had ended up listening on the phone to the details of new baby Milo's birth, from 9-year-old daughter Hannah, who had "stood in" for her father at Robyn's side and gave him a "blow-by-blow" account.

Mel got back to being his sunnier self when Robyn flew in to Thailand following a series of appeals from the actor, who was seriously worried that his drinking would escalate unless she came to his rescue.

As a result of his disagreements with the movie's producers, when it came to pose for a traditional photograph of cast and crew in front of one of the vast Hercules transport planes used during the filming, Mel refused to play. It was his way of protesting against the decision not to allow him home for the birth of his son.

The outcome was a vast photograph showing everyone involved in *Air America* – and an empty canvas chair with Mel's name emblazoned across the back, but no sign of the star.

"He was very angry about it," one British crew member told me later. "Mel felt betrayed and, quite frankly, just like the rest of us, he was desperately homesick by that stage."

His unofficial minder Terri DePaolo confirmed: "We did have a little bit of a problem with Mel on that photo because the producers would not let him go to the birth of his child."

Air America's problems were compounded six months later when the producers decided that the movie's ending was not "upbeat enough" after it had been previewed for audiences in the United States. With just three weeks to go before the film's scheduled release, they tracked Mel down to London where he was shooting the final scenes in *Hamlet*. Awkwardly, he had grown a beard and had his hair dyed for his new role. Carolco were in a state of complete panic and mounted the sort of salvaging operation only Hollywood is capable of.

An *Air America* unit booked into London's costly Savoy Hotel and waited patiently for Mel to complete *Hamlet*. Then they rushed him to Shepperton Studios, on the outskirts of London, and filmed an entirely new scene with co-star Robert Downey Jnr. Mel got $100,000 for the one-day shoot after his agent Ed Limato demanded his client be "compensated" for the extra work.

But when *Air America* finally hit the screens, they need not have bothered. A happy ending was the least of its lacks. Just as Mel had privately predicted, it was a disappointing movie. In fact the most entertaining moments came when veteran Chinese actor Burt Kwouk – star of such classics as

Thunderbirds and the *Pink Panther* films – appeared on screen as a crooked general.

Some claimed *Air America* lacked true direction. Others, like British journalist Christopher Robbins, on whose book, *Air America*, the film had been based, said that Hollywood had ruined the story by sanitising it. "The film is a very trivial comedy about a tragedy – 100,000 people were killed. The one thing, had you asked me, not to do with the book would be to make it into a comedy . . . I just couldn't believe it. I thought that at least it would have been interesting. But it went the way of many things in Hollywood. They put $35 million in one end and a turkey came out the other end."

Australian film critic Matt White, writing in *the Daily Mirror*, said: "It's time Mel took things a little more seriously and showed us some more of the Gibson acting talent that doesn't have to rely on charm and scripted heroics."

More criticism came from the very pilots upon whom the film was supposed to be based. The Association of Air America Veterans said the movie "was not true to the pilots and crews, the customers, the events, the mission, the results, the policies, and the *raison d'être* of Air America". "Apart from that –" as the joke goes . . .

One former pilot accused the movie's producers of making a "political obscenity" and asked, "Did Hanoi make this film?"

But the most damning remarks came from Mel himself when he insisted that Australian showbusiness writer Dan McDonnell switch off his tape recorder during an interview to promote *Air America*.

"He pointed to my tape recorder and said: 'Turn that thing off' and then asked me what I really thought of the movie. I told him it could have been good but it just didn't mean anything," recalled McDonnell.

Then Mel picked up the film's press kit and started laughing out loud.

"He said he hated the movie but he had to promote it. He was very tired and very pissed off. He felt he had just spent four days promoting a film he did not like."

Mel was exhausted after *Air America*. He rejected the lead role in *Ghost* that earned Patrick Swayze world-wide acclaim and at least $10 million. Those earlier problems in the mid-1980s were drifting back to haunt him. He knew he could not afford to burn out again because Hollywood might not give him a third chance. He even admitted that his state of mind was such that he "never wanted to work again". But he would not take such drastic action – yet.

Instead, he planned to take time off, continue breeding his cattle and get to know his sixth child Milo. *Hamlet* was beckoning and he considered that to be the most important challenge and prize of his career.

You quit drinking, you work much better.
Your head is so clear.

Mel's battle with alcohol has been a persistent cloud over much of his career. The star has often given up the bottle for months at a time only to backslide when the pressures are mounting.

But in late 1990 his agent Ed Limato and wife Robyn decided that the time had come for Mel to take positive action to beat booze for ever. They persuaded the star to enrol in Alcoholics Anonymous near the family's main Californian home in Malibu, near Los Angeles.

At first Mel was reluctant to get involved with AA. He felt that the only person who could get him to give up drinking was himself. His attitude towards AA matched his opinion of psychiatric therapists; if you can't sort yourself out then don't bother.

But both Limato and Robyn feared that if Mel did not go completely on the wagon then there was a danger that his career could implode, self-destruct. Stories about his early days boozing were well known because Mel had publicly admitted them. But few people realised that the announcement that he had given up drinking in 1987 had marked nothing more than a temporary truce with alcohol. He had gone back on the bottle with a vengeance.

In the depths of the Thai jungle, his fondness for beer with a whisky thrown in for good measure had stunned colleagues. And while in London making *Hamlet*, there had been similar incidents including one occasion when he turned up at a nightclub, whose owner was later exposed as a drug pusher. With a neat vodka in one hand, Mel leapt on a table and led revellers in a version of "Waltzing Matilda".

According to eye witnesses, Mel started urging three friends, cast members from *Hamlet*, to "have a party". The star eventually rolled out of Brown's Club, in London's West End, at 3.30 a.m.

The main problem was that booze and Hollywood no longer mixed. The days of drunken stars causing chaos in bars across Tinseltown had long since gone. Many celebrities turned teetotal in the early 1980s and studio executives were making it plain that they would not tolerate actors with drink trouble. In some cases, stars were being required to take medical tests to uncover what level of dependency they had on alcohol or drugs. There was a genuine fear that if Mel did not give up the demon drink then he could be blocked out of the system.

Yet Mel – despite all the boozing – was never unprofessional when he was working. He always knew his lines. He was always on time and he never burdened anyone with his "problem".

Lethal Weapon director Richard Donner was astonished when he found that Mel was secretly knocking back five bottles of beer before reaching the set. Coolly, the veteran film-maker made no effort to make Mel feel guilty about his drink problem. Donner went so far as to tell friends that the star drank beer like water and so long as it did not affect his performance then he was prepared to tolerate it.

Photographs in the Hollywood press at the time frequently portrayed Mel as the friendly drunk: eyelids drooping, glass of booze in one hand, cigarette in the other. He started showing up at tacky film premieres "just for the free drinks".

While at the Venice Film Festival in the mid-1980s, Mel bumped into a little-known actor called Kevin Costner in the bar of the Excelsior Hotel. They struck up a conversation and it emerged that Costner was attending the festival to help promote his films *Fandango* and *Silverado*, movies that marked the start of what was to become a phenomenal career. Mel, already deemed a box office attraction, was considerably the more famous of the two at the time. Both men took to each other instantly and started drinking at a most convivial rate.

Costner recollected that the two of them – both married with families back at home – stumbled outside the hotel and decided to "borrow" a couple of locked bikes and go for a spin.

"We went outside, and they were all locked. So Mel went off and found one, but not two. I said: 'I'll ride'; I'd just done this bike picture. And it was great. There we were, on Lido Island, and Mel's on the goddamned handlebars looking like ET! I even think there was a full moon."

Rather sadly, Mel and Costner did not keep up their initial friendship as the Californian actor headed for the same goal of all-out Hollywood stardom and even, to a certain extent, overtook his one-time drinking partner. The two did not keep in touch even though their careers collided frequently in the late Eighties and early Nineties.

In Australia, Mel's drinking continued at a ferocious pace when he consumed vast numbers of tequila slammers in a hotel bar with local pop star James Reyne and his three pretty backing singers.

And on the set of *Tequila Sunrise*, his drink quota steadily rose, although once again, neither his co-stars Michelle Pfeiffer and Kurt Russell nor director Robert Towne were concerned, since he was still delivering superb performances when required.

No matter – in the new, moral Hollywood, few accepted that Mel could continue that way without the booze affecting him eventually. In a town where "being in denial" is considered the worst sin of all, sceptics whispered that he would fall apart sooner rather than later.

Mel had never wanted to be part of the Hollywood system and he had laughed at some of the American stars who pretended to have absolutely no vices. He saw going to AA as an example of that system beating him and he did not want to give in without a fight. There was this inbuilt pride that stopped him doing what everyone else wanted. He has always loved going in the opposite direction.

When he had given up booze in the past it had been he and not anyone else who had suggested it. He had done it himself. He knew how damaging drink was and admitted as much after giving up in the mid-Eighties.

"People think they have a better time when they drink. But alcohol is a prop. It's much more fun without it."

Now Robyn – who had frequently in the past encouraged him to give up (albeit temporarily) – felt that this time it had to work and she would have to be the one to "steer" Mel through. She warned him that their marriage could end if he did not get a booze cure.

Mel's other big fear about AA was that his attendance would become public knowledge and he hated the very idea of anyone finding out that he had been to such a place. But Robyn and Ed Limato would not take no for an answer. They agreed that there was a risk that Mel's membership of AA would become public knowledge, but they insisted that there was no room for excuses and they would face that problem if and when it occurred.

It took a few weeks for a British tabloid newspaper to get an exclusive tip-off about Mel's membership of the Malibu branch of AA. When Limato got wind of the rag's intention to run a story he mounted yet another "damage-control" operation to keep the story out of the press. Tens of thousands of dollars were spent on trying to convince a high court judge in London that if the story were published it would be a serious breach of privacy. After days of legal deliberation, the judge threw out Mel's lawyers' claims and the *Sunday Mirror* carried the following headline in its issue of September 15, 1991: "MEL'S SECRET VISITS TO AA TO BEAT BOOZE HELL".

The paper quoted unnamed fellow AA members about their astonishment at seeing Mel alongside them.

"There he was one day, just sitting with us – then he introduced himself as Mel Gibson and said he had a drink problem," said one AA regular.

Another told the paper: "Mel said a couple of weeks ago that if he didn't get his drinking under control it could start to affect his family. That's why he was there, he told us – because he needs help in fighting this problem. Drinking is the one thing in his life that really frightens him."

The paper recorded that Mel had been attending the Malibu branch of AA – which meets in different locations such as community halls and church buildings – for the previous six weeks.

"When he first came in he looked sad and unsmiling. We could see he had his demons too," said another member. "But soon he was opening up to us. That's part of the therapy. Mel said that he couldn't be with us too frequently because he was dividing his time between his home in Los Angeles and his ranch in Australia."

This member added: "All the girls at the meeting were

bowled over. He looked so cute in his blue jeans and denim shirt."

According to the paper, Mel confronted his problem head on by standing up and talking to the rest of the group.

"Mel told us that nothing worried his wife as much as his boozing, and she encouraged him to join AA. There were about twenty people in the group that night. You could see it was hard for Mel, admitting he had a problem over his boozing."

The *Sunday Mirror* had been startled by the legal battle with Mel's representatives because it was hardly as if Mel's problems with alcohol were novel. But Limato and LA lawyers believed that it was essential to promote a new image of Mel being whiter than white. They also wanted Hollywood to believe that Mel was the victim of a vicious smear campaign. The story came and went, despite them, prompting sympathy for Mel from within the film community. Truth had proved stronger than hype and whitewash.

Mel has been off alcohol for two years now. There are no longer bloodshot or black eyes to be worked on by anxious make-up artists. In their place, Mel's most famous trademark – those exquisite orbs, the colour of bright, fresh cornflowers – gaze out more clearly than before.

"Whenever I'm tempted to go back to my drinking days, I know I can turn to Robyn. One look at her and I know it's not worth it," Mel assured one friend.

Some of his boozing was in reaction to a continual health problem with his back. It all started with a rugby injury at St Leo's nearly twenty-five years before, and was worsened by that time he fell to the floor in a bar brawl in Tahiti during the making of *The Bounty*.

He told friends that the recurring pain was sometimes agonising, but that alcohol offered an escape from it.

He also, of course, discovered that he had been suffering from the yeast-type illness of Candida. It is an infection that makes the sufferer crave for sugar and . . . alcohol. In Hollywood, some cynics suggested that Mel's latest ailment was just a clever publicity device to provide an alibi for all the star's heavy drinking in the past.

But he had been suffering from Candida for more than ten years without even realising it. Fellow NIDA student Linda Newton recalled how Mel used to "completely black out" after drinking just a few beers during their drama school days together. That, according to medical experts, is a classic sign of Candida.

On another occasion he stopped at a Los Angeles hamburger bar, ordered two burgers with chips to take away and downed three bottles of beer while waiting. To the astonishment of other customers, he fell flat on his face and had to be helped to a taxi.

Mel discovered the ailment when he was recommended to a Sikh doctor in Sydney after complaining about feeling run-down and exhausted following the *Lethal Weapon* shoot in Los Angeles in 1986.

The specialist told Mel that his hyperactive behaviour had most probably been caused by Candida and advised the star to give up alcohol completely, as well as sugar, bread, salad dressings and vinegar. Under the new strict regime Mel rediscovered life without constant headaches and even his complexion improved. He removed the bar from his home in Australia as a gesture of intent to Robyn and the kids. But he fell from grace and started boozing again within six months.

Through those difficult days of Mel's induction into Alcoholics Anonymous in the summer of 1991, the actor tried to keep himself occupied, and away from the bottle. He even agreed to record a guest appearance with fellow Aussie Dame Edna Everage – alias actor Barry Humphries.

The television special was being filmed in Hollywood and featured other stars like Julio Iglesias and Charlton Heston.

But Dame Edna's treatment of "her idol" Mel was hilarious and did more than anything else at that time to prove that the old Mel sparkle had not died.

The offbeat chat show host insisted that Mel share a sauna with "her" and grabbed his hand and greeted the actor with, "You're huge, aren't you? Professionally huge. And your Lethal Weapon, well two as a matter of fact – were tremendous. You really are very big, Possum."

Mel was in stitches even though he had to cling to his skimpy towel on getting out of the sauna – in case Dame Edna tried to pull it off.

But "she" insisted she had seen it all before.

"I'm safe – I'm a happily bereaved woman so you don't have to cover up. Women all over the world would kill to be here."

Mel lapped up every moment of it. Usually he tended to be shy and reserved and "hated" one-on-one TV encounters like the disastrous Barbara Walters show he did during the making of *Hamlet*. But, as one of the Dame Edna show's producers said, "Mel was so happy to be amongst other Australians. He seemed so relaxed."

Around the same time, Mel's younger brother Donal took his biggest step towards a major acting prize when he starred in a film produced by Phil Avalon – the same character who had given Mel his first break fifteen years earlier in *Summer City*.

Fatal Bond, co-starring ex-boxer Joe Bugner, was a thriller and Phil Avalon says that Donal, two years younger than Mel, was paid considerably more for his starring role than the $400 Mel did (or did not depending on whom you believe) make from his feature debut. Donal was reluctant to be drawn into comparisons with his famous older brother.

"Mel and I are not the same character and we have different attitudes," said Donal, who also starred in a low-budget movie with Linda Blair, star of the original *Exorcist* film. "It would be foolish to match myself against Mel. Most actors are never going to be as successful as him."

But he did hope that both of them had an ability to turn any part – however small – into something memorable.

"Mel and I can take a part which looks like nothing on paper and do something with it."

Donal has so far refused to venture outside Australia. Many family and friends say that if it were not for being in the constant shadow of his more famous brother then he might be doing even better.

Hamlet is a risk. You open up your shirt and there's a dartboard on your chest – it's dangerous.

The Four Seasons Hotel in Beverly Hills was the fairly un-remarkable setting in which Mel agreed to star in a project that would profoundly influence his career – more than any other film he will ever make. Sitting opposite him in the quiet hotel restaurant was Italian director Franco Zeffirelli, a notoriously eccentric, bombastic man. There was a loaded silence because Zeffirelli had just asked one of the most commercial movie stars in the world if he would like to play the lead in *Hamlet*.

Mel was aghast. His first reaction was that it would be madness to film a play that's been around for four hundred years, that some of the finest actors in the world have failed to master – and then he would be making himself a target for every critic in the world.

However, as the two men enjoyed a light lunch of spaghetti, Mel started to wonder. Maybe it wasn't such a mad idea after all. He was always bemoaning the fact that Hollywood rarely stretched him. Now here was an opportunity to prove that he was capable of anything. In any case, there was something intriguing about Zeffirelli's proposal. He was offering Mel a chance to get back to his acting roots. By the end of that lunch Mel was halfway to being convinced. After a reading for Zeffirelli the next day, he was desperate for the job and refused to listen to agent Ed Limato, who tried desperately to persuade his star not to play the role, even though he had been instrumental in getting the two men together. There were fears in Tinseltown that Mel might damage his lucrative career as an action adventure hero. But the actor did not see it that way.

"I don't care what they say . . . I don't give a shit," he growled.

And Mel had a very distinct handle on *Hamlet* as a serious subject.

"All the images . . . people listening to one another and spying on one another and all the intrigue and blackness and darkness in people's souls. It was almost pre-Christian – Christianity has just arrived – it's dark and decayed and rotten with death everywhere." Mel was very convincing in his explanation of why he took the role.

"I'm very excited about Franco's vision. He'll do it in a very rotten, pre-Christian state of Denmark, where pagan Vikings kill each other and scheme all the time."

Signing Mel for the part was a terrific coup for the Italian director. Now there would be no shortage of financial backers for the project. Some Hollywood sceptics suggested that Zeffirelli's main motive in casting Mel was to guarantee he got the film made. And it was well known that Warner Brothers – makers of the incredibly successful *Lethal Weapon* movies – were hoping to sign Mel (they eventually did in February 1991) to a long-term contract. An investment in *Hamlet* would be their way of showing good faith to Mel. But both men maintain that was not the case and, to prove the point,

Mel's own production company was widely reported to have helped finance *Hamlet* – although it is unlikely that the cash they provided came from anywhere else than Warner Brothers' coffers.

Hollywood showbusiness reporter Dan McDonnell opined, "Warners bankrolled *Hamlet* as a sweetener to get Mel to sign that long-term contract with them."

Zeffirelli emphasised: "Mel put his life and career there. Imagine if he did not succeed. He would have been the joke of the industry."

Mel did not see it in quite such dramatic terms but he was alert to the professional risk of the $15 million project. Yet, taking his father's advice to him as a boy, he was not that bothered. He knew he was going to get some flak but he quite enjoyed the thrill of defiance. He agreed to a greatly reduced fee of less than $1 million (plus a percentage of the profits if it made any money) as a gesture of absolute commitment to the project.

In a phone call to actress Glenn Close, chosen to play Hamlet's mother Queen Gertrude, before any of the actors met for rehearsals, he admitted: "Everyone's laughing at me over here. But screw 'em."

Many people in the industry *were* laughing at him. They saw it in terms that were perfectly reflected by a tabloid newspaper headline shortly after the official announcement of his involvement.

"MAD MAX TO PLAY CRAZY DANE".

The media predicted that massive quantities of egg would end up on Mel's face. Some cynics teased that Zeffirelli was probably intending to sign Sylvester Stallone as Romeo. Others sneered that Mel would turn a soliloquy into a call for the cows to come home. And they kept reminding Mel of stage giants who had made Hamlet their own, over the years: Laurence Olivier, John Gielgud, Alec Guinness, Derek Jacobi,

Nicol Williamson to mention but a few. The role was steeped in tradition. There was a presumption, albeit debatable, that in order to play Hamlet an actor must have attended the Royal Academy of Dramatic Art or the Central School of Speech Training and Dramatic Art, in London.

As Richard Burton once said of the role: "You just have to wait your turn. Meanwhile you stand there with arrows quivering in your flesh."

Mel – whose views on the British were tainted by what had happened to his ancestors at the hands of the Black and Tans – relished every bit of snobbery that came his way. Not only did he have something to prove to the critics who said he was only capable of playing one-dimensional action-packed heroes, he also liked taking on the British establishment, with an outsider's chance of beating them at their own game.

Many of those laughing and sneering at him had conveniently forgotten his background in classical theatre. Shakespeare was part of his staple diet at the National Institute of Dramatic Art, in Sydney. After all, he had played Romeo and been considered for Hamlet, only to be rejected for being too young at the time.

Masterful director Zeffirelli had already successfully translated Shakespeare on to the screen with adaptations of *Romeo and Juliet* (which grossed $90 million) in the late Sixties and *The Taming of the Shrew* starring Richard Burton and Elizabeth Taylor. Zeffirelli had been trying for years to film *Hamlet* and had directed it on stage in 1964; then failed to mount a stage production in Los Angeles in 1979 with Richard Gere in the title role.

Before the cameras rolled on this latest version, starring Mel, the director declared: "I must break with tradition. I never loved this self-masturbating, blond, impotent, supposedly romantic prince who is presented as the definitive

Hamlet. Hell, the role has been so emasculated, it has been played by women. He is fit enough to duel and I think he is the opposite of vulnerable. He knows about the dealings of the world but he has a divided heart. He sees his duty but can't bring himself to do it."

Zeffirelli claimed he was in fact a long-time admirer of Mel's work, including the *Mad Max* films.

"I responded to the energy, the violence, the danger of this character and it made me think of him a bit as an Elizabethan character."

The same went for Marty Riggs, in *Lethal Weapon*. The Italian was said to have been especially moved by that tense suicide attempt.

"He has stature. I was impressed by him. I began to think here is my Hamlet . . . It was the voice. I was madly in love with the voice," enthused the director as word of his "surprise" choice spread through the film industry.

Zeffirelli began signing up Mel's supporting players and they all sounded equally intrigued by the choice of leading man. Glenn Close said her initial reaction was: "Why not? I've always loved his work. I think he has the imagination of an actor who has resources which are yet to be challenged."

British actress Helena Bonham-Carter, who was to play Ophelia, admitted she was "sort of surprised. But then I thought it could have been a genius move. First of all, I realised Mel was not going to be a fool and if he couldn't give a good shot at the part he wouldn't do it."

The star of such diverse projects as *Room with a View* and "Miami Vice" later reversed her stance on Mel by making fun of him just before *Hamlet* opened in London.

"He's got a very basic sense of humour. It's a bit lavatorial and not very sophisticated. His face is wonderful and his eyes are extraordinary but physically he is not in proportion. He's got this odd sort of body. He's got short legs, a slightly over-long body and a concave chest," she told one reporter.

Meanwhile, Mel had to go into training. Once again, he tried to give up smoking and, by all accounts, managed to stay off cigarettes for parts of the five-month shoot. His voice coach Julia Wilson Dickson warned him that the long passages of Elizabethan dialogue were going to be all the more easy if he could regulate his breathing. Having cut out his usual two-packs of Marlboro, he replaced them with jaw-wrenching mouthfuls of nicotine chewing gum that he would only remove when actually speaking his lines.

Another hurdle was the sword fighting. Mel – more used to handling a gun than any other lethal weapon – had to master the ballet-like intricacies of fencing, as Hamlet was a swordsman. Finally, he had to learn to ride a horse – something that the purchase of trail motorbikes on his farm back in Australia had helped him avoid until then.

Before shooting began, Mel was being made painfully aware that he had taken on the Everest of his career. He could not have the occasional cigarette to soothe his nerves and he was starting to be haunted by the character of Hamlet. Mel could not decide precisely how to play the role – and that was bothering him the most.

"I couldn't sleep at night with this character. It was like something that kind of ruled your whole life . . . "

Mel disclosed even more frustration a few months later when he admitted: "There are moments playing Hamlet that make you want to rip your hair out because he is the most confounding character ever written. The only consistent thing about Hamlet is his inconsistency, and you're chasing your tail. You feel like you're going mad – and you do, a little bit . . . "

Just a couple of weeks before filming was scheduled to begin he booked himself and Robyn into the $175-a-night Henlow Grange health farm, in Bedfordshire, to limber up with a few days of seaweed baths, saunas and aromatherapy.

The film was shot at Shepperton Studios near London and at locations in castles along the Kent and Scottish coasts. Mel moved his family into a $14,000-a-month, eight-bedroom house with an acre of land at Ascot, Berkshire, on the outskirts of London. The garden of the $2 million estate was soon strewn with skateboards and bikes and the whole neighbourhood was abuzz with news of the movie star tenant.

Teenager Debbie King got to meet her idol when he strolled into the local newsagent where she worked. "I couldn't believe my eyes. It was just like a dream. He asked me for twenty Marlboro and a packet of mints." So much for abandoning his smokes . . .

Any hopes Mel had – despite his beard and dyed hair – that his stay at the estate might go unnoticed were soon dashed. But then the same house had been rented to singing star Diana Ross the previous year and, according to neighbours, "she was much noisier, with helicopters flying in and out the whole time".

Mel had got into the habit of enrolling his children in schools wherever he happened to be filming. On this occasion he put them into what he later told friends was a particularly "snotty" establishment. Within weeks Mel and Robyn took the three eldest children out of the school because of what they considered the poor quality of teaching and the fact that there were too many children to each class. Privately, Mel was angered by the school's attitude towards him and his wife.

He also claimed that all three children asked to leave because they hated the drudgery. Mel claimed to be appalled by the British school system, saying that it had stifled his children. There was also talk of an incident involving one of the Gibson children and a bullying classmate. Mel was disappointed and somewhat diverted by his children's temporary educational problems. He felt that it was a typical example of British snobbery at its worst.

Very occasionally, Robyn would visit the set with some of the children, but this was not like *The River*, a few years earlier. Tensions on the set of *Hamlet* were intense. Not only were Mel and his classically-trained co-stars trying to concentrate on every move, but emotions in the heat of the moment were running high and Mel felt under enormous pressure.

As usual, Robyn was providing Mel with a little bit of sanity at home. It was his way of escaping the pressure. He even flew his parents Hutton and Anne over for a month. Mel overcame his misgivings about England by strolling around the streets of London sometimes with just Robyn for company – eating in one particular Chinese restaurant on a number of occasions.

He also enjoyed long walks in the Berkshire countryside with the children, and narrowly avoided danger when a bull charged him and three of the children. There was also hide-and-seek with the children in the grounds of the country mansion, which prompted one neighbour to comment: "You'd never have thought this was the man you see in films blasting people with a shotgun."

However some of the family Sundays were ruined by Mel because he was so hyped up over his role, and insisted that Robyn read all the other parts to him as he ran through his lines over and over in a bid for perfection in his performance the next day.

Mel had got his favourite make-up lady Lois Burwell – with him on *Air America* – to join him on *Hamlet*, and together they pressured the producers to allow him to grow the beard he deemed essential for the role. There was anxiety that none of his fans would appreciate a hairy growth but Mel got his way in the end.

For *Hamlet*, Dunnottar Castle in Scotland became Elsinore. But the gloomy weather so carefully emphasised by Shakespeare was nowhere to be seen when cast and crew turned up. Blazing sunshine, cheery blue skies and a holiday camp atmosphere prevailed. Long delays were endured while technicians spent hours attempting to block out the sun. But it was still cold, bitterly cold, and Mel and his co-stars had to trek half a mile to a portable loo every time they needed to go to the toilet. And photographers popped out of the bushes at regular intervals.

Later, back in London, Mel got so fed up with being hounded by one "little bastard" that he had a bet with a friend that if he failed to stay off cigarettes for the duration of *Hamlet* then he would allow the photographer to take his picture. He lost the bet.

The role was proving physically demanding for Mel in many ways; he had to be sewn into his costume which caused him to sweat profusely beneath the hot lights. At one stage he was losing ten pounds of body weight every day. Then his back started playing up again. Filming was delayed for twenty-four hours after he pulled a muscle while lifting another actor.

Mel's on-set relationship with Glenn Close was said by onlookers to be that of soulmates. The actress admitted that she found the most effective way to stop Mel telling incessant bad jokes was to . . . kiss him.

"They weren't sexual kisses. I really kissed him in order to stop him talking!"

Those awful jokes included altering the whole meaning of the movie's library scene which featured Ian Holm (Polonius) with Mel sitting on a ledge above a ladder with Holm climbing the first few rungs as he speaks. With Hamlet's line: "For yourself, sir, shall grow old as I am . . . if like a crab you could go backward," Mel suddenly gave the ladder a push with his foot, knocking Holm to the ground. A brief, tense silence followed, then a smile invaded Zeffirelli's face. "Yes, yes, leave that in and do it again."

One of the most dreadful jokes of all came when Mel

impaled Holm's character with a single sword stroke as he cowered behind "the arras". Mel immediately piped up: "There's an arras-hole for you."

He defended his wisecracking by telling bystanders that he would "go really nuts" if he had to stay in character the whole time.

Despite all that, Mel felt wary respect for the actors surrounding him.

"It was rather like that nightmare where you have been thrown in the ring with Mike Tyson. Well, I felt I was in there with him – only I was awake.

"When I looked around me on the set I was so intimidated. At times, I almost felt like running home because of the illustrious acting company I was in."

And through all this, his co-stars kept up a constant theme of praise to anyone who would listen. Alan Bates, who played Claudius, said emphatically: "Mel Gibson is brilliant. He is going to surprise a lot of people."

Ian Holm (Polonius) said he had nothing but admiration for Gibson. "It's a hell of a thing for a megastar of his magnitude to put himself on the line playing Hamlet with a lot of Brits. He does just fine." (Mel for his part described Holm as "a great guy – for a Pom!")

Helena Bonham-Carter – despite her reservations – conceded, "He's a real clown, a buffoon. He is so relaxed when you're actually with him."

Not for the first time, Mel was using humour as a way to camouflage his deep-set fears. He felt intimidated by the cast that had been assembled in his honour and non-stop praise from his co-stars was starting to sound just a little hollow, patronising. It was almost as if they were saying: "Considering it's Mel Gibson, he's not that bad."

Mel did not want it to be like that. He saw Hamlet as being a logical extension of his stage roles back in Australia –

yet everyone was treating him like some crass Hollywood star trying to prove a point.

He took his role in *Hamlet* so seriously that Universal had to spend an estimated $200,000 flying dozens of journalists into London to interview him about his previous film *Bird on a Wire*, which was about to open.

Explained Hollywood-based reporter Dan McDonnell: "Mel refused to go back to the States to promote the film so we had to go to him. It cost Universal a fortune."

The reason behind Mel's stubborn refusal to travel was that he feared he was close to a nervous breakdown. The stresses and strains of working on three consecutive films had combined with his own insecurity about the *Hamlet* project. He confessed to a film industry figure that he "had run out of gas". It was Mel's own way of saying that if he did not take a long break after *Hamlet*, he might not be in a fit state to make another movie – ever. All that pent-up tension had finally got to him and what was even more frustrating was that he knew he had yet again pushed himself too far. He had recognised the symptoms but he had tried to beat them by slogging on.

When American television's Barbara Walters interviewed Mel on the set of *Hamlet* for a special, aired in the United States on November 14, 1990, he seemed tense and very tired. He told friends he was annoyed when Walters tried to suggest he was a hypocrite for acting in films that did not coincide with his deeply religious beliefs. Mel did vaguely open up about his "dark period" of alcohol abuse five years earlier, but said that was all in the past.

In truth, Mel, who had suffered a dreadful day of take after take performing the difficult soliloquy which starts: "O that this too too solid flesh would melt . . . " was in no mood to be interviewed. His eyes glazed like a rabbit's caught by a battery of lights. He struggled and stumbled and dried up when

Walters asked him: "Can you say a bit of Shakespeare for us?" Mel looked positively relieved when the interview came to an end.

Oh yes, and there was the ghost of all those previous Hamlets. Mel really did believe that the role was "haunted", as was shown by a bizarre incident during the last few weeks of production. Exhausted after another hard day's filming at Shepperton Studios, he headed for his trailer to find a gift-wrapped box awaiting him. Gingerly, he untied the unmarked package to find an elegant hand-stitched shirt with a blood-stain on one sleeve. Mel gasped as he read a note lying on the shirt. It said that here was the very shirt worn by Laurence Olivier in his film version of *Hamlet*. He snapped the box shut instantly.

But later at his hotel, he found himself irresistibly drawn to the package. Once again, he looked down at the shirt and then, unable to stop himself, slipped it on. For a few moments he stared at himself in the mirror. Shivers ran down his back. He felt a strange presence in the room. Hastily, he pulled the shirt off and packed it back in the box and has never opened it since.

Mel has never discussed this incident, but according to one person who met him during the shooting of *Hamlet*, it "completely freaked him out".

"He felt as if the spirit of Hamlet was close by him the entire time," said the source.

When *Hamlet* finally wrapped, he experienced an overwhelming sense of relief. He knew from viewing the rushes with Zeffirelli each evening that he had done reasonably well. In fact, he was quietly confident. But Mel expected that the biggest obstacle of all would be the critics. This was no *Lethal Weapon*, where any amount of criticism would be ignored by the public, desperate to see action. *Hamlet* had to be well reviewed, as the people who read film criticism in newspapers and magazines were the very citizens forming the movie's potential audience.

Within days of finishing filming, Mel also kept another promise to Robyn – to take her for a romantic weekend in Paris without the children. In the French capital, the couple spent two days wandering around shops and restaurants as Mel pondered on what direction his career should take next.

Determined to make *Hamlet* a success, he embarked on an exhausting world-wide publicity tour to promote the film, still ignoring all the danger signs looming in front of him. The buzz surrounding the project was phenomenal. Everywhere he travelled, journalists wanted Mel to talk about *Hamlet*. For once in his life, the actor was happy to oblige. He was anxious to spread the word and his new-found fondness for talking to the press did not go unnoticed. Reporters had not forgotten how awkward he usually was; some were speculating as to whether Mel's new charming front was a signpost to the film's obvious lack of commercial appeal.

Another part of his pre-release preparations was an hour-long education video on *Hamlet*, which he did in co-operation with the students of the tenth grade at University High, in Los Angeles. It was titled *Mel Gibson Goes Back to School* and Mel talked to the students about *Hamlet* in their own language . . . "great story . . . eight violent deaths, murder, incest, adultery, a mad woman, poison, revenge . . . and swordfights."

The students took to Mel's interpretation with great enthusiasm, much to the actor's delight.

"I asked them a lot of questions. They couldn't answer them but it got them thinking about the play. Some of these questions I couldn't answer myself because Shakespeare doesn't come to any answers. He was just raising the questions; that is what is so intriguing."

The video has been a solid seller through Mel's Icon Productions ever since, although teachers don't know if it is because it provides a fresh insight into Shakespeare or simply a showcase for a Hollywood heart-throb.

Then, in December, 1990, just a few weeks before *Hamlet* was scheduled to open in the US, tragedy struck when Anne Gibson – who had been ill for some time with diabetes and a heart condition as well as rapidly failing sight – died at the age of 69. Cause of death was a heart attack in Wodonga Hospital, northern Victoria. Mel was shattered and caught the first available flight from LA to Australia to be with the rest of his family.

In the Kiewa Valley area where his farm was located, friends and neighbours threw a protective screen around the Gibson family. Reporters dispatched from Melbourne for an update on the situation were told to keep away from the Gibson compound.

"They're part and parcel of the community. Fitted in like gloves from the very first day. Mel's just one of us when he's home on the farm," said one neighbour.

In Upstate New York, old family friend Ed Stinson grieved. He had regularly seen Mel's parents and brothers and sisters on their trips back to the area where the actor spent the first twelve years of his life. And he had turned down an invitation to stay with Mel and his parents in England just a few months earlier because of his own wife's illness.

"I tried three times to write a letter to Hutton and the family, but it was too difficult . . . I choked on all three. They're special people, the Gibsons . . . but thank heavens for the memories . . . you can't take them away."

By all accounts, Mel found it very difficult to grieve openly over his mother's death. He admitted to respected writer Linda Lee-Potter: "I don't cope very well with grief. I don't think it's unmanly to cry." But, he added bluntly: "I'm not going to tell you if I ever do."

(His reaction just a few months later to the death of his father-figure Sydney agent Bill Shannahan was very similar. Privately he was knocked for six but publicly he appeared emotionless. Mel was using his considerable acting talents to hide his grief from the world.)

He was particularly saddened because his mother would never get an opportunity to see him in *Hamlet*. The whole family had been proud of the actor when he landed the role. Just a few days after the funeral, Mel surprised Hollywood by putting his grief behind him and flying back to Los Angeles to continue his publicity tour.

"We're surprised that he came back to do this, but of course we're delighted," said a Warner Brothers executive. "It's an indication of how important he feels this film is, that he would lay himself on the line for the press and all the public appearances, at a time when this must be the last place he would want to be."

Journalists at press conferences that followed his mother's death were warned not to mention Anne Gibson or even offer condolences. They all noticed that Mel was back to virtually chain smoking.

"Please don't bring up his mother's death," begged one nervous publicist from Warner Brothers. "Mel is in deep mourning and mention of his mother might cause him to break down."

At one gathering, dressed in a sombre black suit with a black and beige polo shirt, he was asked what it had been like to have Glenn Close, who at 43, was not that much older than himself, playing his mother.

"It was fantastic," came the reply. "She was so good I think I'll adopt her."

Then Mel's voice dropped to a whisper. "She's great to work with . . . but young to be my mother . . . " A silence filled the room as he trailed off. The mere mention of Glenn Close playing a mother had triggered memories of his own mother, and he was close to tears.

A few minutes later, Mel dived outside the room for a puff of a cigarette in a corridor. He looked tense and nervous and told one journalist wearily that he was "gonna stand here and let some steam off".

Later he talked about what he perceived as the similarities between himself and Hamlet.

"He also has this volcanic range of expression bubbling up inside of him. And he doesn't know if it's justified. He's a very honest and just person . . . that's the way he was raised. He holds it in . . . but sometimes it bursts out."

And, it seems, that just about summed up Mel's attitude towards director Zeffirelli by the time the shoot wrapped. There were few public rows between them on set but Mel found the Italian's hysterical method of film-making very wearing. He told friends that the director used to stomp around the set "like a madman who thinks he is Napoleon".

"I don't want to bag the guy . . . we got along all right," was about all he would say when asked about his relationship with Zeffirelli.

With the film days from opening in the United States, Mel anxiously awaited the reviews. He later admitted to having suffered from the biggest crisis in confidence during that period.

In the United States, reviews turned out to be very impressive.

"Gibson's Hamlet is strong and intelligent. The film is controlled by his dignified yet explosive presence . . . a compelling Hamlet," said the *New York Times*.

And *Time* magazine described Hamlet as "being almost perfect for Gibson with his neurotic physicality and urgent baritone".

Meanwhile Michael Wilmington, of the *Los Angeles*

Times, wrote: "His blond hair may seem a conscious tweak at Laurence Olivier's 1948 version of the part, but Mel Gibson shows Shakespearean tools: princely bearing, a resonant and supple voice for verse."

The *New York Post* raved: "Mel Gibson makes a very good Hamlet. It's a doubly pleasant surprise since we've had to judge him by the likes of *Mad Max* and *Lethal Weapon*."

The Los Angeles premiere of the film helped raise $1 million towards the revival of Shakespeare's Globe Theatre in London, after three centuries.

Relieved by the first wave of reviews in the States, Mel returned to Australia something of a hero, especially when he visited his old home ground of the National Institute of Dramatic Art. The main reason for returning to NIDA was to announce the Mel Gibson–Village Roadshow–NIDA scholarship for a student on either technical or creative courses. But he also wanted to talk to and encourage the students.

The school theatre was packed for his appearance and a barrage of questions were thrown at him.

Asked if he would be forever haunted by the role of the tormented Hamlet, Mel stated bluntly: "I'm not going to let the bugger bother me."

One student wondered how he had reacted to the fanfare of jeers that greeted his decision to play the part.

"Who cares? I don't. I'm rich."

But Mel's biggest fear on returning to NIDA was that one of his old teachers would see *Hamlet* and give him a no-holds-barred criticism of his performance. He told a college lecturer he was "quaking in his boots" in case she cornered him.

Mel then got himself embroiled in a row about the recruitment of foreign actors for Australian productions and became a victim of angry responses from the Aussie actors. He enraged the local actors by accusing the Equity union of

Australia of stifling the local film industry by not allowing foreign stars to work.

Actress Penne Hackford Jones accused Mel of "forgetting his roots – the days when he was a struggling actor".

And actor John Hargreaves accused Mel of being "naive."

The star himself pointed out the irony that he was not even an Australian citizen, but insisted that local stars could make it abroad just like he had if they tried hard enough. It took a phone call from his old *Mad Max* and *Summer City* flatmate Steve Bisley to advise Mel to keep a lower profile on the subject. In the eyes of his friends he was treading on very thin ice.

Before the Australian premiere of *Hamlet* in Sydney, Mel attended a party in his honour. For the first time in years he looked relaxed at such a gathering, mingling with guests with a Perrier in one hand and a cigarette in the other. Seven of his brothers and sisters turned up along with Hutton Gibson. For Mel, having his family there was very significant, as he believed that *Hamlet* was the first movie he could truly be completely proud of. Pursuing their own interests as Mel ascended through Hollywood, the Gibson siblings had become, among other things, a professional singer, an X-ray technician, a business executive, a store manager and a moderately successful actor, not to mention two "home-makers".

He told one fellow guest why *Hamlet* was so important to him. "I want this production to be successful because I love Shakespeare and the world needs more Shakespeare . . . because it's full of wisdom, wit and beauty. We need more of that and less of . . . like a weekend trip to a knocking shop."

Following that party, guests moved on up the street to the cinema for the screening of *Hamlet*. Mel did not bother acting the star and riding the few hundred yards in a limousine. He strolled into the auditorium with a handful of relatives, took an unreserved seat well away from the VIP area and disappeared before the end of the final credits as the audience applauded.

Reviews in Australia were glowing.

"This film literally pulsates with dramatic energy. Despite minor wear and tear, Gibson automatically notches up Brownie points as a believably youthful Hamlet," wrote Rob Lowing in the *Sun-Herald*.

But not everyone in Australia was completely won over by Mel's portrayal.

Scott Murray of *Cinema Papers* magazine said: "*Hamlet* is a puzzle. A lot of the favourable reviews were just because he did not muck it up. But it is so thin. It is a big nothing. Every scene is meaningless. Mel did not give it a proper spin. It's neither good nor bad. But I suppose he did help make Shakespeare more accessible to a younger audience."

But Murray insists that making *Hamlet* was "not a good career move for Mel. It was partly ego. He wanted to see if he could do it."

Toughest territory of all for Mel to conquer would be Britain, where the traditions and grandeur of Shakespeare originated. Many critics felt intimidated and appalled by the Hollywood star's decision to play Hamlet.

There was a royal premiere for *Hamlet* at the Odeon Haymarket, in the West End of London. However, Mel – not the biggest fan of the British royal family at the best of times – managed to upset the Duchess of York by being late after getting held up in traffic.

"ALAS, POOR FERGIE AWAITS PRINCE MEL." read the headline in one newspaper, which reported that the Duchess had greeted Mel with the words: "It is very good of you to come."

British reviews for *Hamlet* were predictably lukewarm.

"He makes a plain-spoken rather uncomplicated Hamlet

who sometimes seems scarcely to know what's hitting him but bravely tries to mould fate to his own ends all the same," said the *Guardian*.

While the *Times* critic accused Mel of "enunciating with the unreal clarity of a speaking clock. He is grave, anguished, tender, playful, all the things Hamlet should be. Yet, though Mel Gibson is never for one moment bad, almost everybody in the cast is better. And for all his effort we never get under Hamlet's skin."

Mel told friends that playing Hamlet had a very deep effect on him. Something that will stay with him for the rest of his life.

In a diary he kept during the long and arduous shoot, he wrote: "As I began to fight for Hamlet I started to understand him. In the thick of the fight, with no time to think, only to react, and completely absorbed in Hamlet's actions, I am him. His spirit enters me and somehow we're fighting each other and we're fighting together at the same time. He makes you grow up a little bit."

Hopes were high at Warner Brothers in early 1991 that Mel would be nominated for an Oscar for *Hamlet*. The film was even specially released before the deadline for entries that year. But members of the Academy overlooked him and he has privately admitted his disappointment, although friends say he is philosophical about winning such awards. The one gong he did get was a prestigious Will Award from the Shakespeare Theatre, in Washington. He was the fifth recipient, joining Joseph Papp, Kevin Kline, Christopher Plummer and Kenneth Branagh.

With *Hamlet* up and running throughout the world, Mel retired gracefully to his farm. He badly needed a break after three virtually back-to-back projects. He had to avoid the pitfalls of overwork and he was seriously thinking about what the future held for him.

"You work because you want to work and you're hungry. Then you wait till you're full and you take a break. You have to take a break, to do things that you work for, or you couldn't survive."

"I've got to go away and learn some new tricks. I've got to replenish my creative energy because I'm out of it."

My family means more to me than the artificial trappings of my career. If ever I had to choose between my career and my family, the wife and kids would definitely come out on top.

21

Over-worked, stressed to the edge of burn-out, Mel had to get home to Australia before something very serious happened to his health, following his whirlwind world publicity tour to promote *Hamlet*. Those gruelling back-to-back movies had made him desperate for the peace and quiet of his Victorian cattle ranch. Privately, he was admitting to associates that if he tried to make another film he might have a breakdown. He felt as if he never wanted to go near a movie set again.

Mel even managed a complete reversal in his attitude towards therapists and consulted one in Los Angeles before returning Down Under. It was a remarkable about-turn for someone who had ridiculed psychiatrists so fervently, but he had to take some action to sort himself out. Mel described his sessions as having his body "switched off".

And he told one associate that the visits to the psychiatrist left him totally drained for three days but "after that you feel great, like a dancing bear". Soon he was even able to laugh off his own hypocrisy and has continued receiving regular treatment ever since.

Top of his list of priorities was to see Robyn and their six children. The whole family was aware that Mel was heading dangerously close to burn-out. Showbusiness friends and associates had noticed how much more serious and less inclined to crack jokes and pranks he became in the closing months of 1990. There was none of Mel's inarticulate sidestepping. His eagerness to return to his true home was clear for anyone to see.

Mel was only too painfully aware that the last time he had to take a year off to recharge his batteries was after *Mad Max III* in 1985. This time around, he was even more tired but he seemed a little more in control of his own destiny than in those days which he now described as his "bad period". But the actor was alarmingly open with anyone who asked him if he was feeling the strain.

"I have a hunger to work. To work is to create. But for the moment I have sated my hunger. I need a holiday. A year off," he confessed to one showbusiness writer.

The Carinya (it means Happy Home) farm, in the small township of Tangambalanga near the willow-shaded banks of the Kiewa River in Victoria, represented Mel's little piece of sanity and he fumed every time journalists dared to mention it during his publicity tours. And when U.S. television host Robin Leech (Mel is said to do a brilliant impersonation of him) tried to persuade the star to let his property be featured on "Lifestyles of the Rich and Famous" Mel exploded at the indignity. As far as he was concerned the farm and his family were off-limits to the media.

He was still angry over the way one Australian magazine invaded his privacy by sending photographers to take pictures of his house, plus a team of reporters to question locals and farm workers nearby about their famous movie star neighbour.

The only photographer allowed in to the farm throughout this period was freelance Mark Griffin, after a deal was struck between a local paper and Mel for coverage restricted to his agricultural business alone.

The first thing that struck Griffin was the lax security. "No electronic gates. No barbed-wire fences. It was completely open."

Griffin said, "Mel turned out to be a very affable bloke. I shot him on the tractor and riding his four-wheel motorbike. He was very relaxed."

But Mel changed when the photographer innocently asked about taking some pictures of his children, who were playing nearby. The actor completely ignored the question and changed the subject instantly. However, Griffin said he was impressed by Mel's knowledge of the farming business: "He seemed to really know what he was talking about." After being given a cup of coffee and some of Robyn's home-made cake, Griffin departed and never heard from Mel again.

Gradually, Mel had expanded the red-brick farmhouse with an additional double-storey extension, to cater for his huge family rather than a desire for a grandiose home. Locals note that the farm does not have any of the white-washed post-and-rail fences or huge signs common to many cattle properties where big money has been invested.

In fact, the farm has a fine range of sheds, yards, bales of hay and wrapped silage, and excellent lush pastures (nurtured without the use of chemical fertilisers) . . . the kind of things that are essential on a working farm of 6,000 acres. Then he bought a 2,000-acre property next door, Limerick Springs, followed by about 4,000 acres of rough hill country at Bullioh, in the upper Murray region close by. Finally, Robyn bought a rundown hotel in nearby Yackandandah for a bargain $75,000 at an auction recently. Local gossips are predicting that Mel will refurbish the place in due course and reopen it for business. All four properties are said to be worth in the region of $2 million – and he has still held on to that beach house at Coogee, on the outskirts of Sydney, worth at least another $500,000.

In late 1989, Mel moved his mother and father in to a property on the estate. Tragically, Anne Gibson lived only three more months, but at least she got to be with Mel and his family. Hutton stayed on after his wife's death and became the property's unofficial caretaker when the family were away.

When he first bought the place, Mel had little or no intention of going into cattle breeding in a big way. His only aim had been to find a place to escape that now familiar burn-out scenario. But, he told friends later, the land "needed something on it" so he bought a herd of commercial Hereford cattle.

Then, after a year of making endless mistakes, Mel hired in 28-year-old Peter Ford, a sixth-generation farmer from nearby Dederang. Originally he asked Ford to be farm caretaker, but then Mel decided to give the farmer a full-time job.

Mel also had to face the fact that since making the first *Lethal Weapon* film, Los Angeles had become his main home.

In 1989, he paid $2.4 million for a vast twenty-acre spread a mile into the Serra Canyon, just behind Malibu, that belonged to singer Rick Springfield. It was the perfect retreat for the star and his family with a twenty-four-hour armed guard at the gate to the private road leading to the property – he allows visitors in by invitation only. Mel and Robyn fell in love with the property the moment they saw it because it is surrounded by horse stables and its dusty terrain reminded them of Australia.

There are a couple of tight turns on Serra Canyon that lead to a narrow street that passes the electrified gates to Mel's palatial home. You cannot see the modern building from the road. You identify yourself over the intercom and face a solitary video camera that automatically tightens focus on the subject. Then there's a buzz and the gates swing open. There's lots of green around. In the courtyard a new Mercedes estate with three rows of seats sits on the driveway whenever the family is in residence. The house itself has many floor-to-ceiling windows and at the rear a forty-foot pool provides a natural play area for the children. It's a mix of security and serenity. An elaborate security system encircles the property, and if the beam is broken, the alarms blast off immediately.

But it is an elegant home with an eclectic collection of furniture and the occasional picture hanging on the cream-coloured walls. Everything has its place, although the occasional toy does give away the fact that the owner is far from alone.

Mel was advised to put even more of his many millions into property straight after purchasing the house in Serra Canyon, so he started looking for another place in early 1990. During one bizarre, only-in-Hollywood scene, he spotted a house he liked the look of, in Beverly Hills, and got the real-estate agent to persuade the owners to vacate for one night so that he could sleep over in the house and "get the feel of it". The flattered owners allowed the actor to put them up in a luxurious hotel suite but then Mel changed his mind because he "did not sleep well". He shelled out $3,000 to the owners for their trouble.

Then in February, 1992, Mel purchased what real-estate agents describe as a "beach house filled with rustic charm" in Malibu for $2.5 million. Initially, it was bought just so that Robyn and the kids could swim in the sea in privacy. The sky-blue-painted house – with sixty-five feet of private beach that comes complete with a golf buggy to get down to the oceanside – was built in the 1940s and had three bedrooms and three bathrooms, so it was not even big enough for the entire family to stay in at one time. Neighbours include such

Hollywood luminaries as Sylvester Stallone, Robert Redford, Dustin Hoffman and an immediate neighbour Emilio Estevez. Just like his house a few miles away in the canyons behind Malibu, this one could only be reached by passing an armed guard at the entrance to a private road.

It transpired that Mel had been looking for the perfect, private beachfront property for his family for years and he intends to move the entire family in after conversion work is completed. Building got under way in early 1993 for a Southwestern-style house with a swimming pool and waterfall to be constructed alongside the existing home.

Despite being a property owner in California now, Mel continued to criticise Hollywood.

"You get spoiled in Hollywood, they throw it at you. But it's like joining the police force and trying to stay straight. Sure I like the things they throw at me. I like nice hotels and I like nice food. And I like cars."

But he added quickly, "I like the farm more . . . "

In 1989, he bought the 12,500-acre Beartooth Ranch in Montana in partnership with Queensland breeder Don Anderson. Gradually, Mel developed an interest in the highly controversial genetic engineering of certain breeds of cattle, which had been going on at Beartooth for years. The property had been home to one of the world's finest Hereford studs. Within weeks of buying the farm, Mel invested $120,000 in a prize Saler bull and got himself hooked on genetic breeding.

Former Beartooth owner George Ellis was left in no doubt that the star is serious about running a successful cattle business. "I believe he plans on doing it for a major means of income. He's not just doing it for home entertainment.

"Mel is very athletic and handy with the equipment and anything else he puts his mind to. He's learnt to know the difference between these critters very quickly."

Over the past two years, Mel has poured hundreds of

thousands of dollars into cross-breeding Salers, Gelbviehs and Angus cattle; he and his farming advisers believe that they will eventually make a fortune out of his investment. However, the current world-wide recession has hit Australia particularly badly and Mel has privately admitted that he has lost upwards of a million dollars over the past two years.

"Luckily I don't have to eke out a living as a farmer or I'd go broke trying to feed my family," he says.

But Mel had another, more human motive for raising the cattle – he loved eating the organically-raised beef and vegetables from the garden knowing that none of them had been sprayed with "horrible toxins". Mel fervently believed that avoiding such chemicals would enable him and his family to live healthily and happily to a "ripe old age".

He often jokes that his next plan is to brand the rear end of every piece of cattle with "Mel's Organic Meat". But he may well actually mean it . . .

To Mel, being on the farm was a soothing antidote to the movie business. Riding around his vast estate on a 200cc trail bike, chopping wood, "lugging things around" were the perfect ways to escape the pressures.

The other reason why he was stuck in Hollywood for long periods of time, whether he liked it or not, was that his company, Icon (Mel always proudly announces that it stands for "I con . . . ") was attached to Warner Brothers in Los Angeles and Mel was expected to get involved in many aspects of the day-to-day running of the business. Hundreds of scripts flood in each month for his consideration either as producer, director or star – or all three.

Just a few days before Mel retreated to Victoria after *Hamlet*, he had no idea what he was going to do next. In fact, he wanted to keep his plans deliberately vague to give himself a chance to recover from all that previous work. He wanted to disappear . . .

"Hollywood impedes my ability to be an observer. This visibility you have taints everything. It's hard to explain but if Joe Blow goes into a department store to check out how sales assistants behave and how they do their job the assistants are going to behave differently in front of him than in front of me.

"And this visibility I have changes things for my kids and it is starting to get difficult to take them out. I do. I make the effort but sometimes it's just not worthwhile and that chokes you. If you have a farm, like I do, it's great; nobody's going to come up. Life comes to me rather than me going to it. That helps put everything back into perspective."

There was another thrust behind Mel's decision to retreat into the bush. He worried that there was a danger of over-exposing himself to the public. With his Hollywood agent and other advisers urging him to accept more and more roles for increasingly large fees – they took a healthy share – Mel fretted that people would soon get "sick of the sight of me".

In any case, Mel had spent millions of dollars improving the farm properties – though he proudly told visitors that the main house still had an outside loo, and vegetable gardens where Robyn grows their greens. Not to mention those 200 head of cattle that Mel spends months each year trying to mate with each other.

Sometimes the star would patiently try to coax a bull into feeling romantic about a cow. To Mel's way of thinking it brought him back down to earth with a bump. And he infuriated his agent Ed Limato by refusing to give him the main phone number of the house . . . allowing him to get on with his other career as a farmer. There were auctions to attend and a lot of work to be done. At the Inverary-Nardoo Saler stud he splashed out a further $60,000 on a bull calf and set a record for livestock sales in Australia in the process.

During that year off, Mel organised a cattlemen's field day at his Springbark farm in Gundowring. The actor played host to more than 1,000 locals after announcing he was having the open day "in the interests of better information and improved production for all cattlemen".

Dressed in a checked shirt, blue slacks and slouch hat, Mel welcomed visitors to his property, shaking hands and talking to buyers and other cattlemen as a handful of starstruck teenage girls watched his every gesture. The locals were so protective of their Hollywood star neighbour that they warned anyone against bothering him. But they need not have worried. On this particular day Mel was the perfect gentleman farmer, despite a battery of telephoto lenses pointed right in his direction, constantly. A few months later he turned up at the Royal Easter Show in Sydney, an agricultural extravaganza that attracts farmers from all over Australia. When Australian Channel Ten reporter Angela Bishop approached him for an interview, he entertained a crowd of onlookers by playfully pretending to beat her up and then politely declining the request.

Mel also took over and redeveloped Beartooth International, which was a company that came as part of the package with the Montana farm. The firm is currently building a herd of 650 stud Salers, Gelbviehs and Angus cattle and Mel is paying a handsome annual wage to farm manager Ford to run the whole business during his long absences.

On Sundays, Mel and Robyn hold barbecues for local friends. People who have attended say they are fairly quiet affairs where Mel makes a point of personally handing out dishes of meat and salads and behaving like anyone else there. It all boils down to the type of outback living that Mel hankers after more than anything else in the world.

And he showed just what a local sport he was when he witnessed a hit-and-run accident involving a German Shepherd dog. Mel immediately rushed to the animal's aid and drove twenty miles to the nearest vet where he left a cheque for

$1,300 and asked that they call him if the money did not cover all the expenses.

British-born Amanda Palmer worked as the Gibsons' daily helper/nanny for three years and she provided a peep into the real home life of Mel and Robyn down on the farm.

"Mel only ever wore jeans and a T-shirt and would be barefoot and unshaven with his hair in a mess most of the time. He would love getting stuck in at home, cooking sausages, making toast and frying eggs and bacon. Then he would feed the younger ones and change the nappies."

Amanda Palmer revealed that Mel's household had a strict routine. "I would arrive at 7.30 in the morning and get the children moving, dressed and downstairs for breakfast. If Mel wasn't filming, he'd be down helping with everything. The first thing he said when I started was: 'Do you want a cup of tea?' then went off to make me one!"

She travelled with the family to Los Angeles on a number of occasions.

But Amanda Palmer insists that Mel and his family led a "hermit-like" existence for much of the time at the farm.

"Their whole way of life is no big deal. The house is in a state of semi-chaos."

Mel even insisted on keeping his trusty and rusty old Volvo estate car, according to Ms Palmer.

He is also very strict about what films the children are allowed to watch. All the *Lethal Weapon* films are banned, as is *Tequila Sunrise*, although he did allow them to watch *Mad Max II* because he considers it harmless fun. The only other films of his they have been permitted to view have been *Tim* and *Air America*.

There in the background making sure Mel's feet remain on the ground is Robyn. Mel loves the fact that to her and the kids he's just a husband and father and he absorbs the criticism Robyn regularly heaps upon him.

"She says I've got short, skinny legs, a big bum and a hollow chest. And when she tells me to get out in the kitchen and wash the dishes, I jump to it," Mel brags, masochistically.

Amanda Palmer recalled: "Robyn spends her whole time with the children. She's very much the traditional mother and wife. She just likes to run the home.

"If people saw her, they'd probably be very surprised. Glamour and expensive clothes don't interest her at all. With six children, and given that she doesn't want any staff, it means she's on the go the whole time."

Her husband – despite his family's open break with the current Catholic Church – still believes firmly in God and still insists that if he and Robyn have any more children "God is the only one who knows how many we should have and we should be ready to accept that".

Farmer Mel is not shy about handing out corporal punishment to his children if he deems it necessary. He often smacks or spanks his offspring for bad behaviour. It is something that he learned from his father, who always used to tell him and his ten brothers and sisters not to wake him up before 6 a.m. and try to avoid killing one another!

Mel believes that his children should respect him and corporal punishment is part of that scenario. He has described to friends the type of punishment he hands out to his children as "the type of crack that will sting and bite". But usually he warns each child three times before handing out a punishment.

"He firmly believes that you cannot raise a decent human being without using a little force at times," says one friend.

Yet like most disciplinarian fathers he believes that after hitting a child "you're all back to square one". And his friends and associates have noted that he never talks down to his children.

Mel regularly picks them up from their schools when they are all together in Australia. He holds that constantly moving them around the world with him will do them nothing but good. And both he and Robyn have promised they will never send their children to boarding school.

"I'd rather take them to wonderful places and get a whole new culture spat in their faces," he says. "Make them learn conversion rates and pick up on different cultures."

Mel's philosophy on bringing up children in gypsy fashion may have worked well while they were under the age of 12. But it seems inevitable that eldest child Hannah will soon be enrolled at a school in Australia which she will have to attend the whole year round, meaning that Robyn will remain behind while Mel is away making movies. For the moment the couple are studiously avoiding those sort of separations; Mel is fearful that he might easily fall off the wagon once again if left for long periods on his own.

In lighter vein, he succumbed to pressure from the children and agreed to appear on a Muppets, television special aired in Australia, Britain and America in late 1992. He happily hammed it up as Hamlet in a short comedy sequence with the funny grotesques.

Mel never uses bodyguards or even barbed wire to repel prying fans in Australia. The only time he has ever considered some sort of protective action was when a number of "sick and twisted" letters turned up at the main farmhouse. He took the intrusion in his stride and felt strangely reassured that at least the threats were put in writing. He believes that the ones who don't write are the types who might end up paying a dangerous visit.

A similar problem at the family's main home in Malibu surfaced with a stream of fan mail that frequently included telephone numbers, raunchy letters and even ladies' underwear. Mel sabotaged such approaches by having the mailbox removed from the bottom of his drive-way. All his post is now diverted to his agent's home. He also took security measures that he would never even consider in Australia.

Accordingly, Mel loathes annual lists such as the Forbes world's richest entertainers, which in 1990 proclaimed him the 37th wealthiest person in US showbusiness with a fortune estimated in the region of $24 million. He worries that there are people who read these lists and then target a personaliy.

When, in August 1992, an Australian TV channel decided to run a current affairs programme on how easy it was to computer-hack into personal backgrounds and featured Mel plus one of his Malibu homes as an example, he was enraged.

The programme had a Hollywood private eye using Mel's tax file number to track down personal details on the star, including what he paid for that house in Malibu ($2.4 million on February 24, 1989), when the house was built (1980), and that he was paying $9,000 a year in land taxes alone. Plus the fact that he had purchased another house nearby in Canyon View, Malibu.

One of Mel's sisters saw the trailer for the show and immediately contacted her brother in Los Angeles. Mel was alarmed and approached an old friend, Australian producer Greg Coote, during a tennis game in Los Angeles the same day and begged him to put the station under pressure to drop the programme. They claimed that they were perfectly within their rights to air what they wished. He instructed his lawyers to pursue the situation with a view to getting the programme banned.

"All we have done is put information which is publicly available to air as proof that regardless of how much you try to be private – as Mel does – using legal methods you can find a lot of information. They [Gibson's representatives] wanted to view the programme – which understandably we have not allowed them to do," said executive producer Peter Abbott.

Mel's lawyers launched an all-out bid to stop the

programme. It was a fresh example of Mel being persuaded to waste tens of thousands of dollars on pointless legal battles. Threats of injunctions flew between Los Angeles and Sydney's Channel Seven.

As a gesture of good intent, the show – entitled "You Have No Secrets" – agreed to blank out Mel's specific address and certain other highly personal details. But the incident did provide proof, as if it were needed, of how sensitive he is to the notorious stalker-types who loom up in Hollywood with alarming regularity.

"In the end Mel was quite happy with what we did," claimed a spokeswoman for the snooping documentary.

Mel's obsession with privacy burgeoned. On an Australian internal flight from Sydney to the Gold Coast, he refused to give his autograph to a noisy boxing fan, demanding it for his daughter. When three of the man's burly travelling companions approached Mel in a menacing fashion he still refused to budge and left the plane to a chorus of jeers and boos from them.

Towards the end of his year off, Mel allowed himself to see that it was time to start thinking about work again.

His attitude towards Hollywood had mellowed. It seems to be best summed up by his insistence on wearing a fake Rolex watch, much to the consternation of many so-called movietown players.

In Tinseltown almost everyone wears expensive watches. But not Mel. It is as if he is saying: "Take me as you find me or don't bother," said one friend.

People must be sick of me, or they will be soon.

22

It was one of the biggest-grossing movies of all time, spawning soaraway careers for all the actors and technicians involved. Mel – resting on his farm – eyed the phenomenal success of Kevin Costner's *Dances with Wolves* with envy. As an artist he respected Costner's work. In the hands of a different director he reluctantly recognised that *Dances* would never have been the epic sensation it turned out to be.

When Costner went up and collected his Oscar for best director, it fulfilled the American Dream. Mel had enjoyed his share of that dream but he wanted the same as Costner and embarked on the daunting task of finding a similar project to direct and star in. It had to be something that would close the gap between him and Californian Costner. Mel believed he had it in him to equal Costner's directorial debut. He had the charisma and allure of a major movie star and Warner Brothers would give him a chance if he found the right project.

Mel had his eye on several film properties by the end of

1990. He was particularly interested in finding the sort of romantic adventure that would salute and evoke the days of stars like Cary Grant and Gary Cooper. The frenetic violence and non-stop action of the *Lethal Weapon* series had pushed him in the opposite direction. His partner, friend and accountant Bruce Davey instructed their development executive at Icon Productions to keep a special lookout for such a screenplay. Eventually, Mel settled on a script entitled *The Rest of Daniel* (later changed to *Forever Young*), a fantasy adventure about a man frozen for fifty years in a cryogenics experiment. He committed to the project and, as a measure of how important Mel was (and still is) to Warner Brothers, the studio shelled out an extraordinary $2 million to buy the script from writer Jeffrey Abrams. It became the most expensive script of its kind in Hollywood history when Warners announced they had purchased it specifically for Mel, in November, 1990. Interestingly, he passed on the opportunity to direct it, preferring to wait for something on a smaller scale.

But even multi-million-dollar screenplays have to be polished a little and while Mel awaited a new draft of *Daniel*, he became intrigued by one or two other projects, including a film based on American correspondent George Polk, who was found in a Greek harbour shot through the back of the neck, probably on the orders of the CIA and the then right-wing Greek government. Mel got very excited over the Polk project, buying film rights to a book about the case before it had reached the shops, and persuading controversial Greek director Costa-Gavras to commit to the picture. He had won two Academy Awards for his no-punches-pulled political films *Z*, about the Greek Fascist Colonels, and *Missing*, set in El Salvador.

Other projects were said to include the role of a Sydney photographer who was the only cameraman to get on the island of Grenada when the Americans invaded in 1983.

And besides all this, reaction to *Hamlet* had been so favourable that Mel's asking price for a mainstream movie was now estimated to be $10 million. His investment in making that film for a very modest fee was already paying dividends.

Forever Young – in which Mel co-starred with Jamie Lee Curtis, Isabel Glasser and 12-year-old Elijah Wood – was hardly Mel's most dashing performance, although it did feature his naked rear, running through a building protected only by a strategically placed child's jacket. That provoked countless newspaper articles speculating on just how much his nude bottom might add to the box office takings, but little else. One journalist from the American magazine *Redbook* witnessed an embarrassing moment on the set of the movie when Mel forgot his lines and ended up being comforted by his schoolboy co-star.

The film's biggest publicity coup was to encourage journalists to run countless photo spreads on the efforts of *Forever Young*'s special effects department to age the handsome star from 37 to 80. Headlines like "SEXY MEL TURNS CRINKLY WRINKLY!" summed up the impact of the movie on the public. And when *Forever Young* did reach the screen in late 1992, movie critics gave it a lukewarm reception.

Box Office magazine in the US knocked it for "dripping with the kind of gooey sentiment and melodrama at which Jane Austen would have smirked".

And Georgia Brown in the *Village Voice* dismissed the film as "my candidate for the most inept movie of the year. The final scenes are absolute howlers. Most of the credit goes to the thoroughly absurd, charmless, and fraudulent script by Abrams."

Yet, as usual, Mel avoided any criticism of his role in the film. He could get away with being in a poor movie. It seemed as though his charm and charisma would always pull him through. One of the most memorable things about shooting the film for him was that he became unrecognisable after make-up artists had aged him fifty years, and could eat out in restaurants without anyone realising who he was. The bottom line on *Forever Young* was that its inoffensive plot and obligatory naked backside shot of Mel helped it soar above the critics and take in nearly $100 million around the world.

As one British housewife, Debbie Bettridge, from Taunton in Somerset, commented: "I can honestly say that apart from a rather far-fetched plot this was very good all-round family entertainment. There was no gratuitous sex or violence, just an innocent film for adults and children alike to enjoy, which makes a nice change. Mind you, if gorgeous Gibson had been chosen to star in the ill-fated soap "Eldorado" [a truly dreadful British series] that would have been a success as well."

The film also gave Mel an opportunity to hold a Los Angeles premiere and raise some much-needed funds for two charities that both he and Bruce Davey had become involved with. Hollywood's Recovery Center is a drug and alcohol rehabilitation centre and Mel, presumably in a thinly-veiled reference to himself, admitted that it was a problem near to his own heart.

"Alcoholism is something that runs in my family. It's something that is close to me. People do come back from it, and it's a miracle. And I like to be part of that," he said in a reference to his past problems.

The other charity that benefited from the premiere for *Forever Young* was Santa Monica's Homeless Drop-In Center, which boasts both Bruce Davey and one of Mel's lawyers Nigel Sinclair on its board of directors. In all $70,000 was raised towards both charities.

In the middle of all this, Mel astonished *Forever Young* writer Jeffrey Abrams by inviting the young scribe to join him at the Glendale office of the California Department of Motor

Vehicles while he retook his driving test! It was an experience Abrams says he will never forget.

"When we arrived Mel threw on a big cowboy hat and dark glasses and did an incredible thing – he turned off his charm," recalled Abrams. "His shoulders dropped a little and he became expressionless. The place was packed with all kinds of people. Many looked right at Mel and didn't even notice him."

It turned out that the only reason Mel was having to retake his test was that he had blinked for his licence photo. Somehow, this was not the sort of thing one expected to happen to movie stars.

He passed the test after driving his Mercedes around the test route with a charming housewifely examiner called Mona whose only concern at the end of the examination was whether Mel would be appearing naked in his next movie.

When he was reportedly offered the role of an Israeli secret agent billed as the James Bond of the Nineties, his agents asked for $20 million and the producers rapidly revived their search for a cheaper leading man. He had no intention of taking the role and deliberately priced himself out of the part. Whether it was because of his family's religious beliefs or his complete aversion to playing any role vaguely similar to James Bond we will never know.

Back in Australia, Mel's sister Mary kept up that long-held family tradition of appearing on TV quiz shows by entering the Aussie version of "Jeopardy". But unlike Papa Gibson before her, she did not win.

Warner Brothers were carefully nurturing Mel, whom they considered their number-one star. After all, he had made the majority of his hit movies with them and there was the not inconsiderable matter of making sure the star was "tied in" for *Lethal Weapon* 3. The next step was no surprise inside Hollywood; in February, 1991, Mel's lawyers in Los Angeles finalised an astounding $42 million four-picture deal which could make him one of the most powerful (and richest) actors in the film industry. With his per-movie fee rising to $12 million for the last of the four pictures, it was seen in Tinseltown as "one hell of a deal". And there was also the promise of a lucrative deal which would give Mel a share of the profits from each film as well. The actor and his associates envisage this earning him around $100 million from the package, if the films do well. And the studio had happily agreed to Mel's most important condition – that he gets three months a year off to be with his wife and children. Thrown in is free first-class air travel for him and his family plus assorted helpers so that they could join him at any time. A Warner spokesman said: "Money is not a problem – getting Mel Gibson is."

Part and parcel of the deal was an agreement that Mel's company, Icon Productions, should develop and produce all four movies with Mel being paid not only as an actor but also producer or executive producer. He was now a Hollywood player in his own right and considered one of the three most bankable stars in the world. His name on a picture ensures financial backing for any project and his name on a movie poster virtually guarantees takings of at least $50 million at the US box office alone.

"They'd give you money for Mel's film even if it was a screen version of the telephone directory," said one astute Los Angeles casting director.

On the Warner lot, Icon was given a fine spread of offices. It must have seemed very opulent compared with their previous base in the Santa Monica apartment Mel had bought years earlier and taken some of his women friends to. Mel himself had a dark, somewhat regally appointed office on the Warner lot, decorated with personal memorabilia. *Lethal Weapon* and *Mad Max* posters took pride of place, among a couple of swords, a model fighter plane, two cowboy hats and two top hats. His bookshelves display such unusual items as icons from south-eastern Europe and Sinai. But, perhaps most significantly of all, there are absolutely no photos of Robyn and the children.

(Typically of the way Hollywood operates, Warners signed a similar agreement with Mel's rival Kevin Costner just a few months after their much-heralded deal with the *Lethal Weapon* star. It put Warner in an incredibly strong position.)

Since 1990, Mel's rating in prestigious *Premiere* magazine's list of the one hundred most powerful people in Hollywood has risen rapidly. Only a handful of actors such as Tom Cruise, Eddie Murphy, Arnold Schwarzenegger, Sylvester Stallone, Kevin Costner, Jack Nicholson, Michael Douglas and Warren Beatty command the same sort of respect.

"When it comes to the movie business, power means more than greenlighting projects or grossing big at the box office. What distinguishes the powerful is the influence they wield over others – through respect, admiration or fear. Power is Hollywood's most sought-after quality . . . " said *Premiere*.

Another part of that power is directing and Mel was more and more a frustrated *auteur*. There were increasing numbers of occasions when he felt he could do better than the director he had been working for. With this in mind, and still smarting over Kevin Costner's directorial debut with *Dances with Wolves*, he instructed his executives at Icon to look out for a script that he could direct.

In 1991, he found what he considered the perfect debut project: a modestly-budgeted little movie called *The Man without a Face* in which Mel slated himself to direct and star as a badly scarred burn victim who befriends a lonely 12-year-old boy. Each of them draws from their relationship something that neither has had before – understanding and mutual trust. However, they are forced apart after townspeople develop suspicions about the man's past. It was adapted from a novel written twenty years ago by Isabelle Holland. (Intriguingly, Mel's part was originally supposed to be a gay character, but this was changed on his instruction.) Hollywood wiseacres sniggered that if Mel could make $50 million at the US box office alone with *Forever Young*, when his face was slatered in latex, then a repeat make-up job for *The Man without a Face* would no doubt match that success.

According to cast and crew on the film, Mel achieved a good rapport with everyone. One actress, Fay Masterson, said: "He just gets down to work without any fuss. He is simply wonderful."

Piper Laurie – who had previously co-starred with Mel in *Tim*, thirteen years earlier – was full of praise for him. And his schoolboy co-star Nick Stahl found that Mel's handling was much more "normal" than the usual Hollywood treatment of child actors. Mel said, as always, that he enjoyed working with children. He is probably the only major Tinseltown star who really means what he says.

Ever-loyal Bruce Davey – partner, manager and the movie's producer as well as Mel's onetime drinking companion – reported: "He seems to have been doing this all his life. He's taken to it like a duck to water."

Cynics on the set say they never heard Davey voice anything other than glowing tributes to Mel. But then, he did pluck the accountant out of a grey little office in downtown Sydney and turn him into one of the most powerful producers in Hollywood.

It took Mel himself to admit that directing was not easy.

"It was more difficult than I thought it would be. It's a lot more involved, especially if you are directing yourself. If I was going to direct another film I would not be in it. It drove me crazy because it was too much to do. I had to wear too many hats."

During an interview on Australian televison's "A Current Affair", the actor was even more candid: "Sometimes you wake up in the morning and don't know what the hell you are going to do. I was very lucky to have good people around me. They saved my backside more than once."

Mel even insisted he had tried to find another actor to play the lead role, to allow him to concentrate on directing. But, after three stars had turned him down, he reluctantly agreed to act as well as helm the picture.

Some of the other actors in the $12 million film guessed that Mel hid his innermost fears by behaving the only way he knew how – cracking jokes and making bizarre proclamations. Eventually, he earned a new nickname, "Demento Boy", although everyone agreed that it made a real change to work for a director who joked half the time instead of being extremely ill-humoured – traditional dictator-director behaviour in Hollywood. The nickname simply referred to the moments when "Mel went a little crazy".

He had Robyn and the children with him for much of the film's ten-week shoot in and around the tiny town of Camden (pop. 5,060), Maine and then the seaside community of Bayside. Having been off the bottle for at least eighteen months, Mel behaved impeccably in local taverns where he became known as the "Cappuccino Kid" because he stuck to coffee. When Mel's family travelled back to California shortly before the end of the shoot, Mel attended an AA meeting in the basement of a community centre where he was filming. In the presence of thirty-five people at the Rockland Community Center, Mel introduced himself in the traditional AA way: "Hi, my name is Mel and I'm an alcoholic." Afterwards he shot a few rounds of pool with other AA members before departing for his rented house nearby.

After completion of filming, Mel retreated to France with Robyn and the children to begin editing *The Man without a*

Face. Post-production was one area of which Mel had little experience; the success of a film could depend just as much on the editing as the actual direction. Rumours that Mel had yet again given up smoking (this time after he played tennis with Hutton Gibson and discovered to his horror that his 73-year-old father was fitter than he) seem unlikely, especially because he was about to begin spending eighteen hours a day confined to an editing suite. He told American chat show host Jay Leno he had "quit the weed" but he was soon back on it. Until, in early 1993, Mel went for a course of acupuncture and stayed off cigarettes. For at least two months.

He emerged from the south of France with a better understanding of the language and a quietly confident feeling about *Man without a Face*. He and Robyn booked in for three days at the Thalgo centre in La Baule, where guests pay $400 a day to fight weight problems by having a series of water-based treatments including being hosed down with high-pressure jets of seawater. After emerging from the Thalgo centre and having completed editing of *Man without a Face*, Mel told one associate: "I'm not going to hang myself. I don't want to commit myself to say it's a masterpiece but . . ." When the film was released in the US in August, 1993, the critics seemed to agree. The *LA Times* wrote: "It is a quality, intelligent production – a moving and substantial achievement."

Mel's other quest was to make a western. It had been fuelled not only by the success of Kevin Costner's *Dances with Wolves* but also Clint Eastwood's Oscar sweep in 1993 with *Unforgiven*. He was absolutely convinced that a wild west picture could work for him as well. His interest had been well noted, and agents were flooding the offices of Icon Productions with western scripts and movie treatments, following the $100 million-plus takings of *Dances* and *Unforgiven*. But Mel was nothing if not careful. He surprised Tinseltown by spurning one very high-profile western project, *Bitter Root*, due to be directed by respected helmsman John McTiernan. Sources say that Mel did not like the political content of the script, which was centred around a bloody battle between the US government and the Indians in 1877.

Eastwood's success with *Unforgiven* helped give Mel the green light for a pet project based on the hit television series of the late Fifties and early Sixties, "Maverick". At first, it seemed a strange choice, as the TV series had been a notoriously badly-produced mishmash. Bruce Davey announced the motivation behind remaking *Maverick* as, "Mel has wanted to do a western for some time. What's better than *Maverick*?"

Mel had quietly and carefully assembled a talented back-up team to get the film off the ground. In 1992, his company Icon commissioned veteran screenwriter William Goldman to pen a screenplay based on the TV show. As originator of *Butch Cassidy and the Sundance Kid*, starring Paul Newman and Robert Redford more than twenty years earlier, Mel saw Goldman as the perfect man to knock the project into shape. But there was also another, more personal reason behind his decision to get the famous screenwriter on board: Goldman had written *Adventures in the Screen Trade* – the book that Mel says helped him recover his sanity when he was on the verge of a classic Hollywood nervous breakdown a few years earlier.

Goldman delivered his script in early 1993 and Mel and his partner Bruce Davey set about persuading a top director to helm the project. They did not have to look far; *Lethal Weapon* director Richard Donner could see potential in the project even before he read the screenplay and, in any case, the two men had formed a mutual admiration society during the filming of the three *Lethal Weapons*.

Warners were pleased that Donner and Mel were proposing to join forces once more and immediately gave the project the go-ahead. They saw *Maverick* as *Lethal Weapon* meets *The Wild Bunch*.

As one studio executive candidly confessed: "This is really *Lethal Weapon 4* on horseback, without Danny Glover. We are delighted."

Mel was attracted to the role of the charming, roguish cowboy and gambler Bret Maverick – it was not that far removed from *Lethal Weapon*'s Marty Riggs. Touchingly, he also insisted that Warners sign up the TV series's original star, James Garner, for a supporting role. Then Jodie Foster came on board and the "package" was complete.

But it was the hiring of Linda Hunt for a smaller part in *Maverick* that really delighted Mel. He had never forgotten the pint-sized actress since she played that Oscar-winning performance as a man in *The Year of Living Dangerously*. "Mel was just pleased as punch to get Linda on board", said one insider.

Mel describes *Maverick* as a "kind of Magical Mystery Tour through the Old West. It's fun".

Insiders on location with the movie in Arizona say that Mel spent much of his time playing cards in his caravan with co-star James Garner.

But their off-screen friendship is fast forgotten in front of the cameras because Garner plays a mean-spirited type who tries to steal Jodie Foster's love from Mel.

Warner Brothers predict that *Maverick* will take at least $100 million at the US box office alone this summer (1994). It is being simultaneously released in Europe in a bid to double that figure outside the lucrative American movie market.

Interestingly, little has been made of the pairing of Oscar winner Jodie Foster with Mel. According to one source on the set of *Maverick* "they both keep a friendly distance . . . away from each other" when not actually in front of the cameras.

Another member of the crew explained: "Jodie and Mel are like chalk and cheese. He likes nothing more than a chat and a joke with the crew while Jodie hardly speaks to a soul".

Mel also found it difficult to resist interfering in the director's job after his experience helming *Man without a Face*.

"I had to go into a self-imposed exile. Even when I was screaming to suggest something, I wouldn't do it. Dick (Donner) has been at it so much longer than a nasty little upstart bastard like me". But despite the mega-million dollar fees, Mel still hankers after his first love, theatre. There is even talk of a play with Denzil Washington. In the spring of 1994, Mel was also being touted as the star of a re-make of *A Connecticut Yankee in King Arthur's Court*, which is being developed by director and former Monty Python member Terry Gilliam.

But typically, he had been secretly developing another movie conversion of a western TV series, the famed "Wild Wild West". That was put on ice when Warners announced they had formally greenlighted *Maverick*, in April, 1993.

Other projects that Mel was interested in included the tragic life story of The Who's drummer Keith Moon. Whether Mel intends to play the lead role himself is uncertain. And then there was the long-running saga of another movie adaptation of a Sixties television series, "The Avengers". Mel was rumoured to be keen to play the part of John Steed, made famous by British actor Patrick Macnee.

Actress Joanna Lumley – who played Purdey in one series of the show – was outraged. "Bully for him. I cannot see anyone being John Steed except Patrick Macnee."

Yet Macnee – now a resident of Palm Springs, California – was less opposed to the notion.

"He's a very fine actor and I think he's just right for the part."

Ironically, shortly after these outbursts, it was disclosed that "The Avengers" project was "completely up in the air" and it appears unlikely it will ever be developed into a film.

Another possibility spreading around the Hollywood grapevine was a role for Mel alongside Marlon Brando in an epic feature project being prepared by *Laurence of Arabia* director David Lean. Eventually the project – written by Oscar-winning screenwriter Robert Bolt (who wrote *The Bounty*) – was shelved when Lean died. Then there was *Hiroshima Joe*, which was attached to British director Tony Scott, who made *Top Gun*. But again, initial discussions fizzled out and the project appears to have been shelved. There was even talk that Mel would make the perfect Rhett Butler for the sequel to *Gone with the Wind* but that was nothing more than an entertaining piece of gossip.

But the one rumoured project that really angered Mel was when that old familiar story about him playing James Bond resurfaced during the 1992 Cannes Film Festival. This time, news that *Lethal Weapon* producer Joel Silver was discussing a co-production deal with 007 mogul Cubby Broccoli fuelled the fire. Hollywood sources were claiming that Silver planned to sign Mel to the role in order to rekindle the once popular series of spy movies. But Mel turned down any suggestion of him playing Bond, without even considering a script – would rumours of him playing 007 ever end?

In the spring of 1994, Mel managed to get his second film as a director greenlighted. *Brave Heart* is, according to many Hollywood experts, either going to be an enormous success or an almighty flop.

For Mel it was a project he could not resist. *Brave Heart* is the story of fiery Scot William Wallace, who fought bloody battles against the English in 1270.

With his thinly disguised dislike for the English and his continuing obsession with getting an Oscar, Mel was said to be "ecstatic" to be doing the film.

This is Mel's attempt to emulate *Dances with Wolves* (directed by Kevin Costner)," said one member of his production team at Icon. But, with a $50 million budget and a series of difficult locations in the Scottish Highlands, *Brave Heart* promises to be a very stressful experience for all concerned. "If Mel gets this one right and it makes a fortune at the box office, then he will be in a position to direct anything he wants", added the Icon source.

Meanwhile, Mel had continued his secretive trips to Alcoholics Anonymous in Malibu through the previous eighteen months and, by all accounts, he steered clear of booze throughout that time. However, he was still capable of flaring up when the glare of the public spotlight became intrusive.

During a low key trip to New York City in early 1993, the actor's bodyguard assaulted local photographer James Edstrom when he tried to snap a photo of Mel outside the Tatou nightclub. Sources inside the club say that Mel was drinking Evian water throughout his two-hour visit and he was unaccompanied. But Edstrom believes that the actor's bodyguard reacted against him because he "did not want anyone to know he was in New York".

During the incident, Edstrom says the actor turned to his bodyguard and said: "You know what to do." The bodyguard then allegedly punched Edstrom, stomped on his foot and sent his camera crashing to the ground.

Edstrom is intending to serve a writ on Mel as soon as he can track him down and he insists he did nothing to provoke the attack.

"I am not the kind of guy who harasses people and stalks them. I go by their wishes. I don't know who he thinks he is, coming here and attacking people."

Ironically, a few weeks later Mel was photographed in London stepping out of a limousine exposing what looked suspiciously like a bald patch on top of his head. One New York hairdresser who has cut Mel's hair in the past revealed that Mel is "very concerned about losing his hair".

But his fears have little to do with vanity. "He could not stand the thought of being made to wear one of those ridiculous toupees." And the star has dismissed claims that he wants to be Forever Young as mere gossip.

The truth is that Mel "doesn't give two hoots". He feels the same way about cosmetic surgery, saying that he would rather grow old and withered than submit to "looking like the living dead".

No doubt memories of Sean Connery's long-running battles with the major Hollywood studios to avoid wearing a hairpiece are very familiar to Mel.

During that same trip to London to promote *Forever Young*, Mel upset breakfast television host Paula Yates by refusing to kiss her "because I don't kiss women with tattoos".

The remark was meant as a joke but Paula – wife of Live Aid guru Bob Geldof – was not so sure. Many who were present in the studio believe that Mel was actually being quite serious. Certainly, his friends say he has strong views about earrings and tattoos.

In February of 1993, Mel had the satisfaction of hearing that he was the second-biggest earner in Hollywood after Tom Cruise. Edging rival Kevin Costner into third place was a major breakthrough for Mel. In Australia, the actor made the 1992 list as one of the country's richest residents with a fortune estimated to be in the region of $37.5 million.

He was less impressed to hear that in a poll taken in the United States by the MasterCard Holiday company, women callers voted Mel as the man they would most like to play Santa Claus and come sliding down their chimney.

He was more concerned with the plight of sick and needy children. In early 1992 he began secretly visiting sick youngsters in hospitals in Los Angeles. Mel agreed to the voluntary work after being contacted by soap star Emma Samms, who runs the Starlight Foundation which makes dreams come true for sick children. At first he was reluctant to get involved as he believed that people would publicise his hospital visits and that would simply cause inconvenience for all concerned and do little to help the children. He was also particularly sensitive to accusations that he was using the visits to gain some positive publicity; some stars do that.

After a pledge from Samms that his involvement in the foundation would be kept secret, Mel started making visits to the Los Angeles Children's Hospital. At the bedside of leukaemia victim Adrianna Cervantes he appeared like a guardian angel and sat and talked with the 8-year-old, even agreeing to pose for a snapshot for her family alongside the airtight bubble in which the youngster is forced to spend her entire time.

Then the star moved on to visit other children on the ward, including one terminally ill teenager – who told Mel he was a big Rod Stewart fan.

"He was obviously shocked by the children's condition but he didn't show it to any of them," said one nurse.

The moment Mel got home to Malibu that evening, he called Rod Stewart at his London home and told him about the boy. Stewart followed up Mel's call by sending an autographed soccer ball and a written promise that he would visit when he got back to Los Angeles.

Ever since, Mel has continued visiting children in that hospital.

Back in Australia, he surprised many of his friends and family by agreeing to be the Sydney Opera House's official patron for its twentieth anniversary late in 1993. He said he was happy to act as roving international ambassador for the building and his duties were said to include an appearance at the birthday celebrations.

But in January 1993, Mel confessed that he was no longer certain where his real home was any more. In the first admission that perhaps the Hollywood system had swallowed him up, he said to an associate: "Home is . . . I don't know. I haven't got one."

Mel had given up alcohol, was continually trying to give up smoking, and he had all but given up Australia. He had finally rid himself of that trouble-making image, but was he any happier as a result?

If you can equate life with an automobile trip, I get lost when I'm doing the driving. That's all. You have to be a participant in the trip, yeah, but don't try to drive the car. And that's the hard one to get, because we're creatures of ego, I've gone out and done the driving myself for a while, and I found out it doesn't work.

Epilogue

As Mel careers towards his forties, a lifetime of drinking, womanising, and frenzied overwork has taken its toll. A fine latticework of wrinkles is becoming visible at the corners of his eyes and deep vertical grooves are starting to form at the corners of that famous mouth.

Mel may well be by any definition an original, and one of the most popular actors of our time. His funny/sad persona has already spanned almost two decades of filmgoing.

He is the sturdy, lower-class kid from the wrong side of the tracks who burst on to the movie scene by playing, essentially, himself. The well-read drama student who can talk like an outback farmer or a Los Angeles cop; the shy, reluctant railroad worker's son identified in the public mind with every woman's fantasy; a cowboy-boot-wearing, rugged-looking character with the down-to-earth tastes of a simple man; the Hollywood heart-throb who preaches about God but refuses to attend the house of the Lord because of his father's feud with the Catholic Church; the irredeemable part-time misogynist who admits he prefers the company of women; the redneck, homophobic, dabbler in non-emotional relationships and – most intriguingly – the flagrant anti-social film idol who rose to global fame by being like the guy next door.

Mel is the quintessential quick-change artist, moving from accent to accent and country to country so easily that he defies categorising. In many ways, that is what fascinates so many of us.

In that sense, Mel has always managed to keep one step beyond what was happening in the lives of his contemporaries. In a generation filled with families comprising a manageable number of children, he has gone one step further and bred a mini-army. The arrival of the button-down, money-mad "Just Say No" 1980s made no difference to Mel. He remained the same old-fashioned character who believes that a woman's place is in the home and his children sometimes require physical punishment if they misbehave.

This is the same man who so fervently portrays heroes like Vietnam vet Marty Riggs, even though his own father took Mel and his brothers out of the United States to avoid them being drafted into that conflict.

Closer to home, the luck of Mel has become legendary. Apart from the sad departure of his own mother in 1990, death has rarely touched this remarkably fortunate actor. And all along, Mel has painstakingly chosen the projects he wishes to be associated with.

To promote his obsession with starring in a western, he appeared on NBC's "Saturday Night Live" in 1989. In one skit, he donned a stetson and a bootlace tie to portray a sheriff. Afterwards he urged his associates to watch a video recording of the show because he wanted them to be convinced.

MEL – THE INSIDE STORY

The commercial and (surprisingly) partial critical success of the *Lethal Weapon* series has conveniently deferred his approaching middle age. To be fair, there is no suggestion that Mel fears old age.

However, from him, little is predictable. With an army of advisers urging him on to star in more and more multi-million-dollar movies for vast fees, he is still perfectly capable of turning around one day and walking away from Hollywood.

He has thought about it in the past. Mel even referred to his cattle farm in Australia as his "back-up plan". There is also Robyn and the children to consider. His oldest, Hannah, is in her teens. Switching schools is becoming more and more impractical for the Gibson brood. Mel has made a pledge that he will not spend long periods away from his family. They represent the one secure unit that he can return to after the madness of movie-making. But with high school looming he will have to face some hard decisions about his future and his family's need for more stability.

The notion of Mel retiring before he reaches 40 in 1996 is not so far-fetched. He has always (despite the occasional diversion) remained steadfastly committed to family life. He has hinted that he would be perfectly happy if Robyn had another six children by him. And he has never hidden the fact that he considers the film industry as a job of work and nothing more. Only time will tell . . .

Source and Chapter Notes

The following chapter notes give a general view of the sources who helped in the preparation of *Mel – The Inside Story*, but they are by no means all-inclusive. The author has respected the wishes of many interview subjects to remain anonymous and accordingly has not named them here or elsewhere in the text.

Chapters 1 and 2

Birth certificate came from Peekskill Public Library. Records on background of the town came from local sources and reference material gathered in Peekskill. Other research carried out at Laurens School after access was granted to school records. Also used were city directories, church records plus birth, marriage and death certificates for various relatives and friends. Letters from the Gibson family supplied by one source. Articles from the *Peekskill Star* Jan 3 and Jan 4, 1956. Peekskill directories from 1952 to 1969 were checked as well.

Also interviews with Ed Stinson, Feb 18 and 20, 1993, Kathleen Lyons, Feb 20, 1993 and Pat Grasso, Feb 21, 1993, Ralph McCoach, Feb 20, 1993, Carol Rowell, Feb 18, 1993, Eileen Smith Saladino Feb 18, 1993, confidential source, Feb 20, 1993.

Other source material includes: *Australian Women's Weekly*, Feb, 1987, *Sydney Telegraph*, Dec 22, 1990, *Cinema Papers* magazine, Nov, 1982.

Chapter 3

Interviews with Ed Stinson Feb 18, 1993 and Feb 20, 1993, Kathleen Lyons, Feb 20, 1993, Jeremy Connolly, April 1 and April 10, 1993, Eileen Leiden, April 3, 1993, Mark McGinnity, April 13, 1993, Yvonne Perottete, April 1, 1993, Monroe Reimers, April 4, 1993, Linda Newton, April 13, 1993, Carma Smith, April 14, 1993, Deborah Foreman, April 15, 1993, confidential source Feb 20, 1993, confidential source April 3, 1993, confidential source April 13, 1993, confidential source April 13, 1993.

Articles include: *Australian Women's Weekly*, Feb, 1987, *The Australian*, Jan 1975, *Sunday Telegraph*, Sept 5, 1976, *Sydney Evening Herald*, Feb 1976, *The Sun-Herald*, Sept 12, 1982, *Today*, April 6, 1991, *The Sun*, Nov 4, 1991, *Melbourne Herald*, Nov 4, 1968, *Sydney Daily Mirror*, Aug 8, 1989, *Sydney Sun*, June 20, 1986, *Sun*, Aug 16, 1986, *Australian Alliance for Catholic Tradition*, Dec 1990, *The Black and Tans* by Richard Bennett (Severn House, 1976).

Chapters 4 and 5

Interviews with Linda Newton, April 13, 1993, Monroe Reimers Mar 31, 1993, April 4, 1993, Jeremy Connolly, April 1 and April 10, 1993, Deborah Foreman, April 16, 1993, Eileen Leiden, April 3, 1993, Ed Stinson, Feb 20, 1993, confidential source April 10, 1993, confidential source April 1, 1993, confidential source April 13, 1993, confidential source April 13, 1993, Phil Avalon, April 1, 1993, and April 5, 1993, confidential source April 10, 1993, Carmela Quinn, April 14, 1993, Robert Menzies, April 10, 1993, Pat Lovell, April 4 and April 5, 1993, confidential source April 1, 1993, confidential source April 13, 1993.

Articles include: *Daily Telegraph*, Sept 5, 1992, *New Idea*, April 20, 1991, *Sunday Telegraph*, Oct 18, 1992, *Movieline*, April 17, 1987, Ruther Brotherhood, Aug 17, 1987, *People Magazine*, Feb 4, 1985, *Sunday People*, July 1, 1990, *Daily Telegraph*, July 3, 1987, *Daily Mirror*, August 28, 1985, *The Sun*, June 22, 1987, *Cinema Papers*, August, 1979, *People* magazine, Feb 4, 1985, *Sunday People*, July 1, 1990, *New Idea*, April 20, 1991, *The Sun*, 17 August 1987, *Movieline*, April 4, 1983.

Chapter 6

Interviews with Emil Minti, Mar 31, 1993, John Dowding, April 7, 1993, Mitch Matthews, Mar 30, 1993, Celia Matthews, Mar 30, 1993, Pat Lovell, April 4 and April 5, 1993, Scott Murray, April 8, 1993, Linda Newton, April 13, 1993, Jeremy Connolly, Rhonda Schepisi, confidential source April 1, 1993, confidential source April 13, 1993, confidential source April 13, 1993.

Articles include: *You* magazine, Oct, 1987, *Los Angeles Times*, Dec 30, 1992, *Daily Mail*, Oct 9, 1985, *The Sun*, Jan 3, 1990, *The Australian*, Dec 5, 1981, *Scene*, Jan 2, 1982, *The Australian*, Mar 4, 1986, *Cinema Papers*, Mar, 1983, September, 1985, January/February, 1982, May, 1985, *Evening Herald*, Mar 30, 1985, *The Sun*, Jan 5, 1979, *Variety*, June 15, 1983, June 26, 1985, *Daily Telegraph*, Jan 29, 1985, *Evening Herald*, Jan 29, 1985, *Daily Mirror*, Feb 27, 1985, *The Sun*, July 19, 1984, *T.V. Week*, June 30, 1984, *Daily Mirror*, Mar 20, 1991, *Daily Telegraph*, July 18, 1985, *Financial Review*, Aug 9, 1985, *Herald*, June 5, 1985, *Sunday Telegraph*, Aug 4, 1985, *Daily Mirror*, Aug 2, 1985, *Daily Telegraph*, Nov 20, 1985, *Daily Mirror*, Jan 28, 1986, *Financial Review*, Mar 4, 1986, *Daily Telegraph*, Sept 1, 1986, *Daily Telegraph*, Oct 20, 1986, *Daily Mirror*, Jan 5, 1987, *T.V. Week*, July 22, 1989, *Daily Mirror*, Oct 3, 1990, *Sunday Telegraph*, Sept 23, 1979, *Daily Telegraph*, Dec 13, 1981, *Daily Telegraph*, Jan 8, 1982, *The Sun*, Jan 1, 1982, *Daily Telegraph*, Jan 1, 1982, *The Australian*, Dec 29, 1982, *Daily Telegraph*, Dec 28, 1981, *Daily Mirror*, Dec 24, 1981, *Daily Mirror*, Mar 2, 1982, *Time*, May 10, 1982, *Sydney Herald*, April 6, 1980, *Daily Telegraph*, Sept 23, 1979.

Chapter 7

Interviews with John Philip Law, May 12, 1993, Tim Burstall April 7 and April 9, 1993, Monroe Reimers, Mar 31, 1993, April 4, 1993, Jeremy Connolly, April 1 and April 10, 1993, Pat Lovell, April 4 and April 5, 1993, Scott Murray, April 8, 1993, Rupert Maconick, Jan 10, 1993, confidential source April 1, 1993, confidential source April 13, 1993, confidential source April 13, 1993.

Articles include: *Cleo* magazine, December, 1979, *Sydney Herald*, April 6, 1980, *Sydney Herald*, Dec 24, 1981, *Cinema Papers*, May, 1979, *Australian Women's Weekly*, Jan 17, 1979, *Sydney Herald*, Oct 18, 1978, *Sydney Telegraph*, Sept 23, 1979, *Sydney Morning Herald*, Sept, 1979, *Sydney Morning Herald*, March 29, 1979, *Sydney Morning Herald*, May 20, 1980, *The Australian*, Oct 18, 1978, *Daily Mirror*, Oct 26, 1983.

Chapter 8

Interviews with Rhonda Schepisi, April 9, 1993, Don Bennetts, April 6, 1993, Pat Lovell, April 4 and April 5, 1993, Scott Murray, April 8, 1993, Linda Newton, April 13, 1993, Deborah Foreman, April 15, 1993, confidential source April 4, 1993, confidential source April 5, 1993, confidential source April 13, 1993.

Articles include: *The Sun*, Dec 14, 1981, *Sunday Telegraph*, July 13, 1980, *Sydney Herald*, Sept 9, 1981,*Mode*, Feb/Mar 1981, *The Australian*, Jan 21, 1982, *Australian Film Review*, Aug 8, 1981, *Daily Telegraph*, Aug 8, 1981, *Morning Herald*, Sept 17, 1981, *Sun-Herald*, May 3, 1981, *Daily Mirror*, Dec 1, 1980, *Telegraph Mirror*, May 16, 1992, *Sunday Telegraph*, April 29, 1990, *Variety*, May 5, 1981, *New Idea*, Aug 6, 1989, *Cinema Papers*, July/August 1981, *The Truth*, Jan 31, 1981, *Variety*, June 13, 1981, *Afterdark*, November, 1981.

Chapter 9

Interviews with Rhonda Schepisi, April 9, 1993, Don Bennetts, April 6, 1993, Pat Lovell, April 4 and April 5, 1993, Scott Murray, April 8, 1993, Linda Newton, April 13, 1993, Robert Menzies, April 10, 1993, Jeremy Connolly, April 1, 1993, Dan McDonnell, April 8, 1993, confidential source April 4, 1993, confidential source April 5, 1993, confidential source April 13, 1993.

Articles include: *Australian*, May 26, 1984, *The Sun*, June 1, 1984, *Australian*, Mar 10, 1982, *Daily Mirror*, Oct 26, 1983, *Daily Telegraph*, Nov 9, 1989, *Sunday Telegraph*, Aug 2, 1982, *Australian*, June 16, 1982, *Sun*, June 6, 1982, *Newsweek*, May 31, 1982, *Daily Telegraph*, Dec 16, 1982, *Telegraph*, April 9, 1983, *Hollywood Reporter*, Oct 13, 1982, *Village Voice*, Nov 2, 1982, *Glamour*, Mar, 1983, *GQ*, June, 1983, *Vanity Fair*, July 1989, *Cosmopolitan*, May, 1983, *Moviegoer*, Feb, 1983, *US Magazine*, Mar 14, 1982, *People* magazine, Feb 14, 1983, *LA Times*, Feb 6, 1983, *Herald*, April 21, 1982, *Sunday Telegraph*, June 6, 1982, *Herald*, Dec 10, 1981, *Sun Herald* Dec 19, 1982, *Australian*, June 19, 1982, *Telegraph*, July 4, 1982, *Mode*, June, 1982, *US Magazine*, Mar 13, 1983, *People* magazine, Feb 14, 1983, *Telegraph Mirror*, Dec 12, 1992, *Australian*, June 5, 1982, *Telegraph*, June 6, 1982, *Daily Mirror*, Dec 2, 1982, *Daily Mirror*, Dec 17, 1982, *Daily Telegraph*, Nov 16, 1981, *West Australian*, Jan 5, 1982, *Daily Telegraph*, Nov 20, 1981, *Telegraph*, Nov 23, 1981, *Sunday Telegraph*, Oct 25, 1981, *Daily Mirror*, May 7, 1985.

Chapter 10

Interviews with Maeva Salmon, Mar 23, 1993, Hare Salmon, Mar 23, 1993, Coco Dexter, Mar 23, 1993, Tavaite Vernette Mar 24, 1993, Maimiti Kinnander, Mar 26, 1993, Irene Fuller, Mar 25, 1993, George Logue, Mar 25, 1993, Noetia Guy, Mar 25, 1993, Maco Roometua, Mar 25, 1993, Daphne Fuller, Mar 25, 1993, Maurice Lenoir, Mar 26, 1993, Scan Denis, Mar 25, 1993, confidential source, Mar 25, 1993, confidential source, Mar 24, 1993.

Articles include: *Daily Mail*, Sept 10, 1984, *Sunday* magazine, Aug 12, 1984, *Sunday Express*, June 12, 1983, *Daily Mirror*, May 7, 1985, *West Australian*, Jan 5, 1982, *Daily Telegraph*, Aug 27, 1984, *Daily Telegraph*, July 11, 1983, *Daily Telegraph*, Sept 14, 1984, *Cinema Papers*, July, 1984, *The Bulletin*, June 12, 1984, *Sun-Herald*, July 24, 1983, *Weekend Australian*, May 19–20, 1984, *Sun*, May 24, 1984, *Telegraph*, April 28, 1984, *Daily Mirror*, Feb 6, 1984, *The Sun*, Dec 29, 1983, *Daily Telegraph*, Mar 14, 1984, *Telegraph*, Sept 30, 1983, *Daily Mirror*, Sept 1, 1983, *Australian*, May 12, 1985, *Sun*, Aug 2, 1984, *Sunday Telegraph*, Aug 26, 1984, *Daily Mirror*, July 20, 1984, *Daily Mirror*, July 19, 1984, *T.V. Week*, June 23, 1984, *Sun*, June 14, 1984, *Herald*, July 21, 1984, *Variety*, April 24, 1984, *Herald*, April 28, 1984, *Cinema Papers*, August, 1984, *Sun*, May 28, 1983, *The Truth*, May 26, 1984, *Sunday Mirror*, Sept 15, 1984, *Daily Mail*, Sept 25, 1984, *Daily Mirror*, Feb 3, 1990, *Herald Examiner*, Mar 14, 1983, *Mail on Sunday*, May 13, 1984, *Hollywood Reporter*, Mar 24, 1983, *The Standard*, May 10, 1983, *Variety*, April 5, 1983.

Chapter 11

Interviews with Pat Lovell, April 4 and April 5, 1993, Scott Murray, April 8, 1993, Linda Newton, April 13, 1993, Deborah Foreman, April 15, 1993, Terri DePaolo, May 12, 1993, Andrew Urban, Mar 30, 1993, confidential source April 4, 1993, confidential source April 5, 1993, confidential source April 13, 1993.

Articles include: *Sunday Telegraph*, Aug 28, 1983, *Daily Telegraph*, Dec 19, 1983, *Daily Mirror*, June 13, 1985, *Sydney Morning Herald*, June 6, 1985, *The Sun*, Mar 12, 1985, *Daily Telegraph*, Feb 28, 1985, *Herald*, Dec 24, 1983, *Herald*, Dec 28, 1984, *Sunday People*, Mar 17, 1985, *Sunday* magazine, Dec 23, 1985, *The Sun*, April 29, 1984, *Time*, Feb 7, 1984, *Sunday Telegraph*, April 29, 1984, *Daily Mirror*, May 5, 1984, *The*

Australian, May 4, 1984, *Daily Mirror*, May 3, 1984, *USA Today*, Dec 14, 1992. *Fade Out* by Peter Bart (William Morrow, 1990).

Chapter 12

Interviews with Pat Lovell, April 4 and April 5, 1993, Scott Murray, April 8, 1993, Linda Newton, April 13, 1993, John Dowding, April 7, 1993, Jeremy Connolly, April 1, 1993, confidential source April 4, 1993, confidential source April 5, 1993, confidential source April 13, 1993.

Articles include: *Herald*, Feb 5, 1985, *Time*, July 2, 1984, *Variety*, Aug 23, 1983, *The Australian*, July 20, 1984, *Campus Voice*, Aug, 1984, *Melbourne Age*, June 8, 1985, *Daily Star*, July 27, 1992, *The Sun*, April 25, 1984, *Daily Mirror*, April 11, 1986, *Daily Telegraph*, April 15, 1985, *Daily Mirror*, May 8, 1986, *The Sun*, June 21, 1985, *Daily Telegraph*, April 27, 1984, *Daily Telegraph*, Feb 7, 1985, *The Australian*, July 24, 1984, *The Sun*, Jan 4, 1984, *Daily Mirror*, Dec 14, 1984, *Daily Star*, July 28, 1984, *Variety*, Dec 23, 1985, *The Australian*, June 1, 1984, *The Australian*, Feb 8, 1985, *Daily Mirror*, June 16, 1984, *Sydney Herald*, May 9, 1986.

Chapter 13

Interviews with Pat Lovell, April 4 and April 5, 1993, Scott Murray, April 8, 1993, John Philip Law, May 12, 1993, Deborah Foreman, April 15, 1993, confidential source May 10, 1993, confidential source May 12, 1993, confidential source April 13, 1993.

Articles include: *Sydney Herald*, Aug 28, 1986, *Melbourne Age*, April 4, 1987, *Herald*, Nov 22, 1986, *Australian Women's Weekly*, July, 1992, *T.V. Week*, July 25, 1992, *Telegraph Mirror*, June 9, 1992, *New Idea*, Jan 11, 1992, *Daily Mirror*, Dec 15, 1988, *Daily Mirror*, Aug 27, 1987, *T.V. Week*, Aug 5, 1989, *Sydney Morning Herald*, Aug 10, 1989, *Daily Telegraph*, June 30, 1989, *Daily Mirror*, July 4, 1989, *Daily Mirror*, July 14, 1989, *Daily Telegraph*, July 15, 1989, *Sun-Herald*, July 20, 1989, *Sunday Telegraph*, July 2, 1989, *Sydney Morning Herald*, Mar 14, 1987, *Sunday Telegraph*, Mar 8, 1987, *Sun-Herald*, Nov 9, 1986, *Telegraph*, June 5, 1987, *Sun*, Aug 11, 1986, *Daily Telegraph*, June 30, 1986, *The Sun*, June 10, 1987, *New Idea*, Nov 9, 1991, *Pix*, April 4, 1990, *Melbourne Age*, June 12, 1987, *Daily Mirror*, Aug 16, 1989, *Daily Mirror*, Aug 10, 1992, *Sunday Mirror*, Mar 29, 1992, *Sunday Express*, June 14, 1992, *Daily Mirror*, June 29, 1989, *Variety*, Oct 9, 1986, *Woman's Day*, Aug 17, 1992, *People*, June 15, 1992.

MEL – THE INSIDE STORY

Chapter 14

Interviews with Terri DePaolo, May 12 and 13, 1993, Pat Lovell, Mar 30, April 4, April 5, 1993, Andrew Urban, Mar 30, 1993, Linda Newton, April 13, 1993, confidential source Mar 30, 1993, confidential source April 2, 1993.

Articles include: *The Sun*, May 12, 1987, *Daily Telegraph*, May 18, 1987, *Sunday Telegraph*, Feb 19, 1989, *Herald*, Nov 16, 1985, *Telegraph*, July 20, 1984, June 6, 1987, *U.S.* Aug 7, 1989, *Sunday Telegraph*, Aug 16, 1987, *The Sun*, May 21, 1987, *Telegraph*, Jan 19, 1989, *Telegraph*, June 6, 1987, *Sun-Herald*, Jan 15, 1989, *Telegraph*, Feb 19, 1987, *Telegraph*, Feb 13, 1987, *Sunday Telegraph*, Sept 7, 1986, *Telegraph*, Jan 19, 1989, *Sun-Herald*, Jan 15, 1989, *Telegraph*, Aug 21, 1985, *TV Week*, Aug 27, 1988, *T.V. Week*, Nov 27, 1987, *Sun-Herald*, Sept 16, 1987, *Screen International*, Jan 14, 1989, *Sun*, May 21, 1987, *T.V. Week*, Nov 21, 1987, *Telegraph*, Aug 25, 1986, *You* magazine, Feb 9, 1987, *Screen International*, Aug 20, 1988, *Mirror*, June 13, 1987.

Chapter 15

Interviews with Pat Lovell, April 4 and April 5, 1993, Scott Murray, April 8, 1993, Rupert Maconick, May 12, 1993, confidential source April 9, 1993, confidential source May 12, 1993, confidential source April 13, 1993.

Articles include: *Telegraph Mirror*, May 19, 1992, *Sydney Morning Herald*, Feb 10, 1992, *Morning Herald*, June 29, 1992, *Sun-Herald*, July 14, 1991, *Woman's Day*, Feb 4, 1992, *Sun-Herald*, Feb 10, 1992, *Daily Mirror*, Sept 5, 1992, *Today*, April 20, 1992, *Melbourne Age*, Feb 2, 1992, *Los Angeles Times*, Jan 24, 1992, Jan 15, 1992, *Star*, Feb 4, 1992, *Telegraph Mirror*, Sept 5, 1992, *Sun*, Aug 12, 1989, *Telegraph*, May 6, 1984, *Cosmopolitan*, May, 1983, *Globe*, Jan 12, 1993, *Newsweek*, Aug 24, 1992, *People*, July 9, 1990, *Daily Mirror*, Aug 13, 1992, *Morning Herald*, Sept 5, 1990, *Telegraph Mirror*, Aug 13, 1992, *Woman's Day*, Jan 24, 1989, *Herald*, Jan 21, 1993, *T.V. Week*, Mar 21, 1987, *Cleo*, May, 1987, *Daily Telegraph*, May 27, 1987, *Herald*, July 6, 1987, *Telegraph*, July 6, 1987, *The Australian*, July 6, 1987, *Herald*, April 28, 1984, *Daily Mirror*, Sept 4, 1990, *Herald*, Aug 23, 1979, *Sun*, July 5, 1983, *Daily Mirror*, Sept 4, 1989, *Daily Mirror*, May 28, 1987, *Sun*, May 27, 1987, *Herald*, May 29, 1987, *Time Out*, Aug 9, 1989, *Telegraph*, May 28, 1987, *Daily Mirror*, May 28, 1987, *Daily Telegraph*, May 29, 1987, *Telegraph*, July 22,

1990, *Herald*, May 28, 1987, *Daily Mirror*, May 28, 1987, *Sun*, Aug 11, 1985, *Sunday Telegraph*, May 15, 1992.

Chapter 16

Interviews with Pat Lovell, April 4 and April 5, 1993, Scott Murray, April 8, 1993, Rupert Maconick, May 12, 1993, confidential source April 9, 1993, confidential source May 12, 1993, confidential source April 13, 1993.

Articles include: *Sunday Sun*, May 20, 1990, *Telegraph*, July 5, 1989, *Sunday Telegraph*, Oct 1, 1989, *Daily Telegraph*, Jan 4, 1988, *Telegraph*, Nov 23, 1988, *New Idea*, Jan 25, 1992, *Weekend Australian*, June 10, 1990, *New Idea*, June 16, 1990, *The Bulletin*, June 5, 1990, *Women's Day*, Feb 20, 1990, *New Idea*, June 23, 1990, *T.V. Week*, June 9, 1990, *Daily Mirror*, Nov 30, 1988, *Daily Mirror*, Nov 25, 1988, *Sun-Herald*, Nov 20, 1988, *The Australian Magazine*, Dec 3, 1988, *Sunday Telegraph*, July 3, 1988, *Daily Telegraph*, Mar 18, 1989, *Telegraph*, Feb 10, 1989, *Daily Mirror*, Dec 26, 1988, *The Sun*, Nov 11, 1987, *Daily Mirror*, Jan 3, 1986, *Telegraph*, Jan 25, 1989, *Mirror*, Nov 25, 1988, *Mirror*, Dec 5, 1988, *Telegraph*, Jan 16, 1989, *New Idea*, Dec 24, 1988, *Telegraph*, Feb 28, 1988, *Telegraph*, Jan 12, 1989, *Telegraph*, Nov 23, 1988, *Woman's Day*, Feb, 1989, *Daily Telegraph*, July 15, 1989.

Chapter 17

Interviews with Jim Mitteager, May 21, 1993, Wendy Lee, June 22, 1993, Miranda Brewin (voice analysed) Feb 11, 1993, Michelle Adamson, Mar 31, 1993, Cassandra Kirton (submitted to polygraph) Nov 22, 1992, Deborah Foreman, April 15, 1993, Linda Newton, April 13, 1993, Pat Lovell, April 4, 1993, confidential source May 12, 1993, confidential source, May 13, 1993.

Articles include: *Good Housekeeping*, Jan, 1993, *Daily Mirror*, April 11, 1989, *TV Week*, Feb 11, 1989, *Sun-Herald*, Nov 8, 1987, *Daily Telegraph*, Nov 9, 1987, Nov 6, 1987, *Sunday Telegraph*, Nov 8, 1987, *Sunday Telegraph*, Feb 11, 1990, *Daily Telegraph*, Jan 30, 1986, *Daily Telegraph*, Nov 6, 1987, *Sun-Herald*, June 29, 1990, *Daily Express*, Jan 30, 1993, *GQ*, May, 1991, *News of the World*, Aug 6, 1989, *Los Angeles Times*, Oct 16, 1990, *Variety*, Oct 2, 1987, *Weekend*, Sept 16, 1989, *Sun*, Nov 8, 1987, *Sunday Mirror* magazine, Jan 1, 1989, *Sunday Express* magazine, Mar 26, 1989, *National Enquirer*, Jan 1993,

Globe, Feb 9, 1993, *Woman's Day*, Feb 15, 1993, *New Idea*, Feb 20, 1993, *Sun*, Oct 17, 1990, *Telegraph Mirror*, Oct 18, 1990, *News of the World*, Jan 31, 1993, *Vanity Fair*, July, 1989, *Daily Telegraph*, Oct 21, 1986, *Sunday* magazine, Sept 8, 1992, *Daily Telegraph*, Feb 1, 1993, *The Sun*, Nov 5, 1987.

Chapter 18

Interviews with Terri Depaulo, May 12 and 13, 1993, Dan McDonnell, April 8, 1993, confidential source Feb 11, 1993, confidential source Feb 15, 1993, confidential source Feb 15, 1993, Som Pol Sungkawess, Jan 25, 1993, Charlie Sungkawess, Jan 25, 1993, John Bremer, Feb 8, 1993, Peter Nowlon, Feb 2, 1993.

Articles include: *Variety*, Nov 6, 1989, *Los Angeles Times*, Sept 17, 1989, *People*, Nov 25, 1990, *Daily Mirror*, Dec 19, 1990, *Sun*, Dec 14, 1990, *Mail on Sunday*, Oct 18, 1989, *Woman's Day*, Dec 1989, *Sun*, April 18, 1991, *Daily Mail*, July 28, 1990, *In Dublin* magazine, Oct 25, 1991, *Herald*, Aug 7, 1990, *Hollywood Reporter*, June 20, 1989, *Herald*, Aug 11, 1990, *Mirror*, Dec 16, 1989, *Telegraph*, Dec 21, 1988, *Herald*, Aug 12, 1990, *Entertainment Weekly*, Aug 17, 1990, *Daily Mirror*, Aug 14, 1990, *Telegraph*, Mar 13, 1989, *Daily Mirror*, June 19, 1989, *Daily Mirror*, Aug 21, 1990, *Daily Mirror*, Aug 7, 1990, *Weekend Australian*, Aug 25, 1990, *Daily Mirror*, Aug 7, 1990, *Woman's Day*, Feb 13, 1990, *Sun-Herald*, Sept 9, 1990, *Sun-Herald*, Aug 12, 1990, *Costner* by Todd Keith (Ikonprint, 1991).

Chapter 19

Interviews with Terri DePaolo, May 12 and 13, 1993, Scott Murray, April 8, 1993, Pat Lovell, April 5, 1993, confidential source Feb 11, 1993, confidential source Feb 15, 1993, confidential source Feb 15, 1993.

Articles include: *Telegraph*, Oct 21, 1986, *Telegraph*, Mar 30, 1989, *Herald*, Nov 27, 1988, *Australian*, Aug 11, 1985, *The Sun*, Nov 5, 1991, *New Idea*, Oct 5, 1991, *Telegraph*, Nov 28, 1988, *Daily Mirror*, Nov 25, 1988, *Sun-Herald*, Nov 27, 1988, *Herald*, Mar 30, 1989, *Daily Mirror*, April 22, 1987, *Telegraph*, Feb 26, 1987, *Telegraph*, Sept 23, 1985, *The Truth*, Aug 13, 1989, *Telegraph*, July 20, 1986, *Woman's Day*, Dec 28, 1992, *Telegraph*, July 29, 1992, *Post*, Nov 9, 1991, *Evening Standard*, Aug 9, 1990, *Today*, April 21, 1987, *Daily Mirror*, Aug 24, 1987, *US* magazine, Dec 12, 1988, *Sun*, May 30, 1990, *Sunday Mirror*, Sept 15, 1991, *Herald*, May 24, 1990, *Telegraph*, April 11, 1991, *Daily Mirror*, Aug 27, 1986, *Daily Mirror*, Mar 4, 1985, *People*, Sept 5, 1985, *Daily*

Mirror, Jan 12, 1989, *Sun*, Nov 17, 1990, *Women's Daily*, Nov 29, 1991, *Sun-Herald*, Aug 18, 1991, *Daily Express*, Sept 3, 1991. *Kevin Costner* by Todd Keith (Ikonprint, 1991).

Chapter 20

Interviews with Terri DePaulo, May 12 and 13, 1993, Dan McDonnell, April 8, 1993, Scott Murray, April 8, 1993, Pat Lovell, April 5, 1993, confidential source, Feb 11, 1993, confidential source, Feb 15, 1993, confidential source, Feb 15, 1993.

Articles incude: *Bulletin*, Feb 26, 1991, *Woman's Day*, Feb 19, 1991, *Daily Mirror*, Feb 19, 1991, *Herald*, Jan 27, 1991, *Women's Weekly*, Feb, 1991, *Sun-Herald*, Feb 8, 1991, *Telegraph*, Jan 10, 1991, *Women's Day*, Aug 21, 1990, *US* magazine, Sept 3, 1990, *T.V. Week*, Feb 16, 1991, *Good Weekend*, Feb 16, 1991, *Sunday Express*, Nov 18, 1990, *Daily Mail*, Dec 21, 1990, *Evening Standard*, April 18, 1991, *Daily Mirror*, Sept 5, 1990, *Daily Express*, April 16, 1991, *Today*, April 17, 1991, *Independent*, April 19, 1991, *Sunday Times*, April 14, 1991, *Daily Mail*, April 24, 1991, *The European*, Mar 15, 1991, *Evening Standard*, Mar 27, 1990, *The Times*, April 13, 1991, *Los Angeles Times*, May 6, 1990, *Evening Standard*, April 19, 1991, *US* magazine, Mar 9, 1990, *Herald*, Jan 20, 1991, *USA Today*, Dec 31, 1990, *Daily Mirror*, Jan 9, 1991, *Sunday Mirror*, Mar 24, 1991, *Life* magazine, Feb 1991, *Time Out*, Dec 19, 1990, *Evening Standard*, Feb 9, 1990, *New York Tiems*, Sept 24, 1989, *Parade* magazine, Mar 3, 1991, *T.V. Guide*, Nov 10, 1990, *The Australian*, Sept 1, 1990, *Telegraph*, Aug 11, 1990, *Los Angeles Times*, Jan 10, 1991, *Daily Mail*, April 18, 1991, *Variety*, Dec 20, 1990, *Daily Express*, April 5, 1990 and Mar 15, 1991, *Telegraph*, Aug 11, 1990, *Herald*, Jan 14, 1992, *Daily Express*, Dec 13, 1990, *Daily Telegraph*, April 13, 1989, *Daily Mail*, April 24, 1990, *New Idea*, Sept 30, 1989, *Daily Express*, April 7, 1990, *Sun*, July 13, 1990, *Daily Mail*, Oct 17, 1990, *People*, May 12, 1992, *Hollywood Reporter*, Jan 2, 1992, *Sunday Mirror*, Feb 24, 1991, *Daily Mail*, Jan 2, 1992, *Telegraph*, April 19, 1991, *Telegraph*, Mar 26, 1991, *Daily Mail*, May 1, 1990, *New Idea*, Feb 2, 1991, *Sun-Herald*, May 27, 1990, *Daily Mirror*, April 12, 1990, *Daily Mirror*, April 12, 1990, *Australian Women's Weekly*, August 1989, *Telegraph*, Aug 11, 1990, *Daily Mirror*, Feb 23, 1988, *Herald*, Jan 4, 1991, *Daily Mirror*, July 20, 1990, *TV Week*, July 28, 1990, *New Idea*, July 20, 1991, *New Idea*, May 25, 1991, *Telegraph Mirror*, April 19, 1991, *Telegraph Mirror*, Mar 15, 1991, *Sun Herald*, Feb 24, 1991,

Telegraph Mirror, Feb 16, 1991, *Telegraph Mirror*, Feb 19, 1991, *Morning Herald*, Feb 21, 1991, *Woman's Day*, Jan 19, 1991, *The Australian*, Feb 16, 1991, *Sun-Herald*, Jan 27, 1991, *Sun-Herald*, Jan 27, 1991, *Telegraph Mirror*, Feb 15, 1991, *New Idea*, Feb 2, 1991, *Telegraph Mirror*, Jan 8, 1991, *Time*, Jan 21, 1991, *Telegraph*, Nov 27, 1990, *Sun-Herald*, Dec 23, 1990, *Telegraph*, Nov 11, 1989, *Telegraph*, Dec 23, 1990, *Telegraph*, Dec 13, 1990, *Telegraph*, Dec 12, 1990, *Daily Mirror*, Oct 1, 1990, *Daily Mirror*, April 13, 1989.

Chapter 21

Interviews with Mark Griffin, April 11 and 12, 1993, Dan McDonnell, April 8, 1993, confidential source April 4, 1993, Linda Newton, April 13, 1993, confidential source April 13, 1993, Chris O'Mara, April 15, 1993, confidential source May 12, 1993.

Articles include: *Daily Mirror*, Aug 13, 1990, *New Idea*, Mar 23, 1991, *Telegraph*, Mar 23, 1991, *T.V. Week*, Mar 3, 1991, *Sunday Telegraph*, Feb 10, 1991, *T.V. Week*, Aug 25, 1990, *New Idea*, June 9, 1990, *New Idea*, Nov 10, 1990, *The Bulletin*, Dec 19, 1989, *New Idea*, Sept 22, 1990, *Daily Mirror*, Mar 7, 1989, *Telegraph*, Feb 10, 1991, *New Idea*, Sept 5, 1992, *Daily Mirror*, Nov 23, 1991, *Telegraph*, Nov 23, 1991, Harper's Bazaar, Autumn, 1990, *Daily Star*, July 20, 1992, *Daily Mirror*, Aug 26, 1992, *New Idea*, Sept 10, 1988, *Daily Mirror*, April 6, 1990, *Daily Express*, May 2, 1990, *Los Angeles Times*, Mar 19, 1987, *People*, Aug 27, 1990, *Daily Express*, Oct 16, 1991, *Telegraph*, April 20, 1991, *People*, July 26, 1992, *Sun*, Aug 9, 1990, *New Idea*, April 15, 1989, *New Idea*, Mar 23, 1991, *Herald*, Mar 26, 1991, *Herald*, Mar 24, 1987, *Herald*, Oct 28, 1990, *Herald*, Sept 12, 1990, *Daily Mirror*, April 11, 1989, *Herald*, Nov 20, 1988, *Daily Mirror*, Feb 12, 1989, *Bulletin*, Dec 19, 1989, *Daily Mirror*, Mar 7, 1989, *New Idea*, Sept 22, 1990, *Cleo*, Oct, 1990, *Woman's Day*, Feb 5, 1991, *Australian Women's Weekly*, April, 1991, *Daily Mirror*, Dec 11, 1991, *T.V. Week*, Mar 9, 1991, *Daily Mirror*, Feb 2, 1989, *Sun-Herald*, Oct 22, 1989, *Daily Mirror*, Nov 29, 1988, *Sun-Herald*, Sept 23, 1990, *Sunday Telegraph*, Nov 11, 1990, Feb 17, 1991, *Telegraph*, Nov 11, 1989, *You* magazine, Aug 2, 1992, *US Magazine*, Sept 3, 1990, *T.V. Week*, Feb 16, 1991, *New Idea*, Mar 16, 1991, *Woman's Day*, April 16, 1991, *Telegraph Mirror*, April 15, 1991, *Sunday Telegraph*, June 9, 1991, *Sydney Morning Herald*, Feb 25, 1991, *Sun-Herald*, Mar 8, 1992, *New Idea*, Nov 9, 1991, *Sun-Herald*, April 12, 1992, *Telegraph Mirror*, Aug 26, 1992, *T.V. Week*, Jan 23, 1993, *Sun-Herald*, Aug 30, 1992, *Sun-Herald*, Jan 11,

1989, May 7, 1992, *Melbourne Age*, April 4, 1987, *Melbourne Age*, Mar 6, 1988, *New Idea*, Jan 16, 1993, *The Australian*, Dec 3, 1988, *Daily Star*, Mar 31, 1989, *Telegraph*, Aug 11, 1990, *Sunday Telegraph*, Feb 7, 1991, *Woman's Day*, Aug, 1990, *US Magazine*, Dec 12, 1988, *New Idea*, Mar 7, 1987, *Telegraph Mirror*, Dec 11, 1991, *Today*, Oct 8, 1990, *GQ*, Feb, 1987, *Daily Mirror*, April 16, 1991, *The Sun*, Mar 8, 1991, *Sunday Mirror*, April 8, 1990, *Sunday Mirror*, Feb 16, 1992, *Hello!*, Feb 2, 1991, *Hello!*, Jan 19, 1991, *Daily Telegraph*, April 7, 1990, *New Idea*, April 4, 1992.

Chapter 22

Interviews with James Edstrom, June 22, 1993, Dan McDonnell, April 8, 1993, Terri DePaolo, May 12, 1993, confidential source May 21, 1993, confidential source May 14, 1993, confidential source March 10, 1994.

Articles include: *Telegraph Mirror*, Feb 16, 1991, *Daily Express*, Mar 26, 1993, *National Enquirer*, Feb, 1993, *Mail on Sunday*, May 24, 1992, *T.V. Week*, Sept 5, 1992, *Daily Mirror*, Feb 1, 1991, *Sun-Herald*, Dec 20, 1992, *Sunday Telegraph*, Nov 8, 1992, *Screen International*, Jan 28, 1991, *Telegraph Mirror*, Oct 20, 1992, Oct 13, 1992, *Sun-Herald*, Oct 4, 1992, *New Idea*, Feb 20, 1992, *Daily Mirror*, July 8, 1990, *Sunday Telegraph*, April 19, 1992, *Sydney Morning Herald*, Mar 20, 1990, *Telegraph*, May 15, 1992, *New York Times*, Oct 4, 1992, *Parade*, Dec 23, 1990, *Hollywood Drama-logue*, June 7, 1990, *People*, June 15, 1992, *Los Angeles Times*, Dec 14, 1992, *Hollywood Reporter*, Mar 10, 1992, *T.V. Guide*, May 12, 1990, *Telegraph*, Aug 31, 1992, *Daily Mirror*, Mar 11, 1992, *Daily Express*, May 14, 1992, *Sun*, April 25, 1992, *Sunday Mirror*, Sept 20, 1992, *Sunday Telegraph*, April 2, 1992, *Sunday Mirror*, Mar 7, 1993, *Sunday Telegraph*, Aug 30, 1992, *Mirror*, May 19, 1992, *Today*, July 15, 1992, *New Idea*, June 27, 1992, *Herald*, Dec 13, 1992, *Daily Express*, Jan 29, 1993, *Telegraph*, Aug 25, 1992, *Sunday Telegraph*, Dec 2, 1990, *Cosmopolitan*, Oct, 1992, *Who*, Sept 21, 1992, *Time*, Jan 11, 1993, *Sunday Telegraph*, Jan 10, 1993, *T.V. Week*, Jan 23, 1993, *Weekend*, Aug 14, 1990, *New Idea*, April 4, 1992, *New Idea*, Mar 7, 1987, *Telegraph Mirror*, Feb 25, 1992, *Woman's Day*, Mar 7, 1989, *Mirror*, Dec 2, 1992, *Herald*, Oct 25, 1992, *Mirror*, Oct 29, 1992, *Mirror*, Nov 3, 1992, *Telegraph*, Dec 27, 1987, *Mirror*, Dec 18, 1989, *Herald*, Oct 27, 1991, Nov 3, 1991, *Telegraph*, Jan 8, 1989, *Morning Herald*, May 14, 1992, *Sun-Herald*, Feb 2, 1992, Feb 8, 1992, *New Idea*, June 27, 1992, *Cleo*, April, 1993, *Mirror*, May 2, 1991, *Herald*, Oct 2, 1991, Oct 20, 1991,

New Idea, Dec 28, 1991, *Daily Express*, Mar 26, 1993, *Daily Express*, April 2, 1993, *Mirror*, Feb 2, 1991, *Herald*, Aug 9, 1992, *Mirror*, Aug 10, 1992, *Woman's Day*, Dec 28, 1992, *Variety*, Nov 12, 1990, *Sun-Herald*, Dec 13, 1992, Dec 15, 1991, *Sunday Telegraph*, Aug 23, 1983, *Telegraph Mirror*, Oct 9, 1992, April 13, 1992, Mar 11, 1992, *T.V. Week*, Aug 31, 1991, *Sunday Telegraph*, Jan 27, 1991, *Telegraph Mirror*, Jan 1, 1991, *Mirror*, Mar 20, 1989, *Morning Herald*, Jan 9, 1989, *Telegraph*, Jan 8, 1989, *Herald*, Jan 8, 1989, Mar 24, 1991, *Woman's Day*, April 16, 1991, *Melbourne Age*, Feb 24, 1991, *Mirror*, June 19, 1990, *New Idea*, June 9, 1990, *Bulletin*, July 18, 1989, *Herald*, Dec 15, 1991, *Daily Star*, Jan 6, 1989, *Daily Express*, July 20, 1989, *Redbook*, Nov 1992, *Herald*, Feb 2, 1992, *Mirror*, Mar 11, 1992, *People*, Dec 5, 1988, *Herald*, Mar 8, 1992, *Herald*, Mar 24, 1991, *Los Angeles Times*, May 25, 1992, *Variety*, Oct 6, 1992, Mar 19, 1992, *Today*, Feb 4, 1992, *Telegraph*, May 21, 1992, April 3, 1992, *Daily Star*, Feb 12, 1991, *Telegraph*, May 16, 1992, Dec 27, 1992, *Daily Express*, Jan 13, 1988, *Herald*, Dec 20, 1992, *Herald*, Dec 27, 1992, *Mirror*, Feb 8, 1993, *Telegraph*, June 2, 1991, *Daily Express*, April 7, 1990, *Cosmopolitan*, April, 1993, *Telegraph Mirror*, April 13, 1993, *Telegraph*, Dec 27, 1992, *Mirror*, Mar 20, 1989, *Empire Magazine*, April, 1993, *New Idea*, May 16, 1992, *Sunday Mirror*, July 26, 1987, *USA Today*, Dec 14, 1992, Feb 3, 1992, *Hollywood Reporter*, Mar 19, 1992, *Daily News*, June 12, 1992, *Los Angeles Times*, Feb 2, 1992, Oct 16, 1990, *Hollywood Reporter*, April 19, 1993, *People*, July 13, 1992, May 18, 1990, *Variety*, Mar 19, 1992, *Women's Daily*, Sept 7, 1992, Oct 5, 1992, *Melbourne Age*, Oct 20, 1991, *Mirror*, Aug 25, 1992, *Women's Daily*, Aug 7, 1990, *People*, Jan 25, 1992, *Variety*, April 19, 1993, *Village Voice*, Dec 22, 1992, *Box Office*, March, 1993, *Press-Telegram*, Feb 4, 1993, *Los Angeles Times*, July 7, 1993.

Filmography

Summer City (Australia 1978) Director: Christopher Fraser. Producer: Phil Avalon. Screenplay: Phil Avalon. Photography: Jerry Marek. Editor: David Stiven. Music: Phil Butkis. Released by: Interropic Film Distributors. Cast: John Jarratt, Phil Avalon, James Elliot, Steve Bisley, Mel Gibson, Debbie Foreman, Vicky Hrekimian, Peter McGovern, Abigail.
Fee: $250.00

Mad Max (Australia 1980) Director: George Miller. Producer: Byron Kennedy. Screenplay: James McCausland and George Miller. Photography: David Eggby. Editor: Tony Paterson. Music: Brian May. Released by American International. Cast: Mel Gibson, Joanne Samuel, Hugh Keays-Byrne, Steve Bisley, Roger Ward.
Fee: $10,000

Tim (Australia 1980) Director: Michael Pate. Producer: Michael Pate. Screenplay: Michael Pate (from the novel by Colleen McCullough). Photography: Paul Onarato. Editor: David Stiven. Released by: Satori Productions. Cast: Mel Gibson, Piper Laurie, Alwyn Kurts, Pat Evison, Deborah Kennedy.
Fee: $20,000

Attack Force Z (Australia 1980) Director: Tim Burstall. Producer: David McCallum, Lee Robinson. Photography: Lin Hung-Chung. Cast: Mel Gibson, John Philip Law, Sam Neill, Chris Hayward and John Waters.
Fee: $6,000

Gallipoli (Australia 1981) Director: Peter Weir. Producer: Robert Stigwood, Pat Lovell. Screenplay: David Williamson (story by Peter Weir). Photography: Russell Boyd. Editor: William Anderson. Released by: Paramount Pictures. Cast: Mel Gibson, Mark Lee, Bill Kerr, Stan Green, Max Wearing.
Fee: $35,000
US Box office: $4 million

The Road Warrior (US 1982) Director: George Miller. Producer: Byron Kennedy. Screenplay: Terry Hayes, George Miller, Brian Hannant. Photography: Dean Semler. Editors: David Stiven, Tim Wellburn, Michael Balson. Music: Brian May. Released by: Warner Brothers. Cast: Mel Gibson, Bruce Spence, Vernon Wells, Emil Minty, Mike Preston, Kjell Nilsson.
Fee: $100,000
US Box office: $24 million

The Year of Living Dangerously (US 1983) Director: Peter Weir. Producer: James McElroy. Screenplay: David Williamson, Peter Weir (from novel by C. J. Koch). Photography: Russell Boyd. Editor: Bill Anderson. Music: Maurice Jarre. Released by: MGM/UA Entertainment Co. Cast: Mel Gibson, Sigourney Weaver, Linda Hunt, Michael Murphy, Noel Ferrier.
Fee: $150,000

The Bounty (US 1984) Director: Roger Donaldson. Producer: Bernard Williams. Screenplay: Robert Bolt (from book *Captain Bligh and Mr Christian*). Photography: Arthur Ibbetson. Editor: Tony Lawson. Music: Vangelis. Released by: Orion Pictures Corporation. Cast: Mel Gibson, Anthony Hopkins, Laurence Olivier, Daniel Day-Lewis, TavaiteVernette, Wi Kuki Kaa.
Fee: $500,000
US Box office: $3.5 million

The River (US 1984) Director: Mark Rydell. Producers: Edward Lewis, Robert Cortes. Screenplay: Robert Dillon, Julian Barry. Photography: Vilmos Zsigmond. Editor: Sidney Levin. Music: John Williams. Released by: Universal Pictures. Cast: Mel Gibson, Sissy Spacek, Scott Glenn, Shane Bailey, Becky Jo Lynch.
Fee: $500,000
US Box office: $8.1 million

Mrs Soffel (US 1984) Director: Gillian Armstrong. Producers: Edgar J. Scherick, Scott Rudin, David Nicksay. Screenplay: Ron Nyswaner. Photography: Russell Boyd. Editor: Nicholas Beauman. Music: Mark Isham. Released by: MGM/UA Entertainment Co. Cast: Mel Gibson, Diane Keaton, Matthew Modine, Edward Herrmann, Trini Alvarado, Jennie Dundas.
Fee: $700,000
US Box office: $3.9 million

Mad Max Beyond Thunderdome (US 1985) Directors: George Miller, George Ogilvie. Producer: George Miller. Screenplay: Terry Hayes, George Miller. Photography: Dean Semler. Editor: Richard Francis-Bruce. Music: Maurice Jarre. Released by: Warner Brothers. Cast: Mel Gibson, Tina Turner, Helen Buday, Frank Thring, Bruce Spence, Angelo Rossitto, Angry Anderson, George Spartels, Edwin Hodgeman.
Fee: $1 million
US Box office: $40 million

Lethal Weapon (US 1987) Director: Richard Donner. Producers: Richard Donner and Joel Silver. Screenplay: Shane Black. Editor: Stuart Baird. Music: Chris Brooks (composed by Michael Kamen, Eric Clapton). Released by Warner Brothers. Cast: Mel Gibson, Danny Glover, Gary Busey, Mitchell Ryan.
Fee: $1.2 million
US Box office: $65 million

Tequila Sunrise (US 1988) Director: Robert Towne. Producer: Thom Mount. Written by: Robert Towne. Editor: Claire Simpson. Music: Dave Grusin. Released by Warner Brothers. Cast: Mel Gibson, Michelle Pfeiffer, Kurt Russell, Raoul Julia.
Fee: $1.5 million
US Box office: $28 million

Lethal Weapon 2 (US 1989) Director: Richard Donner. Producers: Richard Donner and Joel Silver. Screenplay: Jeffrey Boam. Photography: Stephen Goldblatt. Editor: Stuart Baird. Music: Michael Kamen, Eric Clapton and David Sanborn. Released by Warner Brothers. Cast: Mel Gibson, Danny Glover, Joe Pesci, Joss Ackland and Patsy Kensit.
Fee: $2.4 million
US Box office: $147 million

Bird on a Wire (US 1990) Director: John Badham. Producer: Rob Cohen. Screenplay: David Seltzer, Louis Venosta, Eric Lerner. Photography: Robert Primes. Editor: Frank Morris and Dallas Puett. Released by Universal. Cast: Mel Gibson, Goldie Hawn, David Carradine, Joan Severance.
Fee: $3.5 million
US Box office: $65 million

Air America (US 1990) Director: Roger Spottiswoode. Producer: Daniel Melnick. Screenplay: John Eskow and Richard Rush (based on book by Christopher Robbins). Photography: Roger Deakins. Editor: John Bloom. Music: Becky Mancuso and Tim Sexton. Cast: Mel Gibson, Robert Downey Jnr, Nancy Travis, Burt Kwouk, Art La Fleur, David Marshall Grant.
Fee: $4.2 million
US Box office: $32 million

Hamlet (US 1991) Director: Franco Zeffirelli. Producer: Dyson Lovell. Photography: David Watkin. Editor: Richard Marden. Music: Ennio Morricone. Released by Warner Brothers. Cast: Mel Gibson, Glenn Close, Alan Bates, Ian Holm, Helena Bonham-Carter.
Fee: $700,000
US Box office: $20 million

Lethal Weapon 3 (US 1992) Director: Richard Donner. Producers: Richard Donner and Joel Silver. Screenplay: Jeffrey Boam and Robert Mark Kamen. Photography: Jan Dee Bont. Editors: Robert Brown and Battle Davis. Music: Eric Clapton. Released by Warner Brothers. Cast: Mel Gibson, Danny Glover, Joe Pesci, Renne Russo.
Fee: $10 million
US Box office: $160 million

Forever Young (US 1992) Director: Stever Milner. Producer: Bruce Davey. Screenplay: Jeffrey Abrams. Editor: Jon Poll. Music: Jerry Goldsmith. Released by Warner Brothers. Cast: Mel Gibson, Elijah Wood, Isabel Glasser, George Wendt, Jamie Lee Curtis.
Fee: $7 million
US Box office: $50 million approx.

The Man without a Face (US 1993) Director: Mel Gibson. Producer: Bruce Davey. Screenplay: Malcolm MacRury; from a novel by Isabelle Holland. Editor: Tony Gibbs. Photography: Donald M. McAlpine. Music James Horner. Released by Warner Brothers. Cast: Mel Gibson, Nick Stahl, Margaret Whitton, Fay Masterton.
Fee: NA
US Box office: $50 million (projected).

Index

INDEX

INDEX

INDEX

WENSLEY CLARKSON was one of Britain's most successful young journalists before leaving Britain for Los Angeles with his wife and their four children in 1991 – an experience which inspired his book, *A Year In La La Land*. His other books include the tabloid newspaper exposé *Dog Eat Dog*, plus his best-selling true crime series *Hell Hath No Fury, Like A Woman Scorned, Love You To Death, Darling* and *Doctors of Death*.